Law and Economics of International Telecommunications

Under the Auspices of the
Max Planck Institute for Foreign and International Private Law
edited by Prof. Ernst-Joachim Mestmäcker
and Prof. Christoph Engel

Volume 42

Christoph Engel/Kenneth H. Keller (eds.)

Understanding the Impact of Global Networks on Local Social, Political and Cultural Values

First Symposium of the German American Academic Council's Project „Global Networks and Local Values".
Dresden, February 18-20, 1999

Nomos Verlagsgesellschaft
Baden-Baden

Die Deutsche Bibliothek – CIP-Einheitsaufnahme

Ein Titeldatensatz für diese Publikation ist bei der Deutschen Bibliothek erhältlich.

ISBN 3-7890-6389-4

ISSN 0935-0624

1. Auflage 2000

Foreword

Opportunities and risks are twins. There are few who would deny the opportunities provided by global networks in general and the Internet in particular. But many fear the concomitant risks, or what they perceive as risks. Racist speech, pornography, and misuse of personal data rank highest in public awareness, but there are many others, ranging from predatory business practices to publication of false and libelous information.

Some concerns are almost universal, such as child pornography. But with respect to others there are at least differences of degree. In the light of its history, Germany has actually banned right wing publications that would be allowed, even if not admired, in the United States. On the other hand, Americans in large numbers deem material pornographic which most Germans would find inoffensive. Privacy is also interpreted in different ways in the two societies. These contrasts lead some into a stark and simplistic assertion: global networks threaten local values.

The reality of global networks, and of their interrelation with local values, is much more complex. This volume explores different paths for understanding global networks, local values and their reciprocal impact. It stretches from cultural theory to law, from systems theory to economics, from sociology to political science. Although technology forecasting is not a central theme or purpose here, we do attempt to incorporate both the potential and the limitations of new technological developments in these broader theoretical discussions.

The volume assembles papers presented and discussed at a symposium held in February 1999 at Dresden. The symposium is part of a larger endeavor financed by the German American Academic Council and jointly organized by the Computer Sciences and Telecommunication Board of the U.S. National Research Council, Washington, and the Max Planck Project Group on the Law of Common Goods, Bonn. The views expressed in the papers are those of the authors and do not necessarily represent those of the organizing institutions. A final National Research Council report, drawing in part on these papers, will be published in early 2001, upon completion of the project.

The overall project is directed by a bi-national Steering Committee whose hard work we, as co-chairmen, would like to acknowledge. The members of the Committee are listed in an Appendix. We are also indebted to Herb Lin (senior scientist) and to Nicci

Dowd (project assistant) of the Computer Science and Telecommunications Board, and to Joachim Dölken, Dr. Lorenz Müller, and Wolf Osthaus (research associates), to John Stanley (native speaker), Thomas Feldkamp (editorial assistant) and Anja Moosmann (project assistant) of the Max Planck Project Group on the Law of Common Goods.

Christoph Engel Kenneth H. Keller

Contents

Note: The papers in this volume were first presented in a workshop jointly Hosted by the Max Planck School for the Law of Non-Private Goods and the Computer Science and Telecommunications Board of the U.S. National Research Council.
However, the views expressed by their authors are those of the authors alone, and do not necessarily represent those of the Computer Science and Telecommunications Board or the National Research Council. A final report, drawing in part on these papers, will be published in early 2001.

Wolfgang Kersting

Global Networks and Local Values

Some Philosophical Remarks from an Individualist Point of View

A very long time ago, when the Greek philosopher Thales was out walking and staring incessantly upwards, in an attempt to study the marvelous vaults of the heaven, he forgot to pay attention to the path he was taking and fell into a well. A witty and pretty maid, who had been drawing water from the well and was obviously well aquainted with realities of life, watched him and burst out laughing at this turn of events. She shouted at the dripping wet philosopher what a strange human being he was: passionately longing for the knowledge of the celestial sphere, but completely ignorant of the earthly things that lay directly before his feet.

Since then, the laughter of that Greek maiden has been ringing in the ears of philosophers. The philosopher is regarded as unworldly, as Johnny Head-in-the-clouds, who stumbles whenever he accidently comes in contact with reality. Along these lines, you too have probably already asked yourself what a philosopher is doing here and what philosophy has to do with problems concerning the political regulation of the internet. Of course, the philosopher has always been a kind of software specialist, an expert of the invisible, dealing with the significance behind the visible signs, with the awareness behind the measurable brain and with the agency behind the perceptible motions of the body. That, however, certainly does not allow for the conclusion that he therefore has an especially intimate relation to cyberspace. A philosopher can only claim a kind of competence regarding the issue at hand, because he is also an expert in normative foundations along with more comprehensive connections and contexts. The examination of these foundations, which you, as members of the technical and scientific community, may now and again lose touch of and actually can rightly ignore in the everyday routine, is in no way detrimental and is sometimes even necessary, when, for example, new technologies cause societal changes as well as ethical and political irritations to such an extent that an inventory and review of our cultural self-understanding is unavoidable.

Technology frees. The societal application of various technologies leads to the continuous improvement and englargement of the freedom of action for an increasing portion of humanity. Within this development you will always find a phase of moral alarmism since technologies, which were hitherto morally unobtrusive, start to become morally conspicuous. The cause of this change is always the same: the new technologies' liberating effects collide with existing values. Such conflicts are unavoidable because values have regulatory effects, whose restrictive extent is determined by past experience in conflicts. Technology is liberating because it pushes back the limits of necessity: where yesterday physical or biological fate still reigned, today you can find freedom of choice. For centuries infertility was a fate one had to accept. Today we have the techniques of reproductive medicine, which have robbed infertility of its inevitability. The same holds true for the progress in communications' technologies. These have torn down the barriers of space and time between individuals and thereby have led to an undreamt-of expansion in our information and communication possibilities. This process began with the printing press, continued with the invention of the telephone and has reached its present peak with the internet. Due to their enormously liberating and freedom-enhancing effects, however, these technologies, by their very nature, affect the moral convictions of society and it depends on one's temperament and one's attitude to modernity, whether these effects are conceived as moral risks or as moral challenges. In the case of the new reproductive technologies, our cultural self-understanding is challenged by the fact that the natural grounds of our self-conception are starting to sway as man begins to select himself as a subject for genetic optimization and hence becomes the author of his own evolution. In the case of the new telecommunication technologies, the changes affect the cohesion of society and the ethical foundations of the citizens' common life. They reinforce the already existing tendencies of atomization and social alienation and under their influence individuals lose their social competence and capability to commit themselves to and be involved in common projects and public affairs.

There are further parallels. Both technologies bring forth contradictory effects. There are some who look at the inner workings of the new technology with utmost fascination and point with shining eyes at the increased freedom of choice. There are others, however, who stare gloomily at the far-reaching and rapidly accelerating changes, longing for the simple social conditions and clearly laid out life of the past. In a nutshell, each influential and significantly life-changing technology evokes utopian as well as catastrophic reactions, due the fact that the diagnostic assessment of its social and cultural impact and the evaluation of its potential for emancipation and risk is shaped by prior value convictions. As a rule, utopians give a benefit-fixated judgment; thus neglecting all questions of costs. Therefore their expectations must necessarily be disappointed. Doomsdayers, however, restrict themselves to a purely cost-fixated view, thus excluding all questions of benefit. Consequently, their fears must also remain unconfirmed. Both are experts at oversimplifying reality.

My tentative attempt to indicate philosophy's relevance for the contextual problems of the internet is supported by the very name of our project. Obviously a threefold assumption is standing behind the formulation "global networks and local values". First, it is assumed that the expanding information structures and communication webs have an impact on society's cultural self-understanding. This is both researchable and worth studying. Secondly, it is assumed that this influence is so ethically and politically challenging, that it is capable of producing deep and far-reaching political countermeasures. The third and final assumption is that the discussion of these disquieting effects and the possible political countermeasures not only has to take into account the technical, economic and legal dimensions of the problem, but also its normative and evaluative facets as well. The foundation for this view is the fact that society does not understand, interpret or present itself descriptively, from an external point of view, but rather evaluatively, from an internal point of view. It does not use the observational language of facts, but the participational language of values.

What is the internet's impact on local values? Does it attack and weaken them? Does it destroy their acceptance and thus erode their validity? Does it lead to social alienation? And if so - how is it to be judged? What are the consequences for our societal praxis and our political action? Do we have to engage in the protection of "Communal Values", in a kind of ethical environmentalism? And if so, in what way? By network participant's self-regulatory initiatives and activities or by legal and stately enforced rules? And what kind of cultural alienation is in question here? Is it about the westernization of the world, with an accompanying eradication of global cultural diversity? Or is it about levelling off the cultural differences within a nation state's borders? Even further, does this alienation question refer to the more fundamental conditions of sociality at all, to the chemistry and composition of society's glue? - To get a clearer view here, I'd like to address in a very systematic manner two problem areas: the conceptual and typological problems of value on the one hand, and on the other hand the problems of legitimate political action, or, to quote Humboldt's famous liberal program book from 1792, the problem of the limits of the state's effectiveness (Humboldt 1968).

I will begin with some introductory remarks on the concept of value. The concept of value is a highly contested term with a very confusing history. It originated in the realm of economics. Furthermore, the theories of value, which for example were developed by Marx and the Austrian school, are much older than the value discussions in social sciences and philosophy. That might seem amazing in face of the fact that currently the concept of value is mainly used to criticize the reduction of human life to purely economic terms. This reduction - in the eyes of the present moral criticism - implies devaluation of the valuable and value blindness. The civilizing of capitalism, so the slogan of the new moralism, means: capitalism as a consumer of morals and destroyer of ethics, must be subjugated to the rule of values. In all of their excitement, however, these critics tend completely to forget - as it will be shown later - that the market not only creates values but also is based on values whose acceptance is crucial for its flourishing. - It is characteristic for the history of modern societies that talks about values come recurringly into fashion. Once again, certain groups are worrying that communal values are in danger of decaying and they preach to the people to look to former values to regain a common conception of morality and respect. We are dealing with the rhythmic recurrence of a phenomenon known since the Enlightenment: the discontent with modernity. Behind the complaints about the erosion and loss of values, a deep sense of social disorientation and a feeling of disquiet with the societal changes destroying the social presuppositions of traditional lifestyles, self-conceptions and worldviews is hiding. What this uneasiness veils is the fact that the self-propagated opposition between an existence enriched and fulfilled through values and a life improverished and nihilistic due to valuelessness is purely theoretical and is to be found nowhere in reality. Talking about the decay of value is nothing more than a partisan interpretation of value change. The concept of value change presupposes that the content of values alters, that traditional values lose their acceptance and new values find recognition thus gaining validity and normatively directive power.

A careful analysis of the usual lamentations for eroding values would discover that the retreat of the so-called secondary virtues in favor of emancipatory life plans, the appearance of post-materialistic attitudes and increasing moral sensitivity are the real reasons behind the mourned loss of values. What has changed is the internal weighting within the tense relation between the two basic human needs: freedom on the one hand and social bonding on the other hand. After the ever expanding market had supplied the individuals' freedom of choice with an ever increasing supply of "new and improved" consumer goods, the individual's need for freedom was no longer satisfied and demanded a further widening of the range of options. In the following period, this freedom of choice was expanded to include non-standard lifestyles, cultural practices and systems of belief. Biographic standardizations became increasingly insignificant; traditional life patterns were broken up, because their age-old forms of binding and obligation lost their attraction. The self-realized man could only satisfy his complementary need for security, belonging, and community in new ways, which were compatible with his decision for a life as autonomous as possible. Therefore new forms of communities and new ways of togetherness appeared, more individualist, more elusive. The natural obligation to belong, which conservative communitarians consistently defend with emphasis, has lost its obliging power. It has been replaced with the revocable decision for a life in voluntary associations and hand-picked communities. Even marriage and family have fallen into this whirlpool of individualization and suffered the according effects and social costs.

The discourse of values's decay erroneously equates traditional values, which have become unattractive, with values themselves. In reality, however, we find that modernization only brings about alterations of our normative semantics, but not a destruction of our normative syntax. It is this normative syntax, with which I am now dealing. If we understand its structure and function, we will be capable of resisting the temptation of modernity's skeptics and see that human society is essentially value-generative and therefore was, is and always will be filled with values. We will learn that we are suffering from a loss of clarity in speaking about values rather than from a loss of values themselves.

What is a value? I suggest a functionalist approach in answering this question, while this approach is useful in seeking the role of value concepts within the context of our rational individual and collective action. Man is an *animal rationale*, an animal, who has reasons - this claim is not only made by philosophy, it is proved by human actions every day. These reasons serve a double purpose: they are necessary for the process of selection and for the process of justification. Selection presupposes a range of options, a given plurality of possible actions. Justification, however, presupposes a public sphere along with a plurality of fellow actors and citizens. Selecting an action equates with finding a reason for oneself, to prefer it to other competing actions. Justifying an action, however, means convincing my fellow citizens of its preferability. It is clear that there is a strict correspondence between selective and justificatory reasons only for completely truthful people. Only saints have a soul like an open book and feel no need to hide their privacy behind adequate rationalizations. We, as members of the more profane portion of mankind, however, are doomed to a justificatory double life, because the reasons that are guiding our decisions are not necessarily identical with the reasons we offer to the public, should our fellow citizens ask for some justification. Proofs of the preferability of a choice can only succeed within an established social practice of justification that is rooted in shared values and common convictions. Arguing for the preferability of something requires standards and generally accepted principles of evaluation. Recognizing such moral rules and principles is equal to holding them for true and being convinced of their rightness. One cannot acknowledge such justificatory rules and evaluatory standards, while at the same time denying them all significance for oneself and one‘s own life. These rules and standards are important to us, because they mirror the normative framework of our social existence. They are important to us, because we are convinced that our way of living together, which they structure and shape, is preferable to every other model of societal coexistence.

Surely, that does not mean that our everyday life is permeated by an ever watchful value awareness; but it does mean that we will come in contact with these normative foundations if we leave our routines of acting and reflect upon our actions and the principles behind them. Admittedly, although we justify with values, these values themselves cannot be justified. These value-based justifications do not have the character of a deductive argument because the semantics of values are extremely porous and therefore lack an unambiguous directive power. This vagueness, however, is not problematic, because our common value awareness is normally a kind of background knowledge remaining in the dark. And these background convictions can kept hidden as long as the inconspicuous everyday routine isn't queried and no need of justification or clarification arises. But if this value background is disturbed by urgent requirements for justification caused by any significant social, political or cultural transformation, it will step forward and require a clear definition. This semantic clarification, however, can only be reached communicatively within the social discourses of the interested fellow citizens. Therein an elaboration of the corresponding values' meaning in each and every individual case is reached. Therefore evaluative justifications are always generally accepted and situation-related value interpretations that determine what is political, legal or moral due in the present situation. Our definition of our essential values therefore converges with the history of their exegesis. I am choosing this term deliberately; the religious associations are intended. Our fundamental value convictions, our human rights egalitarianism and our belief in sovereignty of the people is a kind of secular, civil religion. At least it justificatorily functions as religious belief systems do. They offer sense and meaning for the individual and the collective life. Guiding all justifications, they themselves cannot be justified. Being semantically open and undetermined they are dependent of interpretation which puts the values in concrete and situation-related terms. But as in the case of religions, which also have their history and are nothing outside of their history, this dependence on actualized interpretation or interpretative actualization does not lessen the social stability or politically and ethically orienting power of our values.

In the past, people believed that the correct rules for communal living could be learnt from the eternal rhythm of existence, from an eternal value order hanging amongst the stars, or from divine will. At the very least, they were convinced that the obligational power of historical authorities and traditional directives could be trusted. In modern times, we have lost this belief and know that the societal necessity of justification can not be met by an appeal to God's will or a natural value order. The fading of the theological worldview, the disappearing of the traditional teleological concept of nature in face of the new mathematical physics, the desintegration of a tightly-built and highly integrated societal order under the attacks of economic reductionism and individualization - all of these tendencies demand a reorganization of the cultural justification mode. They demand a replacement of the traditional stock of values with new ones that correspond to the new intellectual foundations of the modern world and the newly shaped self-understanding of modern man. The systematic backbone of this new and modernity-adapted conception of justification is normative individualism. Normative individualism vests the individual with moral autonomy. This autonomy is only restricted by those laws, which he has agreed upon with his equals within the framework of fair procedures and negotiations. It is not surprising that under the conditions of normative individualism contractual agreement becomes a central justificatory symbol of modernity. The idea of a contract gives the justificatory intuitions underlying normative individualism an authentic expression (Kersting 1984).

Modern man is a sort of ontological drifter, homeless, no natural place to go, without bindings produced by a given order. He has to fend for himself and can only call his own, what he is carrying around with himself. He is forced to operate with his reason and interests in order to meet the cultural need of justification. Making himself the presupposition of sense and value, he relegates social orders and political institutions to a secondary position with justificatory dependence. Social orders and political institutions can only be justified if their functions and accomplishments mirror the individuals' rationality and need. Social orders and political institutions are only justified if they turn out to be useful instruments for the realization of individuals' preferences. This is the fundamental rule for open societies: *open societies are characterized by an individualist justification method.* They demand that we justify any statements about the common good or the collective interest solely by how it advances the individual welfare of each and every citizen. It is a reliable and distinctive mark of closed societies, past as well as present, that their justification practice is based on a holistic account that treats the common good as an independent property or attribute of an ontologically superior collective entity, such as history, society or mankind, and whose rights and interests define and restrict the individuals' legitimate claims.

If we ask the question which institutional order is preferable from an individualist point of view, we quickly come across the familiar systems of the competitive market, democracy and the rule of law. To demonstrate this, we need only to carry out the contractual thought experiment asking which rules of coordination and collective decision-making rational individuals would agree upon when faced with the task of unanimously outlining the institutional design of their future society. The idea within this argumentation that on the one hand pleads for the supplementation of the free market with a regulatory political framework demands on the other hand that this regulatory framework be strictly defined and limited. The exertion of political power is legitimate only under the condition that its effects serve the interests of as many individuals as possible. Therefore, decision-making rules about supplying and financing the common weal should, when possible, find the agreement of all, but, at the very least, they should have the support of solid majorities, in order to be established. Of course, direct democracy would be highly desirable from an individualist point of view, since a plebiscitarian democracy, which made decisions unanimously, would be the only truely non-discriminatory democracy (Buchanan/Congleton 1998). Thus, surprisingly, it is exactly the economically oriented individuals, who most strictly observe the political legitimation criteria that was developed by Rousseau for his social contract.

The individualist's conception of liberty is negative; liberty is first and foremost being free from restrictions. Individualists are therefore maximalists regarding liberty and minimalists regarding political rule. Not only are they always endeavoured to reduce the state's intervention in the citizen's private sphere to the mere political essentials, but they are also concerned about clearly limiting the state's power. The fundamental benchmark of legitimate politics is the enabling or maximizing of individual liberty. Regulatory politics therefore carry a heavy burden of proof. In the face of the existing thicket of regulations - especially here in Germany- the individualist's tool can only be one thing: deregulation. The individualist is particularly suspicious when conservatives call for more and new laws to protect endangered values. In an open society, the general task of politics is system upkeep, which entails establishing and maintaining a framework for the economic interactions as well as securing the society's ground rules by protecting all of its sub-systems from wear and tear. The state has to deploy its political and especially its legal instruments to prohibit any damage or impediment to the continual development of coordination and cooperation within the societal system. In view of the increasingly accelerating speed of society's transformation, it must not be forgotten, that this political programme of constitutional care must also cultivate learning skills and the development of flexible patterns of political reaction.

Since the particular systems of economy, law and politics are organized by individualist normative principles that give legitimacy to state actions and at the same time define these systems' inherent ideal form, in an open society, state activity also has to orient itself on values. Values, however, are thoroughly universalist and claim ethically invariant, culture-transgressing validity. Because they have allied themselves with pre-cultural man's "natural" rationality and interests, their validity cannot be restricted by any peculiar cultural interpretations of human needs. But where does culture fit now in this individualist value model? What role do local values play in it? How are politics related to local values? And what is the relationship between local values and internet? It is evident and without doubt that the internet harmonizes splendidly with the individualist value system of the free market and the universalist value system of the rule of law and democracy, since the improved possibilities provided by the internet of getting information, of communication, of coordinating interests and organizing economic actions world-wide raise the individual's chances of liberty and rationality. Likewise, it cannot be maintained, that the internet possesses a special or privileged status; that it is an unlegislated area where the enforcement of the legal rules, which coordinate the individuals' actions and balance their particular basic rights, can be abandoned.

But what about the local values? The concept of local value can be understood in three ways. First, it can refer to the world's cultural diversity. Second, it can refer to modern western societies' ethical-religious pluralism. And finally, it can refer to the factually unavoidable historical and cultural determinedness of every occurrence of the aforementioned economic, legal and political order. This last meaning is clearly the least obvious, while at the same time, the most intriguing one. In the first case, we are dealing with the fact of cultural pluralism: men have different conceptions of world, reality and divinity and different convictions about personality and good life. These different conceptions are partly incompatible, partly convergent with smaller and larger zones of overlap. Cultural pluralism generates problems when civilizations draw nearer to each other, especially when they have to live together in the same political space. Under these conditions, cultural self-understanding can see itself under pressure and in danger. Special conflicts can then appear, which are very threatening, because they are not conflicts of about material goods that can be defused by appropriate distribution mechanisms, but rather are conflicts about existence and where the cultural identity is at stake. Huntington, for example, is convinced that tomorrow we will witness a world-wide clash of civilizations, which seems unavoidable due to the fact that western culture is unable to desist its striving for hegemony (Huntington 1996). The conflict constellation which results from this reads: the West against the Rest. Fukuyama, however, already proclaimed the end of history earlier because the notions of liberalism, market economy, rule of law and democracy, would irresistibly spread over the globe and lead to a general pacification by cultural unification. His device reads: the West goes global (Fukuyma 1992) .

Is the internet an agent of western culture? Without a doubt. It supports the spread of free markets, enlightenment and democracy and makes the consumption of western communication habits and cultural products as well as the picking up of western views and evaluation modes easier . Above all, the internet is a partisan of the open society. It favours the internal and external opening of society and serves to increase individuals' autonomy by providing possibilities for the widening of their knowledge and for the improvement of their cognitive skills. The people's freedom of movement is resistible; the radio waves' freedom of movement however is irresistible. The unnerving reactions of the Chinese government with regard to the growing access to the internet in their country as of late have shown how eminently important it is for the people's desire for freedom and intellectual dignity to be able to receive any and all available information without having to fear for one's life. Besides, the establishment of English as global language by the ever-growing internet does not necessarily imply a linguistic imperialism or that in cyberspace only English will be spoken. Rather, I think the current situation of coexistence between English on the one side and the various indigenous and vernacular languages on the other side will repeat itself in the cyberspace. Thus, although the main activity of the internet will be the spread and globalization of the English-speaking culture of the West, it will also occur that Non-Western societies will partially check this move by occupying certain cyberspace regions and thereby maintain themselves locally. This assumption is grounded in my general conviction that the processes of modernization - with globalization and the spread of telecommunication networks as perfect examples- can never simplify the individual and social conditions of life but will rather always complicate them. This increase in complexity is due to the effects of differentiation as well as to the well-known phenomenon that every tendency reliably generates a counter-tendency and thus deepens the numerous paradoxical structures of our society on the other side.

What ensues from the aforesketched cultural partiality of the internet, from its inherent bias towards the ideal of an open society? Do friends and supporters of the internet have to accuse themselves remorsefully of cultural imperialism and admit that their external and internal enemies are right? Are they required to exercise restraint and to restrict the communication reach of the internet to the culturally domestic areas for the sake of respecting the right to cultural autonomy? Not at all. On the one side, such politics of cultural protection – assuming that they are even technically feasible - would be an illegitimate intrusion upon the citizen's rights. On the other side the positive impact of the global telecommunication networks on the spread of the model for open societies is eminently desirable, since the fundamental principles of the open society, the core values of the Western culture are universalist and reasonable for everybody. Their spreading will certainly make it more difficult for the cultures with societal discriminations and political apartheid to survive, but it will not in the slightest lead to a cultural uniformation of the world. Globalization is not only compatible with localization and regionalization; globalization often leads to a rise in the endeavours to maintain and strengthen local or regional particularities and loyalties. Both appear side by side. Neither Huntington nor Fukuyama is right. They hold a complementary simplicism that has already been surpassed by the structural complexity of today's developing world society. Understanding is possible between different cultures, though not because they are all disappearing or merging into the one remaining western monoculture, but because they can coexist and because men will learn to speak several languages and to live in several worlds at the same time. They will cope with the internet and nevertheless carry on trusting in their gods. The contact with modern life that the elites in the Near and Far East and in South East Asia presently enjoy will be available to increasingly more people when the necessary structural reforms enhance the rule of law, democracy and systems of education. The internet is a device with the help of which we can tackle the cognitive-communicative projects that we are pursuing for whatever reason or purpose in a considerably enhanced manner. The internet is no Midas, who deprives those entangled in the word wide web's electronic threads of his indigenous cultural traits and transforms him into a westerner.

The debate about the 'Asian Values', which communitarians and other remorseful cultural relativists like to call upon the witness stand to testify for their anti-universalist convictions, plainly shows that globalization of economic and communication does not pose a threat to cultural identity but rather to the given authoritarian political structures (Senghaas 1998; Habermas 1998). It makes clear how important it is to unravel the mixture of culture, modernization and power politics and to be aware of the special political interests behind the propaganda campaign for cultural particularity. It is telling that Asian values have been conjured up at that time when the relationship between capitalism, confucianism and autocratic politics loosened and the economically modernized society, calling for the corresponding political modernization, wanted to throw off the bonds of developmental dictatorship. Asian values are not incomprehensible for us. No culture-transcending efforts are required to grasp their meaning, no self-obliterating immersion in an alien value cosmos is necessary. These values were ours but yesterday. For centuries they formed the normative grammar of our traditional social world; therefore it is not in the least surprising that presently they are being offered by communitarians as medicine for the wounds of modernization in a nearly unchanged form, supposedly in order to moderate the speed of societal transformation, to mitigate the strains of individualization and to stop the running dry of the moral resources of solidarity. The Asian values which have been exposed and defended in this debate contain nothing more than the value profile of a traditional, culturally homogenous and highly integrated society. Their propagandists are not found in the areas of society which are responsible for the production and reproduction of culture, because these values - as a programme of identity politics - are an invention of the ruling political class, an ideological contrivance of the existing autocracy. The political class succeeded in modernizing the economy by a combination of an educative and developmental dictatorship, but then shyed away from the social and political consequences of the initiated modernization and wanted to lure the intellectuals, bourgeois' and labourers away from their demands for rule of law and democracy by a political scenario demanding cultural self-assertion. The function of the Asian values scheme was to extinguish the citizens' rebellion against a solely economic modernization by means of an opportunistic cultural relativism. This relativism undermines the human rights' foundation of the political criticism and discredits the demands for rule of law and democracy as cultural alienation and foreign infiltration. The criticism of the defenders of Asian values is not addressed to the human rights universalism of the West but to the West in their own countries, to the democratic demands of the capitalist market societies in South-East-Asia. The asian societies, however, cannot permanently enjoy the benefits of the capitalist modernization without taking advantage of the accomplishments of the individualist legal order and granting the citizen fundamental rights to individual and political autonomy. The propagandistic thesis of an irreconcilable conflict between asian values and the western culture of human rights is nourished by the illusion that capitalism without fundamental individual rights and democracy is possible in the long run. This illusion hides the conservative motive of the ruling class to break down the internal connection between individualist economic order, individualist legal order, democratic participation and individualist, right-based legitimation of state rule in order to protect their own political power from the egalitarian human rights and politically emancipatory implications of the individualist concept of legitimation.

Leaving the problem of global cultural diversity and going to the multiculturalism of the western nation states, a similar picture appears. The important question here concerns the problem of the state's activity in the face of an increasing cultural and ethical pluralism. Is it possible to hold on to the proven and well-established politics of indifference, as liberals demand or do we have to give up this strategy of political neutrality and, as the friends of cultural identity suggest, draft and implement a policy of difference-sensitivity to handle the deepened multiculturalism? Politics of indifference in the language of the contemporary political philosophy means the political obligation to ethical abstinence. The state has to restrict itself to securing non-violent coexistence of different cultures and lifeforms on its territory and is only allowed to intervene, if the political activities of culture groups lead to a violation of the constitution and the citizens' rights. The religious and ethical truth is strictly private. The individuals' conceptions of a good and sensible life, therefore, must not concern the state. The opponents of this liberal politics of indifference, however, demand a policy of difference-sensitivity, which amounts to a kind of reverse discrimination for the majority culture (Benhabib 1996). They want particular political constraints for the others as well as licenses for themselves to correct the inegalitarian effects of the liberal ethical neutrality. The difference-sensitive politics within multicultural societies is about cultural self-assertion and self-maintenance. Its aim is the complete parity between the different culture groups and the majority culture. More specifically, this political intervention endeavours to end the structural advancement of the majority's individualist, secular and liberal life pattern through the emphasis on group rights and the launching of compensatory programs (Kymlicka 1995). They believe that theses measures will prevent the ethical marginalization of minority cultures in a society shaped by liberal indifference and the state's ethical abstinence. The underlying motif of this conception is the accumulation of so much political representation and social power that these minority groupings, which often belong to an earlier evolutionary stage of social development, are able to survive in a hostile cultural environment. That the demanded right of self-assertion and cultural self-defense is in actuality a privilege, or more openly stated, an inequality deviating from the egalitarian principles of the liberal legal order, is suggested by the consideration that such special group rights represent in their very essence internal restrictions on the legal freedom of group members as well as an external restriction on the legal freedom of everyone else, in order to secure the minority culture's authentic survival. Because there is a significant difference between the desired political guarantee of the culture's survival and continuity on the one side and the individual right to live in accordance with one's faith and cultural traditions within the framework of the existing liberal legal order on the other side, the granting of individual rights to cultural autonomy and religious freedom does not in any way guarantee the continuity of a culture or the survival of individual ethnic-religious groups. In a nutshell, the individual human right to cultural autonomy and religious freedom cannot prevent the extinction of cultural species. Since the claim of being protected as a member of a cultural group and not as an individual interested in the free exertion of basic human rights is not necessarily contained in the fundamental right to cultural autonomy and religious freedom, the establishment and implementation of group rights would cause considerable modifications to the liberal rights system. Admittedly, I cannot see how a reorganization of the internet and a political control of its contents in a manner that would satisfy the adherents of group rights could be managed without grave violations of an individual's fundamental rights. Each culture group has free access to the internet and can, with the possibilities found therein, present itself, can secure its own identity, and can strengthen its internal group cohesion, while situating itself within the pluralist cultural spectrum of society. That the pressure to assimilate, which is exerted by the majority culture on the minor culture groups, will grow through the increasing use of the internet, is both evident and unavoidable. Here we must also remember, however, that the internet is but one tool of modernization amongst others: it will not destroy cultural particularities, it will merely aggravate the living conditions of those individuals who have not yet finished their workload of modernization by increasing the requirements for flexibility, reflection and the capacity for coordination and organization. Living in modern times is psychologically challenging and therefore extremely risky for authoritarian cultures. It demands the cultivation of special virtues. In particular the development of a socio-cultural competence for dealing with ethical pluralism, the ability to carry out several different roles in life, and the capability to be present in different social worlds at the same time is required. The internet intensifies the urgency of cultivating these skills, while at the same time making it easier to acquire them. We have to learn to become the creators of our own identity within the wide framework of an open society. Identities are no longer pre-packaged bundles of sense and meaning provided by an unquestioned past and distributed by cultural authorities. Identities must be worked out autonomously and responsibly.

Hitherto, I have reviewed international cultural diversity and interstate multiculturalism in order to outline the concept of local value and to get a better understanding of the problem pertaining to the relationship between a global internet and local values. Remaining is the central problem of social integration. This problem is best handled by dividing it into two separate questions. The first question is what integrative significance local values may have for the socio-cultural reproduction and the maintenance of the economic, legal and political orders within a historically determined society. The second question is what influence the increasing expansion of the internet will have on the social validity of local values and thus the reproductive capability of societies. Furthermore, what are the consequences of the internet on the development of the abilities, competences and conduct patterns which citizens have to possess to a sufficient extent in order to ensure the self-continuation of society? Does the internet weaken the cohesive power of the social cement? Is it a cradle of new forms of community which will nevertheless produce the same integrative effects as the old and traditional ones? Or can we perhaps even expect an optimization of our community's democratic quality, a flourishing of civic virtue from the internet? Will it finally end the people's growing disenchantment with politics? Will it change the onlookers into participants and transform the often deplorable spectator democracy into a participatory democracy? (Leggewie/Maar 1998)

Of course, the question of social integration and of politics' democratic quality are interrelated: in an open society, civic virtues and social virtues are to a great extent, one in the same. Nevertheless I'd like to differentiate these problem areas conceptually by separating the question of whether the internet is a social paradox from the question of whether the internet is a communicative paradox. In discussing these questions it is very useful to make a distinction between the internet‘s impact on the one side, which is caused by its contents, and the internet‘s effects on the other side, which arise solely through the pure usage of this medium. Regarding the content question, it is not probable that the internet will take in, hold and make accessible information, which cannot also be found in non-digital media. Of course, the internet enhances distribution considerably by providing a completely private, immediate and thus uninhibited access. However, we are merely dealing here with a formal and purely technical optimization of the communication flow, which might lead to a quantitatively increased consumption of such contents, but which does not as such call for political regulations and legal constraints. What is illegal and prohibited outside the internet is also illegal and prohibited within the internet. There are no vices that are only flourish in cyberspace and the internet has not given birth to any new forms of pornography, hate speech and other legally and morally incriminating activities that would not find a home in another medium outside of the internet. Therefore it is not in the slightest necessary to enhance the regulatory density of our legal order. The regulatory problem arising here is only of a technical nature: how is it possible to make up for the provider's and user's advantage of elusiveness with the help of corresponding control and/or filtering technologies. Cyberspace does not give the libertarian dream of anarchy a new chance; it cannot be treated as a regulation-free zone. Cyberspace participants are not better human beings than the inhabitants of the real world. On the contrary, a number of real world citizens transform themselves into a netizen in order to hide themselves behind the veil of anonymity and to do and say things that he or she would never dare to do or say when confronted face to face with a fellow living, breathing citizen. It is therefore an illusionary belief that cyberspace participants would suddenly form a self-contained group that could completely internalize the social and moral costs of its activity. What failed under natural condition-- namely the spontaneous generation of a moral order or at least a form of self-regulating coexistence incapable of harming anybody economically or morally – will certainly not succeed in cyberspace. But that does not mean that new laws are required. Rather it only means that we need the appropriate technologies for enforcing the well-established laws in the elusive reaches of cyberspace.

In dealing with the problem of the internet's socially and communicatively paradoxical effects, however, we are thinking less of pornography, hate speech or National Socialist propaganda, which, by the way, is distributed world-wide by some Canadian resources. We are thinking not of content, we are thinking of the effects which are generated by the pure use of internet itself. We are thinking of social alienation, of uprooting, of atomization and isolation, of the increased weakening of the human capabilities to judge and discern and of the decreased abilities to trust and commit, with one word: we are thinking of the loss of social competence, social responsibility and civic virtues. Why is the internet suspected to cause paradoxical sociality and paradoxical communication? It is true that virtualization rescinds all spacial confinements, thus enhancing the physical possibility of sociality and communication, but with their extended dwelling in cyberspace and cyberworld the people's factual capabilities to create and cultivate social relationships successfully and to enrich their lifes through communication will vanish. The delimitation of our common world by virtualization generates exactly the opposite effect: the internet is isolating and alienating people and thus destroying communality. This process will lead towards complete social and communicative inability: the cyberspace dweller is going to loose contact to reality, fall silent and each encounter with a real human being will scare him to death. Obviously sociality demands for sensibility; sociality must be experienced. It can only flourish in an embodied world, on the basis of a face-to-face communication.

What does that have to do with local values? Local values refer in this context to the entire area of cultural identity constitution, which encompasses, besides the principles of normative individualism and the forms of its economic, legal and political organization, the people's history, myths of origin and self-understanding narratives as well. History, origin myths and self-understanding narratives are the material out of which nations build their self-conception. Both tracks of identity building are equally important. The cultural self-conception has to be passed on as carefully as the systems of economy, law and politics have to be looked after. Otherwise the political community won't be able to hold its standards and to reproduce itself on the normative level which it has set out for itself (Kersting 1997). Of course, the foundations of the organizational models, which the normative individualism is arguing for, are universalist; capitalist economy, rule of law and democracy are legitimatorily rooted in human rights egalitarianism. But the economic, legal and political systems of an open society only exist in a particular , historically shaped form. Thus each political community has its special historical flavour, its special cultural markedness. Individual and collective identity building in the framework of modern western society therefore is always a cooperation between individualist and universalist values on the one side and local values on the other side. We are more than just an aggregate of homo oeconomicus, rights-bearing subject and participant of the people's sovereignty; we are socially embedded, historically determined and culturally formed citizens who act economically in a more or less prudent manner, who respect themselves as free and equal and who exert their political rights of democratic participation. Since we are such complex beings our readiness to cooperate socially depends on the presupposition of our granted cultural participation, conversely the entire political community's fate is dependent on a sufficient degree of the citizen's social cooperation and on a sufficient amount of civic virtue and social competence.

The internet skeptical dystopians allege that on account of the above mentioned disintegrative and alienating effects the common public places will become deserted and the ressources of social cooperation and solidarity will run dry. They are afraid, that the public will be obliterated and the formation of cultural identity will be abandoned since culture can only survive in an inhabited social space. Surely, our systems of exchange, of law and of democratic voting will still function for a while, but at some point, the ethical internet critics fear, the entire common wealth will implode and perish on accont of internal, isolation-caused hollowness (Barber 1998). In their eyes, the internet is a value-destroying machine. In thematizing the problem of whether the internet is conducive to democracy this criticism will become clear. Especially this question gave rise to enthusiastic reactions, and politicians from Al Gore to Newt Gingrich expressed their expectations that the internet will have a positive impact on politics by improving democracy and making better citizens. They think of a significant expansion of political communication and hope for a substantial enhancement of political judgement in an everincreasing number of citizens. They think of the dissemination of information, of the easy and inexpensive way to accomplish great organizational effects by building political groups through recruitment and retention of members and supporters with the aim, to gain political influence through the exertion of political pressure and the lobbying of the government. These internet enthusiasts obviously hope for effects of politization. They confidently expect that the citizens' deplorable cognitive capabilities which have been lamented by the realist democracy theoreticians since the days of Schumpeter, can be elevated through the enlightening effects that the internet will necessarily produce. And they also think of using the internet technology to make democracy more plebiszitarian and thus more democratic. They are in all seriousness convinced that the internet of all things would open the gate to the new participatory age, which Barber and the friends of a strong and deliberative democracy are dreaming of, and provide citizens with the readiness to political commitment and involvement that a flourishing democracy is urgently in need of (Barber 1984).

Of course, it can be objected, that willing and interested citizens could also acquire all information they might want in pre-digital times. It is surely naive to expect an improvement of democracy by frequent button pressing on a huge scale; this expectation is based on something what could be called the technological fallacy of democracy theory (Hill/Hughes 1996). And this technological fallacy of democracy theory is only a special case of a more general error which is often made by technophile utopians in evaluating the moral and cultural impact of technological changes: they mistakenly correlate technological progress with moral improvement, but the instrumental expansion of our freedom of action which is made possible by the new technical devices, does not automatically generate any moral or cultural effects of supervenience. It was one of the favorite illusions of the believers in progress that technological development would bring the solution of all great problems of mankind in its wake, that technological development would become the locomotive of mankind's continual cultivation which would ultimately lead to the establishment of a global rule of human rights. We know in the meantime that technological development does not automate the continual progression of culture. We know only too well that civilizations can fall victim to barbarians who know everything about the newest techniques. We know, that technologies are means, instruments which can be used beneficially or with the most devastating effects, but which can never guarantee cultural and moral progress by itself. Nevertheless with the appearence of each great technology this foolish game starts anew; its supporters cherish the greatest cultural and moral hopes whereas its opponents conceive it as a fiend from hell.

It seems very advisable to avoid all dramatization and to meet the emphatics' and catastrophics' exaggerations with sobriety and a chastened view of human nature and affairs. The internet does not confront us with unknown problems. The telecommunications technology only heightens the tension between benefits and costs, which has been engraved in modernity from the very beginning, and which impedes the balancing of liberty and bonding. It is indisputable that the internet enhances the liberty of the people. Especially under the conditions of a globalizing world economy access to information and unrestricted communication is of decisive importance. And an internet that shrinks the real world to the keys on a keyboard contains unimaginable possibilities to abandon the restrictions in communication and obtaining information that existed to date. On the other side the internet will surely not lessen the negative social consequences that are unavoidably connected with modernization. On the contrary, it will intensify them. In general the costs of modernization are perceptible as the waning of societal cohesion power and disappearing of social solidarity. Thrusts of individualization are constantly challenging social integration. The increase of choice necessarily leads to growing cultural fragility and more flexibility with regards to traditional strategies that meet society's integrational needs. But we should not underestimate the capability of learning, which modern societies have developed in the meantime. Up til now this exciting construction has withstood all ups and downs of modernization and produced the requisite amount of cohesiveness and communality that prevented it from atomistic implosion.

And what is the result of my considerations about the relations between the impetuously developing internet on the one side and the different web of values on the other side? It is hardly possible to get beyond the following banality: the internet offers chances as well as socio-cultural challenges. The chances are to use prudently; and the socio-cultural challenges are to be evaluated with sobriety and to be met with confident pragmatism. As no societal formation before modern society compells itself to ever-lasting learning, to an unstoppable accumulation of cognitive competences. Incessantly transforming itself modern society is bound to take care of its fundamental requirements of self-preservation on the one hand and the normative standards of its basic functions on the other hand under ever-changing conditions. Chastened by philosophy of history's past efforts to prognose and evaluate the ever accelerating transformations of modernity we should endeavour to spare our society old promises and old fears. Admittedly, there are people who are addicted to television; and a growing number of our fellow citizen is well on the way to becoming mobile phones addicts; and I am certain that some already have a really pathological relation to the internet and suffer from a digital turkey in case of power failure. But as abusus non tollit usum the restrictions of freedom caused by a possible internet pathology must not be brought to bear against the effects of enhancing liberty which will reliably be produced by sensible use of the internet. The internet won't bring us particularly closer to the democratic paradise of a free association of well-informed, enlightened and rationally and morally mature individuals. But it won't particularly increase the dangers of civilizational fragility, atomistic isolation and societal disintegration which are endemic risks of cultural modernization and inherent to modern societies, either. Individuals have to develop special virtues and skills in order to make reasonable use of modernity's possibilities; they have to aquire capabilities and attitudes that enable mobility, flexibility and the virtuoso change of perspectives, that, however and above all, allow them to handle the given pluralities, to develop a management of cultural-ethical pluralism. No multiple personality will be generated whose identity is broken into shards; but identity formation, the individual as well as the collective one, is under modern conditions and thus in an increasingly culturally inhomogeneous environment a more flexible, more open, more unsteady process. And without a doubt the dealing and living with the internet will considerably further this modernization of our individual and collective psychological and socio-cultural constitution.

Bibliography

Barber, Benjamin: Strong Democracy. Participatory Politics for a New Age, Berkely 1984

Barber, Benjamin: A Passion for Democracy. American Essays, Princeton 1998

Benhabib, Seyla: Democracy and Difference. Contesting the Boundaries of the Political, Princeton 1996

Buchanan, James M./ Roger D. Congleton: Politics by Principle, Not Interest. Towards Nondiscriminatory Democracy, Cambridge 1998

Fukuyma, Francis: The End of History and the Last Man, New York 1992

Habermas, Jürgen: Die postnationale Konstellation, Frankfurt a. M. 1998

Hill, Kevin A ./ John E. Hughes: Cyberpolitics. Citzen Activism in the Age of the Internet, Lanham 1996

Humboldt, Wilhelm v.: Ideen zu einem Versuch, die Grenzen der Wirksamkeit des Staats zu bestimmen, in: *Humboldt, W.v.*: Gesammelte Schriften, Bd.1, Berlin 1968

Huntington, Samual P.: The Clash of Civilizations, New York 1996

Kersting, Wolfgang: Die politische Philosophie des Gesellschaftsvertrags, Darmstadt 1994

Kersting, Wolfgang: Recht, Gerechtigkeit und demokratische Tugend, Frankfurt a. M. 1997

Kymlicka, Will (ed.): The Rights of Minority Cultures, Oxford 1995

Leggewie, Claus / Christa Maar (eds.): Internet & Politik. Von der Zuschauer- zur Beteiligungsdemokratie, Köln 1998

Senghaas, Dieter: Zivilisierung wider Willen, Frankfurt a. M. 1998

David J. Farber

Predicting the Unpredictable – Technology and Society

I have been asked to examine the likely information based technologies that will arrive over the next decade. Note the decade time scale was my limitation since predicting outside that that time frame is unlikely to be realistic. For each technology I will discuss what the impact will be on society with particular emphasis on the international aspects. I have chosen to organize this paper as a set of bullets rather than a narrative in the interest of clarity.

Each bullet will be proceeded by a date and a probability. These are my estimates of when the technology will attain large-scale deployment and how confident I feel it will actually achieve that deployment. I will also start with large scale technologies that have major national and international impact and then focus more on technologies that will directly impact the average citizen.

Ultra high speed all optical networks

With the steady progress in the technology that underlies optical networks it is now feasible to predict with some certainty the future directions. Terms like multiwave fiber networks with speeds in the 40-gigabit per wave and number of waves in te 100 range are not beyond the rational dreams of technologists. The inclusion of optical amplifiers makes it feasible even now to remain in the optical domain for continental distances. Current work in all optical switches strongly suggests that we may within the first decade of the 21st century achieve source to destination communications systems in which the signals remain entirely in the optical world. This raises a set of very interesting questions. Some of them are technical; some economic and some societal. I will examine each of these in turn.

Multi-Gigabit speeds have raised a whole new set of very difficult technical issues. Designing and building switching devices and interface devices, which can operate at these speeds, is not simple. It pushes both hardware design and VLSI technology to their limits. As a result, it has been necessary to take innovative architectural approaches to even hope to achieve speeds nearing a gigabit. Perhaps most interesting, though, is the conclusion that many of the ideas developed over the past twenty years in computer architecture, operating system design, and networking protocols seem to be ineffectual when applied to such high speeds. It is worth observing that these communication speeds are of the same order of magnitude as the main memory bus speeds of modern workstations. Thus it is not surprising that we have run into problems. When streams of data arrive at memory speeds, it becomes difficult, given the protocol systems currently in use, to get the data into memory, to allow the processor enough processing bandwidth to examine the data and move it, and still to have processing power left over for other tasks. I will not elaborate in this piece on the solution Others and I have proposed for this problem. But basically, the solution revolves around the creation of a geographically dispersed distributed machine, the components of which would be interconnected by high-speed networks. This approach has been well documented.

What is more important than a particular solution is the challenge of facing a future in which gigabit speed networking will be considered slow, in which our communication infrastructure will consist of multi-gigabit, low error, high-latency networks, in which our processing units, while growing faster, will not keep up with increasing communication speeds. It is too easy to just remove a few instructions, hack a few cures, and show that one can operate not too badly at current speeds of communication. Perhaps this is equivalent to saying, "let the next generation solve the problem." I believe that there is a challenge facing the computer communication field of at least the same magnitude as the challenge the field faced in the very early days of networking. Attacking this problem will require the talents of people from every area of both the computer and communications fields – people willing to experiment and willing to face the same set of challenges those in the fifties faced with the then-new computers.

The major impact will be on industry. The changing of technologies forced by these ultra high speed all optical systems will expose existing industrial leaders to the same pressures and dangers that main frame manufacturers of hardware faced in the 70s. Many of them failed to respond to those challenges and several of the then leaders are no longer forces in the computer business. Attempting to continue to market buggy wipes in the era of fast cars is a formula for becoming obsolete. The same is true of software. As the focus shifts from large slow, by future standards, operating systems and individual software applications to the lean and mean systems required by the future high-speed communications, many companies will be come obsolete. Applications will tend to become much more distributed as communications capabilities expand and costs, and maybe even price, decrease dramatically. Such changes will upset the current national industrial strengths and will push the need for increased numbers of IT trained people to compete in this New World. Countries which are fast to adopt, have a pool of investment capital and have a pool of flexible trained people will most likely emerge as the leaders.

In the communications space things are much more complicated. When one adds to the all optical backbone infrastructure the increase in slower speed but still multi-megabit data rate technology capable of delivery to the last kilometer – to the home and business, dramatic changes in the communications world becomes possible.

Bits to the Home/SOHO (small office/home office)

Over the past several years, a major change has started in the last kilometer connection area – the so called local loop/last mile... Prior to that time, the notion was that the last mile was either telephone services or cable TV services. In both cases they were monopoly-regulated services that offered little or no data services beyond what was available via analog modems. While ISDN was in theory deployed, for a number of reasons it failed to be a major player. The reasons were some technical – ISDN still used the telephone local switch and tended to overload it and some economic – prices were held high and deployment was sparse. In addition as analog modem technology matured the speed differential between it and ISDN narrowed.

Recently two technologies have become economically and regulatory feasible – at least in the US. These have been TV cable based data services and the XDSL capabilities over the copper telephone wire. They both offer the potential of always connected multi-megabit two way data services to the home at prices, again in the USA, that are affordable for certainly the SOHO area and many homes.

These create the possibility of providing significant last mile access to the future optical wide area networks. A note: there is the possibility of optical connectivity directly to the home via plastic fiber etc. However it is not clear that this is feasible economically duie to the cost of installation in all but new concentrated construction. If it is feasible then things are just better and my following argument just gets more interesting.

What will be the impact on the public and industry of this enhanced last mile capability. Again it threatens to attack the business base of several important industries. The most susceptible to economic damage is the telephone industry. The ability to carry telephone traffic over packet switched networks has been amply demonstrated even though in the current internet the performance is less than standard telephone quality. That differentiation will vanish on future technology internets and even now the capabilities of cable and xdsl strongly suggests that as a local telephone company bypass for at least non local calling, it could be deployed now. Since the capabilities to access these data services will tend to focus initially on the SOHO marketplace, a number of serious impacts suggest themselves.

Perhaps the serious is the draining of the long distance income and even local service fees that will be lost by the removal of the business use. That will most likely force the telephone companies to raise their fees. Such raised fees will impact more strongly on the less advantaged segment of the population. Also in the long run, the telephone industry wedded to circuit switched equipment with long life times will find itself in more and more financial difficulties as more efficient competition arises utilizing much cheaper technology. Since the telephone industry is both a large employer and in many countries a significant source of government monies, it is not at all clear how this will resolve itself. Attempts to preserve the old infrastructures will most likely cause decreased international competitiveness. While the telephone industry is threatened by new technology for the last mile another treat is arising via wireless systems in the world/city and house.

Wireless and mobility

Wireless technology is one of the fastest growing areas of communications technology. For many years we have been offered the vision of being connected via a digital path at all times. Unfortunately for a long time the technology, regulators and the market place did not combine to deliver the promise. There are several new technologies coming into the marketplace and laboratories that may radically change the wireless world. First, and this is US centric, there are market forces at work that are changing the way wireless is used. The bulk tariffs that are now offered by almost every cellular carrier have changed the balance between the wire world and wireless cellular service. In many cases especially in urban areas the need for a wire line telephone is decreasing. The costs of wireless with a large allocation of talk time, about 600 to 1000 minutes per month with no toll charges and no roaming bring often the cost of cellular below that of wire service. That will have two effects. One is that again the "cream" market will be skimmed off the wire telephone service and what is left is the low margin "lifeline" service and second it will force the costs of conventional toll down to a level to match that of the flat rate cellular – that is happening already. All this, at least at a nation level, will bring reduced costs and increased capability to the public and the advantages of wireless systems in emergencies, storms etc.

Internationally life is a good deal more confused. The new GSM is moving along along with several competitive systems. The only bright spot in my view is the fact that technology makes it feasible to produce handsets, which are multi-standard, capable. That is they will operate on any of the worldwide standards given of course the licensing authorities within the country allows their operation. The lack of a sensible roaming system makes it much more difficult to live in this environment internationally.

LEO, low earth orbit, systems such as Iridium are coming online and at some time in the future may reach a price point where it will force the rationalization of the normal cellular systems with respect to international roaming. The potential of satellite systems for high speed data is just being explored in the commercial world and one predicts a slow start due to the high initial investment required.

The role data in the current generation of cellular wireless systems is at best secondary. However proposals for the next generation cell systems talk about data rates that could hit a megabit per second and higher largely due to the small cell size of future systems. In the arena of satellite systems, Hughes and others have been talking about Direct Broadcast systems that allow two way links with modest speed uplinks. Such systems are still not available and it is unknown what the price and performance will be. The use of Satellites for multicast applications seems much more desirable than direct point to point usage. Systems under study use such multicasting for Snow Crash like applications.

Satellites are by their nature transnational and thus raise all the issues of cultural identity, religious rules and national control. These will become ever more of an obstacle to the free exchange of material over networks be they ground of earth orbit.

Home and Personal networks

The wireless world is often focused at mobility in geographic distances such as cities, sates etc. The advent of short range very inexpensive radio links such as Bluetooth and equivalent systems.

From http://www.sss-mag.com/ssnews.html#3:

Bluetooth Technology Highlights

- Based upon a small, high performance integrated radio transceiver, each of which is allocated a unique 48-bit address derived from the IEEE 802 standard.
- Operate in the unrestricted 2.45GHz ISM 'free band', which is available globally although slight variation of location and width of band apply
- Range set at 10m to optimize for target market of mobile and business user
- Gross data rate 1Mbit/s, with second generation plans to increase to 2 Mbit/s
- One-to-one connections allow maximum data transfer rate of 721 kbits/s (3 voice channels)
- Uses packet switching protocol based on frequency hop scheme with 1600 hops/s to enable high performance in noisy radio environments. The entire available frequency spectrum is used with 79 hops of 1Mhz bandwidth, analogous to the IEEE 802.11 standard
- Low power consumption drawing only 0.3mA in standby mode enables maximum performance longevity for battery powered devices. During data transfer the maximum current drain is 30mA. However during pauses or at lower data rates the drain will be lower

The technology represented by Bluetooth opens up a wide and exciting variety of applications. Essentially everything in a house can now be equipped with network access. Personal devices such as watches and calendars can communicate to other systems in the home and office. An ID card can become an active badge that identifies the user to the environment they are in. Locks can open, lights can come on and temperature can be set to an individual taste when they enter a room. (As a side comment the badge can require a pin prior to becoming active so as to insure the rightful user is using it.). TV sets can restrict the program material depending on who is viewing. Thermostats can sense occupants, outside weather etc and properly adjust the house saving significant fuel.

More important is the ability for devices to organize themselves into interesting new systems. For example, a PC equipped with a Bluetooth can detect that the PDA (Pilot like personal device) belonging to me (via use of my personal ID card) and update its data base with new appointments etc. The possibilities are huge and will start a new round of innovation at a much more personal level that that of the PC.

As with each of the technologies I have mentioned there is a societal impact. The privacy of the individual will be constantly under attack. If I have an active ID card which constantly announced to all that will listen, or all that will ask, who and where I am, there is an excellent opportunity for massive violations of my privacy. Each of these threats to the individual has a corresponding technical solution and unfortunately the potential for these solutions to be blocked by national laws. For example, most of the applications envisioned by such wireless links would greatly benefit from or require strong encryption. Yet in many nations strong encryption is banned or controlled. Also in many nations the export of such technology and thus damage the marketplace for devices with that capability.

Computers

While I have focused my attention in this paper at communications technology since that is the arena where the most change will take place in the next decade, it would be inappropriate to ignore looking at computers and software.

The end of history in computers has often been predicted based on limits of line width etc on semiconductor devices. Each decade we predict the end of increased capability due to these effects and each decade it keeps growing. At least for the next 5 years we can expect increased speed and capability out of our microprocessors. Architectures that used to require rooms of equipment are now in a small chip. Further we see yet again the blending of software methodology with hardware architecture as computers that require complex and capable compilers are entering the marketplace. We can expect to see this sophistication increase and begin to see optical interconnects between components to overcome the limits of wire connections. Further we will see increased use of multi-processor architectures to gain increased performance from commodity components as well as increased capability to provide security on the chip. The limitations on computing, at least at the non-supercomputer end, will come from software.

A major limit to innovation has always been our ability to produce reliable working software. The scale of software systems enabled by the modern computer and communications systems has stressed our abilities to create such systems. This problem started in the 60s and has gotten worse. Further as such systems have embedded themselves in critical tasks often managing life-supporting systems. This lack of a viable software engineering methodology is currently the major limit to the greater infusion of computers and communications into our society. Numerous attempts to understand the planning and development of large complex software systems have failed to achieve any meaningful success. The USA in its IT^2 research initiative will devote significant resources in an attempt to solve this problem. However the size and complexity of systems may out race our abilities under the best of circumstances to get software under control.

Repeated failures of key software systems even after the 2000 issues will have societal impact on people and nations. This impact ranges from the loss of credibility on the part of the public for computer based devices with increased pressure not to continue our technologically enables society up to and including massive damage done by nuclear plants and missile control systems which fail.

Some social comments

While I have been asked to address the technical issues and their impact on society, I can not finish this paper without making some social comments. These comments originally were made at a meeting of the AAAS in 1996 and are modified for 1999.

Cyber-rights

John Perry Barlow is credited with having observed that *"Our Bill of Rights is but a local ordinance in Cyberspace"*. He was referring to the fact that the basic rights which "we hold self evident" in the USA are only self evident to our society and are not accepted worldwide. Similarly our notions of morality, law, right and wrong are European centric and are not accepted uniformly worldwide. Our society is individually oriented. The rights of the individual often take priority over the rights of society as a whole. This view is certainly not a world wide view. Asia, especially Singapore, is fond of pointing out that the Asian view puts the group first and the individual is viewed in the light of what is good for the group. What "side" will Cyberspace citizens take in this very profound cultural argument? Can both views live compatibly in a closely coupled cyber-world?

In Cyberspace individual national laws and customs, which are often different and contradictory, may conspire to limit the ability of individuals and corporations to freely interchange information, ideas, images and spoken works even when those items are legal and appropriate in the nation of one of the participants. Many societies currently, for example, limit the availability of satellite dishes. Several governments have equated internet access. along with the fax machine. as the prime vehicles for external disturbances to their control of their society and have stated that in the event of any future internal disturbances they will severe the internet connections rapidly. What will be the impact of such attitudes on international commerce and learning?

The privacy laws that many governments have reasonably instituted to protect their citizens from having their personal information flow outside the control of the laws of their nation raises many difficulties when on is engaged in a Internet environment. The establishment of directory structures which involve some nation's citizens may be in violation of the laws of that nation. Libel laws are traditionally national yet in Cyberspace, libel is instantaneous and globally damaging. Is there a notion of global liability? How do I sue a person in another nation? If I can, do we achieve the lowest common denominator? Is there a global "right to privacy"? How is it enforced? What happens to global commerce if there is not a common understanding?

Many nations and cultures have dramatically different perceptions of what is "proper" and not proper for its citizens to possess or to view. Consider an extreme case — child pornography. We in the United States have strong laws which forbid the distribution, possession etc. of such material — other cultures may not agree with us or have different notions of the control of such material. Suppose citizens of two such countries send each other such material and the material transits the United States; is storage on a US computer (without the knowledge of the owner of the computer) against the law? etc. Can or should the US intercept such material and "delete" it, should they arrest the people when they next enter the US, should they close down the computer used to store the material.

Is there an international agreement on the transport of cryptographic material across national boundaries? Is there a right of "innocent" passage — that is , it is bound for another nation and just stops for a short stay — mail relays for example? What is the right of a nation to monitor the contents or addresses of electronic communications that is transiting their nation?

The Cyber-economy

As the Internet becomes more a part of the everyday business of the nations, it will become more and more necessary for commerce to take place among the users of the infrastructure. We can expect in a very short period an international electronic marketplace where goods of all types — merchandise, information, software etc. are being bought and sold.

Historically there has always been a need to create a way of paying for such goods in order to motivate the supply side of the marketplace. Currently our primitive electronic marketplaces have no very effective mechanisms for paying for goods.

This creates an interesting and exciting opportunity to examine just what is needed to supply a mechanism for the exchange of electronic currency and how such a mechanism can exist in a national and international arena.

The issues raised by the potential existence of ***an international electronic marketplace*** (IEM) are not limited to just how to pay for things. There is the need to have the equivalent of credit cards, checks and paper money with it various shades of traceability and privacy. There is the need for escrow mechanisms and international exchange etc.

The additional issues raised by the IEM include:

⇒ The use of small payments as the mechanism for enabling the marketing of hypermedia documents where the links are access paths to updated and marketable property. The crossings of the links require the payment of a fee (electronically and capable of allowing very small payments). For example having accessed the information once if I copy it and give it to a colleague I have lost the ability to search for sub-links and automatic updates.

⇒ authentication of sellers and buyers when necessary and the protection of that information when required

⇒ privacy and personal freedom issues as to what I buy and from whom.

⇒ the integration of any such system into the domestic and international banking and funds transfer systems as well as the different laws and regulations of states, countries and needs of law enforcement

⇒ the need to internationalize buyer protection laws

Cyber-education

Nowhere are the challenges greater than in the possibilities that the Internet offers in education. There is no better way to create international understanding, friendship and exchange than communication and cooperation between schools and students all over the world at all levels. Education applications cover most potential uses of the INTERNET and impose demanding requirements on the infrastructure. Education is also an area where the public interest is evident.

The role of the universities in educating the citizens who will lead their nations into this future calls upon them to pioneer the exploration of the benefits to be gained as well as the problems to be faced in this new world. Exploration of the Modern Worldwide Multi-Campus University-University of Cyberspace-interacting with lower grade schools and continuing education to provide individual-centered lifelong learning, should therefore be included in the G-7 vision. The intent should be not to just perform experiments with exchange of courses over the network but rather to explore, understand and solve the complicated issues of inter-organizational operation, economics, national laws and tradition that must be solved in order to create such an extended University. Perhaps most important, however, we must understand how such an organization can enrich University life for the students as well as the faculty. The design of the University must address this issue with highest priority if it is to be a success.

A group of Universities strongly believe that the lessons to be learned from this effort will show the way for better understanding of how industry and governments can use the INTERNET.[1] This effort will contribute to new strategic knowledge necessary to

---

1 *The Distributed University* David Farber, Moore Professor of Telecommunications The Moore School University of Pennsylvania USA and Bjorn Pehrson Professor and Chairman Department of Teleinformatics Kungliga Tekniska Hogskolan Sweden, Dec. 1994

cope with the global structural change of the telecommunications, media and information industries which is expected to lead to an information society. This rapid change calls for extraordinary programs in research and education to provide the competence necessary in government, industry, among users and all parts of society. However, the most important outcome will be to create a new generation of future leaders who have lived and learned in the borderless world of the Internet and who thus will be better prepared to understand and control the structural changes being created by the information society in order to secure fuller more meaningful employment and social welfare for their people.

Paul A. David

The Internet and the Economics of Network Technology Evolution

1. Introduction:The information technology revolution, the Internet and 'creative destruction'

A new set of global economic activities, structures and organizational arrangements is emerging from the dual impacts of the revolution in computing and telecommunications technologies and of the worldwide movement toward liberalization of the regulatory regimes affecting communications networks. The converging technological development driving this process have made it feasible quickly and very cheaply to retrieve codified knowledge ('information') rapidly from geographically far-flung sources; to assemble and transmit it to places where it may be further processed; to transform it extensively so that it may be utilized for other production and service delivery purposes; and to re-catalogue and store it for speedy retrieval and re-use. Concurrent with these technical transformations, a global trend in economic policy has emerged during the past two decades, favoring the loosening of national regulations on international and inter-regional flows of goods and services, finance, and technological information; coupled with this has come a movement toward the privatization of former public utilities — including the national telecommunications networks previously operated by postal, telephone and telegraph (PTT) agencies.

Network technologies and the business activities based upon them hardly can be thought to be new, and many features of the economics of modern telecommunications services have interesting and sometime illuminating precursors in the historical experiences of older, physical network industries. At the same time, as Jens Arnbak (1998) has recently emphasized, digital information and communications technologies (ICTs) do offer a quite singular combination of features and options that carry potentially enormous economic significance:

- speed-of-light transport (in contrast with roads, canals, railways, pipelines)
- mass transport at vanishing marginal costs, without degradation of quality of service (unlike electric power)
- instant copying/broadcasting, bundling and re-routing/ refiling of information (uncommon to postal services, printing and non-electronic publishing)
- complementary customer-access options, providing choice between wired access (which have strong economies of scale, scope and/or density) and wireless

networks (providing area coverage, e.g. via cellular mobile networks, and wide-area broadcasting either with or without conditional access)

- lightweight and compact terminal devices that permit customization for the individual user (in contrast to sea, air and rail network termini).

This combination of properties affects both the relevant *geographical* markets for many information goods and services, which can now extend much beyond national and regional jurisdications, and it concurrently is transforming the boundaries of *product/service markets*, as technical convergence via digitization facilitates the bundling of formerly distinctive commodities. Little wonder that these developments have seen a popular revival of interest in Schumpeter's concept of innovations as unleashing economic and social forces of "creative destruction."

a. Synergies between technological and institutional innovation affecting telecommunications

An apparent synergetic interaction has marked the dynamics of the technological and institutional innovations affecting the proliferation and elaboration of information networks. On the one hand sharp declines in unit costs and price performance ratios have been permitted by exploiting the convergence of digital computer technologies with advanced telecommunications techniques utilizing direct broadcast satellites, terrestrial fibre optic networks, and cellular radio for transmission; as well as the enhancement of the capacities of both — through improved software permitting switching, multiplexing and data compression, and sophisticated routing and network management algorithms. These advances affecting the data transport and network services layers of the infrastructure have, in turn created a commercially feasible basis for new "value added network services" offering access to digital information service vendors who package and deliver "telematic content." On the one hand, liberalization of the regulatory environment has opened the field to new enterprizes seeking to enter lines of business — whether in network service provision, or in content distribution — whose incumbents former were 'protected' by the barriers imposed by licensing requirements and other regulatory costs. Reciprocally, a broaden range of technological opportunities has induced the formation of new forms of enterprise, and challenges to the economic significance of the sphere of control assigned to existing regulatory authorities.

Thus, the appearance of many new, and experimental business ventures attempting to take advantage of these opportunities has placed pressure on pre-existing monitoring and regulatory agencies intended to protect consumer interests, and so increased the attractiveness of the political trends favoring relaxation of the social control of business. Still more striking has been the undermining of the pre-existing regimes of telecommunications regulations by the widening menu of technical options for providing customer access.

There are some profound implications for institutional restructuring that may be seen as corrollary to the famous "Negroponte switch" — the proposition that in the new digital communications environment "everything that came to you through wire and cable will come to you through the air, and everything that you used to receive through the air will be delivered via wire and cable." The point is that each of those technological domains had associated with it an array of regulatory regimes (national and international), characterized by particular goals, operating principles and bodies of technological and business expertise relevant to the provion of specific kinds of services. The migration of services to quite different kinds of networks does not automatically bring about an accompanying migration of control structures. Thus, "regulatory by-pass" may be an unintended and socially disruptive consequence of the expanded sphere of technological choices that have been made available for the designers of information technology systems, and the options open to consumers of the services that they will be able to deliver.

b. The Internet Explosion

The growth of the Internet, and the explosive proliferation of services offered on the World Wide Web (WWW) forms only one facet of the information technology revolution, but it is so striking as to have become emblematic of the larger developments. Today the Internet is composed a collection of utilities that allow the transmission of data, images, video and voice. There are seven principal components: FTP (file transfer protocol), Telnet, Netnews, E-mail, Gopher and WWW. Until the late 1980's the number of Internet hosts worldwide (defined as a domain name which has an IP (Internet Protocol) address assigned to it, i.e., any computer connected to the internet) remained very modest, so that there were but 159,000 hosts by October 1989. This number had increased more than ten-fold to 1.776 million by July 1993, and four years later (in July 1997) stood at 26.053 million. Within the following twelve months, another 10.7 million hosts were added, implying that there were approximately 60 to 70 million users in July 1998 (see data from Network Wizards: http://www.nw.com).

The growth rate of internet hosts in the US and in the EU alike appears to have stabilized at a proportional pace that brings slightly less than a doubling every 12 months. At that pace Europe is lagging the US in the absolute number of hosts by some 15 months, but the parity in their rates of advance implies there is no immediate prospect for the US lead to shrink. But over the course of the mid-1990's the rate of increase recorded in Japan, Canada and Australia, and a fringe of other, smaller markets, was appreciably faster than in the US and the EU (see data from RIPE NCC: http://www.ripe.net). The growth of the WWW since the early 1990s has been widely advertised in the popular and business press, and, indeed, the pace of expansion in the volume of WWW traffic has been spectacular even in relation to the total flow of data on the Internet backbone: in March 1995, when the NSFNET ceased publishing such statistics, the WWW accounted for about a quarter of the total data flow, whereas an estimate made two years later conservatively put the share in the neighborhood of two-thirds (see Geuna and Steinmueller, February 1997: http://www.analysis.co.uk/acts/fair). Projections of these trends suggest that by the early years of the coming century some 600 million people, or a tenth of the world's population will be users of computers connected to the Internet. Even if this is somewhat overstated it is clear that the Internet is unprecedented in terms of the extent of global penetration within the span of a decade, and that it is likely to have some profound economic and social impacts. What the immediate commercial significance of the diffusion of this set of communication utilities, and particularly the extent of expansion of electronic commerce on the WWW, remains far from clear at present despite the many optimistic forecasts stimulated by the rapid rate of uptake of nascent tele-shopping services.

2. The emerging GII environment: visions, challenges and choices

Business and government policy leaders in the developed nations are converging on a common vision of the future of telecommunications. Privatisation and competitive entry are expected to create the economic incentives for construction of a telecommunications infrastructure capable of delivering broadband connectivity to all subscribers. National information infrastructures will be stitched together to form a 'global information infrastructure (GII) extending broadband connectivity throughout the world. At both a national and global level the fabric of the new information infrastructures will be sewn together using technical compatibility and interface standards, the subject of this paper. The ambitions for the GII are extraordinary. Standards frameworks, open network access (ONA) in the USA and open network protocol (ONP) in Europe, are expected to resolve technical inter-connectivity and inter-operability issues and to allow the upgrading of capacity without resorting to a central planner, the traditional role of the telecommunications network operator. It is generally understood that the vision of broadband interconnectivity will be achieved incrementally, with business services leading the way in two-way high speed access and consumer services initially based upon asymmetric connections (with high capacity incoming and lower capacity for return). Even with these limits, a vast array of new services is expected to emerge, a foretaste of which may be found in developments ranging from the WWW to corporate desktop video conferencing. These developments are expected to increase the productivity and competitiveness of business enterprise and lead to a faster rate of employment growth than would occur otherwise.

Achieving the GII vision will require reconciling its ambitions with the institutions and market mechanisms that have been created during the past century of voice telephony, and with more recent developments stemming from rapid technological progress in both information and communication technologies. The current approach to effecting this reconciliation is the substitution of standards of inter-operability and inter-connectivity for the traditional central planning of Public Telecommunication Operators (PTOs). *Technical standards* affecting the compatibility of information system components and network *inter-operability* (as distinguished from mere interconnection), are likely to have an especially critical role if more than incremental progress is to be made towards the fulfilment of the GII vision.

a. Technology standards and the emerging GII environment

As is commonly understood, the creation of the GII will entail a substantial upgrading of the present telecommunications network. There are three main aspects of the transformation that is envisioned. First, it will make it possible to deliver new services based upon substantially greater bandwidth than is available currently using voice telephony or basic rate ISDN connections. Such services include video on demand, interactive video (multimedia), and video-telephony. Second, it will support growing use of inter-networked data communications like those now offered by the Internet, as well as new generations of value added network services for users of computers and other networked digital equipment. These services span a wide range of business, residential, and public sector 'tele-activities — for example, tele-working, remote learning, tele-shopping, and tele-medicine. The foregoing two sets of expectations form the basis of the demand side argument for the commercial viability of GII construction. Meeting those expectations, and thereby paying for the substantial investment costs of the upgrade, will require a highly dynamic development of the supply of new services.

Third, the upgrading of the network is linked to the policy aims of enhancing and accelerating the prospects for competitive entry in all facets of the telecommunications industry. Entry will require the enforcement of standards for inter-operability and inter-connection to make it possible for entrants to inter-connect at almost any 'location in the network. Despite considerable evidence that the supply of, and access to, advanced telecommunication services at present is both concentrated and unevenly distributed, it is widely believed that the GII will present few entry barriers for innovators, and that access will be nearly universal in industrialised countries. Thus, the threat or reality of competitive entry is expected to reconcile demand and supply.

These three features of the new telecommunications network 'vision represent marked departures from past experience in this field. Historically, a common and centralised control was exerted by national PTTs, or by regulated monopolies that in every country were responsible for the development of the telecommunications network for voice telephony, and that also had supported, in varying degrees, the creation of advanced services such as data communications. Current efforts, by contrast, are focusing on the task of defining global standards for a variety of purposes: (a) to permit switched broadband telecommunications, (b) to extend and upgrade data communications standards, (c) to resolve differences among proprietary data communication standards inherited from the past, and (d) to establish the means of implementing performance standards supporting interconnectivity. Collectively, these efforts amount to a novel attempt to control and manage the development of telecommunication networks through common agreements on interconnection standards. This new control regime would, if realized, supplant the historical regime: planning and implementation by more-or-less monolithic national agencies which coordinated their international communications business through international treaty organisations such as the ITU.

b. The Aim and Organization of the Paper

If we are to rely upon hopes that the GII vision is to be achieved, careful attention to the processes that will create these inter-operability standards is necessary. This matter is all the more serious because the GII fabric is not being woven anew, but instead must be sewn together as a patchwork of pre-existing national telecommunications infrastructures that are based largely on voice telephony, and are undergoing upgrading individually as a result of national initiatives to extend advanced telecommunication technologies and services. The following sections examine the array of economic and quasi-political mechanisms through which standard-setting, as a critical form of technology selections affecting telecommunication network evolution, takes place in practice, and the public policy issues that are raised by those processes.

The nature and function of technical standards, and their parallels with norms of social behavior are the subject of Section 3, immediately following this. Section 4 surveys the nature and performance of the so-called standards development organizations. These are the family of institutional arrangements that historically performed the task of setting telecommunication network standards to effect international connectivity and inter-operation, and which represent a formal cooperative approach to technological systems design. Section 5 examines the significance of network externality effects for the performance of technical systems; and the consequent strategic importance of interface or compatibility standards in coordinating the formation of distributed networks in the absence of the internalization of those effects under natural monopoly construction and operation. The dynamics of positive feedbacks driven by network externalities' effects in competitive markets and their influence on the strategies of rival standard-sponsors are treated in Section 6. That discussion, further, evaluates the widely shared expectations of network inter-operability, summarizing the economic and technical issues that often make this goal elusive. The most promising instances of 'uncoordinated standards developments, the Internet and the WWW are examined in Section 7, which offers some assessment of the prospects for the emergence of alternatives to the Internet/WWW as a basis for GII development. By way of a conclusion, after recapitulating several of the main points regarding the public goods functions of technical inter-operability standards in network evolution, Section 8 briefly considers the implications for public policy of treating social communication norms as analogous commodities.

3. Standards: a strategic information good for networks

Seen from the most general theoretical perspective, the analysis of technical standards properly belongs to the domain of information economics. Establishment of standards has greatest significance when economic agents cannot assimilate without substantial costs all the relevant information about the commodities that may be exchanged with other agents, and the processes by means of which those goods and services can be produced. Many features that have been noticed as problematic about the demand for "standards," and the supply thereof, are not peculiar to standards as such. They are, instead, generic attributes of information as a commodity. Lack of super-additivity is one example: just as having the same bit of information twice does not convey more information than having it once, so having two standards for the same thing does not mean one has more "standardization" — indeed, quite the opposite may be true. Specifying a technical standard has high first costs, which are fixed in nature, but the subsequent costs of each application of the information thus provided are negligible, so that the average total cost cost fall continuously as the standard is more and more widely adopted. Furthermore, once a standard has been promulgated it is difficult (costly), and generally unrewarding to prevent its contents from becoming ubiquitously accessible.

Broadly construed as information, standards may be held to have the function of reducing transactions costs. "Voluntary standards" is a term used in reference to technical documents formulated with this ostensible purpose; they have been described as "agreements intended to facilitate communication within an industry" (Link 1983, p. 393). Having a standard can lower transactions costs by making it simpler for all the parties to a deal to recognize what is being dealt in, and also by limiting the scope for the exploitation of informational asymmetries through practices such as giving short weight, short measure, adulteration, debasement of payment media, and so forth. Private agents' costs of information acquisition obviously can be reduced by the elimination of variety, so, "standardization" — the action of bringing things to a uniform standard — has the effect of facilitating economic transactions. Elimination of variety also may yield savings in unit costs of physical production, as is the case when achievement of greater uniformity permits economies of repetition, more intensive (larger scale) utilization of fixed facilities, and reductions in the relative importance of setup vs. operating time.

a. Technical compatibility (interface) and other standards: a taxonomy

The term "standards" has been used here in more than one way. It is employed substantively in the ordinary, dictionary sense, when referring to the means used in determining "the way things should be." This is broad enough to include something established by authority, customary usage, or general consent as a model, exemplar, or criterion; as well as something which has been set up and established by authority as a rule for the measure of quantity, weight, extent, value, or quality. In modern parlance the noun "standard" also has acquired a special meaning, which is the one invoked when the International Standards Organization, or the US Federal Trade Commission (1978) uses it to refer to *a technical document* intended to describe design, material, processing, safety or performance characteristics of a product. In all of these usages it is evident that "standards" are objects of intentional or unintended "selection," and that the choices made among alternative formulations define the features and performance characteristics of technological systems of greater or less complexity.

A great diversity of standards is subsumed under the foregoing general rubric, and some distinctions of potential economic interest among them are bound to be obscured by concentrating theoretical attention upon their shared properties. In a seminal paper on this subject Charles Kindleberger (1983) suggested that the distinction between the two economic effects just noticed — reducing transactions costs and realizing physical economies of scale in production — provides a basis for categorizing standards. Some practical problems arise with this particular proposal, because a given "standard" evidently can perform both functions: the dimensional standards for lumber would appear to fall into one category at the sawmill and the construction site, but into the other when considered at the retail lumber yard. There is a more serious objection, however, against starting out to classify standards according to their ultimate economic effects. The latter should not be prejudged for the purpose of locating a standard within a taxonomic framework; rather, the question of the effects upon market structure and industrial performance is a proper subject of applied economic analysis, and so must be permitted to remain unresolved in particular instances.

Virtually the same objections may be lodged against selecting as a taxonomic principle the manner in which a standard comes to be set up — that is, whether it has been formalized *de jure* (through legislative mandate, administrative decree, legal ruling), or established without force of law by explicit voluntary agreement, or arisen *de facto* through customary usage or the congruence of many individuals' independent actions. This, too, is an important matter which is better left for a more systematic politico-economic inquiry than can be embarked upon here. Moreover, the origins of particular standards are likely to turn out to be as much a product of the institutional and market contexts as of any intrinsic qualities of the standards themselves.

How then might the various forms of standards be better represented for purposes of formal economic modeling? If one focused upon the aspect of standards as measures of one sort or another, a standard's relevant features could be described mathematically as involving the establishment of one of the following:

(1) an ordinal scale or measure against which the relative extent of some quality dimension is compared, of which gradation measures of the quality of many consumer products are typical;

(2) a cardinal scale for a quality against which some minimum or maximum bound is defined, as exemplified by the typical environmental standard;

(3) dichotomous sets, one being compatible with a standard and the other not, which typically holds for standards intended to assure compatibility among components or products. Standardization of technical interfaces characteristically falls into this category.

It must be acknowledged that this formalism does not overcome the problem of lack of mutual exclusivity: a given "technical standard" could be placed in more than one of the three foregoing categories. For example, being greater or less than some bound establishes two dichotomous sets, and the notion or "partial compatibility" further blurs the distinction between class (3) and classes (1) and (2). This is somewhat disappointing because drawing distinctions along these lines might prove useful in applied studies where enforceability of standards is a matter of interest; it may be that it is easier to insure conformity with a cardinal scale, because monitoring is cheaper to effect when it has some foundation in a scientific procedure, even though only an ordinal property of the standard (not giving short-weight) has major interests for the customers. Conformity to the standard of accuracy for the weighing-machine at the butcher-shop is of less relevance to shoppers than the standard's ordinal property: that the machine should not overstate true weight.

The foregoing suggests that a taxonomy helpful for economic analysis might be constructed using the two orthogonal principles of classification: one that refers to the nature of the things with which the standard is concerned, and another that refers to the informational function performed by the standard in reducing transactions costs. We may begin by dividing standards between instances in which the standard deals with features of an inanimate object (principally its material and design properties), and those in which the standard describes human behavior, procedures, and performance. This distinction creates a major separation between the entire class of *technical standards*, which are easier to specify *ex ante* in a fully quantitative manner, and standards for human behavior, which are typically codified *ex post* and generally retain greater elements of ambiguity.

The indicated separation may have some heuristic value, in calling attention to the fact that several distinctions that appear within the family of technical standards can be extended with little difficulty into corresponding distinctions among *behavior standards*. Social experience with the latter may then clarify our thinking about the former, but analytical propositions regarding the economics of technical standards may carry some insights for a discussion of the implications of culturally constructed norms for human social interaction (a matter to which we will return in the concluding section).

Thus one can distinguish three general categories or types of technical standards. First comes the category of reference standards, within which we may place definitions, terminologies, and classification and labeling schemes. A key feature of a *technical reference standard* is that it functions as a reference point in only one dimension; the informational categorizations or definitions alone serve to divide objects into sets. These sets can have either mathematical representation in a cardinal scheme such as weights and measures, and conventional dimensions (as in the case of 2 x 4 lumber, which has been standardized to be 1½" x 3½," sawn and dried); they can simply be a categorization scheme, such as chemical properties, or the grades of wheat, and meat. Thus, this class is more general than measurement type (1) above. (The behavioral counterparts of technical reference standards would then include such things as specific precedents in the law, and standards for the identification of agents performing specialized complex services, as in the case of professional licensing and accreditation standards.)

The next general class of standards can be viewed as providing information in the form of sharply drawn dichotomies. Technical standards belonging in this category generally involve the combination of a numerical and a categorical reference standard, in order to categorize objects on the basis of a *minimum admissible attribute*. It is a combination of measurement modes (2) and (3), because the designation of a dividing line turns a numerical standard in one dimension into a dichotomous classification scheme in the same dimension. (While it resembles the categorical reference class of standards because of the existence of a rule for inclusion and exclusion, the rule employed in the numerical case is an inequality.) The satisfaction of a safety level for the operation of a technological system, and the existence of technical safety features in an individual product or device, are exemplars of technical standards of this sort. Standards assuring some minimal level of quality in products belong here, too — such labeling standards fix a maximum for the proportion of chicken allowable in a "beef frankfurter," or the amount of gum arabic that can be present in a product sold as "mayonnaise." Among the behavioral analogues of this category of standards one would want to place legal codes that separate licit from illicit conduct, and job qualifications such as minimum educational attainment levels.

The third functional class of standards, and the one of greatest present interest, provides information required to facilitate physical interactions and behavioral "transactions" at interfaces between objects, or between agents, and also between objects and human agents (as in the layout of airplane cockpits, the oft-cited case of typewriter keyboard layouts and touch-typists, and the screen presentation of computer spread-sheet programs). Technical standards here may possess all the measurement features found in the first two functional classes, but they are more complex and present in more than one dimension. One feature of this class of standard is the multiplicity of judgements and labels that typically go into the exclusion and inclusion rule, but it is possible to think of special instances in which a single-dimensional minimal admissible attribute standard functions as a standard assuring the compatibility of components — e.g., in receipts for food preparation.

Rather than risk over-simplification, however, it seems better to consider the following illustratively complex example from the filed of microelectronic circuit design: the "TTL" standard, to which a large class of integrated circuits conform. Features of TTL ICs include the universal use of 5v. supply voltages, designation of 3v. or greater as a binary state of unity, and of 2v. or less as a binary state of zero. Although the standard itself is named after the original circuit design (Transistor-Transistor Logic) employed in fabricating a type of IC device, an IC can be classified as TTL if it conforms to the interface specifications that assign those voltage ranges to the binary codes — regardless of whether or not its actual circuitry uses transistor-transistor logic to perform logical functions. Notice that although here the "physical design of interfaces" standard stops at the boundary of the IC with its external environment or interface, functional compatibility depends upon the standard of signal levels which is defined in terms of minimal admissible attributes (2v. = '0', and 3v. = '1'), and the 5v. supply reference standard. Moreover, the performance and operating cost of an electronic *system* built with TTL-standard ICS is by no means determined when the interface issues are resolved by specification of that standard; because the operating speed of a system is often limited by the component device whose "switching speed" is the slowest, system performance may be determined by specification of a reference standard switching speed. Thus, in realistically complex technological systems, although the attributes of constituent design standards may be labeled according to the proposed taxonomic scheme, the type of standard controlling the construction of systems appears to be distributed arbitrarily across the main categories that have been distinguished.

Technical design interfaces, such as those between spark-plugs and automotive engine cylinders and electrical circuits, or the thread-sizes of nuts and bolts, and formal codes (like computer languages), are perhaps more familiar members of this category, and many of the most difficult economic policy questions surrounding interface standards concern the way that compatibility among components affects the benefits and costs of forming and operating complex technological systems. These will occupy the discussion in the two following sections, but, as the taxonomic framework notices, there are significant parallels that may be drawn in this regard between technological systems on the one hand, and the organization of commercial, social, and political networks, on the other hand. (Some of those parallels will be briefly explored below,in the concluding section.)

Whereas 'standard agreements' must be negotiated explicitly, 'standards' more generally may arise in other ways. One is the widespread passive acceptance of a set of specifications that has been promulgated by a single agent acting unilaterally. Alternatively a standard can emerge spontaneously, through an undirected competitive process in which many individuals exercise their choices among a potentially wide array of alternatives.

'Standards', therefore, may be established by the widespread acceptance of any of the following: (a) *unsponsored* standards, these being sets of specifications that have no identified originator holding a proprietary interest, nor any subsequent sponsoring agency, but nevertheless exist in a well-documented form in the public domain; (b) *sponsored* standards, where one or more sponsoring entities holding a direct or indirect proprietary interest – suppliers or users, and private cooperative ventures into which such firms may enter – creates inducements for other firms to adopt particular sets of technical specifications; (c) standards agreements arrived at within, and published by voluntary *standards development organizations* (SDOs); (d) *mandated standards*, which are promulgated by governmental agencies that have some regulatory authority. The first two of the foregoing outcomes emerge from market-mediated processes and are referred to generally as *de facto* standards. The latter pair usually issue from political ('committee') deliberations or administrative procedures which may be influenced by market processes without reflecting them in any simply way; both are sometimes tagged loosely as *de jure*, although the standards have the force of law behind them only in the last case.

4. Institutionalized cooperative standard-setting: committee consensus vs. market selection

Standards development organisations (SDOs) underlie most of the world's standardization activity and operate across nearly all product areas. Their creation, whether by government as public agencies or through private negotiation, can be viewed as a response to the difficulties of achieving coordination in a purely market-driven process. Further, inasmuch as the "products" of the SDOs themselves belong to the category of information goods, their production and distribution are subject to many of the sources of inefficiencies that are inherent in the treatment of information as a commodity. In contrast to the *de facto* process, however, rather less attention has been given to the operation and performance of the SDOs, their interactions with market-driven standardization, and the potential problems of "institutional failure," as opposed to "market failure" in the formation of compatibility and inter-operability standards. Moreover, it is apparent that these institutions find themselves having to cope with problems unprecedented in their history, and that at the national, regional and international levels the standards-setting regime currently is in something of a state of transition. Criticisms of performance, and proposals for restructuring and reform have, to date, been debated largely within the narrow venues of the various organisations concerned. But, the issues clearly have a much wider economic significance and raise concerns as to whether the changes in institutional structure and procedures will address the underlying problems in adequate and timely fashion.

a. *Voluntary standards development organizations: structure and scope and procedural ethos*

Today, formal SDOs operate at the national, regional and international levels. The world's first national standards body (NSB), the British Standards Institute (BSI) was founded in 1901 to create a forum within which industry, government and consumers could debate issues of standardization and arrive at some kind of consensus. This provided an institutional template (indeed, we might say a "standard") that was soon adopted around the world, with BSI's German (DIN) and French (AFNOR) counterparts forming in 1917, and 1926, respectively. Worldwide, there are currently more than 81 NSBs, which, typically, have been given responsibility for coordinating national standardization activity across all industry sectors.

The international SDOs, in contrast, typically are specialized along industry lines — as is evident from the identities of the leading representative of that category of institutions: the International Telecommunications Union (ITU), the Consultative Committee on International Telegraph and Telephones (CCITT), and the International Electrotechnical Commission (IEC). The reasons for their specialized functions and separation are largely historical. At the turn of the century, reaching national consensus proved to be challenge enough for most sectors. In the areas of telecommunications systems, however, there was an immediate need for common standards between countries to ensure the safety of equipment and the interoperability of networks. As a result, specialized international coordinating *fora* in these areas typically predate the generalized NSBs.

The International Telecommunications Union (ITU) can trace its roots back to the International Telegraphy Union which was founded in 1865 by a group of European national telegraph authorities convened in Paris. It was first established as an intergovernmental treaty organisation because the leading continental European telegraph systems of the day were government run, and so, it is not only the oldest specialized international organization in the communications field, but, arguably, the oldest in any field of endeavour. The ITU provided an institutional model for subsequent intergovernmental collaborations long before becoming an agency of the United Nations in 1947. Its'original remit was to facilitate international communications through the standardization of the technical, operational and tariff aspects of international telegraphy. Today, it performs analogous duties for the range of wired and wireless communications. Following a major reorganization in 1992, the ITU now has three main functions — standardization, regulation and development. Initially the ITU's voting members (the so-called "Big-Ms") comprised the monopoly PTOs. Many countries, however, have since separated telecommunications operators from government administrations, and as a result the tasks of the big-M members are now increasingly entrusted to national telecommunications regulators.

It was an early recognition of the need for compatibility, and perhaps even more crucially safety standards in the field of electricity that led in 1906 to the creation of the second international SDO: the International Electrotechnical Committee (IEC). The IEC now sets all electrical and electrotechnical standards and draws its membership from national electrotechnical committees; many of which also predate their respective NSBs. The first international steps towards coordinating other areas of standardization came in 1926, with the formation of the Federation of National Standardizing Associations (ISA), a U.S.-inspired organization whose activities were focused largely upon mechanical engineering standards. ISA activities ceased in 1942, owing to the Second World War. Following the end of hostilities, in 1947, a new body, the International Organisation for Standards (ISO) took up the work of the defunct ISA. Today the ISO deals with all areas of standards-setting other than the telecommunications and electrotechnical fields, drawing its membership from the various NSBs.

The industrial divisions upon which the ITU-IEC-ISO framework was erected are tending to become less meaningful as a consequence of technological developments and various structural changes in the world economy. These organizations have been slow in responding to this blurring in the boundaries between their areas of "responsibility," and, in particular, long resisted embracing the jurisdictional implications of the ongoing convergence of telecommunications and computer technologies. Some limited inter-organizational steps, however, have been taken towards accommodating the new order: in 1987, for example, the ISO and IEC formed the Joint Technical Committee 1 (JTC1) to oversee work in the area of information technology;, whereas that, previously, had fallen between the remits of the two organisations. This and other kindred coordination efforts, nevertheless, have stopped well short of a full-scale reallocation of responsibilities that some analysts see as being necessary to meet the standards needs of an upgraded, Global Information Infrastructure (GII).

The formal SDOs operate across the entire range of the generally accepted taxonomy of technical standards, producing (a) reference and measurement standards, (b) minimum quality and performance, including product safety standards, and (c) compatibility and interoperability standards. Their basic function is to provide a forum for coordinating the choice between competing technological alternatives, and for developing technical specifications. They offer a channel for communicating information about the technical capabilities and commercial implications affecting the preferences of the individuals and firms participating in the committee process, and a mechanism for effecting a compromise when their interests, technological perceptions, or business preferences diverge.

A set of shared principles has shaped the development of the formal SDOs. These are:

- *Due Process.* Since the exercise is largely one of consensus building, strong emphasis is placed on observing due process;
- *Fairness and Transparency.* SDOs operate according to published rules and procedures that are fair and transparent. Moreover, participation is open to all on a non-discriminatory basis;
- *Consensus.* The general objective is that the output of the SDO should reflect, as far as possible, the consensus of opinion among all stakeholders. Decisions are generally made on the basis of unanimity, particularly at the level of the technical committees;

- *Voluntarism.* The process usually is considered as voluntary in the two-fold sense that all participants are volunteers, and that the implementation of any standard is not biding upon the membership.

These guiding principles have been reflected in the formation of SDO's internal procedures, which typically are based upon a hierarchical organizational structure. At the top lies the General Assembly (GA) which determines strategic objectives, and acts as the final arbitrator of any dispute. Below this comes the Technical Assembly (TA), which has the responsibility for devising specific work plans, and for ensuring that these meet with the general guidelines laid down by the GA. Finally, the technical committees (TCs) have the task of writing and agreeing the technical specifications to be submitted for approval as standards. TCs may also form sub-committees (SCs) and working groups (WGs) to undertake different aspects of their work.

As far as concerns the work carried on by the technical committees and their sub-groups, an important distinction can be drawn between efforts to select among and harmonize existing technologies, and the development of totally new specifications. The former can be conceptualized as bargaining activity over selecting a coordinating point for producers of interoperable technological systems. Of course, in order to achieve a compromise between competing technology sponsors who have proprietary interests in existing product specifications, it sometimes is necessary to develop a new design that combines some technical features from each of the contending parties. The latter situation arises especially in the course of writing *anticipatory* standards, that is standards in advance of the formulation of technical products that are ready to be marketed. Anticipatory standards development work, although carried on by the same NSBs and formal organizations, really is quite different in nature from the optimization of mature technologies and reduction of superfluous variety in designs and specifications; it has be viewed as being and rather more closely akin to cooperative, "pre-competitive" research and development — without a binding commitments on the participants.

b. SDO performance issues

The intent of these institutional arrangements, if not always their effect, is to very clearly separate the *political* from the *technical* aspects of the SDO's decision-process. In broad terms, the *political* power or voting rights are vested in the upper levels of the hierarchy, and made the responsibility of groups that would meet rather infrequently.. The GA's of international SDOs, for example, used to meet only once every four years. In contrast, the *technical* work is undertaken at the lowest level of the organisation within the TCs, SCs and WGs. These typically meet on a more frequent and regular schedule. Consequently, once a *technical* agreement on a draft standard has been reached within the TC, the process effectively grinds to a halt as the specification passes back up the hierarchy for circulation among the members, comment, and ultimately *political* approval and publication.

The opportunities for delay and stalemate that are present in both parts of the process, undoubtedly, are exacerbated by a technocratic ethos that frowns upon resort to legislative stratagems such as "linkage" and "log-rolling" as mechanisms for resolving conflicts. Traditionally, this was the dominant ethos within the SDO's, and a technocratic stance continues to be viewed as appropriate and highly desirable by many participants in the work of the technical committees. From the economist's viewpoint, a critical problem for voluntary standard-setting via committee consensus is that it simply may not be possible to achieve agreement without arranging for elaborate "side-payments," especially when it is necessary to resolve conflicts among interested parties that involve the *distribution* of the benefits that standardization would provide. This is compounded by the institutional rules of organizations conforming to ISO principles, particularly, the requirement that participation in committee deliberations be open to all potential stake-holders.

In the computer and telecommunications field, the standards arrived at in this way often are the ones that allow participants to earn some quasi-rents on the respective "components" of the network in which they had developed a special competence. Such compensation will be needed, generally, to induce the cooperation of firms who believe they would surrender a valuable competitive advantage by relinquishing their freedom to switch to the use of some new proprietary standard; or that rents which they enjoy as integrated system sponsors would be competed away once standardization permitted easy entry into the market by suppliers of separate components. Feasible arrangements for side-payments among "stake-holders" could be facilitated by changes in anti-trust policy, favoring formation of joint ventures among rival system suppliers for the purpose of developing industry standards. These, however, soon begin to assume the features of a cartel which, in turn, would call for some measure of continuing governmental oversight.

However difficult it may be to achieve confined cooperation in a timely fashion, voluntary standard-setting is nevertheless viewed by many as the appropriate public policy course because it represents the lesser of two evils. The greater evil, in this case, is regarded to be the potential efficiency losses arising from governmental imposition of "wrong" standards. It is pointed out frequently that public authorities do not generally possess the technical expertise required to write technical standards, and so must in any event rely upon information obtained from sources closest to the technology in the private sector.

Voluntary standard-setting through formal committee negotiations are an alternative to market-driven standards, but there is growing concern that this mode of creating standards is proving ineffective in achieving inter-operability in telecommunication services. Inability to anticipate adequately the standards needs of emerging markets, failure to stop the exit of important sub-coalitions of producers into private standards-making consortia promoting their own '*de facto* standards, long delays in producing recommended standards, and failures to achieve closure on particular standards are among the criticisms levelled at the performance of existing voluntary standards development organisations.

These criticisms would be fully deserved if it were true that the delays and blockages in voluntary standards negotiations arose from petty committee disputes among experts who were not acting in the interests of the companies that backed their participation; or that in representing those interests (e.g., refusing to agree on standards that would be disadvantageous to their company) they were imposing private costs upon rival companies and social costs upon potential users. In practice, however, many of the performance problems of the voluntary standards process reflect the workings of the same economic incentives that obstruct the achievement of inter-operability through 'de facto or market-driven standard-setting. Private interests are not united in desiring immediate standardization, and are at odds over whose is to be made 'the standard, and this compounds the opportunities for committee disagreements to arise over technical differences of opinion. Further complicating the problem is the fact that the technical and economic implications of decisions are subject to considerable uncertainties due to rapid technical change.

Both voluntary standard-setting and market-driven and processes elicit strategic behaviour in furtherance of private business interests. At present, there are no clear guidelines available from economics for structuring the work of the voluntary SDOs, or for assessing the public welfare implications of its performance. It will be clear from the discussion in the following section, however, that market mediated standardization has the potential to produce anti-competitive outcomes that may need to be remedied by active competition policy for the telecommunication and information service markets. By extension of this observation, it should be appreciated that the recent tendency for corporations in ICT industries to by-pass the SDOs' procedural principals by forming private anticipatory standards development consortia has opened a path that may result in cartel-like control over the future evolution of telecommunications technologies. To understand the dynamic market forces that may speed the selection of technology standards, but can do so at the cost of commiting users to choices constrained by system parameters that are technically or organizationally inferior, we must turn now to examine the economics of 'network effects' and the positive feedback processes to which these and related positive externalities can give rise.

5. Market competition and standardization processes in the presence of network effects

The technical interrelatedness of the components that form, say, a communications network, requires strict compatibility at each interface, node, or linkage point, in order for the system as a whole to perform efficiently in an engineering sense. Hence the functioning of any component of an integrated technological system cannot be evaluated in isolation, and its within-system performance can be affected by the attributed or behavior of other components. A second point to notice is that the existence of system scale economies, or benefits of more extensive network integration, means that the economic value of any technically defined variant of system design can in some degree be enhanced for those using it be enlarging the size of the user-community. When technically interrelated components of a system are supplied by independent economic agents, both features give rise to "network externalities."

The first form of externality impacts immediately upon the technical performance of the particular system as a whole, and feeds back to affect the costs and profits of other characteristics upon users' demand for it in comparison with alternative technologies. The second form operates directly upon the demand side of the market, where the benefits derived by users increase with the number of others whose decision to use compatible products enlarges the coverage of the network. The paradigmatic network externalities, discussed for the case of telephone systems by Rolphs (1974), involve both "call externalities" and "subscriber" externalities: the greater the number of network members by whom one may be contacted, and the greater number of fellow-subscribers who one may contact, the greater is the value of the communication service.

Adding a marginal subscriber should thus be expected to generate some incremental willingness to pay for the service on the part of the existing subscribers, inasmuch as it tends to increase with the number of others on the network. Indeed, considerations of this kind lead to the rule of thumb known as "Metcalfe's Law"— attributed to Robert Metcalfe, the inventor of the Ethernet — which holds that if the private benefit of providing an individual subscriber with a connection remains constant, the value of the network to the totality of its members must increase approximately as the *square* of its membership size. This follows from the face that the number of potential pairwise interconnections in an network of size N is N(N-1), so that if each interconnection is valued symmetrically, the maginal *social* benefit of adding a member is proportional to 2N. The exclusive provider of network membership services would thus strive to expand network size so long as at the margin the positive externality effects ran ahead of the incremental costs of providing capacity to avert the rising negative externalities, in the form of congestion effects.

a. Network externalities and interface standardization: statics

Yet, as economists widely appreciated, externalities (of any sort) create problems when resource allocation is left to market price competition. We may note, before putting to one side the existence in telecommunications and other information service industries the implications of large fixed costs for infrastructure facilities, and low marginal costs of production. Price competition tends to be unsustainable, as prices are driven towards marginal costs, leaving unit fixed costs uncovered. At the same time, the tendency towards marginal cost pricing of access to the network may induce expansion to continue until high and rising congestion costs are being sustained by all users.

Beyond that there are difficulties more specific to the provision of network compatibility standards that are required to coordinate the activities of the suppliers of the components of an open, distributed network system. First, there is the generic problem that the provision of interface specifications, or communication protocols needed to interconnect existing terminals and to form networks of networks, would yield "public goods-like" benefits that whoever undertook the development of the standard generally could not expect to appropriate fully — particularly if a measure of competitive were preserved. Perfectly competitive suppliers would be unable to capture those gains, and hence would be incrline to free-ride on the standards development investments of others. Second, to the extent that existing subscribers to a network would derive incremental benefits from the enlargment of the subscriber list brought about by effecting compatiblity with another network, their gain would be far smaller than that of the members of a much smaller network. Thus, although providers of network services that were proprietary, i.e., "privately sponsored standards," might have profit-seeking motives that encouraged network integration, these incentives are likely to be substantially weaker in the case of dominant incumbents than they were among smaller network sponsors. The value of the effective network expansion is much greater for the customers of the latter class of network operators, but it is in the interest of the dominant network operator to refuse them the connection.

Thus, as is now widely accepted, competitive markets are likely to work poorly as mechanisms for quickly ahieving the degree of compatibility or standardization required to maximize the benefits obtainable with an already existing network technology. This is not to say that uncoordinated networks will never arise via the decentralized profit-seeking actions of agents who will not or cannot be bound by enforceable contracts to maintain stipulated interface standards. What is most likely to happen early in the development of a network technology is that there will be a multiplicity of configurations, each of which is not fully compatible with the others. In the early days of the computer boom, for example, although peripheral equipment such as tape drives had to be designed to interface with central processing units (CPUs), little was done to allow data recorded on one type of machine to be read by another: by 1960 there existed fifty models of tape drives, with physical tape widths ranging from one-half inch to two inches and the number of parallel data tracks ranging from seven to forty-eight (Brock 1975, p. 77). More prosaically, the owners of Nikon and Pentax SLR cameras on an outing today can lend 35mm film to each other if one of them has an extra roll and the other has run out; yet they cannot share lenses unless they have equipped themselves with special adaptors.

Societal advantages which could justify government action to induce interface standardization are therefore seen to lie both in the greater benefits afforded to those users who would adopt the new technological system in any event, and the marginal benefits derived through the extension of its use to others who otherwise would have had to bear the costs of installing adapters, or "gateways" to achieve ex post network integration. Further, standardization of component interfaces sometimes can allow customization which better suits the varied needs and tastes of users, as has proved to be the case with hi-fidelity audio systems. Beyond these, there may also be generic standardization gains for complex system users: design information and engineering costs may be reduced, along with search costs and uncertainty regarding system performance. Greater price, and/or quality competition among suppliers of standardized components is more likely to ensue, supposing that the latter can enter the market more readily than can firms who must undertake to provide an entire system. Market structure and conduct may well be improved by the standards for interchangeability which restrict the scope for "tying" arrangements (Leland 1979, Lecraw 1984).

On the other hand, in a pure market environment, coordinated network technologies may be developed through the private sponsorship of a set of interface standards which are embodied in a proprietary system: all the necessarily interrelated components of a consumer product or a production facility can, in many instances, be readily packaged together by a single provider. Such a supply-agent may be referred to as an integrated system sponsor; and the particular product of service supplied as a system variant. An obvious difficulty arises, however, where the entailed capital costs are so large that they pose effective barriers to the entry of rival system variants, and so give rise to natural monopoly systems such as exist in the paradigmatic network industries: railways, telephones, electric utilities. Hence the problems of achieving standardization can be replaced by those of regulation that emerge where firms acquire great market power.

b. *Regulated monopoly and mandatory standards: problematic solutions*

Where technological innovations offer the possibility of contesting established market positions by offering cheaper or superiour quality network services, such as mobile telecommunications services, effective competitive restraints upon an incumbent's exercise of market power require that the regulatory authorities assure that an entrant's access to potential customers can be gained through inter-connecting with the incumbent's network on terms that are economically viable.

The literature on the economies of standardization recognizes an alternative route to network coordination, which may look attractive in eschewing the creation of natural monopolies requiring regulation: public authorities may hope to foster network integration *ex ante*, and so to promote competition among suppliers of network components, by promulgating uniform interface standards for systems purchased by government agencies, or by mandatory imposition of standards in regulated industries — such as has been the case in regard to broadcast telecommunication media that (also) are assigned portions of the electromagnetic spectrum. That losses of potential efficiency may result from the legislative of administrative setting of technology standards, and also from governmental efforts to induce cooperation among firms in the voluntary setting of standards, is generally regarded as the central dilemma facing public policy-makers in this arena.

6. Positive Feedback and market-driven emergence of de facto standards

The discussion to this point reflects a largely static conceptualization of network industry economics, in which the core problem is seen to be the fact that market competition does not lead to enough standardization to optimize the efficiency of existing network technologies. Yet the world takes on a very different appearance when one turns to consider the dynamics of market rivalries among alternative variants of a network technology — whether these are sponsored or unsponsored. Such an approach seems especially appropriate to the current economics of the internet and the emerging global information infrastructure (GII).

An extensive literature emerged in economics since the mid-1980's devoted to analyzing phenomena and policy issues that arise when standardization processes display increasing returns (to the marginal adopter) in the number of existing adopters. Increasing returns to adoption occur either through demand side externalities, network effects, or installed base effects, or more generally through cost reductions attributable to experience-based learning, or to the attainment of system scale economies. An overriding theme in these analyses is that situations with increasing returns differ fundamentally in the dynamics of development, and in the comparative statics of their outcomes, from situations characterized by constant or decreasing returns in the extent of adoption. At the macro-level, dynamical systems of the former kind display 'positive feedback', whereas, in the latter two cases, respectively, there is no feedback (state independence) or negative feedback. As a general proposition, it is known that where there are strong positive feedback effects, the system will possess a multiplicity of stable attractors, or equilibria. Those points of equilibrium (in relative market shares held by the various technological standards) need not be situated at the extrema, where *de facto* standardization on one or another of the relevant alternatives is complete.

a. Unsponsored de facto standardization processes

More specifically, it has been shown that under conditions of competitive entry of network service providers, and in the absence of governmental intervention to mandate inter-operability standard and set inter-connection access charges, the existence of significant increasing returns in system scale can give the result that one variant will drive out all the others and so emerge as the de facto standard for the industry. This may occur quite spontaneously, that is to say, without the presence of a 'standard-sponsor' who pursues a pricing policy, or other marketing strategy aimed at pushing the market share, or 'installed base' of adopters beyond some 'critical mass' point. Individual purchasers of hardware, or of software – whether operating systems or applications, typically will make their selections sequentially rather than simultaneously, and therefore do so within the context that has been formed by the preceding durable commitments of other agents. In order to enjoy the positive externalities of compatibility and inter-operability, their choices may well diverge from those which they would have made had they been free to choose in isolation; or had they been able to enter into some contractual arrangements that would have induced their predecessors in the market to considered their (different) preferences and predilictions among the available variant systems.

Of course, the typical situation is one in which the first choices are made, at best, under uncertainty as to what technological options subsequently may become avaiable, and inter-temporal contracting among successive cohorts of users is entirely infeasible. Consequently, the technological solution that emerges as a market winner, and whose victory is sealed by the endorsements of later compatibility seeking purchasers, need not be the most efficient among the available alternatives, nor te one which adopters would have chosen – if a different historical sequence of choices n the part of others had preceded their own. The problematic layout of the QWERTY keyboard bears witness to the practical relevance of such theoretical considerations; similarly prejorative comparisons have been made about the technical features of information and computer system variants that triumphed in market contests: Sony's Beta-Max VCR format, compared with the JVC design; MacIntosh's operating system, compared with MSWindows; the BASIC programming language, compared with many alternatives, and so forth. Although some among the latter instances clearly involved sponsored (proprietary) standards, examination of the specific case histories suggests that the eventual market outcomes were not strongly shaped by deliberate strategies pursued by the protagonists; rather, the market competition that evolved was shaped by decisions, and some extraneous events in the early phases of the technologies' elaboration, sometimes before it had become clear to the players that network externality considerations would become preponderant.

b. Sponsored standards: strategic business behaviors and competition policies

The existence of 'bandwagon and network externalities in the adoption of compatibility standards for telecommunication services suggests a variety of possibilities for strategic business behaviour in the emerging GII. Two interesting possibilities, in addition to the efforts to manipulate compatibility standards to generate additional profits, are the potentials for anti-competitive pricing and efforts to capture the lead in '*de facto* standardisation by 'super-setting existing standards.

The problem of anti-competitive pricing is particularly difficult in industries where costs and demands are dynamic. What conditions are necessary to demonstrate that a firm is pricing below costs with the intention of damaging rivals ability to compete? When prices are linked to the adoption of a compatibility standard that is mutually incompatible with those of rivals, there is a potential and acceptable rationale: social benefit from 'penetration pricing (which might be perceived clearly as predatory) in the form of the encouragement of the production of complementary content that meets the predator s compatibility standard, and thereby magnifies the impact of the pricing strategy in accelerating the adoption of a service. Since many of the costs of both service and content are likely to be fixed, initial low prices simply may represent an optimistic view of what the level of demand is likely to be after the market develops. Therefore, it becomes virtually impossible to determine whether or not a particular (low) price reflects anti-competitive intent, rather than simply an aggressive effort to develop a larger and profitable market. In an international context this sort of issue is particularly contentious, as has been illustrated by the problems of international competition in the integrated circuit industry.

In addition to relying on pricing as a strategic instrument to engage and augment the effects of 'bandwagons and 'installed base network externality effects, firms also may choose to employ quality competition and, in particular, feature 'super-setting to attract a loyal following of users. As noted earlier, super-setting preserves some of the network externality advantages of inter-connection while permitting access to additional functions not included in the 'basic package of a GII-related product or service. Super-setting disrupts standards to the extent that it creates information flows that are not inter-operable with other applications or hardware connections. This strategy, however, already is broadly employed on the Internet, where there are now available many 'add-ons to the (*de facto*) standard 'browsers and other tools. Netscape, the leading vendor of such browsers, initially employed an extreme version of 'penetration pricing , by freely distributing its software to the academic community (and, in effect, many other users). Having thus established an enormous user base, Netscape now is in the process of building its share of the commercial market for 'add-ons and business-oriented applications related to its 'platform product. By recurrently upgrading their product and bundling into it more functionality, they are pulling ahead of companies that offer simpler tools for Internet access. Gaining a lead of this type makes it possible to define the product characteristics and technical compatibility standards in ways that disadvantage rival vendors, and so establishes substantial market power in the provision of a (improved) service — one that at the outset was offered freely in an inter-operable form that maximised the network externalities.

Pricing, and quality competition through 'super-setting, are only two of the possibilities for exploiting network externalities and 'bandwagon effects to reinforce proprietary compatibility standards and generate a strong market position. They also illustrate the potential for deep conflicts between the hopeful vision of an enhanced and inter-operable GII, and the immediate commercial interests in attaining various proprietary compatibility standards. A closer examination of the most promising development in 'uncoordinated standard-setting for information services, the Internet, suggests further ways in which technical standards can exercise major economic leverage upon the dynamics of network development; and also illustrates the potential costs of market myopia.

c. *Theory and reality: the elusiveness of global inter-operability*

Telecommunications networks are already among the world s most complex technical systems, and increases in the functional complexity of these networks will require major efforts not only to establish technical compatibility standards, but also to monitor their interaction and performance. Standards play a central role in efforts to maintain service quality while accommodating a greater variety of service offerings from a growing array of competitive entrants. Ideally, such standards will not involve tradeoffs between service quality and variety, but will knit together advanced telecommunication networks in a seamless web of inter-operable technologies and services. In practice, however, there are many reasons why such a construction may prove difficult to achieve.

The economic reasons for the elusiveness of inter-operability as an emergent property of decentralized choices in these network markets are to be found in three types of incentives that face producers and users of advanced telecommunication services. The first is the traditional incentive to innovate, created by the expansion of the technological opportunity set. Innovation creates differentiated services that may be incompatible technically, but, nonetheless may be chosen by users because they improve performance or meet an idiosyncratic need. The innovating producer profits by gaining a lead over rivals, through first-mover advantages of becoming identified with developing a new market, through cost-reductions from moving down a 'learning curve', or from intellectual property rights protection of their innovation. Intervening in this process to suppress 'non-conforming products or services, and thereby achieve higher levels of inter-operability, will produce a direct loss of welfare for those producers and customers who otherwise would have benefited from innovative alternatives. Political pressure groups may readily form against the *de jure* imposition of standards in new areas, since potential vendors in many specific product areas can perceive a common interest in keeping the field(s) open.

A second set of incentives favours individual, uncoordinated efforts to 'standardise a service by seeking large-scale adoption of a particular technology. Both 'bandwagon effects (in which users cope with uncertainty by imitating one another) and 'network externalities (in which users enjoy a benefit in consequence of the previous adoption decisions of other users) provide dynamic mechanisms leading to widespread adoption and thus tend to support the creation of '*de facto* or market-driven standards. Such standards will tend to reduce the rate of radical innovation as they will 'lock in users to a particular product or service, often including its subsequent upgrades. The appearance of markedly superior services may undermine the equilibrium achieved through mass adoption, and thereby set off a new wave of adoptions that leaves a significant number of users 'orphaned by the discontinuation of vendor support for the former '*de facto* standard. The risks of social losses from the 'creative destruction of established standards do tend to diminish, however, as the pioneer technology becomes elaborated and users perceptions of their business needs, and tastes, become adapted to it.

The third type of incentive affecting the realization of inter-operability is the attractiveness of 'super-setting existing standards to create a differentiated product that preserves compatibility with incumbent 'de facto standards, while offering incompatible features that provide 'value added for new adopters. Although this incentive leads to outcomes that nominally preserve existing compatibility standards, it also creates user-communities based on incompatible services.

Substantial complexity in outcomes will be generated by the foregoing three, relatively simple inducement mechanisms; and the theoretical economics literature on this subject has demonstrated that spontaneous convergence to a common standard is possible only when network externality or bandwagon effects are large and the net opportunity cost of switching is low· The variety of possible outcomes available under market-driven or 'de facto standards processes suggest the likeliness of coordination failures, frustrating the adoption of standards permitting universal inter-operability.

Is there a possibility of attaining higher social welfare by intervening in the process to mandate standards that represent a socially optimal trade-off between variety and the benefits of inter-operability? Unfortunately, the answer to this question, most likely, is 'no. The requirements for intervention are the ability to accurately specify the social opportunity costs of a mandated standard in suppressing innovative variety, and the ability to enforce such a standard. There is little basis for assuring that at an early date we would know the social opportunity costs of 'locking in users to any particular mandated standard, and it is clear from the history of earlier standards (such as the NTSC standard for North American television or the frequency allocation for voice telephony circuits) that such social opportunity costs can be high.

In the case of telecommunication services, there also are problems of enforceability. Large businesses already are capable of configuring existing technology to deliver many advanced telecommunication services. Mandating that they should be 'locked into an inter-operable standard with lower performance would directly conflict with the aim of liberalising the competitive environment of telecommunications. In addition, these users may simply 'exit from public network services if faced with an unattractive mandated standard.

7. The Internet and other routes to the GII

The meteoric increase in the numbers of Internet hosts and usage suggests that a set of '*de facto* standards for achieving the GII 'vision may be already well along in the process of widespread acceptance. The TCP/IP communication standards for data communications and, increasingly, the NCSA-sponsored standards for the WWW may be a robust basis for the future of the GII. This is suggested by the enormous size of this telecommunication network, as well as its accommodation of a wide variety of 'super-set type compatibility standards that maintain basic compatibility while permitting experimentation and variety.

All three of the components of the GII vision appear to be within reach through the incremental development of the Internet, and, in particular, the progressive removal of the 'bottleneck of local access speed for users that are unable to share a common high-speed data link to the Internet 'network backbone. When utilised in a local area network environment with high-speed local access, the Internet is capable of supporting new broadband-like services such as interactive video as well as voice telephony. The Internet is the benchmark against which inter-networked data communications services are measured, providing excellent e-mail and computer file transfer capabilities. The Internet also appears to be a model of decentralisation and competitive entry, with low entry barriers to new service providers and important entry opportunities for both value added network service providers (such as Internet access providers) and telecommunication network operators (including mobile and cable television operators). This happy vision, unfortunately, is marred by serious problems that appear when the Internet model is examined more closely. The pricing model for Internet services is based upon a fixed access charge to the network and no traffic-based charges on usage. A zero price for additional data transmission creates an incenti ve to devise services without regard to the demands they place upon network transmission capability. The potential for congestion problems on the Internet is a much debated question. Economists (see e.g. MacKie-Mason and Varian 1995) tend to argue on first principles that congestion is inevitable with the current pricing rules (although they tend to ignore other constraints in the system that may practically 'ration away the problems of backbone congestion, as well as possible institutional practices having similar effects). But the economists' arguments from principle are echoed by skeptical forecasts about the Internet's future from some highly knowledgable network engineers (see e.g. Metcalfe 1995). Centainly, one evident result of the pricing structure has been service innovations such as software-based Internet telephony, audio, and video applications as well as the growing use of graphic displays in network transmissions, all of which make heavy draughts upon available bandwidth. The other, related result is an explosive growth in Internet traffic, raising the potential of congestion effects in the network 'backbone provided by publicly subsidised 'bulk transmission lines connecting large servers, many of which also are publicly subsidised. These developments have been reflected lately in the wry popular re-interpretation of the WWW acronym as: "World Wide Wait."

The potential for the continued growth of congestion presents public authorities with three choices. First, they may choose to raise the costs of Internet access for connections with the publicly provided backbone, thereby setting in train increases in Internet access charges for private customers, and higher charges for public institutions (e.g., 'research universities) which governments would have to absorb. This is the average cost-based pricing solution — tally the total costs of capacity and divide it among the users. Second, the governments that fund the Internet 'backbone may elect to adopt usage-based pricing, so that higher charges would be levied for larger transmissions. Such pricing rules would, in effect, distribute the costs of building additional capacity non-uniformly, with those making the heaviest use of the system bearing a proportionately larger share of the costs. But, as MacKie-Mason and Varian (1995) have pointed out, this approach is not a 'marginal cost charging rule, since the marginal costs of using the backbone are essentially the same as the average costs; it is, instead, a means of distributing the costs of capacity according to usage. Larger-sized transmissions do not significantly raise the costs of electricity or other inputs into the operation of the 'backbone , but do impose higher costs on users who must cope with congestion effects. The reservation prices of these users for relief from congestion, which is the true marginal costs of capacity utilisation, cannot be determined in advance, however, since the congestion is an externality generated by users of high-volume datastreams, the "bursty" characteristics of which impose large and costly margins of excess capacity upon network providers who seek to avert severe slowdowns in service.

The third approach is continue to increase the public subsidy for the Internet 'network backbone, recognising that shortfalls in capacity will lead to rationing through congestion costs, i.e., utilisation of the Internet for some purposes will become unattractive due to response delays.

Average cost-based pricing itself would not remove the present incentives contributing to congestion. The prospect of increasing prices due to average cost distribution may, however, lead to changes in 'acceptable use policies in universities and other institutions. Such policies create costs in their enforcement and will only govern the behaviour of a subset of Internet users. Average cost-based pricing is likely to foster user access charges with a direct relationship between service quality and price. Only the higher service levels would support graphics and other bandwidth-intensive services, a development that would reduce the current incentives to behave as if Internet services were being conveyed on a high capacity GII.

Adopting comprehensive 'usage-based pricing for the Internet raises a different set of problems. The standards defining the Internet were devised without a direct concern for usage metering. To depart from this standard, a whole host of 'intelligent network features, such as those being deployed in the publicly switched telecommunication network, will have to be imposed on Internet traffic. Usage-based pricing for the Internet would require the adoption of new standards that would lead to a convergence between the practices of public telecommunication network and Internet. Such practices would include (a) the negotiation among Internet service providers of 'settlements depending upon traffic, (b) the accounting mechanisms to track these settlements, and (c) a means of billing these 'settlements back to users. The costs of billing under such a system would be substantial, although this method does provide the most direct inducements for innovations that would reduce congestion effects.

That, however, is not the end of the matter. If either average cost- or usage-based pricing is employed, there is no reason for the Internet to remain a largely public network. Already, many of the users of the Internet are accessing it through 'firewalls behind which lie extensive private networks. Attempting to pass on growing costs of the Internet to this heterogeneous community creates an exit incentive for large private users, which ultimately could leave public institutions and private individual users (i.e., those without institutional affiliations) to bear the fixed costs.

Thus, it would seem that the Internet is destined to become either another 'pay per view telecommunication service, suitable for re-integration in the public switched telecommunication network, or a pure public good in which usage is for the most part rationed through congestion costs. The much-praised self-organisation of the Internet is therefore not a panacea for the problems of centrally coordinated standards administration. Instead, precisely because of the open-ended standards the Internet employs, it is heading toward major difficulties in maintaining service quality and/or affordability.

a. Paying for the infrastructure: mass market standards, conditional access, and other routes

The absence of high capacity local access for advanced telecommunication services (in particular, universal broadband communications) makes it impossible to know whether demand is adequate to finance creation of such capacity. Promoters of the construction of broadband capacity argue that the market potential is large for services like the ones being developed on the Internet, as well as other, more specialised 'tele-services. Critical observers, however, note the relatively immature state of development of these applications and the absence of effective compatibility standards for delivering them. Still another group maintain that the revenues necessary for the construction of a broadband infrastructure can only come from the development of mass markets in home entertainment — including extension of cable television, video on demand, and interactive multimedia such as computer games.

In the cases of consumer services, it is clear that compatibility standardisation will be necessary to develop mass markets. A key issue is the definition of the technologies that will permit 'conditional access or 'pay per view types of services to proliferate, and whether these services will extend market access to consumers or restrict it. Conditional access systems present opportunities for restoring the model of control by a central actor in the development of advanced telecommunication services. This may be done directly if the provider of the 'set top box, or other access technologies, can dictate the terms and conditions by which competing content providers are able to access customers. (In countries like the U.S., The Netherlands and the United Kingdom, where there is a high penetration of cable television, one means of creating high-speed access is upgrading the cable network. But this comes with the prospect that the cable television company will install 'set-top boxes that effectively control user access to services.)

This form of overt control of customers on the GII is likely to reproduce the situation already apparent in the cable television industry, where local monopolies are often accused of offering limited service at high costs. At the same time, it is unclear that effective market development for home entertainment services can be accomplished by the decentralised methods observable on the Internet. Even if a compromise is attainable that allows unrelated parties to deliver services to residential customers, a possible outcome of compatibility standardisation in this area is that the design of user interfaces would 'channel users toward particular services (much in the way that flight reservation system operators were alleged to have favoured certain airlines). It is questionable whether existing regulatory institutions and competition policies are adequate for dealing with these issues.

Mandating broad compatibility standards or achieving a voluntary standard through industry consensus for advanced telecommunications services are the only routes that seem to offer a viable alternative to the progressive upgrading of Internet standards to provide broadband services. Individual countries may act to retain national identity, language, and culture through the creation of national systems for delivering advanced communication services, but no nation has yet committed itself to such a strategy. Thus, for consumer markets, the alternatives seem to be between upgrading the Internet to broadband services and creating 'purpose-built mass entertainment systems such as video on-demand or interactive game channels.

For businesses, the main alternative to Internet usage is the use of the public telecommunications infrastructure for connecting private networks. The impact of the Internet has been to accelerate both the development of private and public networks with the 'intranet, or institution-specific information network playing a growing role in large corporations. Private networks offer direct solutions to the problems of standards-setting, since they reproduce at smaller scale the centralised control that previously was available from a central communications manager. This 'solution leaves unanswered the problems of inter-organisational communications, particularly for services more complex than e-mail. These problems, often depicted as a failure in the standard-making process, are the result of the high costs of resolving inter-organizational differences in business practice and culture — except under the broadest and least constraining standards such as those governing the Internet or (X.400) e-mail systems. They also are an instance of the coordination failure that occurs as businesses opt for specialised and mutually incompatible solutions at different times in the evolution of their data communications needs. Further movement toward Internet usage will not necessarily

resolve these issues, especially now that a plethora of technical compatibility standards may be defined which are Internet-compatible.
The foregoing examples all share the private incentives problems previously identified, in Section 5. Adopting a common standard reduces variety and the benefits that may be obtained in providing specialized services using incompatible systems. Since in each of these cases, the user is required to make complementary investments in specific skills or knowledge to take advantage of a particular service, they are at least partially 'locked into that service due to the costs of switching. Thus, compatibility standards become a means of leveraging the control of one or another complementary component of the emerging GII into a position of market power in delivery of other goods and services. The same basic principles apply whether we are talking about the set-top box, the user interface for selecting advanced communication services, or the preservation of market share in private networks by equipment and service suppliers.

8. Conclusion: information technologies, social communication norms and the state

As the foregoing should have managed to suggest, important consequences — both private and public in their natures — are bound up with the economics of information technology selection and its impact upon the evolution of telecommunication networks. That the explosive growth of the Internet and the WWW are part of a profound restructuring of the pre-existing global telecommunications infrastructure should be just a evident as is the point that interdependent processes of technological and institutional innovations, particularly in the sphere of regulation, have acted as dynamic drivers in these developments.

We would be mistaken in trying to forecast the future simply by considering the implications of the new technological context into which we have moved, or the presently perceived balance in the economic interests identified with different groups of nations. One of the main conclusions of recent research on the evolution of technological networks — and one that legitimately can be applied in the analysis of social network structures — is this: the eventual outcomes are powerfully controlled by the persisting influences of seemingly small details of the particular historical paths which happened to have been followed. So, one may at least be confident that way the emerging global networks will impinge upon the cultural diversities found today among the world's peoples will be strongly shaped by their respective histories, and, as part of that heritage, the scope for intervention allowed to the nation state.
In approaching the latter question, and considering the rational basis for state policies that would circumscribe the development and deployment of emerging network technologies within their respective balliwicks, it may be useful to bear in mind the several parallels that can be drawn between the need for technical inter-operability in telecommunications systems and the role played by social communication norms in the effective functioning of social and political systems. By way of a conclusion, this line of thought can be elaborated further in the form of the following series of propositions.

(1) Culture provides an efficient information system basis for the nation-state. National cohesiveness and identity derives in large measure from the existence of a group or groups among whom social communications are easy and reliable. Obviously, such informational communities offer a substructure that facilitates the coordination of specialized production and distribution activities, fostering division of labor and increasing productive efficiency among the population identified with the nation.

(2) Network integration can be achieved by developing and maintaining uniform communications standards, and also via "gateways" or "translation" facilities that patch together distinctive local networks. But, at the national or community level, ex ante uniformity proves to be the most efficient arrangement supporting communications.

(3) Social communications standards have the properties of pure "public goods", which in general will not be not adequately supplied by the private self-interested actions of community members channeled through markets. Thus, the state itself may in some instances be called upon, as it is in other cases involving pure public goods, to assume the role of provider — or reinforcer — of the underlying community's sense of cultural identity; in other words, national leaders may have social as well as private purposes in heightening a people's sense of their cultural distinctiveness, and seeking to associate it with "national consciousness."

(4) However, it is also true that where choices among alternative communications networks are involved, coordination may be achieved "spontaneously" through decentralized self-interested actions. Thus, individual decisions made in the context of interpersonal relations, and the interactions of producers and consumers under perfectly competitive markets conditions readily can result in too much voluntary standardization too soon, as well as too little, too late. In other words, in the case of public goods like social communication standards, the form that "market failure" takes is not necessarily that of an insufficient degree of standardization; and there may be no need whatsoever for compensatory collective actions to further improve social communications by engaging the political apparatus of the state.

(5) Extensions of the sphere of social communications via voluntary actions in the context of international market competition can conflict with the preservation of national distinctiveness, which itself may be viewed as a local public good. Acceptance of informational standardization transcending regional and national boundaries — and thus eroding the former distinctions among communities created by gaps in social communications — increasingly is becoming a requirement for the economic viability of producers in many industrialized and industrializing nation's, and for the ability of consumers to enjoy the benefits of global division of labor.

(6) There is thus a paradoxical aspect in viewing the standardization of channels of social communication as providing public goods, inasmuch as it seems possible for groups to have too much access to such standards even though such access is

free. This paradox is part of the public goods supply dilemmas that government bodies encounter in trying to frame national policies affecting the preservation of distinctive linguistic and cultural norms, or supporting symbolic institutions that enhance social communications and a sense of national identity. It is essentially the same problem that arises when economic and political entities (business organizations and nations) find themselves having to chose among alternative strategies regarding the technical conformity or incompatibility of their information processing and communications facilities with international computing and telecommunications standards.

(7) Governments today are thus especially beset with new complications caused by the effects of the "information revolution"; falling information costs have rapidly raised the informational content of many of the goods and services being produced and exchanged among nations. Once upon a time, it was entirely possible for population groups to remain culturally distinct and fully in control of economic transactions crossing their borders. They could deal with one another through economic intermediaries, diplomatic protocols, and other "gateway" devices, while remaining far from socially communicative with other groups. This could be done without greatly sacrificing the benefits of the global division of labor, that is to say, without substantially hindering their people's participation in exchanges of commodities — like cloth, wine, pepper, or steel rails — which had little or no intrinsic informational content. But, the option of remaining only minimally communicative is daily becoming less and less viable as a national economic strategy. At the same time, advances in the technology of telecommunications and computing are creating conditions in which the very ability of existing nation-states to maintain control over their cultural identities and effectively pursue their economic, social, and security interests, are felt to be under challenge.

(8) The roots of the dilemmas arising from the impulse of states to preserve their peoples' cultural individuality in a world of rapidly falling information costs, obviously, lie in the historical origins of the national groupings that presently exist. New cultural groupings, supporting new national political alignments could emerge under the formative pressures of increased social communications made possible through the continuing dramatic advances in information technology.

(9) Perhaps the most compelling economic argument for the creation and perpetuation of cultural distinctiveness, and correlative linguistic diversity, is one that parallels the case made for the protection of bio-diversity at the global level. The key point is that different languages are formed in cultural contexts that render them less than perfect sustitutes for the expression of particular ideas, and, likewise for the conveyance of particular human emotions. Precise articulation of these are achievements in which human kind at large may be held to have an interest, so there is some tension between the (diverse) cultural circumstances that may be best suited to generate man exemplars, and the (homogenous) communication conventions that would permit their widespread

dissemination. As for the former, we are talking about illuminating and novel cognitive and affective expressions, and the corresponding literatures that a language's native speakers are most likely to create. These are not simply alternative encodings of the same, universal content, even though, once expressed in a given tongue, it may be possible to convey the distinctive ideas and sentiments in another language — thereby rendering accessible to a wider population. Diversity of natural languages contributes in this way to the *totality* of human expression and understanding, rather than simply protecting the rents that native-speakers of the existing assortment of tongues may enjoy by virture of their mastery of one or another of those modes of expression. This argument will be recognized by economists to be somewhat analogous to the proposition that technological standardization is inimical to the generation of innovations, even if it is most conducive to the widespread realization of the benefits of innovation through their adoption.

Our present national groupings arose from historical circumstances reflecting very different technological conditions, which influenced patterns of "social communications" and provided particular cultural substrata supporting political coalitions. New cultural groupings supporting new political alignments could well emerge as a result of the revolution occurring in information technologies. Alternatively, some existing nation-states may be propelled by special economic interest groups to create and maintain incompatibilities in their technologies, preserving territories from international competition in the provision of communications and information processing systems. And there may be powerful pressures on states to respond to perceived threats to the "integrity" of their cultural foundations, or to the erosion of their ability to monitor and control information flows, in ways that will reinforce a distinctive identity based on moral, religious, linguistic, or other "traditional" bases for social communications and ethnic or national self-consciousness.

Because the information revolution is rapidly undermining the distinction between "exchange societies" and "cultural communities based on informational exchanges," the economic costs of pursuing the goals of maintaining old patterns of distinctiveness or individuality in social communications are growing. The potential benefits of the global division of labor increasingly are coming to depend on information-commodity exchanges. So, there will be heavier costs imposed on consumers and workers by autarkic policies that react against the spread of trans-national information and the spontaneous emergence of *new* patterns of cultural programming.

In noticing the "public goods" nature of both (i) cultural standards supporting domestic communications and political cohesion, and (ii) compatibility standards for international communications, the difficulty of achieving a balance between "individuality" and "conformity" — at the societal level, as well as in one's own consumption activities — has implicitly been acknowledged. The public goods aspect of the problem makes it tempting to jump to the conclusion that market failure will take the form of underprovision of standards; whereas in the case of network connectivity, markets may result in too much, spontaneous standardization.

But, a deeper dilemma persists. While individual action through markets cannot be relied upon to achieve the optimal balance between diversity and conformity, it does not follow that national governments can be trusted to do a better job. Not only are national governments often subject to, or captives of special economic interest groups; the historical record should remind us that they often are biased representatives of the deeper interests of people, and that they have been tragically destructive promoters of nationalistic prejudice, enmity, and war. Especially when confronted with decisions regarding the delineation of national individuality, there is a real danger that national governments are responsive to the worst of human instincts. Even if their rivalries and aggressive assertion of the "national interest" (as they define it) do not precipitate international conflict, one must worry that national governments in this setting could impede the opportunities for progress towards greater social communication and sense of community among the world's people — opportunities that a wider sharing of information and information technologies could transform into realities.

Michael Hutter

The Commercialization of the Internet
A Progress Report

A. Introduction

The Internet has gone through a period of rapid, even accelerating growth over the past ten years. The number of networks connected grew from 217 in 7/88 to 32.370 in 5/94 (Merit Network). The number of hosts connected to the networks increased from 1.000 in 1988 to 2 mio in 1/94, and to 19.5 mio in 7/97. The number of domains jumped from 30.000 in 1/94 to 1.3 mio in 7/97 (Sarkar 1996; Hormozi, Harding and Bose 1998).

The geographical distribution of users is still very skewed and will stay that way: out of the 4.8 mio host s connected in 1/95, 3.4 mio were located in North America, 1 mio in Europe and .35 mio in Asia and the Pacific rim (Internet Services Group, in Karakaya and Karakaya 1998). However, some unusual new patterns appear. Users from countries like Finland are unusually active, and social subgroups in otherwise strongly isolated countries use the access to a global communication network. The distribution according to organizational purpose is shifting rapidly: in 1994, the ratio of educational to commercial to governmental sites was still 6:5:2. But since then, the number of commercial site has virtually exploded.

In 1994, fewer than 1.000 businesses in the U.S. were listed with web sites. A year later, the number had increased to over 15.000, "with an average of 73 sites added to the list daily". Aggregate revenue forecasts for the "Internet industry" were posted at $ 5.8 bio (Karakaya and Karakaya 1998:10 and 11). The growth takes place in all possible fields of application. The number of professional Net providers in the UK alone increased from 160 in 8/96 to 291 in 12/98 (Internet Magazine Dec. 1998:31).

During only one decade, the Internet has grown from a tool of science to a major new economic resource. Given the continuing, still accelerating rate of expansion, there is no telling where the frontiers of the new domain may lie. It is not surprising, then, that all sorts of attempts have been started to turn the potential of the Net into private monetary revenue. This is the process which we will call "commercialization", without intending to pass any value judgment on such activities.

For further and more detailed studies of Net commercialization, it is useful to distinguish three different kinds of goods and services. The three categories have different degrees of publicness – a concept that will be of critical importance in the discussion below:

(1) The service of using the Net itself
(2) Goods and services that make up the Net or are transmitted through it
(3) Goods and services that are advertized, ordered or executed using the Net.

I have studied the economic literature that accompanies the process of commercialization in these three market categories. The basic tenet in that literature is the presumption that individual economic agents will react to changes in their constraints and to changes of expected value alternatives in their environment. Using standard tools of the theory, one would expect that many access rights, copying rights and communication services which are all hitherto free will be priced and sold. However, the process of introducing prices in new commodity domains is slow and groping. It is complicated by the fact that we are observing networks rather than single objects, and by the fact that the networks do not transmit steel or cars but communication. Therefore, the solid solutions of commodity market allocation under private property regimes do not hold anymore.

The challenge of the new developments has led to a flurry of academic contributions to the "Economics" of networks, particularly computer networks, particularly the network of networks known as the Internet. The field features two impressive websites (Varian, Economides), it has been promoted by the contributions to a MIT workshop, published in 1996 in the *Journal of Electronic Publishing* and it will have its own European journal, *Netnomics*, starting in 1999. In addition, valuable contributions to economic ussues have come out in on-line journals aimed at Net users.

Still, the total set of contributions is rather small. It does not distinguish well between scientific analysis and academic advice to policy makers or business persons. To make things more difficult, the object under observation changes monthly right under the eyes of its observers: information traffic on the Net has increased a hundredfold since 1988.

All that can be aimed for under such circumstances is a "progress report" that tries to structure the available material along lines that help to estimate the paths along which the commercialization of the Internet is likely to proceed. To provide a basic structure, I will distinguish between the discussion (1) surrounding the installation of specific price regimes, (2) the discussion surrounding the emergence and change of market forms and (3) the discussion surrounding the installation and self-emergence of rules and institutions.

B. The Report

1 Price Regimes

1.1 Analytical Structure

There is general agreement in the literature on the basic economic treatment of a resource like the Internet. The Net is a network of nodes that connect communication hosts with each other and routes information packets between them. The value of a network increases exponentially with the number of nodes added. Shapiro and Varian (1999:183) suggest v(n)=n x n -n as an approximation.
In a network, the social benefits exceed private benefits as more users join the network. Since the network effects do not accrue to specific owners, they constitute "adoption externalities". Because of the externalities, the size of the network in competitive equilibrium is smaller than the socially optimal size (Katz and Shapiro 1994).
The "non-rivalry" and the "non-excludability" with which the positive effects are received qualifies the Internet as a public good (Dybvig and Spatt 1983).

The Internet qualifies as a public good not only because of its network properties, but also because of its content. The Net routes information packets. Information, unlike material objects, can be copied without losing its value to those who receive it: there is non-rivalry in consumption. The access to information can be controlled. But that often involves very high costs with less than perfect protection: non-excludability is at least a possibility. Therefore, the content transported on the Net has strong properties of a public good as well (Arrow 1997).

Public goods are not produced in private markets with "symmetric prices" i.e. prices that are the same for the buyer and seller (Hallgren and McAdams 1996). Their production is characterized by high initial costs for those who build up parts of the Net, or for those who invent the information contained in program that run on the Net . The high initial costs are followed by marginal costs approaching zero, as new hosts are hooked up to a network and users join a "software community" while maintenance costs remain constant. There is a strong incentive for actors to free ride on such efforts. If the net is small enough then there is a good chance that proprietary rights on the network or the software use allow the capture of all network effects. That is the case for the network of users of a specific PC program, or the users of software linked to specific hardware (Katz and Shapiro 1994). But for very large networks, or networks of networks like the Internet, the probability of such a strictly private solution is very low. The traditional strategic answer in such situations is "asymmetric pricing": the price paid by every single buyer is less than the amount paid to the seller because contributions are extracted from the members of a tax base in order to invest the funds in the maintenance and in the innovation of such public goods. In what follows we will focus on the Internet, although the results apply to under large communication networks as well.

The Internet is an example for a successful application of the economics of public goods: the Net was built up in the public domain of universities and research institutions. The NSF, a U.S. institution, funded the ANS TS backbone, a key part of the Net's physical infrastructure until 1994. That year, the NSF accounced that it would phase out its funding. The four Network Access Points and the new high speed backbone vBNS were to be operated by private companies (Sarkar 1996). Thus, the precarious initial phase of building up the network was stabilized by contributions that were taken out of general tax income of the USA. Once critical size was reached, the operation was turned over to private suppliers, both commercial and non-commercial.

Underinvestment is not the only public good problem of the Net. It suffers from a serious side effect of non-excludability: congestion. As long as the Internet is a free domain, there is no system of priority, i.e. of valorization, attached to the information packets on line. But the bandwidth of the Net's lines is limited, and the demand for sending and receiving high volumes of information has multiplied since real-time video can be sent over the net using cheap standard equipment, "pumping out up to 1 megabyte per second" (Sarkar 1996). The Net is not infinite. It is, in the terms of an analogy to environmental resources suggested by Hallgren and McAdams (1996), "depletable".

It seems appropriate, therefore, to interpret the Net as a "constrained" or "impeded" public good, something for which the term "common good" is fitting. Pricing is an effective means for regulating the allocation of a resource which has become constrained and thus scarce. In fact, Net congestion and its correction through pricing is the most prominent topic in the literature on the "Economics of the Internet". [1] But, as we shall see, adequate solutions are more complex than in the case of other common goods in the history of Western society.

1.2 Pricing the Net

This section deals with the use of the Net itself, not with the specific software and hardware needed to perform certain operations on the Net. The key players are the Internet Service Providers (ISP). They charge those who employ their services.

ISPs have traditionally used flat charges per host. Flat charges are easy to administer, but they do not discriminate with respect to volume or content of the information packets. They are a fixed charge related to access to, but unable to regulate traffic within the Net.

The most common alternatives in the debate are transaction-based and usage-sensitive charges (Knight and Bailey 1996, Brody 1995). Transactions are more differentiated than access, but they still do not distinguish between priorities. Therefore, usage-related pricing is commonly at the center of attention.

The technical pricing options available are too numerous to discuss in detail (MacKie-Mason and Varian 1995). The simplest approach would use parameters like distance and number of nodes employed, as in phone networks. That approach is hard to implement and inflexible. A more sophisticated approach would determine priorities in specified precedence fields. Many suggestions fall under this category. It remains open, however, how the field specification can be established without favoring some of the players. To avoid such difficulties, MacKie-Mason and Varian suggest a process whereby prices are established in a continuous process of bidding for slots on the Net. The Net would, in effect, contain the software which determines the constantly shifting charges for its use: "Each packet would have a "bid" field in its header wherein the user would indicate how much he is willing to pay. ... During congestion, users would bid for access and routers would give priority to packets with the highest bids" (Sarkar 1996).

The bidding approach makes the highest demands on technological sophistication, but it is feasible. However, Sarkar points out that in order to function such a market for Net priority has to be supported by "regulatory oversight" to keep those in control of bottlenecks from manipulating load factors. He also points to another, more fundamental strategy for avoiding congestion: technological innovation and input cost may allow vast increases in bandwidth, thus muting the issue. With such superwide information channels, flat fee providers would again outcompete providers with congestion charges.

Actual experiments with usage charges are at a technically simpler level. For example, Brownlee (1996) reports that the Net in New Zealand operates with a backbone that is run by a non-profit membership society called Tuia. Tuia charges according to long-

1 See the extensive bibliography by Economides 1998.

term traffic volume, differentiated in a few basic categories. The Accounting Meter and its Manager/Collector Programs (NeTraMet) can be downloaded for free since 1993.

A final constraint on the introduction of differentiated pricing is the cost of establishing and maintaining a payment technology. In phone networks, billing used to account for half of total operating cost (Brody 1995). That ratio will not change much unless ways are found to transfer payments through the Net, not through traditional banking channels as in credit card payments or prepaid charge accounts. Breakthroughs on that front are not forecast for the near future (Hughes 1995). This is, of course, an issue which concerns the development of markets in the Net and with the Net as well. But the strongest impact of payment in the Net would be on the pricing of Net use itself because of the high level of "granularity" at which single uses of the Net take place.

A viable way out of the charging problem may be the offer of tailor-made long-term contracts. Particularly private line providers offer huge discounts for customer commitment. Therefore, Gong and Srinagesh (1996) speculate that "the market may be moving towards contract carriage based on term/volume commitments and increasing efforts at differentiation, and away from the ideal of an unbundled bearer service."

To summarize: inspite of the very concrete danger of congestion, usage-sensitive prices for information load factors at specific times are slow in coming and may be outpaced by technological advances which alleviate the problem for a while, or by institutional innovations which help to channel funds to the growth of the Net.

1.3 Pricing in the Net

The debate on pricing for software and hardware in the Net hinges primarily on an aspect of the public good property already mentioned: High initial cost are followed by marginal cost close to zero once the network of users expands, or the "navigation tool" becomes the standard in its application function.

Shapiro and Varian (1999) take this condition as the starting point for a very practical exploration in the strategies that are open to entrepreneurs given that "information is costly to produce but cheap to reproduce" (21). They begin with various methods of price differentiation, supported by various product versions. They continue with approaches that go beyond pricing: the management of rights, of lock-ins and of positive feedback, the establishment of standards through cooperation and through aggression, and the constraints through competition law and government intervention.

The range of strategies is particularly relevant to companies operating in private property markets. Basically, competitors will try to "reduce average cost by increasing volume through reuse and resale". (28) They will also consider selling display rights to other producers, thus capitalizing the value of their network volume of users (Hutter 1997).

There exists, however, a radically different approach to pricing in the Net, namely, the "open source" approach (Raymond 1997). Its proponents argue that the benefits for the total Internet community and for the originator of a new tool are largest when the tool is made available at zero price, possibly with aids for easy downloading. This way, the largest possible distribution is achieved. Private revenue can still be generated through special services, like customized installations, proprietary licenses and exclusive training courses. With such an approach, new tools can be improved and updated by all their users (O'Reilly 1998). Open-source appeals to the university-based inventor who considers it part of his responsibility to distribute the knowledge contained in a publicly funded project, and it appeals to commercial competitors who are not large enough to defend their own network.

There are thousands of open-source projects, ranging from web servers (Apache), languages (Perl, Python) and programmers' tools to operating systems (Linux, BSD UNIX). Open-source strategies became a serious options for big players when Netscape disclosed and made available the source code of its browser in 1/1998.

To summarize: There is a market for commercial Internet tools using specific net-tailored pricing strategies. But the size of that market is constrained by companies both in the profit and the non-profit segment that practice an open-source policy and thus keep the prices for information tools (and content?) close to marginal cost.

1.4 Pricing Commodities connected with the Net

This category is so diverse in itself that it will be helpful to start with some differences.[2]

First, there are commodities that are produced for transmission on the net.[3] An example would be an electronic postcard, complete with sound and personalized features, sent to someone's email account, or a software program on accounting, advertized and transmitted through the Net, or pornographic images.[4] These commodities could be distributed in other ways, but their specific competitive advantage consists in being tailor-made for the Net transfer. We should expect that the domain of these commodities expands rapidly during the coming year. The major constraint will again be the available payment technology.

Second, there are commodities that cannot be digitalized and transmitted. These goods, consumption as well as investment goods, are distributed and shipped along traditional channels. But the advertizing and the ordering takes place via the Internet, which is, in turn, interconnected with the computing networks of producers and costumers. Some of

---

2 This has to be distinguished from the service providers discussed in 1B. The use of the Net itself is a service as well, and ISPs typically sell also general services like electronic mail. As greater generality is approached, the common good properties of the general service grow stronger.

3 Dertouzos 1997 distinguishes between direct and indirect electronic commerce.

4 It is inevitable that those kinds of trade benefit most which are inhibited by artificial transaction costs, as in the case of pornography.

the goods are off-line versions of Net products. Some are custom-made or just-in-time items. Most of them are the same goods that can be found in the mail-order catalogues of large distributors.

The new communication channel gives a comparative advantage to existing mail-order houses. It also leads to an expanded application of data-base marketing: customers are not anonymous anymore, and future offers can be directed to precisely defined target groups. Finally, the rate of growth will be greatest in sectors where the quality of the product is precisely definable. The success of book distributors on the Internet is an example.

Thirdly, there are commodities which are not material goods but services rendered. The Net is a communication medium, and it will therefore show its maximum impact in making communication possible in fields where communication was heretofore impossible or cumbersome. Examples are spezialized news services, chat rooms, discussion groups, Netgames, data bases, auction mechanisms and other aids to the execution of complex commercial transactions.

We should expect an increase in market volume in all three categories. Prices will be set around traditional steady market equilibrium in category 2, and along the typical, rapidly declining price path of information products in categories 1 and 3. Market expansion will, again, depend on the availability of payment on the Net. The cost of usage-based payment will, particularly in category 3, lead to strategies with heavy third-party advertising on the programs that are made available. The advertisers buy the opportunity to direct attention and links to their products while the "free programs" are being used.

To summarize: Increased commercial activity will certainly take place as more goods and services are connected with the net. But here, we are dealing largely with private commodities, where rights to material or intellectual property are fairly clearly established. Therefore, market process itself is not changed in its form. One major exception are information products that follow the logic of decreasing marginal cost in their pricing.

2 Market forms

2.1 General analytical structure

Market theory has traditionally studied two static cases: the case of competitive markets with many producers selling similar goods, and the case of monopoly markets where one producer has the right or the ability to sell a unique good. In both cases, there exists a stable solution. Markets with few producers of similar products do not have clear solutions. More recently, the strategic interdependence in such oligopolistic markets has been analyzed in game-theoretic models (Tirole 1989).

The study of information products in a network, however, leads attention away from equilibrium structure to the process of organizational change which accompanies the life cycle of such products. Every innovation is by its nature the potential object of a monopoly market. It competes with other potential monopoly products until one product captures the network benefits and "takes the market". Such net monopolies are temporary. The pressure of decreasing marginal cost leads to a diffusion of the gains: perfect copies appear, service loses relevance, technical progress generates superior substitutes. Thus, product markets connected to the Internet transform themselves along a pattern of competitive innovation, monopolistic domination, competitive imitation and new competitive innovation. Even the relative stability of oligopolistic skirmishing for market share is, as we shall see, the exception in product markets connected to the Net.

2.2 *The Net as a market: Access, rights and lock-ins*

The use of the Net itself seems difficult to monopolize. But the network properties generate continuously opportunities for temporary monopolies.

The Internet, although a free domain, can be accessed only through specific gates. The gates are under the control of commercial, educational and governmental providers. Access providers can extract monopoly rents from those who are locked into certain access gates.

The major cause of monopoly is customer lock-in. "Customer lock-in is the norm in the information economy, because information is stored, manipulated, and communicated using a "system" consisting of multiple pieces of hardware and software and because specialized training is required to use specific systems." (Shapiro and Varian 1999:116) Aspiring monopolists know the positive feedback effect of growth through lock-in, and they work hard to bring it about. Loyalty programs, for example, have begun to proliferate for that reason.

Information products like software can be protected from copying by being granted a temporary intellectual property right. Under that protection, an ingenious form of asymmetric pricing takes place: the monopolist's high initial prices can be maintained for awhile, thus rewarding the producer for the invention. It is not clear, however, whether copyright protection is always the most effective strategy given network effects: the trade-off consists in the slow-down in software diffusion due to the prohibition of free reproduction.

Temporary market leaders will follow strategies intended to perpetuate the domination. Such strategies are all the more promising when the financial power of market leaders like Microsoft or Intel has reached a volume that places them among the world's largest corporations. But this is not the end of the economic argument concerning argument, as sec.3 is going to show.

2.3 *Markets in the Net: Profit vs. Non-Profit*

Markets for software and hardware which is used to operate or "navigate" on the Net are not very different from the kind of markets observed just above. Of course, as the tools become more specialized, proprietary rights gain in relevance. Still, there is the same basic structure of lock-in as networks of users of a particular software product expand, promising potentially profitable monopolies. We therefore observe increasingly aggressive competition between net and program system providers, resulting in rapidly fluctuating patterns of market domination (Katz and Shapiro 1994). But we also observe, and that is a surprising fact, the successful operation of non-profit competitors.

Non-profit competitors come usually from a university background. They have built up their assets through public funding, and find themselves in a position to control a tool that has become a standard. In that position, the decision is made to make the tool available without payment and to raise the funds through a membership society.

An example for such a strategy is reported by Hallgren and McAdams (1996). The case concerns GateD, a program "designed to listen to different routing protocols and to choose the best route for traffic to a given network". GateD, originally developed at Cornell University, has become a "defacto standard for Internet connectivity". GateD is distributed freely. "Instead of "marketing" the software as a product with a licensing or royalty fee, Cornell has created a consortium to raise the necessary funding for GateD. This has answered the needs of the community, while remaining consistent with the economic realities of the good." Members of the consortium are the NSF and other grant-giving agencies, as well as members from industry, government and academia who pay substantial "fees". In addition, private-good style benefits, like technical briefings, are offered to the members. The authors claim that the strategy was successful. They admit, however, that the funds critical for further enhancements and updates are not yet secured, and that free riding of major users is a problem.

Membership societies can be an alternative to commercial production when an inventor is able to identify the members of a "community in the Net" which benefits from the use of the invented tool. It is a frequently notice property of communication networks that users and providers are difficult to distinguish as all of them participate in developing the network (Brill and de Vries 1997; O'Reilly 1998) Behavior in the communities follows the "University Model", i.e. an incentive structure appropriate to the creation of public goods such as knowledge and innovation. In fact, "the Internet has grown up in response to incentives that fit the University Model, not the private sector market model of patents, trade secrets, high prices, destructive rivalry, etc." (Hallgren and McAdams 1996).

Non-profit organizations, funded by a mixture of private, commercial and governmental members therefore stand a good chance in competing with profit-driven enterprises. They can use the alternative of "opening the source", thus leaving the development of a network tool to the community of users, and they can supplement their public activity with income-generating services.

It remains doubtful whether non-profit organizations will be able to withhold substantial portions of t he Net from commercialization through such "community efforts". As the total value of new developments and the cost of continuous enhancement increase, non-profits will consider sellling out or granting pervasive licenses to commercial operators. They will consider that alternative all the more willingly if the hosting university is in financially dire straights.

2.4 Markets on the Net

Among the Net uses listed in the Business week survey of 1997, entertainment, news and hobbies hold potential for business on the Net, while investing and shopping are linked to markets external to the Net.[5] There are two major reasons for long-term market domination in this category. First, the financial stakes are much higher. Mass consumer products are on sale. Secondly, the players in the markets on the Internet are extensions of already existing conglomerates in the media field, and the players in markets off the Net are extensions of the large distribution conglomerates. Reliable, recent data on market shares in these markets are difficult to get. But the theoretical argument clearly points to this emerging domain as a hotspot for potential antitrust action.

3 Rules in and for Net Markets

3.1 General theories of institutional change and self-regulation

The past two decades have seen a rapid revival of interest among economists in the emergence of rules. It is by now generally acknowledged that the process of establishing a market, no matter for what product, must be accompanied by a simultaneous process in which the rules of the market are established. Otherwise, the stability of expectations necessary for that market to exist will not be achieved.

Very roughly, the contributions to an economic theory of rule emergence can be distinguished into two categories. First, there are approaches which explain new rules as a response to high transaction costs. Exchange is inhibited and transactors come up with rules for more efficient exchanges. In general, rules relating to the exclusivity and transferability of commodities are suggested and adopted, as these commodities become scarce and increase in economic value. This "new institutionalist" strand has its beginnings with Coase and has by now spread to the theory of organizations (Williamson, Milgrom).

Second, there are approaches which explain rules as the result of a continuous process of self-regulation among those participating in market exchanges. Negative feedback, self-organization and self-reference are the fundamental principles in a fully decentralized, evolutionarily contingent process of constantly emerging and vanishing rules. This "self-organization" strand has its beginnings with Hayek and has been boosted by models of game theory (Schelling, Schotter, Selten) and complex systems theory (Arthur).

5 The survey, quoted in Karakaya and Karakaya 1998, lists the following percentages of Net use: research 95%, education 90%, entertainment 77%, news 83%, hobbies 83%, game playing 50%, information about computers and software 76%, socializing 49%, investing 46%, shopping 36%.

The Net seems to be a perfect candidate for the "commons explanation" popular among new institutionalists: a domain has been created which is free of norms because nothing like it ever existed before. As in the case of the medieval commons, congestion sets in and spots or slots on the domain become scarce and valuable. But here the comparison ends: Fencing or other forms of privatization cannot alleviate the "market failure" observed in the network domain. The Internet was intentionally designed to subvert or, better, circumvert any attempt at domination. Any player who declares his proprietary net off limits to all other players must expect to be simply left out, as the information packets travel around his property. It is conceivable that someone's network is so powerful that it is hard to substitute. But that adds only a retarding factor – the time it takes to hook up channels that are designed to weave around the gap created by whoever attempted to fence in parts of the Net. The difference between the two types of domains, then, is the difference between pasture and channel.

The channel metaphor suits the self-regulation approach. In that view, the technical process of net governance is accompanied by a social process of Net governance. That process does not assume the introduction of certain rights and rules through specific, usually dominant players. It assumes a constant exchange between members of a community of channel users which eventually leads to a gradual acceptance of informal standards and formal rules for that community. The process includes conflicts and narrow decisions. But it is still able to respond swiftly to new, hitherto unknown strategies of participating players.

The cases reported from the history of the Net rules seem to fit the second approach better than the first. The "Net community" is a commonly observed phenomenon. But can this rather quaint, research-oriented community survive as a generator of rights and rules when the number of commercial players and thus the stakes of the game increase? The answer to this question will turn out different depending on which of the three market levels is considered. In consequence, commercial strategies designed to influence rule development will find different grounds and leverage points from which to start such efforts.

3.2 Rules for the Net and its Services

Hoffmann and Kuhlmann (1994) give an account of regulation and self-regulation on the Internet which turns that history into a stunning example for self-organization. They emphasize the decentralized and hierarchical nature of the Net, and the fact that the relations to be observed are customer-customer relations rather than customer-provider relations, which are more clearly regulated in traditional commercial law. They take their examples from Usenet. Usenet is a collection of thousands of interest groups that exchange news among each other. The admittance of a newsgroup and the acceptance of a item for posting in a new group follows an internal process of selection.

Until 1987, the selection process was under the control of administrators of the technical backbone. Controversies among the administrators led to a new set of "guidelines" that now regulates the introduction of new groups and the freedom of speech in the groups in a more "democratic" way, with rules for general votes of participating members and judiciary panels for guideline interpretation or violation sanctions.

The set of rules and guidelines is called "Netiquette". It ranges from rules of courtesy in exchanging messages to quasi-legal norms and sanctions. It regulates technical procedures, the structure and the content of communication. The aspirations connected with its practice are far-reaching: Netiquette is intended "to communicate a feeling for the impact of one's actions ... on scarce resources" (2). But even if the hopes of instituting an alternative to the allocation of scarce resources via markets are not fulfilled, Netiquette is still an indispensable institutional background for market operations, and it is an impressive example for the ability of net communities to regulate themselves.[6]

With the expanding number of Net users and with the advent of a multitude of wide area network providers, the reliability and applicability of informal Netiquette decreases. But there are other institutional means, particularly agreements and standards.

Agreements are an essential tool for providers who want to increase their interoperability and thus benefit from network effects. Bailey (1996) reports, not too surprisingly, that bilateral agreements are favored by large providers, while smaller networks prefer cooperative agreements. Agreements with third party administrators suffer from principal-agent-problems. In any case, we find that providers typically develop complex "agreement structures" to stabilize multiple interconnection architectures.

Agreements contain cooperatively determined rules for the application of technical standards that insure compatibility, a very valuable economic good (David and Greenstein1990). The alternative are non-cooperative strategies of threat, preemption and "expectations management". The object is to convince the user community that one contestant will emerge as a winner from the "standards war" (Shapiro and Varian 1999, ch.9). Evidently, such wars are costly. On the other hand, the de facto decision for a certain technical standard might determine the economic survival of a company. Therefore, such conflicts will continue to erupt.

Up to now, only self-instituted rules and agreements were discussed. But the usual situation is more likely to be one in which possible conflicts and rule violations are determined by another major social institution, namely the Law. Issues regarding the impact on the Law are not the subject of this paper. Yet, the relevance to the question of institutional background for markets is such that some general remarks are inevitable.

6 As a further example, see Hoffmann und Kuhlmann 1994 and Mefford 1998 for an account of the RFC mechanism as a medium for descision making.

The applicability of traditional Law to operations on the Net is in doubt. Mefford (1998) points out that national jurisdictions lack legitimacy in international transactions, that they have no power without physical control and that effects of actions cannot even be attributed to physical boundaries. The Net "ought to be treated as a separate and discrete jurisdiction with its own rules and its own laws that reflect its unique character." (5) In fact, the beginnings of such a process can be observed. They consist in basic forms of contract law – reminiscent of the medieval Lex Mercatoria and complete with "virtual arbitration" through the *Cyberspace Law Institute* – and of tort law, although the latter remains at the conceptual stage. Sanctions could be fairly easily enforced as long as the "net-courts" control the access points to the Net and thus are able to banish violators from the domain. [7]

Although Mefford may forecast the long-term development quite accurately, the short-run changes focus more strongly on existing legal forms, and on existing international trade agreements. To date, there is considerable evidence supporting the opinion that the demands of commercial suppliers using the Net, with their rather traditional concerns, prevails over the demands of non-commercial Net providers with technologically new concerns. If commercial suppliers prevail, then path dependency for the development of legal institutions is locked in and ambitious new legal concepts become improbable. [8]

A strongly commercial pressure on the legal and judiciary system surrounding the Net would lead to attempts for strengthening the concept of property. Copyright law, licensing law and tort law are possible venues. A prime example for such efforts is the *Digital Millenium Copyright Act* that has recently been approved by U.S. Congress (Rötzer 1998). Representatives of the Net communities, in turn, attempt to strengthen the rights of non-profit organisations and to achieve official international status for the functions carried out by membership institutions.

This brings us to a dimension of institutional context that has not yet been mentioned: the force of political intervention. That force is implicit in the impact of legislation on the performance of the legal system. It becomes explicit in the actions of executive state agencies. Governments play an active role in both fields. With respect to the Net, one of the prime issues of institutional design is the legislation surrounding the payment technology. Even minor stipulations in the versions currently under discussion can have far-reaching effects on the viability of instruments like stored value cards, or the authority of banks on the Net (Fisher 1996, Bernkopf 1996). The role of executive agencies is most prominent in basic research. After all, government-operated and

---

7 An interesting example is the strategy used agains spamming,i.e. the flooding of newsgroups with unauthorized advertising. The practice was stopped when, in the famous "Canter & Siegel"-case, a Norvegian student invented a program that deleted the message from most news servers. A retaliation on the technological level succeeded where intervention on the behavioral level failed (Hoffmann and Kuhlmann 1994).

8 An example is the modification of existing copyright law — originally aimed at books — to suit the needs of software producers.

government-funded institutions are responsible for most of the development of the Net until very recently.

To summarize: The making of rules and, thus, rights is currently the most actively pursued aspect of Net commercialization. The activities make economic sense: before stable markets can be installed, the institutional "hardware" has to be in place. Still ahead are major battles between proponents of narrow property rules and proponents of open source rules. The outcome will determine the evolutionary trajectory of Net institutions for the years to come.

3.3 Rules for Commodities on the Net

The inadequacy of existing informal and formal rules is, expectedly, the strongest in markets which transact software on the Net. This applies to software which helps to "navigate" the Net itself, like browsers or shopbots, and to software that is of any other content, but copied and transmitted through the Net, like music or images or data.

Market failure results in all these cases from the public good property of information products: they can be copied and modified at zero marginal cost, and reproduction can only be excluded at extra cost. The first concern is therefore with property. Information property has no physical shape. It must be constructed as an informational "firewall" (Hormozi, Harding and Bose 1998), or as a legal fiction. The legal fiction needs some objective criterion. The dominant criterion for patent protection is "inventive step". Copyright protection is given to precise works of "creative" character (Dyson 1994, Hutter 1996). Copyright law comes closest to the demands for virtual property protection. But there are two major defects: first, the fiction of intellectual property was intended for artistic creation; its extension to any creative work has no plausible limit to avoid the protection of any human expression. Second, if artistic integrity is not an issue, then a modification of the original work just large enough to evade protection violation will be cheap to find.

If we consider software markets on the Net in a temporal dimension, we encounter issues of reliability. The identity of the user is, by the logic of the Net, not anonymous, and making it anonymous is an intentional transaction feature. The seller cannot present himself and his product with the kind of signaling used in physical markets. The performance of software products over extended periods of time cannot be ascertained with the certainty of long tested material products. Activities to overcome these obstacles to functioning markets are made both on the private and the governmental side. Private companies experiment with insurance contracts that accompany the commodity and shift the risk to the producer (Lai, Medvinsky and Neumann 1996). Governments initiate legislation that outlaws pirating and electronic fraud, and that legitimizes claims against violations of anonymity and for damages incurred.

Another section of Law bound to undergo major changes is corporate law. The number of legal actors will multiply through the construction of alliances, ventures, coalitions and non-profits. Some of them are set up to maintain and distribute only one product, others control major sections of the entire market as a form of self-governing authority. Agents on the Internet will be even more confused once the technical and institutional security needs of payment transfer are fulfilled. Then, all kinds of financial operations will become part of Net traffic. As a consequence, the distinction between companies and banks, between real and financial agents must be drawn in new ways (Bernkopf 1996, Hughes 1995, Schreft 1997, Brill and de Vries 1998).

As discussed in sec.2, the cost structure of software products leads necessarily to temporary monopolies. Once established, the monopoly itself is an incentive to maintain the barriers to entry that kept prices at such profitable levels. Competition policy and antitrust policy, usually armed with national executive agencies, are the traditional instruments to counter such developments. Public good problems are not new to the agenda. Public utilities from electricity to telecommunication have been at the center of attention in many countries. Therefore, Shapiro and Varian (1999) are optimistic about the ability of existing antitrust legislation and policy to deal with potential conflict. However, the situation is less comforting when a less domestic perspective is chosen. National jurisdictions can be evaded easily, and many parts of the world do not having functioning competition protection. Technological progress will therefore continue to be the best antidote against market manipulation.

To summarize: many fields of commercial law will have to be modified to accommodate the needs of markets on the Internet. The issues mentioned here are only indicative and exemplary. The slowness of such changes will inhibit commercialization. It will also make non-governmental forms of litigation, arbitration and standard setting a viable alternative.

3.4 Rules for Commodities by means of the Net

Markets for goods and services advertized and ordered through the Net should be sufficiently served by existing commercial law. An exception are services that rely on the properties of the Net, like web site naming and maintenance, Email advertising or online bidding. Here, new legal ground is to be broken.

The lack of existing formal rules does not have to be a deterrent to the growth of such markets. As long as informal rules function, commercial action proceeds without running into conflicts over liability or contract content. The more general rules of commercial law would still apply. When an impasse is reached, there is a good chance that products offered and players involved change faster than going through formal legal action. As in the case of commodities sold for and in the Net, the traditional, national legal systems will be supplemented by other, supra-governmental or private systems of adjudication.

C. Conclusions

We started from the observation that the growing value of the Internet attracts users and providers who try to transform that value into monetary revenue. The growing commercialization of the Net is an inevitable accompanying effect of the Net's expansion. How has that effect changed the Net, and how is commercialization going to change it in the future?

The outcome of the survey is that we have only tentative answers to a complex set of questions. The sudden increase in demand for Internet resources leads to problems of congestion; pricing has been introduced as a proven method to allocate efficiently resources that have become scarce. therefore, not only a drive for new profit opportunities but also a more general interest of providers in using charges as a rationing device can be observed. But market prices allocate only efficiently under private property regimes. Such a regime does not exist on the Internet, and it would not even make sense, given the public good property of the Net and the zero cost reproduction property of information products. Moreover, the legal and political institutions which market participants take for granted are not in place, or they have created difficult conceptual challenges to legal and political science. It seems that the "community enthusiasm" of veteran Net users/providers is more than the typical enthusiasm of freshly emerging research scenes. It is supported by the logical structure of the Net and its operation, and it is supported by the material facts of electronic data reproduction.

If we were to forecast an equilibrium, or an equilibrium path solution for the Internet as a resource and as a marketplace, we could exclude either of the "pure cases": a fully commercialized Net is technically feasible. But eventually, the higher value priority of commercial traffic would drive out the information traffic of the research communities. The lack of continuing innovation would slow down growth and eventually end in stagnation. On the other hand, a Net in which the research communities keep the traffic free of all charges would lose commercial attraction while being choked by congestion.

I therefore expect a composite solution, i.e. a state in which private and public elements are strongly mixed. The development of the PC-software industry might be a blueprint: a formerly research-dominated domain turns commercial, but inventors are kept active in "golden cages" within larger corporations. The five leading corporations generate 80% of the revenue, but an active, rapidly changing independent inventor scene survives in their periphery, supported by a capital market for high risk ventures. All of this is would have to be stabilized, to a much greater extent than in the software industry, by forms of self-adjudication in order to prevent free-riding and to reward Net additions. The relative share of public and private elements would probably different in the three categories of Net markets surveyed: markets for Net service will be strongly public, markets in Net commodities will have either characteristics side by side, and markets in commodities through the Net will be predominantly private.

The value change connected with this process will be tremendous. Most clearly observable is the exponential growth in economic value. That dimension can be documented by realized transactions, as part of GNP, but it is even more impressive when it is documented by the stock market values of companies working on and with the Net, even though this indicator omits the value of all the companies not traded on the stock exchange. Moreover, the growth leads to a shift in the relative contribution of different economic sectors. The growth of the Net furthers the transition from steel plants and automobile assembly lines to communication providers as primary source of economic value at least in modern, post-industrialist economies.

The shift in economic value creation can only be documented on an aggregate level, but it takes place on the level of local values. In every single financial market, in every negotiation for research or development funds, value estimates are communicated and determined. As these values become part of individuals' lives, the individuals change their own value scales or "preference orderings". They begin to act in ways which help the Internet to expand. The Net, as a communication brain, will reproduce the values of individuals, economic and non-economic, needed for its own reproduction.

References

Arrow, Ken: Economic Welfare and the Allocation of Resources for Invention. In: *D.M. Lamberton* (ed.), The Economics of Communication and Information. Cheltenham: Edgar Elgar 1997

Bailey, Joseph: Economics and Internet Interconnection Agreements. In: Journal of Electronic Publishing 2, May 1996, <http://www.press.umich.edu/jep/works/BailEconAg.html> (9.11.98)

Bernkopf, Mark: Electronic Cash and Monetary Policy. In: First Monday, 1996, <http://www.firstmonday.dk/> (2.10.98)

Brill, Andreas / Michael de Vries: Virtuelle Produkte. Links, Rights und In-Betweens. In: *D. Baecker*, ed., Wittener Jahrbuch für ökonomische Literatur, 1997

Brill, Andreas / Michael de Vries (eds.): Virtuelle Wirtschaft. Opladen: Westdeutscher Verlag 1998

Brody, Herb: Internet at Crossroads. In: Technology Review 98 (May 1995), 25-31

Brownlee, Neville: New Zealand Experiences with Network Traffic Charging. Journal of Electronic Publishing 2, May 1996, <http://www.press.umich.edu/jep/works/BailEconAg.html> (9.11.98)

David, Paul / Shane Greenstein: The Economics of Compatibility Standards: An Introduction to the Recent Research. In: Economics of Information and New Technology 1 (1990), 3-41

Dertouzos, Michael: What will be. New York: HarperCollins, 1997

Dybvig, Philip / Chester Spatt: Adoption Externalities as Public Goods. In: Journal of Public Economics 20 (March 1983), 231-47

Dyson, Esther: Intellectual Property on the Net, Release 1.0, Dec. 1994, <http://www.edventure.com/release1> (13.11.98)

Economides, Nicholas: The Economics of Networks. In: Int. Journal of Industrial Organization 14 (March 1996)

Fisher, Rosalind: New Payments Technology. 1996, <http://www.cato.org/moneyconf/> (2.10.98)

Gong, Jiong / Padmanabhan Srinagesh: The Economics of Layered Networks. Journal of Electronic Publishing 2, May 1996, <http://www.press.umich.edu/jep/works/BailEconAg.html> (9.11.98)

Hallgren, Martyne / Alan McAdams: A Model for Efficient Aggregation of Resources for Economic Public Goods on the Internet. In: Journal of Electronic Publishing 2, May 1996, <http://www.press.umich.edu/jep/works/BailEconAg.html> (9.11.98)

Hoffmann, Gero / Dirk Kuhlmann: Regulierung und Selbstregulierung im Internet. 1995, <http://gromit.prz.tu-berlin.de/ derek/internet/> (17.11.98)

Hormozi, Amir / William Harding/Utpal Bose: Is the Internet Feasible and Profitable for Small Business? SAM Advanced Management Journal (Summer 1998), 20-27

Hughes, Eric: A Long-Term Perspective on Electronic Commerce, Release 1.0, March 1995, <http://www.edventure.com/release1> (13.11.98)

Hutter, Michael: On the Construction of Property Rights in Aesthetic Ideas. In: Journal of Cultural Economics 19 (1995), 177-185

Hutter, Michael: On the Consumption of Signs. In: *M. Bianchi*, ed., The Active Consumer, London: Routledge 1998, 236-257

Karakaya, Fahri / Fera Karakaya: Doing Business on the Internet. SAM Advanced Management Journal (Spring 1998), 10-14

Katz, Michael / Carl Shapiro: Network Externalities, Competition, and Compatibility. American Economic Review 75 (June 1985), 424-440

Knight, Lee / Joseph Bailey: An Introduction to Internet Economics. In: Journal of Electronic Publishing 2, May 1996, <http://www.press.umich.edu/jep/works/BailEconAg.html> (9.11.98)

Lai, Charlie / Gennady Medvinsky / Clifford Neuman: Endorsements, Licensing, and Insurance for Distributed System Services. In: Journal for Electronic Publishing, May1996, <http://www.press.umich.edu/jep/works/BailEconAg.html> (9.11.98)

Mac-Kie-Mason / Hal Varian: Pricing the Internet. In: *B. Kahin / J. Keller* (eds.), Public Access to the Internet. Cambridge: MIT Press 1995

Mefford, Aron: Lex Informatica: Foundations of Law on the Internet. 1997, <http://www.law.indiana.edu/glsj/vol5/no1/mefford.html> (24.11.98)

O'Reilly, Tim: The Open-Source Revolution, Release 1.0, Nov. 1998, <http://www.edventure.com/release1> (13.11.98)

Raymond, Eric: The Cathedral and the Bazaar. 1998, <http://tuxedo.org/~esr/writings/cathedral-bazaar.html> (8.1.99)

Rötzer, Florian: Copyright – made in USA. In: Telepolis, 1998, <http://www.heise.de/tp/deutsch/inhalt/te/1587/1.html> (13.10.98)

Schreft, Stacey: Looking forward: The Role for Government in Regulating Electronic Cash. In: Federal Reserve Bank of Kansas Economic Review (Fourth Quarter 1997), 59-84

Sarkar, Mitrabarun: An Assessment of Pricing Mechanisms for the Internet – A regulatory Imperative. Journal of Electronic Publishing 2, May 1996, <http://www.press.umich.edu/jep/works/BailEconAg.html> (9.11.98)

Shapiro, Carl / Hal Varian: Information Rules. A Strategic Guide to the Network Economy. Boston: Harvard Business School Press 1999

Tirole, Jean: The Theory of Industrial Organization. Cambridge: MIT Press 1989

Dirk Baecker

Networking the Web

Abstract: In order to be able to ask whether there are hopes, and fears, that the World Wide Web of the Internet (or Web for short) gets commercialised the article takes a long detour in first asking how to conceive of the Web in a scientific way at all. It then identifies the basic loop which is constraining the Web as a tool for purposes of communication. The next step is to ask what it means to communicate by the means of the Web. The Web is understood as a mass communication medium which is not a social system in itself but a "perturbator" disturbing, and attracting, the "iterations" of other social system. The question then is in which respects the Web may be a mass communication medium that demands a completely new "coding" by social communications in order to understand what type of information and utterance the Web is featuring. The conclusion is that the fears of a commercialisation of the Web are not justified since there is no way to completely turn a mass communication medium into a market, and that the hopes of a commercialisation may do well to beware of a type of communication which underlies a market that asks for a new type of goods and features a new type of consumers as well as of producers.

I. Sciencing the Web

Approaching the World Wide Web of the Internet in a *scientific* way means to watch it in terms of *functions*. Following a distinction of science creating functions from philosophy creating concepts, and art creating sensual units (Deleuze 1990, 168), we immediately enter a type of thinking which asks neither for the essence or substance of a phenomenon nor for the identification of certain causes which bring it forth, or of effects which it produces. Instead the phenomenon is taken as a variable whose value is dependent of the values other variables are realizing (Korzybski 1958, 133 ss.). There is a further distinction to be drawn which opposes dependent and independent variables, but the more important step in considering functions consists in looking for *relations* between these variables which now and then may be dependent or independent, depending on case, situation, and complexity.

In observing functions science is to be understood not as an objective statement about data and facts but as a way of dealing with certain experiences according to certain assumptions and with certain techniques. That is why Leslie A. White (1969, 3) speaks of science as *sciencing*, that is as an activity which indeed is operating on itself as well as on the subject it is observing. That does not free science from the claim to distinguish true from false sentences, but that is a claim which already internally regulates or codifies the way of proposing, deducing, and rejecting sentences (Luhmann 1990a). Using Andersen's (1998) graph which we will introduce later we can visualize the process of sciencing as it is shown in Fig. 1:

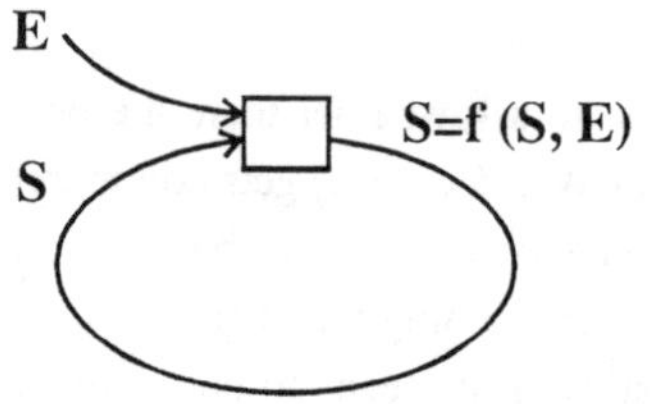

Fig. 1: perturbed recursion in science

with **S** denoting science, **E** denoting environment, and **f** denoting a function that is capable to recursively reproduce science out of computations of its former states in dealing with possible perturbations arriving from the environment of science.

Functions are not self-evident objects of observations. Distinguishing variables and identifying relations between them is not an innocent activity. We understand functions in their mathematical sense which has nothing to do any more with a causality in disguise (à la Bronislaw Malinowski, or, for that matter, Talcott Parsons) that claims the function of a phenomenon to be the cause of other causes bringing it forth as their effect. Instead we view functions as sets of possible behaviours among which a *recursively closed, that is, selfreferential system* may choose in order to produce further operations, reproduce structure, or check constraints. They are a matter of *observation* but that does not mean that they are morphogenetically unimportant since observation itself is an operation and is related to other operations which reproduce the system (Luhmann 1995a, 298 ss.; Nietzsche 1991, 2, § 12).

Thus we regard functions with respect to systems and thereby leave the realm of causal explanations, and enter the realm of cybernetic explanations which is an explanation by constraints, or by negative selection, instead of by causes, or by positive selection (Bateson 1972, 399-410). We begin by drawing the all-important distinction between system and environment (Luhmann 1995a) and then go on watching phenomena as functions of systems producing their own distinction from their environment. Any function, of course, may be a *dysfunction* in other respects, depending on observation, that is on the interest we cultivate (Weick 1979, 55). And any function, contrary to Wittgenstein (1963, 5.251), may re-enter its own set of possible behaviours as an argument of itself (Luhmann 1962; Luhmann 1964; von Foerster 1976). Luhmann (1997, 77-78) distinguishes functions from themes. Both play an important role *in communication*, yet whereas themes select which contributions belong to certain communications, functions allow to observe the actual state of the autopoiesis of communication and the structures (i.e., expectations of further communication) which are able to reproduce it. We may talk *about* the Web, selecting it as a theme of our communication and then observe any contribution anybody may propose with respect to our understanding of the theme. Yet we may also watch, that talking about the Web fulfills the function of reproducing our way to communicate in a historical situation that is deeply impressed by the appearance of a new medium of communication.

In the terms of Andersen's (1998) graph, the Web appears as a date of **E** and enters the states of **C** (communication) which reproduce **C** as a function of **C** and **E** (Fig. 2):

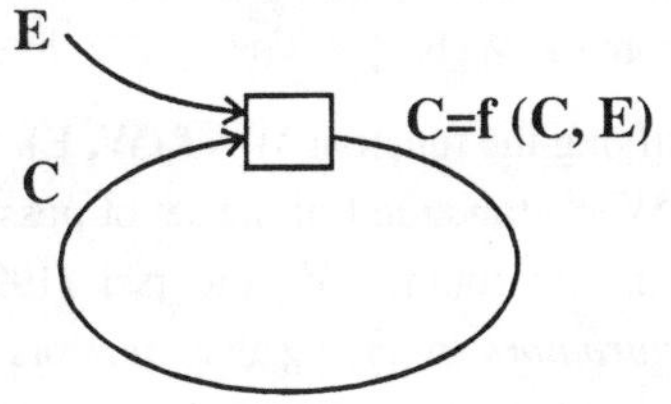

Fig. 2: perturbed recursion in communication

Sciencing the Web thus means to watch the Web as a function with respect to certain systems among which it may be possible to observe the Web as a system in its own right (depending on the possibility to identify, that is distinguish, operations of the systems which reproduce it). It brings forth constraints that either enable or hinder itself and other systems to reproduce their structures.

II. Constraining the Web

We begin by observing the Web as a function of itself in order to be able to distinguish constraints which we may introduce into other systems when asking how their operations and structures may be changed by using the Web. We confine ourselves to observing the Web as a *social* phenomenon, that is as a phenomenon which somehow alters *communication.* We do not observe the Web as a technical phenomenon, that is we do not go into the details of the question how machines, hardware and software, are to be understood and to be connected in order to constitute and maintain the Net. We as well do not enter questions of history, knowing that the present state of the World Wide Web is the result of the development of different other nets like the ARPANET, the BITNET, and the INTERNET and thereby bears traces of the loosely coupled, decentralized, and highly self-substitutable "post-apocalyptic command grid" (Bruce Sterling) as devised by the US Pentagon and the text-and-mail biased communication tool of the High Energy Physics community as devised by CERN, Genf (Hardy 1993).

Peter Bøgh Andersen (1998, 11), whose graph of perturbed recursion we already used, has described the Web as a function of itself by analysing the recursive loop constituting it as a sequence of operations of Request and operations of Response: A client uses the Web by searching ready-made documents which lie with servers and that are requested by addressing the appropriate URL which responses by sending the requested document. These documents, as long as they are texts, feature further links to other texts which may be used, by clicking on them, to request the documents the links go to. That is why the World Wide Web basically is a *hypertext.* Yet, there are further features of a document, such as playing a sound or a video clip, or acting out certain programs enabled for instance by JAVA-scripts. The operations carried out are always constrained by the resources of the computer machine used by the client who may add on these resources by downloading further ones from the Web.

Thus, we may start by identifying the function **W = f (W, E)**, which reads: What is actually being done in the Web **W** is a function **f** of the set of possibilities of the Web **W** and perturbations arriving from the environment **E**. Andersen (1998, 15-16) proposes to distinguish *iterators* from *perturbators* in saying that iterators recursively reproduce the system, and perturbators irritate the reproduction without adding (that is, "influencing") operations to the system. One may visualize the recursive function as perturbed by an as yet unspecified environment with Andersen's (1998, 15) graph (Fig. 3):

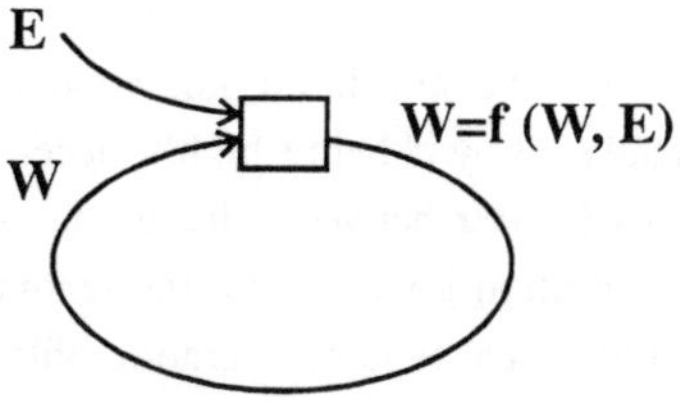

Fig. 3: perturbed recursion in the Web

The question now is how to conceive of the Web. Is it a system in its own right, as Andersen (1998) claims by demonstrating its recursivity, genetical evolution (Web pages out of Web pages), and self-referentiality (addresses consisting of addresses, links linking links, meta-languages being of the same type as the object-language HTML)? I would claim that these features are not enough to call a phenomenon a system as long as one essential one is lacking, which is the identification of *a type of operation* which actually is able to produce, and reproduce the system autopoietically (Luhmann 1995a). That is a question of much debate since the original notion of "autopoiesis" (Maturana/Varela 1975; Maturana/Varela 1980) asks for a network of elements able to produce the network *and* the boundaries of the system which themselves are part of the network (Maturana 1981). Nobody actually knows how to conceive of the idea of "production", let alone "auto-production", even if Humberto R. Maturana's original idea was to answer the question how life is able to bring forth life. If one looks at the criteria defining "autopoiesis" (Varela/Maturana/Uribe 1974; Zeleny/Hufford 1992), the matter of production is carefully avoided, and certainly rightly so. Instead the neighborhood of components that constitute a network is taken as *an indicator* of a production going on.

Yet that does not solve our problem of knowing whether to deal with the Web as a system or not. That is why we started to analyse it as a function in the first place, avoiding the question of system. We don't know whether it "is" a system, yet we regard it as a function of itself, identify iterators like web sites, program languages (HTML, JAVA), and links, yet do not know how to identify the perturbators since we do not know what "environment" to conceive of as long as we cannot define the system. Thus, at this state of analysis we just end up with an idea how the Web is a function of itself by constraining what is being done on the Web through its recursive Request/Response-loop.

We may call this first result of our sciencing of the Web a possible "demystification" of it. In other words, we reduce its phenomenal complexity to a basic recursive loop whose working indeed may be able to produce a whole new complexity of communication in society.

III. Introducing the Web

If the Web is a function of itself we still do not know what type of operation produces, and reproduces it. Technically, even if being highly decentralized, it consists of rigid couplings between machines (*cables* between clients and servers) and between documents (*links*). There is no selection going on on the technical level of the Net which means there is no hint of a technical type of operation able to produce, and reproduce, the Net as a technical system. Indeed, the *loose coupling* of the set of possibilities which is necessary for operations to be able to *select* links, that is to mould certain forms into it, is not introduced technically but on the level of communication.

One has to *use* the Web – designing a page, surfing the sites, trailing a sequence of hypertexts, using a search-engine, switching browsers (see I/O/D's Web Stalker for a look at the structure of the Net instead of at the content of the Web: www.backspace.org/ iod) – for being able to watch it becoming "alive". What kind of life is it? Do you experience the artificial life of a machinery? Do you liven up your mental imaginations? Or is it a kind of communication you follow up between you requesting documents and servers sending them, ready-made, to you. It seems to be richer than broadcasting since you are able to select much more selectively, but poorer than conversation since you only get the ready-mades or "customized" ready-mades (Andersen 1998, 12-14).

Of course the "life" you see depends on how you observe the Web. The Web is a function of itself and its environment regardless whether you look at the machinery, at mental imagination, or at communication. It does what it does, yet what it does depends on how you look at it. You may act as a philosopher working on your concepts, as an artist trying to figure out, or interfere with, sensual artifacts, or as a scientist watching out for functions. It is always you who is introducing what you are doing into, or better: with, the Web.

My choice is to watch communication. I regard the Web as a communication medium like language, writing, and print, and as distinct from them depending on how you look at those (Esposito 1995; Esposito 1998). That is, I propose to switch perspective and to put the Web into the environment **E** of communication **C**. Thus, we have as our basic idea to start with the function $\mathbf{C = f\ (C, E, E^W)}$. Communication still is recursively produced by iterating communication which is ridden by its own *undecidabilities* (von Foerster 1980; Derrida 1990; Luhmann 1997) and uses these undecidabilities – or its oscillation between self-reference and other-reference, between information and utterance, between constative and performative speech acts, and so on – to deal with perturbators arriving from an environment which features a new phenomenon, called the Web ($\mathbf{E^W}$) (Fig. 4):

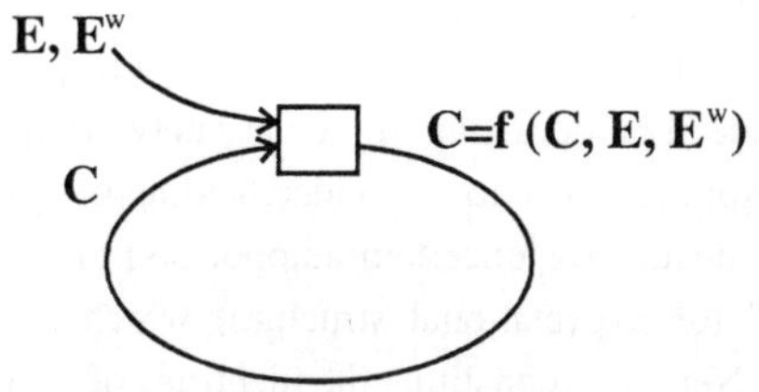

Fig. 4: perturbed recursion in communication featuring

an environment containing the Web

That seems to be an understanding of the phenomenon which bears a lot of resemblance to our present situation. Somehow the Web indeed actually *is* altering the way communication is reproducing itself. But in order to know *how* it is altering this way we ought to know a lot more about (a) the iterators reproducing the communication recursively and (b) the way perturbators are handled by communication. One of the questions to ask is how $\mathbf{E}^{W}$ is to be distinguished from **E**. That is a distinction drawn by **C**, that is a distinction participating in the recursions of **C**, and it makes a lot of difference whether and how this distinction is drawn. It makes a difference whether this distinction in drawn in terms of communication media, for instance, thus distinguishing the Web from television, print, or spoken "interactive" language. And then what the Web looks like depends on how one looks at television, print, or spoken words. Each social system will have its own thematic and functional preoccupations in dealing with the Web, that is in iterating its own operations and in handling the perturbations it is able to account for. Certainly a military use of the Web is distinct from a political use, and the hope of business is distinct from the sorrows of education, and vice versa.

We have to look at social systems and their actual handling of their self-reproduction by perturbed recursion in order to be able to tell more about the possible functions the Web is fulfilling in communication. We will talk about the "networking" of the Web and try to be explicit about the fact that it is only social systems which network the Web and whose networks are changed by the Web. It is not sufficient to technically, by rigid coupling, connect nodes when one tries to make a network. It is the way to introduce the Web into the communicative reproduction of social systems which turns it, or more precisely, the parts actually used, into a function of a social network.

We use the term "network" (see White 1992) because it relates to the structural coupling of social systems to their environment. Networks select different nodes, which are not only persons, but also institutions, organizations, ideologies, stories, beliefs, concepts, or whatever (i.e., covering and combining structures as well as semantics, events as well as ecologies), and constitute a reliable, yet uncertain pattern of reproduction among these nodes, persons becoming dependent on ideologies, events and their shadows dependent on ecologies, beliefs and disbeliefs dependent on organizations, and so on. These networks, as once Parsons's (Parsons/ Shils 1967) social systems, constitute social action – with this social action indeed participating in the very network that produces, and reproduces, it. The term "network" is close to our understanding of "function", since it relates to observations of the "outside" (or uncertain autopoiesis) of social systems in distinction from their "inside" (or expectational structure) which is observed by "themes" (Luhmann 1997, 77-78). Networks constitute the identities of social actions that are used to control the disciplines which are necessary to maintain these ever uncertain and necessarily ambiguous identities (White 1992). They try to turn perturbators into iterators or to keep them at a safe distance without possibly being sure about a success of either attempt.

IV. Mediating the Web

Switching from a perspective which conceives of the Web as a system technical or social, in its own right, to a perspective which regards the Web as a function of other social systems, we conceive of the Web as a communication medium. Any communication in any social system is a form, a rigid coupling of references to information, utterance, and understanding (Luhmann 1995a, 139 ss.), that depends for its "coding" (Luhmann 1995a, 142) on the possibility to distinguish between coded events, or iterations, and uncoded events, or perturbations. The Web as a communication medium consists of loosely coupled, even if technically rigid coupled, events which compel the communication, insofar as it takes recourse to the Web, into the situation to distinguish between coded and uncoded events presented by the Web. Yet this is a distinction which can only brought about by the communication itself. "The environment contains no information; the environment is as it is" (von Foerster 1981, 263). That means that there is no communication by the means of the Web, or inside the Web, no page-designing, surfing, searching, and requesting which is not already coded by some communication addressing the Web.

It demands communication to turn the technically rigid coupling of the Web into the loose coupling of possible communicative events. Only then specific forms, a communication here and then, can happen at all, since communication presupposes the distinction of form from medium. It uses this distinction to operatively produce communication, that is to select it out of a set of more or less specified possibilities (Shannon/Weaver 1961; Baecker 1999) and to connect it recursively to previous and further communication (Luhmann 1997, 195 ss.). The distinction between form and medium (Heider 1959) replaces the older conception of a "transmission" of messages by "communication" between sender and receiver. Now communication is all production, and maintenance, of *redundancy* (Bateson 1972, 406 et passim), that is a bringing forth of meaning (iterations) in order to handle surprises (perturbations) (Luhmann 1971; Douglas 1989).

Any communication presupposes such a code that distinguishes coded from uncoded events. Since it presupposes it it does not take note of it as long as everything works fine. The code is used as an "unwritten cross" in the terminology of G. Spencer-Brown (1972), and communication does not focus on it but on the distinction of information, utterance, and understanding which "enacts" (Weick) the code, so to speak. The code constrains what information, utterance, and understanding are possible. And vice versa we can only look at information, utterance, and understanding when trying to find out the redundancy structure of the code (Titscher/Meyer 1998).

These rather complicated yet necessary considerations lead us to the expectation that the appearance of a new medium of communication, such as the Web, for the time being does not change anything in the "process" of social communication. It indeed *cannot* change anything. It is just a perturbation, an uncoded event, awaiting its coding, its introduction into the iterations of communication. Oscillating between theme, as in this article, and function, as in social process, the Web is "out there" and "in here" and the only thing we know is that it will take much time to be able to watch possible effects of it, as it took centuries for writing and printing to be better understood in their function for the reproduction of communication (Ong 1971; Ong 1977).

It is just the other way round that one may learn something about already existing social systems by looking how they are using the Web, that is which form they are putting into it, and which form they get out of it. Watching the Web thus means to employ a very simple heuristic to reveal the redundancy structures of the society, both on the side of those using the Web and those watching the effects of its use with the users (the parents and teachers of children surfing the net, for instance). Indeed, it is not a knowledge of the Web which leads to the hopes and sorrows of those watching it. It is a knowledge, or something like it, of social systems on their run to the Web which leads some to expect a further step towards emancipation and participation, and others to suspect the next turn of an ever-winning capitalism. And both are right, since they know their lot.

On the other hand, this does not mean that the Web in the long run *will* not change the social process of the society. There may be features of this medium of communication which may encourage yet unknown forms of communication to appear. Yet this would mean that the coding of communication would have to change. The relationship between coded and uncoded events would have to shift thus bringing forth new types of information, utterance, and understanding and possibly leaving behind others.

V. Coding the Web

The Web is a mass communication medium. Like writing, print, and television before it reduces the improbability (Luhmann 1981) to reach somebody by communication. Reducing the improbability to reach somebody does not mean to be able to reach everybody, of course. Here we should not be trapped by euphorical self-descriptions of broadcasting media. As any mass communication, the Web is highly selective. One needs a lot of machinery, quite some knowledge, and still a lot of time to use it (go http://www.hotwired.com/web101 for a beginner's introduction). A lot of journals offline and online (for instance see Wired or http://www.wired. com) are actually journals working on the attractiveness of the selectivity of the Web. They may not only be read as media that make us literate both on the computer and on the Web. They actually work out the code that allows us to introduce the perturbations of the Web, both with respect to its sheer existence, to its contents, and to its pragmatics, into the iterations of our communication. These journals as other publications on the Web in the Web are perfect examples of the self-referentiality of the Web (Andersen 1998). They experiment on the forms that are imaginable and possible in the medium of the Web.

It seems not to be possible to already name the code that is emerging in transforming the perturbations of the Web into the interactions of communication. If we leave aside the military use of a self-substituable net, the scientific community's use of a fast posting and mailing medium, that is uncomplicated in matters of communication since it is free of organizational considerations, and the use of the Web for illegal cataloguing and marketing of arms and pornography, all of which just extend the codes of their social systems to a new medium, we hit upon certain new kinds of information, utterance, and coding which might be worthwhile to have a closer look to.

With respect to information it seems to be the image of a "new world" which is the most interesting for people surfing the Net. It is a new world with respect to persons one can reach without ever actually meeting them, with respect to places one can explore without ever actually going there, with respect to organizations both public and private whose programs one can look at without having to invest heavily into search and mailing costs, and with respect to unknown possibilities of playing around with one's own computer when downloading software turning one's machine into a multimedia tool.

With respect to utterance it seems to be the possibility to self-select the use of a broadcasting medium. There is no Request/Response-loop without every participator being marked as one who utters these requests and responses. The addresses linked by the Web are highly specified by URLs, by being a client or a server, while at the same time the Web shares with other broadcasting media the characteristics of anonymization. One may put one's requests using a nickname, one may send out an "agent" doing the search and downloading actions in a pre-programmed and anonymous way. And one can never be sure that the homepages of individuals and organizations one hits upon are the pages of real or fake individuals and organizations. The Web thus embodies one of the most fascinating features of modern world society which is an almost free floating communication that is only loosely coupled to "actors" doing the utterances. There is no communication without somebody uttering it. But the communication itself is almost free in identifying anybody as its utterer. Which of course means that there is much need to make up on matters of identity, sincerity, and authenticity on the Web. And nothing is more attractive than faking a convincing identity.

With respect to understanding the Web seems to work on a code that combines the uncertainties of ambiguity with the uncertainties of ambage, that is the cultural uncertainty of interpretation with the social uncertainty to avoid certain communications and go elsewhere (see White 1992, 103 ss.). What is one looking at when looking at a page in the Web? How fast is one going to decide to surf on? What is going on when somebody understands a page, that is becomes able to distinguish between its informational content (other-reference) and its state of being uttered (self-reference of communication) (Luhmann 1995a, 139 ss.)? How is the communication in the Web going to decide whether any understanding took place at all, that is how is it going to distinguish between perception (somebody looking at text or pictures, listening to a sound...) and communication? These are theoretically important questions since without understanding there is no communication going to happen.

Maybe it suffices for an understanding coming along with actions of search, surf, and click that the two Web-specific aspect of information and utterance actually get distinguished and thereby identified. That means that the communication begins to understand the forms that are possible in the medium of the Web as soon as it combines the observation of the emergence of a "new world" with the experience of social and cultural uncertainty. Whether this understanding is a fascinated or scared one is a question of secondary importance, as is the question whether the communication happening in the Web gets accepted or rejected. The important point is that the Web gets translated into, and introduced with communication as soon as the communication is able to develop a sense of the undecidablity between a social and or cultural uncertainty of "the new". Maybe the Web is the scout of modern world society posing exactly that question. It is not the answer which then is important but the asking of the question itself. To ask and maintain this question which presents a certain coding of communication by communication may be the function of the Web for modern world society.

One may then go on and differentiate the selection of understanding producing a communication by looking at its factual, temporal, and social meaning dimension (Luhmann 1995a, 74 ss.). Are there new "objects" emerging in the Web, a new addressing of time horizons future, present, and past, a new handling of the distinction of *alter ego* from *ego*, that is of consensus and dissensus? What is the new world like which is produced by the understanding of communicating with the Web?

These are questions which may be addressed by a reading of science fiction literature (for instance Gibson 1984; Gibson 1986; Stephenson 1992). The objects this literature is dealing with are objects which try to serve both interests in the programmable artificiality of things, bodies, behaviour, and spaces and in the life-like and authentic experience of impressions. They are virtual objects which are both made by man and able to surprise their creator. They are explorations in an artificial life (Bourgine/Varela 1992) that adapts autonomously and is able to pose new problems never thought of. They are explorations in the cognitive abilities of computation.

The time horizons of the Web are extremely malleable. The future as an unknown one, yet technologically already envisioned one is always present. Yet the present is fugitive like almost no present before, as everybody can verify by trying to hold certain states of the Web by for instance downloading pages: The next time one logs into the Web, the pages already are vanished or at least they are changed. A great deal of the fascination of the Web indeed consists in the appearance of an almost interaction-like fugitiveness, individuals come and go, pages pass, everything somehow is a site "under construction". Only the bugs seem to be stable. Most disturbingly perhaps, as compared with an unknown future and a fugitive present, is the enormous capacity of the Web to store the past. Thanks to the machines, both clients and servers attached to it, the Web is acting like its own archive and at the same time producing a "*mal d'archive*" (Derrida 1995; Fuchs 1998) of its own in exposing all possible problems in feeding, interpreting, embedding and disembedding the archive. In its handling of all three time horizons the Web features a synchronicity (Luhmann 1990b) which is so demanding that it should not come as a surprise that the Web is beginning to develop its own time structure which is differentiated from the time structures of the surrounding life. One gets sucked into the Web, quickly looses a feeling for time, forgets about the most ordinary body functions and finds oneself virtualized faster than any virtual reality tool may be able to develop.

Yet the most difficult question perhaps relates to the handling of the social dimension of meaning, that is to possibilities to experience, and act out, consensus and dissensus, in the Web. Somehow this seems to be a dimension which is strongly underdeveloped due to the request/ response-structure of the Web and thus can only be regained in a somehow artificial manner in chat rooms and forums. The famous problems of "netiquette" have to do with the Web not leaving much room for disagreement, let alone conflict. One just clicks one's way away from the sites one does not like, at the most leaving a commentary (yet why?) that nobody reads (and if?). That is perhaps why there are a lot of "liberal" hopes coming along with the Web: There is just a presenting of opinions, and you like or you don't, but you don't get the chance to do anything against it. Of course there are sites which strongly oppose a certain policy, public or private, or campaign for certain conflicts. Yet even these sites will be called on mostly by people agreeing with their purpose – and others searching for information about them. The use of the Web already seems to integrate people into a "multiverse" (Neal Stephenson) which is more unifying than any "universe" has been. Or better, the Web is turning all conflicts going on into conflicts carried out in arguments. That is already calming them down, and if you don't like it you don't use the Web.

Thus both *ego* and *alter ego* turn into "avatars" (Neal Stephenson) which you only fight in game since they are as fragile as you are. Indeed, there seems to be no space for double contingency (Luhmann 1995a, 103 ss.), so the most catalytic problem for any communication to emerge is absent. It is eclipsed by the machines already running.

In all these matters of understanding and of meaning communication in the Web extends on the already known attempts to adapt itself to the restlessness of a consciousness watching the communication. Adaptation, as Luhmann (1995b, 124) emphasizes, does not mean that the communication tries to play along with the desires of the mental systems in the environment of the communication. Instead it forces the consciousness into the situation to choose to either accept the communication or to reject it in a way which is to be understood by communication. Thus, it is difficult for a mental system not to comply with communication. Both ways it is already trapped.

With respect to the Web the consciousness trailing along with its thoughts finds itself in a situation visualized once again by Andersen's (1998) graph (fig. 5):

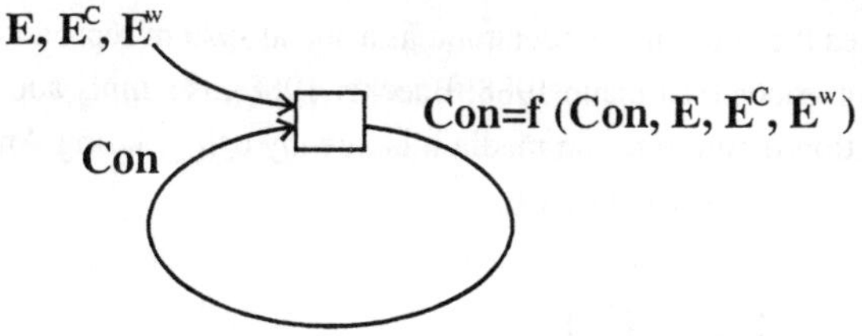

Fig.5: perturbed recursion in consciousness with respect to an environment featuring communication and the Web

The consciousness **Con** reproduces itself as a function of itself, **Con**, and an environment **E**, which is enriched by communication $\mathbf{E}^C$ going along and a Web $\mathbf{E}^W$ attracting its users. We won't go into details here but just note in passing that the interesting feature of the Web for the consciousness may consist in the distinction between perception and communication which it shares with pictures, movies (Baecker 1996), and other multimedia. It is as easy to turn a text into some graphic impression as it is possible to read the pictures of the Web and to indeed understand that they contain information uttered by somebody. It is nevertheless the blending into each other of text, sound, and image which is so attractive for mental systems watching that they enjoy perhaps addictively the oscillation between perception and communication.

That again may be a hint to the actual coding going on of the Web by communication: The "new world" is to be understood as a world which is much more adapted to the almost simultaneous capacities of mental systems to compute vastly heterogeneous impressions in a very fast way than the older text-based world has been. Communication by the means of the Web is extremely speeding up, orbiting the earth in all its respects, or so it seems, and yet always offering the option to extremely slow down and let everybody have a real close look.

VI. Commercialising the Web?

There is no problem in commercialising the Web as long as that means nothing else but the recourse of the economy to the Web. Of course, the Web can be used for offering jobs, offering commodities, offering services. And it is and will be used to purchase them. The Web steps in where ordinary business of the real-interaction type could be done as well. And it steps in when a business of a more clandestine type is looked for. Producers can use the Web to extend on their facilities to observe what competitors are offering, and how they are presenting their offers. And consumers can go on a long tour of comparisons of price and advertisement (there is no link to check on the quality, but who is willing and able to check the quality the first time he buys anyway?) without leaving their chair and as long as their patience and curiosity is not running out.

In these cases the economy, understood as a social system reproducing itself by means of payments for goods (Luhmann 1988; Baecker 1988), is simply adding the Web as a mass communication medium to the media it is already using. Using Andersen's (1998) graph the situation is as follows (Fig. 6):

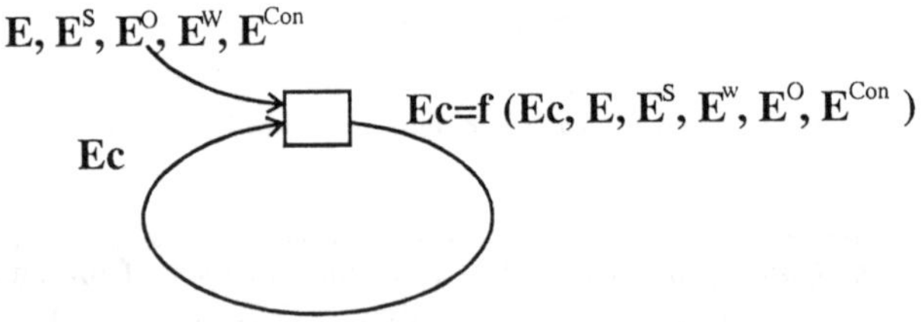

Fig. 6: perturbed recursion of the economy in an environment featuring the rest of the society, the Web, and mental systems

The economy **Ec** is reproducing itself recursively by iterations which are a function of the economy **Ec** and a general environment **E**, wherein one may distinguish the rest of the society $\mathbf{E^S}$, including other mass communication media like writing, print, and television, the Web $\mathbf{E^W}$, business organizations (companies) $\mathbf{E^O}$, and lots of mental systems (or consciousnesses) $\mathbf{E^{Con}}$. Of course this is a sharp selection of matters relevant.

When asking the question of a possible commercialisation of the Web two different questions become relevant which mark the two sides of one coin. The first question is whether there is a possibility that the Web, taken as a mass communication medium as sketched out in the pages above, may be overtaken by the economy, or by companies acting on its behalf, that is which search out options to reproduce payments sensibly and profitably. The second question is whether it might make an important distinction for the economy, or its organizations, or both, that there is a new mass communication medium emerging. The first question may read as well like this: Is the Web going to become another market? And the second question may read as: Is the Web a different market than those already known of?

Using our analytical tools we tried to sketch out in the previous paragraphs, both questions are easy to answer, namely: No, and Yes, respectively.

There is no way to turn the Web into a market because there is no way to completely turn a mass communication medium into a medium focusing exclusively on the triggering of payments. Nobody can buy the Web since nobody owns it – which does not exclude that companies buy servers, search engines, browsers, and so on – and these are already companies. It is as impossible to turn the Web as a whole into a market as it is impossible to have journals or billboards only communicate the desire to buy, and sell. The symbolic communication medium used by the economy, money, works only under the condition that there are other symbolic communication media working as well, power for instance, or truth, or love, or maybe trust. Mass communication media are distinguished from symbolic communication media in that they can not simultaneously select and motivate communication as the latter do (Luhmann 1997, 316 ss.). One can use the Web for purposes of advertisement, and indeed heavily so, but that's it.

But indeed, yes, the Web seems to be a market very different from known markets. It is a marketing tool which depends on consumers requesting the documents offered by firms. That is why advertisements are about to appear everywhere where surfers usually have to stop to go on, for instance with search engines. And that is why firms try to feature everything possible on a sophisticated multimedia level to attract the kind of people who is surfing the Web these times, namely people interested in the technological possibilities of multimedia much more than in searching out best offers (with selling software and hardware it seems to be different: here the web sites have not to be sophisticated but fast and reliable in their building up of the pages). But if one does not wish to stop with certain firms one just does not do it, as in any ordinary market.

All this is common sense. The question of a commercialisation of the Web becomes interesting as soon as one asks whether the different type of coding which is developed by communication with respect to the Web might imply possible other objects (goods) to deal with and a possible different understanding among consumers to take account of. There is an "economy of context" (Dyson 1995) emerging which begins to view contents as free, since they will be copied anyway as soon as they can be copied, and focuses instead on the creation and maintenance of attentiveness, which indeed is the scarce resource of an economy with information overflow.

The difficulty to do business in the Web stems from the necessity to induce the requests which can only be made by the clients (in both senses of the client machine and the client as a customer). So the business is done by a sequence of luring, servicing, and selling that distributes some information for free, helps to introduce (iterate) that information into an already existing structure of information, and then sells the solution to the problem the new piece of information is causing inside the already existing structure. The all-revealing paradigm for this kind of business is the market for software. It is a matter of implanting parasites (Serres 1980) that one knows one never needed as soon as one discovers that there is no way to get rid of them again.

Bibliography

Andersen, Peter Bøgh: WWW as self-organizing system. In: Cybernetics and Human Knowing 5, no. 2 (1998), 5-41

Baecker, Dirk: Information und Risiko in der Marktwirtschaft. Frankfurt am Main: Suhrkamp1988

Baecker, Dirk: The Reality of Motion Pictures. In: Modern Language Notes 111 (1996), 560-577

Baecker, Dirk: Kommunikation im Medium der Information. In: *Rudolf Maresch / Niels Werber* (eds.), Kommunikation, Medien, Macht. Frankfurt am Main: Suhrkamp 1999, 174-191

Bateson, Gregory: Steps to an Ecology of Mind: Collected Essays in Anthropology, Psychiatry, Evolution and Epistemology. San Francisco: Chandler 1972

Bourgine, Paul / Francisco J. Varela (eds.): Towards a Practice of Autonomous Systems: Proceedings of the First European Conference on Artificial Life. Cambridge, Mass.: MIT Pr.

Deleuze, Gilles: Pourparlers: 1972-1990, Paris: Ed. de Minuits 1990

Derrida, Jacques: Vers une éthique de la discussion. In: Limited Inc. Presented and translated by *Elisabeth Weber*. Paris: Galilée 1990, 199-285

Derrida, Jacques: Mal d'Archive: Une impression freudienne. Paris: Ed. Galilée 1995

Douglas, Mary: A Typology of Cultures. In: *Max Haller / Hans-Joachim Hoffmann-Nowotny / Wolfgang Zapf* (eds.), Kultur und Gesellschaft. Frankfurt: Campus 1989, 85-97

Dyson, Esther: Intellectual Value. In: Wired 3.07 (1995), 136-141, 182-184

Esposito, Elena: Interaktion, Interaktivität und die Personalisierung der Massenmedien. In: Soziale Systeme: Zeitschrift für soziologische Theorie 1 (1995), 225-260

Esposito, Elena: Fiktion und Virtualität. In: *Sybille Krämer* (ed.), Medien Computer Realität: Wirklichkeitsvorstellungen und Neue Medien. Frankfurt am Main: Suhrkamp 1998, 269-296

Fuchs, Jürgen: Magdalena: MfS, Memfisblues, Stasi, Die Firma, VEB Horch & Guck. Berlin: Rowohlt 1998

Hardy, Henry Edward (1993): The History of the Net. Master's Thesis. School of Communications, Grand Valley State University, Allendale, Mich. (http://www.vrx.net/usenet/ thesis)

Gibson, William: Neuromancer 1984

Gibson, William: Burning Chrome 1986

Heider, Fritz: Thing and Medium. In: Psychological Issues vol. 1, no. 3: On Perception, Event Structure, and Psychological Environment. Selected Papers. New York: International UP 1959, 1-34

Korzybski, Alfred: Science and Sanity: An Introduction to Non-Aristotelian Systems and General Semantics, fourth edition. Lakeville, Conn.: Institute of General Semantics 1958

Luhmann, Niklas: Funktion und Kausalität. In: Kölner Zeitschrift für Soziologie und Sozialpsychologie 14 (1962), 617-644

Luhmann, Niklas: Funktionale Methode und Systemtheorie. In: Soziale Welt 15 (1964), 1-25

Luhmann, Niklas: Sinn als Grundbegriff der Soziologie. In: *Jürgen Habermas / Niklas Luhmann*: Theorie der Gesellschaft oder Sozialtechnologie: Was leistet die Systemforschung? Frankfurt am Main: Suhrkamp 1971, 25-100

Luhmann, Niklas: Die Unwahrscheinlichkeit der Kommunikation. In: Soziologische Aufklärung 3: Soziales System, Gesellschaft, Organisation. Opladen: Westdeutscher Verl. 1981, 25-49

Luhmann, Niklas: Die Wirtschaft der Gesellschaft. Frankfurt am Main: Suhrkamp 1988

Luhmann, Niklas: Die Wissenschaft der Gesellschaft. Frankfurt am Main: Suhrkamp 1990a

Luhmann, Niklas: Gleichzeitigkeit und Synchronisation. In: Soziologische Aufklärung 5: Konstruktivistische Perspektiven. Opladen: Westdeutscher Verl. 1990b, 95-130

Luhmann, Niklas: Social Systems. Translated by John Bednarz, Jr., with Dirk Baecker. Stanford: Stanford UP 1995a

Luhmann, Niklas: Was ist Kommunikation? In: Soziologische Aufklärung 6: Die Soziologie und der Mensch. Opladen: Westdeutscher Verl. 1995b, 113-124

Luhmann, Niklas: Die Gesellschaft der Gesellschaft. Frankfurt am Main: Suhrkamp 1997

Maturana, Humberto R.: Autopoiesis. In: *Milan Zeleny* (ed.), Autopoiesis: A Theory of Living Organizations. New York: North-Holland 1981, 21-32

Maturana, Humberto R. / Francisco J. Varela: Autopoietic systems: A characteriziation of the living organization, Urbana, Ill. 1975

Maturana, Humberto R. / Francisco J. Varela: Autopoiesis and Cognition: The Realization of the Living. Dordrecht: Reidel 1980

Nietzsche, Friedrich: Zur Genealogie der Moral: Eine Streitschrift. Frankfurt am Main: Insel 1991

Ong, Walter J., SJ: Rhetoric, Romance, and Technology: Studies in the Interaction of Expression and Culture. Ithaca, NY: Cornell UP 1971

Ong, Walter J., SJ: Interfaces of the Word: Studies in the Evolution of Consciousness and Culture. Ithaca, NY: Cornell UP 1977

Parsons, Talcott / Edward A. Shils (eds.) Toward a General Theory of Action. Cambridge, Mass.: Harvard UP 1967

Serres, Michel: Le parasite, Paris: Grasset 1980

Shannon, Claude E. / Warren Weaver: The Mathematical Theory of Communication. Urbana, Ill.: Illinois UP 1963

Spencer-Brown, G.: Laws of Form. New York: Julian 1972

Stephenson, Neal: Snow Crash. New York: Bantam 1992

Titscher, Stefan / Michael Meyer: Text und Gegentext. Die Differenztheoretische Text-Analyse (DTA): Ein Methodenvorschlag. In: Soziale Systeme 4 (1998), 445-479

Varela, F. J. / H. R. Maturana / R. Urib: Autopoiesis: The Organization of Living Systems, Its Characterization and a Model. In: BioSytems 5 (1974), 187-196

von Foerster, Heinz: Objects: Tokens for (Eigen-) Behaviors. In: Cybernetics Forum 8 (1976), 91-96 (reprinted in *Heinz von Foerster*: Observing Systems. Seaside, Cal.: Intersystems, 1981)

von Foerster, Heinz: Epistemology of Communication, in: Kathleen Woodward (ed.), The Myths of Information, Technology and Post-Industrial Culture, Madison 1980, 18-27

von Foerster, Heinz: Notes on an Epistemology for Living Things. In: Observing Systems. Seaside, Cal.: Intersystems 1981, 258-271

Weick, Karl E.: The Social Psychology of Organizing, second edition. Reading, Mass.: Addison-Wesley 1979

White, Harrison C.: Identity and Control: A Structural Theory of Action. Princeton, NJ: Princeton UP 1992

White, Leslie A.: The Science of Culture: A Study of Man and Civilization. Second ed. New York: Farrar, Straus & Giroux 1969

Wittgenstein, Ludwig: Tractatus logico-philosophicus. Frankfurt am Main: Suhrkamp 1963

Zeleny, Milan / Kevin D. Hufford: The Application of Autopoiesis in Systems Analysis: Are Autopoietic Systems also Social Systems? In: International Journal of General Systems 21 (1992), 145-160

Michael Thompson

Global Networks and Local Cultures: What are the Mismatches and what can be done about them?

Contrasted pairings of social solidarities are as old as social science itself: Durkheim's (1893) *mechanical* versus *organic* solidarity, Tönnies' (1887) *Gemeinschaft* and *Gesellschaft* and Sir Henry Maine's (1861) historical transition from *status* to *contract*, to mention just three. Nowadays, the favoured contrast, echoed in this symposium's distinction between private and non-private goods, is between *markets* (autonomous actors freely bidding and bargaining with one another) and *hierarchies* (the benign authorities who ensure that the necessary conditions for this market game – a "level playing field", for instance – are in place) (eg Lindblom 1977, Williamson 1975). However, though the "masters" and their latter-day incarnations have all drawn dualistic distinctions – dualistic distinctions that clearly are persuasive and clearly are tapping into something fundamental – you will go mad if you try to map their formulations onto one another. Only if you double-up, from two to four, can you accommodate them all in a way that does not give rise to serious contradictions or Procrustean amputations.

This "mapping of the masters" is the speciality of my colleague, Steve Rayner, and I will not go into it here.[1] Instead, I will just point out that, since markets institute equality (of opportunity, that is) and promote competition whilst hierarchies institute inequality (status differences, that is) and set all sorts of limits on competition, a full typology of

1 But see Table 4.4 (p.327) of Thompson and Rayner 1998.

solidarities will have to include the other two permutations: equality without competition (which is called *egalitarianism*) and inequality with competition (which is called *fatalism*). If you think of the Brent Spar saga, Shell was the actor from the market (or *individualist*) solidarity, the government experts who okayed the deep ocean disposal were the hierarchical actors, Greenpeace (whose eleventh hour intervention drastically upset this negotiated outcome) was the egalitarian actor, and those (like myself) who found themselves totally convinced by whoever they last heard arguing the case on television were the fatalists (Figure 1).

There is, of course much more to this fourfold scheme than this (this typology is but one component within what is called Cultural Theory[2]) but this is all I need to hang my global networks/local cultures argument on.

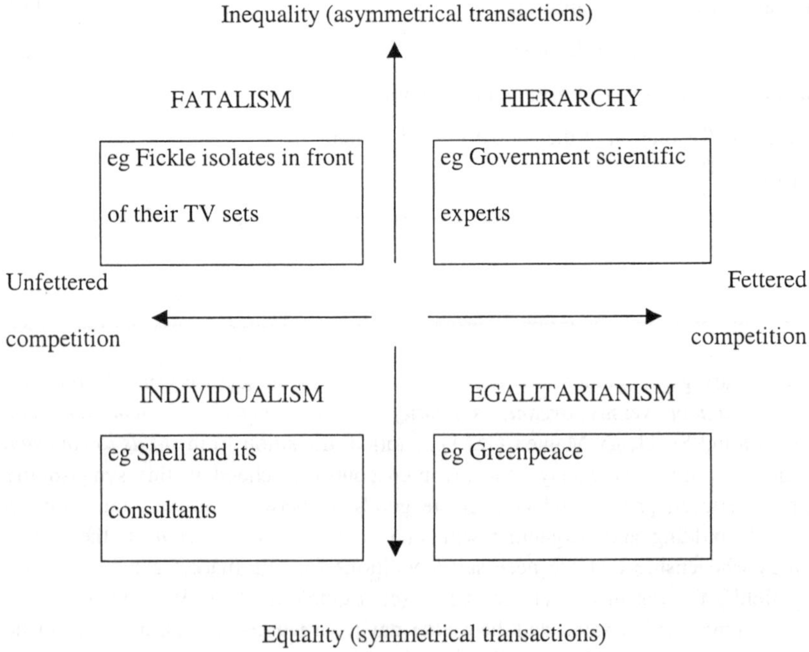

Figure 1 *The Four Forms of Social Solidarity that Underlie Most of Social Science.*

2 See Part I of Thompson, Ellis and Wildavsky 1990, and the introductory chapter of Ellis and Thompson 1997.

Goods and Solidarities[3]

The first step in the argument is the obvious one: that *non-private goods* – the goods with which we are concerned in this symposium – come in three distinct forms, each as different from the other two as they all are from *private goods*.[4] Private goods are distinguished from non-private goods by virtue of their high *excludability* and low *jointness of consumption* (Snidal 1994) and they are commonly contrasted with *public goods*, which are characterised by low excludability (if the lighthouse is there everyone can use it, even if they have not contributed to its costs) and high jointness (the lighthouse is just as bright for the nth user as it was for the first one). The market can readily produce private goods but, according to the conventional rational choice argument, it will underprovide public goods and so the hierarchy will have to step in if we are to have enough of them. But, of course, there are two other permutations – two other varieties of non-private goods: *club goods* (high jointness, high excludability) and *common-pool goods* (low jointness, low excludability). An example of the former is, of course, a club; if you belong to it you enjoy all its amenities, along with all the other members. An example of the latter would be the grazing on a salt-marsh to which all the surrounding farms have access, and there has recently been an enormous amount of research on these sorts of goods: goods that, since their provision requires equalised voluntary restraint and local (and often tacit) knowledge, are something of an affront to both markets and hierarchies[5] (eg Ostrom 1990, Keohane and Ostrom 1995, Goldman 1998).

These four kinds of goods map onto the four kinds of social solidarities: markets providing private goods, hierarchies providing public goods, egalitarian arrangements providing common-pool goods and fatalised margins making club goods viable by the ease with which they can be excluded from them.[6] And in mapping these goods onto this fourfold scheme we turn it into what is called a "contested terrain": each solidarity arguing that life would be much, much better if the goods that are being provided by the other solidarities were provided by it instead. This brings me to the second step in my

---

3 At various stages in this paper I borrow shamelessly from some of the contributions to a shortly to be published book (Thompson, Grendstad and Selle, 1999). Much of this section (up to, and including, Figure 2) is borrowed from Verweij, 1999.

4 To be precise, two of these three (club goods and common-pool goods) are as different from each other as the third (public goods) is from private goods: both pairs differ on both discriminating criteria, excludability and jointness. These two are then half as different from both public goods and private goods as they are from each other, differing on only one of the two discriminating criteria.

5 Voluntary restraint implies that people sometimes prefer a smaller bundle of goods to a larger one, which transgresses the *non-satiety requirement* of the economic theory that explains how markets work. And the idea that those towards the bottom of a hierarchy have access to certain vital knowledge that is inherently inaccessible to those at the higher levels contravenes one of the defining requirements for hierarchical organisation: *asymmetry* (see Gross and Rayner 1985).

6 If the fatalistic solidarity provided goods of any kind it would not be fatalistic! Club goods could be readily explained by some interplay between the market and hierarchical solidarities, were it not for the fact that hierarchies claim to be all-inclusive and markets claim to give everyone an equal chance to participate. Since club goods depend on excludability, they simply would not be possible if there were only the markets and hierarchies!

argument: that these four kinds of goods are *socially constructed* and *essentially contested*. In other words, there is nothing inherent to the goods themselves that will tell you which category they fall into. Goods do not *fall* into categories; they are captured into them and, at some later stage, liberated from them. Even lighthouses can be privatised, and private goods soon cease to exist in a social setting where everyone has become convinced that all property is theft! (Figure 2).

Social life, we can now see, is a never-ending struggle between these four solidarities, each usually managing to keep some of its goods uncontested, but all of them doing everything they can to pry the less firmly-attached goods away from their present categorical anchorages and into the ones they variously prefer. So social arrangements in different localities are always plural in terms of solidarities. In that sense they are all the same, but they will then differ in the relative strengths of the four solidarities (Ireland, for instance, is the most hierarchical European Union country, France the most fatalized, Germany the highest on both individualism and egalitarianism, though of course they are changing all the time[7]). Specific communities will also differ in the distribution of particular goods among the four categories. Thus, even if the strengths of the solidarities in two locations happen to be the same, the cultures can still be very These latter differences are the *particularities* of different cultures, and they are then compounded by history having led people in some localities to value certain things that are not valued at all (or are even negatively valued) in other localities. The French eating frogs' legs, for instance, or Cambodians tucking into platefuls of man's best friend. Likewise with non-kosher individuals munching their way through well-buttered ham sandwiches, and non-Hindus merrily masticating their beefsteaks and dripping-fried chips.

Such differences can certainly lead to problems, and not just with global information networks. Indeed, these sorts of cultural problems are now so well recognised that business people and diplomats can go on special courses on which they learn how to avoid committing terrible gaffes in the countries they are about to visit. Since the providers of global information systems can, and no doubt already do, avail themselves of these sorts of solutions, I will say no more about them. This will leave me free to concentrate on the really serious problems that they (and those of us who are on the receiving end of it all) face: those that stem from major mismatches between the pattern of solidarities inherent in the production and operation of these global information networks and the patterns that are found in the various localities that those networks are beamed into. There is no quick fix for these problems, because they have to do with *the democratisation of technological decision making*.

Information Technology and Democracy[8]

Global information networks are not inevitably locked-in, by their underlying technology, to just one way of operating. Indeed it is the flexibility of the new media (as they are called) that distinguishes them from the old media – radio, for instance,

7 See Grendstad (1990) and Mamadouh (1999).

8 Much of this section (up to and including Figure 4) is borrowed from Hendriks and Zouridis (1999).

FATALIST

Why should we contribute to the financing of this lighthouse? None of its economic benefits will come our way. These, as always, are sewn-up: by the construction companies, the shipping magnates and the bankers.

HIERARCHIST

The proposed lighthouse is a collective good. Everyone will benefit and no one will be excluded. Since individuals will not contribute, the government has to step in. Otherwise the development of the whole region will suffer.

INDIVIDUALIST

The market can do all this. Ships of countries or firms that do not contribute can be refused right of passage through territorial waters. Also, technological developments - radar and eventually satellite positioning systems - will render the proposed lighthouse obsolete (probably before it has even been built). In the meantime, marine pilots (for whom there is a ready market) will fill the gap.

EGALITARIAN

We need to look at things holistically. The lighthouse will spoil an area of outstanding natural beauty and will consume lots of energy. And oil spills, and other problems related to increased shipping and reduced on-board vigilance, may destroy the ecosystem of the entire coastal region. A lifeboat, maintained and crewed by the local fishermen, is what is needed, not the unsustainable "top-down" lighthouse or the high-tech, growth- crazed innovations.

Figure 2 The Provision Of A Lighthouse As A Contested Terrain.

newspapers and one-way television. Satellites and glass-fibre cable networks, computer hardware and software, and other interactive communication and information devices now support things like electronic mail, direct mail, on-line databases, teletext, interactive television, teleconferencing and instant polling (Van de Donk and Tops 1995). Moreover, these new media, according to Abramson, Arterton and Orren (1988), have all sorts of implications for politics and democratic decision making.

- They increase the quantity and accessibility of information for politicians, bureaucrats and citizens.
- They accelerate the gathering, distribution and storing of information, thereby diminishing the constraints of time and space (and facilitating both "community without propinquity" and the much less desirable "propinquity without community").
- They enable the receivers of information to exert more control over that information (empowerment, in other words).
- They enable "narrowcasting" as well as broadcasting on the part of the sender of information.
- They enable decentralisation.
- They enable interaction between sender and receiver and between applier and application.

These characteristics are deduced from what are seen as the inherent properties of the new media, but Cultural Theorists insist that technology can never be fully separated from us in this way; technology is always, to some considerable extent, socially and culturally constructed (Schwarz and Thompson 1990). The new media, for instance, can also enable centralisation. They can globalise as well as localise, and what they actually end up doing is crucially dependent on the way in which they and the different social solidarities are bound up with one another. This, in turn, will likely have a major influence on the way in which these technologies evolve, since each solidarity, left to its own devices, would lock us into a distinctive development path. What this means, quite simply, is that the avoidance of these sorts of lock-ins – the maintenance of technological flexibility – is one and the same as the never-ending task of caring for, and strengthening, democracy.

This vital linkage – perhaps constructive, perhaps destructive – between new technological developments and democracy is clearly evident in the current framing in terms of "Athens versus Orwell":[9] the idea that we are currently at a fork in the road, one way leading to a wonderfully participatory electronic *agora*, the other to a nightmarishly controlled future in which the reins are firmly in the hands of a skilled and knowledgeable elite. Cultural Theory, however, encourages us to reject this framing, and it does this by showing that, since information is socially constructed, information technology is nowhere near as deterministic as the "Athens versus Orwell" formulation requires it to be. It also, for good measure, shows us that democracy is an essentially contested notion and that if we were to actually find ourselves in the participatory utopia we would no longer be democratic because there would be no contestation of that particular image of democracy.[10] So, if Cultural Theory is right, those who are currently

9 An overview of this framing is provided in van de Donk and Tops (1995).

10 For a description of these different images of democracy, and a salutary account of what happens when just one is imposed and the others excluded, see Jensen (1999).

so concerned about the anti-democratic potential of information technology are actually doing everything they can to realise it!

The Social Constructions of Information

It is no use talking about information as if it is "out there": something that is defined for all of us by its inherent properties, and that we then relate to in different ways. Rather, we need to recognise that people draw the line between information and "noise" in a way that, so far as they can judge, will help strengthen their solidarity and weaken the others. Were information not socially constructed in this way there would be no such thing as *information rejection*: the active (and inherently political) putting into the noise category of something that is already information to someone else: a phenomenon so common it has given rise to a host of stock phrases: "Never argue with someone who *knows*", "There's none so blind as those that will not see", "I don't wish to know that" and so on. Information handling styles therefore have a two-way character: they vary in the way we construct the information and they vary in the way we relate to the information we have constructed.[11] We can set out these information handling styles by adding the two missing permutations to the classic dualistic typology proposed by Van Gunsteren (1985): learning based on analysis and instruction (A & I learning) and learning based on variety and selection (V & S learning) (Figure 3).

FATALISM (S & M Learning)	HIERARCHY (A & I Learning)
• World operates without rhyme or reason, and people are not to be trusted. To waste resources looking for order and trust is to lessen your chances of *Survival* in a chaotic environment. • Information is not selected or rejected in any systematic way. Rather, it is *Macerated* so that any regularities that would enable people to get in sync with things become indistinguishable from the surrounding disorder: "What you don't know can't harm you".	• Focus on normality and appropriateness, with information that cannot be classified on basis of normal science and organisational routine being rejected. • Errors detected and corrected through meticulous *Analysis* and detailed *Instruction*. • Ideally, this would be completely automated in a perfectly informatised hierarchy. The boundary between normality and perversity would be under permanent electronic surveillance, and information signalling the crossing of that boundary would automatically lead to corrective instructions.

11 This two-way character, which also holds for needs and resources (we make these vital ends before we make them meet), is one of the most important predictions from Cultural Theory. See Thompson and Wildavsky (1986).

INDIVIDUALIST (V & S Learning)	EGALITARIANISM (E & R Learning)
• Highly pragmatic and utilitarian, with information as a political resource, selected or rejected on the basis of its expected return. • Detects and corrects error in a process of *Variety* and *Selection*, those most skilled quickly combining disparate bits of information into profitable undertakings. • Requires both a broad network that taps into many different sources and a set of adequate desk-clearing principles (shifting less important data to those on the periphery of your network, for instance).	• *Exposure* (of the failings of the other solidarities) and *Revelation* (good and bad in black and white). • Selection of information confirming that the world is getting out of control, together with "monster-barring": blanket rejection of information that would introduce shades of grey. • Conviction, not correction (which goes against their authority-rejecting grain), is the coin egalitarians exchange in their communicative processes.

Figure 3 *Four Information Handling Styles*

The Social Constructions of Democracy

Unsurprisingly, in view of their propensity to learn such different lessons, act in such different ways, produce such different goods, and (as we will see in a moment) sink costs into such different paths of technological development, the upholders of these different forms of solidarity have very different ideas about what democracy should be. These different models (or images) of democracy have long been familiar to political scientists, most of whom have thrown their scholarly weight behind one or other of them. More recently, there has been a growing awareness that there is nothing fruitful about this struggle to decide which model is the right model, and that the fruitfulness is in the struggle itself.[12] In other words, the essence of democracy is in its contestation: a nice insight that simultaneously explains "Levin's law" (which states that any country with the word "Democratic" in its title isn't) and the non-convergence of countries that are undoubtedly democratic (Britain, for instance, being rather more towards the hierarchical model than the United States, Switzerland more towards the egalitarian model and so on) (Figure 4).

If we accept this positive and anti-judgmental view of the struggle to define true democracy then we can crudely assess technological innovations (and other changes – policies, for instance) according to whether they are likely to strengthen (desirable) or diminish (undesirable) the contestation. For instance, a technology (nuclear power, say) that has been designed entirely on hierarchical criteria (as is evident in its large scale,

12 An awareness that was first expressed by Wildavsky (1993) and that is taken up as a unifying theme in Thompson, Grendstad and Selle (1999).

long lead time, high capital intensity and major infrastructural rearrangements[13]) would set our alarm bells ringing. Conversely, a technology that has what advertising people call a "take-out" for each solidarity – the Internet is probably a good example, and Unilever's "Frish" lavatory rim-block certainly is[14] – would receive a favourable assessment.

We can also use this contestation idea to assess the extent to which a global development will mesh with, or jar with, specific local cultures, but for this more subtle assessment we need some sort of measure of the relative strengths of the solidarities inherent in that global development *vis-a-vis* the various patterns that exist in different localities. This is an area of inquiry that goes by the name "political culture", and quite a wide range of techniques for achieving such measures have now been developed.[15] The crude assessments alert us to the sorts of modifications that are desirable in the global information networks themselves. The more subtle assessments alert us (on a one-by-one basis) to the sorts of modifications that are desirable at the points where those modified global networks reach down into specific localities: a sort of "sauce for the goose is not necessarily sauce for the gander" principle.

FATALISM (The *Non*-model)

- True to its learning style (see Fig 3), the upholders of this solidarity waste no time building a model of democracy.
- And true to their conviction that all goods are really club goods (from which they are excluded), their verdict on democracy is not enthusiastic: "It doesn't matter who you vote for, the government always gets in".

HIERARCHY (The *Guardian* model)

- Sides with Plato and his "philosopher-king". Only right that those with superior insight and virtue should make the decisions.
- Democracy should be indirect, representative and majoritarian, the political class being given primacy over public affairs on the basis of popular elections every few years.
- This elite should act as "trustees" (Burke) focusing on the long-term general interest, not short-term individual or factional claims and interests.
- *Loyalty and complaisance* are the crucial virtues.elite should act as "trustees"

13 These are actually Collingridge's (1980, 1992) four technical indicators of inflexibility. They have now been complemented by four organisational indicators: "single mission" outfits, closure to criticism, hype and hubris (see, for instance, Gyawali 1998).

14 The rim-block story is set out in the first chapter of Schwarz and Thompson (1990), and again (in connection with the essentially contested nature of democracy) in Ney and Thompson (1999).

15 For an overview of political culture see Thompson, Ellis and Wildavsky (1992). For the tools themselves see Thompson (1997), Grendstad (1990), Dake and Thompson (1993), Marris et al (1996) Grendstad and Selle (1997) and Linnerooth-Bayer and Fitzgerald (1996).

INDIVIDUALISM (The *Protective* model)	EGALITARIANISM (The *Participatory* model)
• Self-determination is crucial. Paternalism is therefore anathema and plebiscitary processes attractive at first glance. • But such processes tend to crude majoritarianism, which can result in even large minorities being denied self-determination. • Hence need for measures to protect individual and minority rights and interests. • Government's *raison d'être* is "the protection of individual rights, life, liberty and estate" (Locke). • The prime desideratum is that people be able to carry out their plans.	• No place for deference and no support for indirect or majoritarian modes of decision making. Choice must be by direct and broad participation. • Decisions should be agreed by all, ideally in a small-scale, face-to-face way and at a single level: the grassroots. • Leadership is resisted and equality prized. • The *equal right to self-development* is the overriding principle.

Figure 4. The Essential Contestation of Democracy.

The Social Constructions of Information Technology[16]

Bordewijk and van Kaam (1982) have arrived at a fourfold typology of information flows and information relations by way of two pairwise distinctions: two answers to the question "who decides on the topic, timing and pace of receipt of the information?" and two answers to the question "From whose databases are the data retrieved?"

- Where there is simultaneous transmission of centrally constructed information to a number of destinations, with the timing and pace of receipt being determined centrally, we have *allocution* (more familiarly, broadcasting). One-way television is an example of this type of information flow.
- When there is a central collection of information from a number of sources, with the topic, timing and pace of receipt being determined by the centre, we have *registration*. Elections and consumer surveys are examples of this type of information flow.
- In what is the opposite of registration, the 'destinations' retrieve from the centre information about a topic which is selected by each destination, with each destination determining the timing and pace of receipt. This is *consultation* (more familiarly, data-picking). Examples of this type of information flow would be citizens and others (politicians, for instance) consulting newspapers and magazines (and perhaps cutting out or highlighting items of particular interest).

16 Much of this section is borrowed from Hendriks and Zouridis (1999).

- In *conversation* we have the exchange of information between two or more sources-cum-destinations, with a mutually agreed pace and timing. Correspondence, by letter, e-mail or fax, between two or more friends is an example of this kind of information flow.

In Figure 5 these four kinds of information flow have been arranged so as best to depict their affinities with the four solidarities (as they are conventionally depicted). It is not a perfect fit, but broadcasting (as has already been suggested) is supportive of fatalism, registration of hierarchy, conversation of egalitarianism and data-picking of individualism. The fit is not perfect because, except in the symmetrical case of conversation, we can expect different solidarities to be supported by the centres and the peripheries: fatalists at the periphery of broadcasting, for instance, and hierarchists and individualists at the centre (as the impressively ego-centric pundit, Malcolm Muggeridge, shrewdly observed, many years ago, 'the whole point of television is not to watch it but to get on it!').

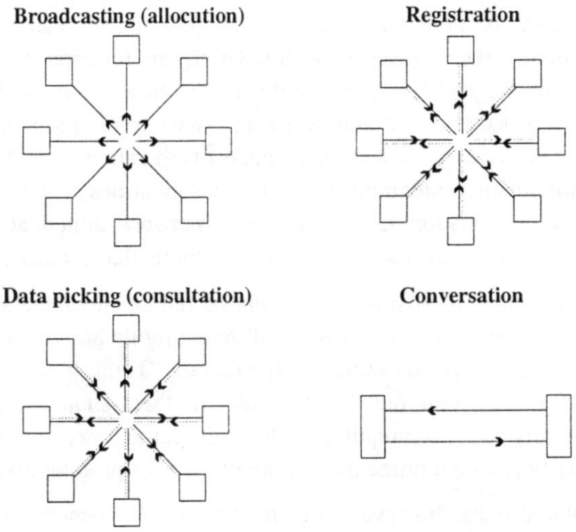

Figure 5 *Four Types of Information Flow*

Hendriks and Zouridis (1999) have gone on from here to a number of case studies – instances where one or other of these four types of information flow have been implemented, technologically, in the field of application that goes by the name "teledemocracy", and whose development is viewed with such optimism and pessimism by the Athenians and the Orwellians, respectively. I will zoom in on one of these case studies in a moment, but first of all I should point out that this diagram, together with its case studies, makes clear that there is tremendous scope for each solidarity to get from the available technologies the things that it wants (and to avoid getting the things that it does not want).

At the same time, this diagram prompts us to take a closer look at the *global information networks* which are the focus of this symposium. Do these fit into just one of these four boxes (broadcasting) and have an affinity with just one solidarity (fatalism)?[17] Or do we find them, in quite different forms and with affinities across all the solidarities, in all of the boxes? The latter, I would say. Of course, powerful actors may be pushing one form rather than other possible forms, but spotting that this is what is going on, assessing the extent to which if it continues it will seriously distort the local patterns of solidarities, and then intervening to avert that undemocratic path of development (and to prevent technological lock-ins that will then lock out other available and desirable options) is precisely what a *Law of Non-Private Goods* should be designed to do.

An Egalitarian Resolution of the Global/Local Problem

The Global Eco-village Network (GEN) links into a virtual community a number of real communities that are much concerned with education and the desire to integrate ecology, sustainability and community development. Their interest, in other words, is in the production of common-pool goods (and in the building of resistance to private, public and club goods). Each "project" within GEN can function as an eco-village training centre, and the range of skills represented by the projects (and in the settlements they link) cover "all aspects of community living" (www.gaia.org/thegen/index.html). Such a network, given its explicit aims and mode of operation, is unlikely to attract members of the individualist, hierarchical or fatalist solidarities, but that is the whole point of it! It is an information technology-based network aimed at extending the egalitarian form of solidarity beyond the sorts of local limits that usually constrain it.

Founded in 1994, and open to anyone (individual or settlement) interested in ecology and sustainability, it has grown in size while still retaining its horizontal character and conversational style. Explicitly committed to the dictum "Think global, act local", the network enables real local communities to maintain their small-scale, face-to-face interactions (community with propinquity) while, at the same time, achieving, in virtual terms, global solidarity and commitment (community without propinquity).

Other environmental groups, however, use the Internet in a more combative way, exchanging information not just for community-building (the production of common-pool goods, that is) but for the mobilisation of support for action to undermine the other solidarities (the destruction, as it were, of private, public and club goods). Greenpeace's electronic alarm system is a fairly mild example that probably does little more than keep the opposition on its toes: more of a service than a disservice, in that it helps promote constructive argumentation among the solidarities. However, the more extreme examples can have rather different effects, both for the activists and for those they hope to undermine.

17 At the periphery, that is. Individualism and or hierarchy at the centre.

- Carrying the struggle too vigorously into the enemy camp can exacerbate incipient tensions (between the *realos* and the *fundis*, for instance in the German Green Party) within the activist groups. This happened recently with the American organisation, Earth First!, which has torn itself apart with acrimonious schisms and accusations of eco-fascism.[18] While the underlying dynamics are still not clear, it seems likely that these more extreme activities can sometimes carry the practitioners across the thin line that separates their egalitarian groups from simple (and simplifying) hierarchies: voluntarism and openness giving way to authoritarianism and the forming of "rejectionist fronts".
- The Internet has also opened up new avenues of political activism, sometimes called "cyberactivism". Electronic mail, for instance, is well suited for the quick and effective mobilisation of large numbers of sympathisers. It can be used for electronic petitions, which can be signed by a simple mouse-click, and, with massive e-mail bombing, it is even possible to sabotage the Internet sites of companies that resist the demands of environmental organisations or refuse to communicate with them.

Though the various solidarities currently co-exist on the Internet (a state of affairs that, by the democratisation criteria I have been arguing for, is highly desirable) it could be that it will eventually end up supportive of just one of them, the others having been bombed out of existence (an outcome that, by the same democratisation criteria, is highly undesirable). Here, then, is a possible peacekeeping role for hierarchy: the solidarity that most observers see as being least supported by this technology. This is a democracy-enhancing argument that gains further support from those individualists who see "off-planet" banking, and even more routine commercial transactions, not developing if the Internet remains unregulated.

Conclusion

The above analysis, and the prescriptions derived from it, are seriously at odds with those that are arrived at by way of the "Athens versus Orwell" framing. Hierarchy, for instance, is something to be got rid of, not conserved, if the goal is the fully participatory model of democracy. And if democracy is defined in just one way then no consideration will be given to the contending models of democracy, and to the need to ensure that they too are granted legitimacy, and that ways are found by which they can make their distinct and constructive contributions to the pluralized and contentious whole. Let me finish, therefore, with a handy tool that will help us to distinguish between the sorts of framings we need and the sorts of framings we need to be rid of.

This tool has been developed for *discourse analysis* and *scenario planning*, where the problem is to ensure that you are sufficiently reflexive, and that your analysis incorporates the requisite plurality. It consists of a 3 x 3 matrix, with the columns being "who is looking" and the rows being "who is in charge" (the fatalist solidarity is not included, because it has no voice in policy debates and is splendidly unconcerned about

18 For some discussion of Earth First!, and of how it differs from other activist environmental groups, see Ellis and Fred Thompson (1996, 1997).

"visions of the future"). So the columns describe the way the world is – able to bounce back from anything we chuck at it (individualism), everywhere fragile (egalitarianism), stable within discoverable limits (hierarchy) – and the way people are – irredeemably self-seeking (individualism), caring and sharing (egalitarianism), redeemable through firm and nurturing institutions (hierarchy). And the rows describe the rational and morally justifiable behaviour in such worlds – *laissez faire*, trial-and-error (individualism), precautionary principle, trial-without-error (egalitarianism), statutory regulation, look before you leap (hierarchy) (Figure 6).

WHO'S LOOKING

		Individualist	Egalitarian	Hierarchist
	Individualist			
WHO'S IN	Egalitarian			
	Hierarchist			

Figure 6 *The Handy Tool*

In each of the three cells along the diagonal the world is indeed the way the people who are in charge are convinced it is. Likewise with human nature. The future therefore turns out pretty much as expected, and there are no nasty surprises. So these are the three *utopias*. But, in the other six cells, both the world and the people in it are very different from the way those who are running things are insisting they are, which means that it is most unlikely that things will turn out as expected and highly probable that there will be all sorts of unpleasant surprises. So these are *dystopias*, two of which support each of the three utopias. A thorough discourse analysis, or a requisitely variegated exercise in scenario planning, would fill out all nine cells. At the very least, it would ensure that the three utopias were considered.

Now, when we offer up the "Athens versus Orwell" framing to this matrix, we can see that it consists of just one utopia (Athens) and elements from just two dystopias (Orwell). The utopia is the egalitarian one and the two dystopias are the dystopias that support that egalitarian utopia: (what would happen if those idiotic individualists and hierarchists were in charge). In other words, far from describing the historic fork in the road, and the entire range of options we have before us, it is setting out just one row from the matrix, when what we need, if we are to keep our democracies up to scratch and our technologies flexible, is the vigorous contention of all three rows. Nor, of course, should we entirely ignore the fatalist solidarity and the vital contributions it can make.

References

Abramson, J.B. / F.C. Arterton / G.R. Orren: The Electronic Commonwealth: the Impact of New Technologies upon Democratic Politics. New York: Basic Books 1988

Bordewijk, J.L. / B. van Kaam: Allocutie. Enkela Gedachten Over Communicatievrieheid In Een Bekabeld Land. Baarn: Bosch and Kenning 1982

Collingridge, D.: The Social Control of Technology. Milton Keynes: Open University Press 1980

Collingridge, D.: The Management of Scale: Big Organisations, Big Decisions, Big Mistakes. London: Routledge 1992

Dake, K. / M. Thompson: 'The meanings of sustainable development: household strategies for managing needs and resources'. In: *Wright, S.D. / T. Dietz / R. Borden / G. Young / G. Guagnano* (eds.) Human Ecology: Crossing Boundaries. Fort Collins, Colo.: The Society for Human Ecology 1993

Durkheim, E.: De La Division du Travail Sociale: étude sue l'organisation de Sociétés Supérieurs. Paris: Alcan 1893

Ellis, R.E. / M. Thompson (eds.): Culture Matters: Essays in Honor of Aaron Wildavsky. Boulder, Colo.: West View 1997

Ellis, R.E. / F. Thompson: The Culture Wars by Other Means: Environmental Attitudes and Cultural Biases in the Northwest. Paper presented at the annual meeting of the Western Political Science Association, San Francisco 1996

Ellis, R.E. / F. Thompson: Seeing Green: Cultural Biases and Environmental Preferences. In: *Ellis, R.E. / M. Thompson* (eds.), (1997) op.cit. 169-190

Goldman, M. (ed.): Privatizing Nature: Political Struggles for the Global Commons, London: Pluto 1998

Grendstad, G.: Europe By Cultures: An Exploration in Grid:Group Analysis. Graduate Thesis, University of Bergen 1990

Grendstad, G. / P. Selle: Cultural Theory, Postmaterialism and Environmental Attitudes. In: *Ellis, R.E. / M. Thompson* (eds.), (1997) op.cit 151-168

Gross, J.L. / S. Rayner: Measuring Culture: A Paradigm for the Analysis of Social Organisation. New York: Columbia University Press 1985

Gyawali, D.: Patna, Delhi and Environmental Activism: Institutional Forces Behind Water Conflict in Bihar. In: Water Nepal 6,1 (1998), 67-115

Hendriks,F. / S. Zouridis: Cultural Biases and New Media for the Public Domain: Cui Bono? In: *Thompson, M./ G. Grendstad/ P. Selle* (eds.), (1999) op.cit.

Jensen, L.: Images of Democracy in Danish Social Housing. In: *Thompson, M. / G. Grendstad / P. Selle* (eds.), (1999) op.cit.

Keohaner, R. / E. Ostrom (eds.): Local Commons and Global Interdependence: Heterogeneity and Co-operation in Two Domains. London: Sage 1995

Lindblom, C.E.: Politics and Markets: The World's Political-Economic Systems. New York: Basic Books 1977

Linnerooth-Bayer, J. / K.B. Fitzgerald: Conflicting Views on Fair Siting Processes. In: Risk, Health, Safety and Environment 7,2 (1996), 119-134

Maine, H.S.: Ancient Law, London: John Murray 1861

Mamadouh, V.: National Political Cultures in the European Union. In: *Thompson, M. / G. Grendstad / P. Selle* (eds.), (1999) op.cit.
Marris, C. / I. Langford/ T. O'Riordan: Integrating Sociological and Psychological Approaches to Public Perceptions of Environmental Risks: Detailed Results from a Questionnaire Survey. CSERGE Working Paper CEC 96-07, University of East Anglia, UK 1996
Ney, S. / M. Thompson: Consulting the Frogs: The Normative Implications of Cultural Theory. In: *Thompson, M. / G. Grendstad / P. Selle* (eds.), (1999) op.cit.
Ostrom, E.: Governing the Commons: The Evolution of Institutions for Collective Action. Cambridge: Cambridge University Press 1990
Schwarz, M. / M. Thompson: Divided We Stand: Re-defining Politics, Technology and Social Choice. Philadelphia: University of Pennsylvania Press 1990
Snidal, D.: Relative Gains and the Pattern of International Co-operation. American Political Science Review 85 (1991), 701-726
Thompson, M.: Cultural Theory and Integrated Assessment. Environmental Modelling and Assessment 2 (1997), 139-150
Thompson, M. / R.E. Ellis / A.Wildavsky: Cultural Theory, Boulder, Colo.: West View 1990
Thompson, M. / R.E. Ellis / A. Wildavsky: Political Cultures. In Hawkesworth, M./M. Kogan (eds.): Encyclopedia of Government and Politics, London: Routledge. Vol.1 (1992): 507-520
Thompson, M. / G. Grenstad, G. / P. Selle (eds.): Cultural Theory as Political Science, London: Routledge 1999
Thompson, M. / S. Rayner: Cultural Discourses. In: Rayner, S. / E.L. Malone (eds.) Human Choice and Climate Change (in 4 vols), Columbus, Ohio, Battelle Press. Vol.1 (1998) 265-344
Thompson, M. / A. Wildavsky: A Cultural Theory of Information Bias in Organisations. Journal of Management Studies. 23,3 (1986), 273-286
Tönnies, F.: Gemeinschaft and Gesellschaft. Darmstadt: Wissenschaftlich 1887 [Translated by C.P. Loomis as *Community and Society*. East Lansing: Michigan State University Press 1957]
Van de Donk, W.B.H.J. / P.W. Tops: Orwell or Athens? Informatization and the Future of Democracy. A Review of the Literature. In: *Van de Donk, W.B.H.J. et.al.* (eds.): Orwell in Athens: A Perspective on Informatization and Democracy. Amsterdam: IOS Press 1995
Van Gunsteren, H.R.: Het Leervermogen van de Overheidi. In: *Bovens, M.A.P. / W. Witteveen* (eds.): Het Schip Van Staat. Zwolle: Tjaenk Willink
Verweij, M.: Whose Behaviour is Affected By International Anarchy? In: *Thompson, M. / G. Grendstad / P. Selle* (eds.), (1999) op.cit.
Wildavsky, A.: Democracy as a Coalition of Cultures. Society 31,1 (1993), 80-83
Williamson, O.: Markets and Hierarchies: Analysis and Anti-Trust Implications. New York: Free Press 1975

Kenneth Keniston

Cultural Diversity or Global Monoculture

The Information Age in India*

The coming of the "Information Age" is the topic of thousands of books, articles, and conferences. Predictions range from outrageous optimism to dire pessimism; we have analyses from a Marxist, a neo-liberal, an anthropological, and many other perspectives; we have advocates and critics; we have more words on the subject than any human being could possibly absorb.

But what we do not have, at least not in sufficient quantity or depth, are analyses of the cultural implications of the new information technologies. By "cultural implications" I mean their relationship to the basic presuppositions, fundamental myths, unstated assumptions, linguistic taken-for-granteds, historic grounds and creation myths that unite a society: all of those conceptual, linguistic, imaginative, literary, musical, artistic, and intellectual threads that bind people together to make them feel "of one kind." "Culture" in this anthropological sense, then, is a core part of our identities as human beings, connected to our mother tongues, to our families as children, to our root assumptions about life and the world, to our links to our ancestors, and to the fundamental texts, written or unwritten, of our social world. It is the glue that binds us together with those whom we recognize as being "people like us." It is what makes a set of individuals a people and not simply a gathering of strangers. In centuries ahead, when the history of these early years of the Information Age is written, I believe that its relation to culture will be among the features most discussed.

---

* Originally given as the opening Talk of the Technical Conference of "IT.COM" in Bangalore, Karnataka, India, in November, 1998.

Yet if we search through books, conference proceedings, and meetings about the Information Age, we find precious little on the subject. The technological challenges of rapidly developing information technology are so fascinating, so intellectually demanding that they alone are worth lifetimes of individual effort, to say nothing of countless international meetings. The economic implications of a world of global networks, of instantaneous communication, of electronic commerce, of households "wired" at a rate that doubles every year, of international monetary markets and economies linked electronically – these implications, too, are worthy of and receive intensive study. And not least important are the legal problems of reconciling the standards for the Information Age of more than one hundred countries, of determining what is right, proper, secret, public, pornographic, militarily dangerous, privately owned, obscene, subversive and so on. These problems (what is sometimes called the "new electronic world order") increasingly attract some of the best legal minds in the world. Were the German authorities right to arrest the German head of Compuserve for permitting the electronic entry of allegedly illegal materials from abroad via Compuserve? Is the U.S. justified in trying to prevent the electronic export of encryption devices? How can we develop international rules to deal with transborder confidentiality, pornography, the drug trade, national security, subversion, terrorism, censorship, and property rights in an era of electronic communication? These cross-national legal problems merit and receive attention.

But "culture" is rarely mentioned. I serve on the German-American committee of the American National Academy of Science and the German Max Planck Institute whose agenda is "Global Networks and Local Values." Apart from myself, the German and the American members of the group are extremely competent technically. Some are international lawyers; others are economists and economic historians. Still others are the men and women who can anticipate (indeed are designing) the technologies of the future. Our discussions of the technological, economic, and legal problems of the Information Age are enormously informative.

But there is a "cultural" issue in this committee which is only rarely discussed. Specifically, it is the issue of feared American cultural hegemony even vis-à-vis so similar, so technological, so advanced a partner as Germany. It is related to the commanding technological and economic position of the American hardware industry; it is connected with the dominance of American software even when translated into German. It is related to the fact that, according to one estimate, more than 90% of all Web sites in the world are in English. And it is connected to the broader worry that what is often called "American culture" sometimes seems (even to Europeans who by Third World standards are very much like Americans) to be an invasive, alien, or even subversive force that weakens, undermines or marginalizes traditional cultures – even of "Western" nations like Germany, France, Italy, or Spain. One question in the German-American group, then, is How does one preserve cultural diversity (i.e., "local values") in an era of "global networks" in which the English language and "American culture" play so dominant a role?

This is the issue I wish to address, focussing on neither Germany nor the United States, but India. India is probably the best place in the world to examine such issues. For since

Partition, not only has India been the world's largest democratic state, but the most linguistically and culturally diverse. It has preserved its unity as a federal nation, while at the same time encouraging the distinctiveness of the separate Indian states. Moreover, as a developing country India has two unusual characteristics. First, it has the world's second largest pool of scientific manpower, reflected in the dynamic information technology industry centered in Bangalore and Bombay. Second, it is a nation where the English language plays the special role as the link language of the nation, to the point that some fear the vulnerability of India's traditional languages and cultures to an Anglophonic tide. This threat is defined in several ways: the role of the English as the language of power and wealth in India; or of satellite TV that brings the antics of American millionaires in Hindi to thousands of Indian rural villages, or the hegemony of English-language, American-based information technology.

Four Cultural Orientations

Let me now try to outline a framework that may prove helpful for this discussion. As an oversimplification, imagine a spectrum on which we place four outlooks of the cultures of the modern world.

1. Cultural Imperialism

At one extreme is what we may call "cultural imperialism." This is the policy, extant in some nations today, of insisting legally on a single culture and prohibiting all other cultures, including all languages that are not the language of the dominant group. There are, as you know, nations where to speak or write publicly in a language deemed subversive may mean years of imprisonment. More commonly, linguistic imperialism entails making it simply impossible to do business, to be educated, or to conduct any but the most intimate aspects of family life in any language other than the mandated and "official" language.

One author has claimed that the teaching of English as a second language after the World War II in developing countries had many features of linguistic imperialism. Others might argue that in India, the role of the English language as the link language of the Nation, the language of the higher courts, the Lok Sabha, the higher civil service, of nationally based as well as international business, and of higher education – that this role amounts to a de facto linguistic and by extension cultural imperialism because it effectively excludes from power, wealth and influence the great majority of those Indians – perhaps 95% – who do not speak fluent English. The point is surely debatable, for against the role of English as the link language of India, we need to set the opposite linguistic policies of the Indian states, with their requirements that state business be conducted in the vernacular language, and also the extraordinary linguistic pluralism of India's great cities.

2. Global Monoculture

Farther along the spectrum lies a second orientation, which we may call "global monoculture." By global monoculture I mean the de facto dominance of a single culture across all the important sectors of the world.

Coercion is absent; many languages are tolerated; multiculturalism is officially extolled. But the power of the dominant global culture is such that it tends to overwhelm, or reduce to a status of inferiority, all local cultures. Such was the case with Roman-Latin culture during the apogee of the Roman Empire; such was the status of Moslem culture and the Arabic language during the greatest epoch of Islam. And such, some claim, is the power of today's global monoculture, embodied in satellite TV, World Cup games, CNN, the Three Tenors at the Baths of Caracalla, Hollywood, Murdoch, Bollywood, Microsoft, Intel - a culture where 90+% of all Web sites are in English, and a world where, in contemporary India, unless one speaks, reads, and writes good English it is virtually impossible to use a computer much less send email.

The political scientist Barber terms this world "MacWorld," combining MacDonald's and Macintosh into a single epithet. Barber notes that even in France, with its proud cultural nationalism and its brilliant tradition of film-making, 90 to 100% of the most popular films each year are American. We could add today the role of CNN, the popularity of American dramas translated into languages like Hindi or Swahili or Spanish, or even Indian MTV, hosted by a laid-back young Indian who speaks English with an American accent. The singers and the languages of the songs, to be sure, are Indian; but the concept is not in origin Indian.

How should we evaluate this global monoculture? The Japanese scholar, Toru Nishigaki, argues that despite its appearance of multiculturalism, today's global culture is in the last analysis an American monoculture, founded on the enormous appeal of Hollywood films and American TV, on the dominance of the American entertainment industry and on the technological, economical, and military power of the United States. Nishigaki argues that we are witness to the spreading, subtly or directly, of "American" values of "free enterprise," materialism, consumerism, political liberalism, and so on. For Nishigaki, this American plague threatens to infect or relegate to insignificance all other cultures.

An alternative view has been stated by Samuel Huntington in a recent and controversial work. He claims that far from being unified into one "Western" or "American" monoculture, the world is increasingly polarized around multiple regional cultural-religious centers - a Confucian world in East Asia, an Islamic world in the Middle East and North Africa, a Latin American world in South America, et cetera. Huntington's work is understandably popular with leaders of nations like Singapore, Malaysia, and the People's Republic of China, who claim that there exist something called "Asian values" (distinct from so called "Western values"). "Asian values" allegedly stress patriarchal family deference, community loyalty, a disciplined and obedient citizenry, and an authoritarian state. According to this view, "Western" values like human rights, human dignity, freedom of the press, religion, and speech are alien impositions that have no rightful place in an "Asian" context.

As is often true, the experience of India puts such views to the test. How can it be, if an obedient citizenry and an authoritarian state are "Asian" values, that Indians are so firmly attached to political democracy, that Indians are almost as undisciplined as Americans, and that Indians have shown so dedicated a commitment to freedom of speech, multicultural tolerance, and freedom of religion? The experience of India on the one hand affirms the importance of different cultural patterns; but on the other hand it raises doubts that all values can be neatly classified as American values, Indian values, Asian values, or what have you. Indeed I myself believe that such values as the dignity of human life, the right to a decent living, the right to choose one's rulers, to education, to literacy, to freedom of speech, the press and religion - that these values are not American, Islamic, Asian, or Indian, but simply human.

Many, including myself, agree with Nishigaki that there is a danger of a global, covertly American monoculture that relegates all other cultures to inferiority, antiquity, or second place. And it is easy, and not entirely inaccurate, to caricature this global monoculture, especially as seen in television and the World Wide Web. It is a world of individuals with platinum Visa cards checking into five star hotels, of glittering luxury sports cars whose dashboards sparkle with subtle green gauges, of viscous shampoos that promise fragrance, body and romance, of soaps that turn grime to pristine whiteness, of politicians who promise whatever they think will enable them to win. It is a world of freely downloadable pornography, of search engines encumbered with advertisements, of information so vast in quantity as to overwhelm the most brilliant and devoted computer user.

It goes without saying that this world is offensive, even obscene, when 300 million Indians and a billion other humans go to bed each night hungry. Indeed, so shallow is this monoculture that we are within our rights to ask whether it is truly a culture at all or, as one colleague has proposed, "only an interface."

But we also need to ask whether the average person, rich or poor, really takes these tele-worlds and cyber-worlds very seriously. More plausible is the claim that these worlds occupy the same place in the minds as ancient mythologies and foundation myths, popular fictions and rituals. Indeed, I suspect that the Indian villager who watches "Dallas" does so with the same mix of amusement, interest and distance with which he previously viewed the televising of the great Indian epics. Neither are models to be emulated in his ordinary life, but legends, cautionary tales, entertainment.

In any event, there is another side to how we evaluate the "globalization" of culture, and once again, India proves a test case. In the last half century it has been convenient for Indians to use English as a link language for the diverse peoples of this subcontinent. Indeed, in the absence of some language that in a sense has "belonged" to no one state or people in India, it is hard to see how the business of this diverse Nation could have been conducted. Moreover, the linkages of India with the rest of the world would have been more difficult if this subcontinent did not possess the second largest English speaking population in the world. There are obvious advantages to sharing a common culture and language, even as a second culture and language, with the rest of the world. Without that second language, Bangalore could not have happened.

A personal anecdote may be relevant. Through a mutual friend, I read the scholarly work – in English – of a Pakistani author. His book was so outstanding that I found his email address and thanked him for his work. Not knowing Urdu, I naturally wrote in English. (In any event, email in Urdu is difficult if not impossible.) He replied in the fluent English for which educated South Asians are famous. An email friendship resulted: We now exchange writings, views, and even fragments of our autobiographies; I truly feel that I today have a new friend in Pakistan.

All of this presupposes a "global monoculture" in which we both participate, based on email and the English language. My Pakistani friend remains in Pakistan because it is his homeland and he wants his children to be reared there. Is he the less a Pakistani because his English is fluent and we communicate in that language? Do Indians cease to be Hindus, Jains, Muslims, Parsis, or Christians because they speak good English? Does the desire for an electric fan, a refrigerator, a television set, decent medical care, a motor scooter, a car, shampoo, or a computer constitute capitulation to the consumerism of "global monoculture?"

India again provides a test case. To a foreign observer like myself, it seems that Indians live more peacefully, more comfortably, with multiple cultural identities than any other people on earth. Long before contemporary "global monoculture" was imagined, Indians lived easily with multiple cultural frameworks, shifting languages, and even plural personal identities. The Indian experience suggests that it is possible to take part in a global culture which has, as Nishigaki indicates, many "American" or "Western" aspects, yet at the same time to retain one's identity and rootedness in one's own particular culture.

3. Cultural Diversity

The next point on the spectrum is also well defined by contemporary India. I will call it "cultural diversity." This is a society – or a world – that contains and supports many distinct cultures, each with its own particular strengths and weaknesses, its own language and educational system, and its own capacity to instill in its members a sense of identity based on rootedness in their culture.

Such a world is not one in which people are necessarily monocultural or monolingual. It is possible to be rooted in one's culture and yet to collaborate with, to understand, to participate in, other cultures as well. India is again the world's best example of the possibility of multilingualism, which is a proxy for multiculturalism. In no other country of the world do people live so easily as in the major Indian cities with multiple linguistic and cultural groups. In no other country can people shift so easily from one to another cultural frame of reference, including that of their childhood and their mother tongue. India can provide a model for what the rest of the world could be like, a point to which I will return.

4. Exclusionary Cultural Nationalism

Finally, at the far end of the extreme of this cultural spectrum, we have what Barber calls "Jihad" and what I will term "exclusionary cultural nationalism." By this I refer to the emergence of regimes, groups, or parties - in a few countries the ruling parties - which make the purity of their culture, their religion, their ethnicity, their tradition, and/or their language the central theme of their ideology and their politics. Cultural pride, in itself a benign and probably necessary base for community and identity, is here perverted into an intolerant and even violent exclusion of all that is not orthodox. In Western Europe and America we have examples of this in the Medieval Inquisition, in American anti-Communist "witch hunts," or in Soviet efforts to extirpate "revisionists" and "agents of imperialism." Such tendencies exist, needless to say, in many other countries.

The characteristics of exclusionary cultural nationalism are well known. First is the creation of an imaginary past in which the culture was unsullied, in which foreign and modern influences did not exist, when cultural power extended over vast regions, and where the cultural, social, and political rules of society were uniformly obeyed. Compared to that Golden Age, the present suffers, and the cultural goal is to return to that imagined past. The chief enemies are therefore aliens, foreigners, subversives, cosmopolitans, infiltrators, fifth columnists, disloyal citizens. Their crimes are to introduce subversion, to challenge the hegemony of the culture, to produce pornography, to defile women, to violate sacred places and customs, to seduce children, to consort with foreigners and adopt foreign habits, foreign dress, foreign ideas. Purity is the goal, and the pursuit of that holy goal may even justify holy wars or movements of exclusion and even extermination - what Barber calls Jihad.

Where does exclusionary cultural nationalism come from? In part, from the sense that one's culture is threatened, undermined, disvalued, and depreciated; in part from the belief or fact that the members of one's culture are disabled, blocked, disenfranchised, or disempowered. All these feelings have much to do with the emergence of intolerant cultural fundamentalism. This is understandable: to support our core sense of our own value and identities, we need to know that our identities rest on a valued culture. When that culture is disvalued or deprecated, it is not surprising that people turn ugly, intolerant, vicious, even murderous and genocidal. To explain is of course not to justify. But it is to warn that if cultural diversity is undermined by global monoculture, then a kind of ugly exclusionist cultural nationalism can result.

Strengthening Cultural Diversity in India

What does this excursion into the realms of a kind of cultural theory have to do with information technology? With "global networks and local values"?

An answer is that along with its economic, technological, and other features, the impact of Information Age is linked to the cultural spectrum I have tried to define. Let me mention a few of the linkages, and conclude with an exhortation.

First is the extraordinary role of the English language amongst Indian elites and the inaccessibility of the Information Age to the average Indian who does not speak good English because of the absence of local language software.

India, as seen by an outside observer, faces very critical choices with regard to software. There are probably more inventive, creative, and energetic software engineers and designers in India than in any other country except possibly my own. But most major Indian software firms, for excellent reasons, have chosen to focus on the export market rather than the domestic market. And the major American software firms (with the exception of IBM's DOS localization to Hindi) have not produced, and as far as I know have no plans to produce, full localization to any of the Indian languages - not even to Hindi, with as many speakers as live in the entire European Union. The Indian Internet situation is even more confusing, with many creative proposals, but few following the standard of ISCII, and most incompatible the one with the other. ISCII itself has been challenged, and efforts to modify it so as to adapt it to contemporary computing needs and to the languages of the Southern States have not yet borne fruit. The Centre for Development of Advanced Computers (CDAC) and the National Centre for Software Technology (NCST) the two principal Government of India agencies pursue different approaches to localization; and there are also at least a dozen more. The result for Internet in Indian languages is, at present, an emerging tower of cyberbabel. There is an urgent need, recognized by many at a September CDAC Conference in Pune, Maharashtra, for Indians to come together to standardize codes for the most important of India's 14, 16, or 18 official languages.

The alternative to localization is clear: lacking local language software, computers in India in the Information Age will be merely one more aspect of a move toward global monoculture. Only English-speaking Indians, already the most powerful and wealthy group in India, will have access to the power-increasing Information Age. The gap between the empowered and the powerless will grow, and so will the devaluing of local languages and cultures. For this to happen is to risk the transformation of India's benign and generous cultural diversity into uglier forms of intolerant cultural nationalism, forms that are visible in my own country, in Europe, indeed in every country of the world. Localization (and its prerequisite standardization) is therefore critical if the Information Age is to reach and benefit broad sectors of the Indian population - what my friend Venkatesh Hariharan terms "the forgotten 95% of Indian computing."

Another conclusion emerges from conversations with major American software producers and with officers of some of India's cutting edge firms. In America, for complex reasons, the Indian "market" is not currently seen as sufficiently large as to justify the expenses of full localization of, let us say, Windows NT to languages like Hindi, Bengali, Kannada, Telegu, or Tamil. I believe this belief is incorrect; but it means that what we are likely to see in the near term (and indeed already see) is the lesser step of "locale coding," which still presupposes a knowledge of English in order to run the computer (although it permits using the Qwerty keyboard to enter, for example, Devanagari script). In India, the most dynamic firms have concentrated on the export market, and their long-term strategic plans usually involve shifting toward packaged software rather than focusing on the potentials of the domestic market.

These economic decisions mean that the most creative approaches to localization are not likely to be taken by major firms in the U.S. or India, but rather by small, "back-street" operators in India - smart people with a dozen or so collaborators who are already producing innovative email programs, localizations, et cetera. The problem is, of course, that they are small, that they lack venture capital, and that the solutions each proposes is incompatible with the solution of his neighbor. But the inventiveness is there, and I suspect that it is from these "back alley" operators that eventually localization will come. For example, from one such firm I have already begun to receive email in Gujerarti, Marathi, and Hindi (none of which I can read, unfortunately), and indeed even the embedded code and keyboard layout which would permit me, were I fluent in these Indian languages, to reply in one of them.

Finally, a word about the relationship of economics, market forces and the role of public authorities. My friend Harsh Kumar, best known as the inventor of the localization code known as Bharat Bhasha, sees a vast potential market for vernacular software in, for example, the small and medium sized merchants who work in Gujerati or Marathi in Bombay, who have the financial means to buy a computer but not the English to use English-based small business packages. Kumar rightly points out that in software, potential demand does not necessarily generate supply in the short run. If there is no software in Gujerati, there can obviously be no demand. Kumar tells the story of the two shoe salesmen who visit a rural Indian village of a thousand inhabitants. The first salesman returns to his company headquarters deeply depressed. "It is hopeless," he says, "there is not a single person in the whole village who wears shoes." The second returns to his company headquarters excited and jubilant: "What a marvelous opportunity," he says, "we can sell a thousand pairs of shoes!"

Kumar is doubtless right that if the vernacular software existed there would be many who would buy it. But my own prediction is that the driving force behind the creation of standards and localization will be public authorities, and in particular the Indian states. Many outside India are familiar with the ambitious plans of Chief Minister Naidu, and the ongoing work to computerize all land records in the State of Andhra Pradesh. But if this work is to be useful to the average Andhra Pradesh peasant, then it must be in Telegu rather than, or in addition to, English. Or, to take another example, the Government of the State of Maharashtra has plans to link via email all of the district offices in that state. I recently had the privilege of speaking with one of the officials in charge of this plan, and asked what language would be used. "Marathi, of course," he said. I asked if they had Marathi email software up and going to permit communication between all of the many dozens, indeed hundreds, of district offices. "CDAC will provide it," he said. But at CDAC it emerged that this software is not yet fully functional.

My point has to do not with the work that remains to be done, but with the fact that only the state governments, and at the centre, only the Government of India, have the authority, the capacity, and the economic power to produce that standardization which is essential for the production of software in the rich and ancient languages of India. The technical problems of vernacular software in South Asia are, I am told, no more complicated, perhaps less so, than those of localizing to French, German, or Spanish – to say nothing of a language like Japanese, which is a localizer's nightmare. Indian languages are phonetic; the Northern languages have a common root in Sanskrit; the study of the grammar and structure of Indian languages from Panini onwards is very advanced; and localization, although it is always costly and time-consuming, presents no special technical challenges. Thus I think that the push underway from states like Karnataka, Andhra Pradesh, and Maharashtra is the force most likely to produce usable vernacular software and thus to make the Information Age accessible to the peoples of India.

My colleague at MIT, Michael Dertouzos, the Director of the Laboratory for Computer Science, has written a book entitled "What Will Be." Dertouzos is a technophile; he believes that the Information Age will empower people; he and his group have been at the cutting edge of technological innovation for the last 30 years, and remain so with, for example, the location of the Web Consortium at MIT. But Dertouzos makes the critical point that whatever the benefits of the Information Age - and he believes there are many - the Information Age will not solve the traditional problems of humankind. The gap between the poor and the rich, political oppression and injustice, hunger and disease, cultural intolerance and genocide - none of these have a necessary connection to the Information Age. Indeed, these problems may grow in importance in the Information Age, he suggests.

To be sure, every new technology awakens utopian hopes. It was said that the telegraph and telephone, by encouraging communication, would prevent all future international misunderstandings. It was written that the automobile would eliminate the chief problem of the cities by eliminating horse manure (as indeed it did, but at some cost). Many claimed that electricity would eliminate factories and permit the decentralization of production to agreeable rural sites. The nuclear age would bring "electricity too cheap to meter." And now, the Information Age will produce a time when, as another of my MIT colleagues puts it, we will all be better for "being digital."

Dertouzos' warning is well taken with regard to culture. Technologies do not have necessary social or cultural effects. How they are deployed, how they are used, how they are shaped and perceived depends upon human, social, cultural political will and decision. In our current euphoria about economic liberalization and the market, we cannot rely exclusively on blind market forces. We also need the active intervention of corporate and business leaders who possess vision and commitment to the well-being and the vitality of their cultures, and of political leaders who know how, and are willing, to moderate the forces of the market so as to achieve goals of which the Information Age knows nothing - the elimination of poverty, the universalization of education, political freedom and democracy, and the preservation and deepening of cultural diversity.

Miles Kahler

Information Networks and Global Politics

An outline of the changes in information technology that have altered economic and social landscapes in the 1990s is not subject to much dispute. Rapidly increasing desktop computing power and high-speed communications networks have converged to produce integrated systems that transmit information at radically reduced cost, what Peter Cowhey has labeled the distributed information revolution. (Cowhey 1995, Estabrooks 1995). A technological revolution of this kind inevitably spurs a search for its broader implications. For many observers, these technological changes represent a shift toward less hierarchical and more global forms of organization, systems "that are inherently transboundary where traditional ones were nationally or regionally oriented, differentiated horizontally across strong networks rather than vertically between weak ones, and organized around communications rather than hierarchies." (Rochlin 1997, 72). Such a transformation, if it takes place, would have profound effects on international politics.

These technological changes also occurred as the Cold War ended, the century's third wave of democratization swept the globe, and economies opened to international economic exchange in unprecedented numbers. In order to evaluate the independent effect of transformations in information and telecommunications technology and their consequences for global politics, four alternative futures are examined that range from modest change to radical transformation. In the first, nation-states and their governments remain the uncontested dominant actors in world politics. The effects of the new technologies are reflected in the *capabilities* of nation-states and the new *vulnerabilities* that threaten those states at the hands of other actors. A second scenario can be labeled economic globalization: new and binding *constraints* are placed on national governments by technologically driven market integration. A third and more fundamental alteration of world politics would result if technological change produces a new transnational politics, creating for the first time a global civil society that extends beyond any single national polity. Finally, *identities* may be transformed through the expansion of information networks, as barriers fall to the creation of new communities or the rediscovery of old. The effects of technological change on the transformation of the existing international system increase in this array from a modest reinforcement of the existing hierarchy of existing states to an undermining of an international system based on territorial nation-states.

Unfortunately, when one scratches beneath the polemical debris that covers these subjects, one discovers important impediments to an investigation of the effects of networked information technologies at the global level. Neither the adoption of the new information technologies nor many associated economic and political trends are genuinely global. Although figures on Internet penetration are difficult to evaluate, it is clear that Internet connections, although rapidly expanding, are heavily concentrated in North America and northern Europe. A recent study of corporations in a sample of largely middle-income developing countries found more than one-third of the firms responding connected or planning to connect to the Internet, but few individuals within each firm had access to the Internet.[1] In similar fashion, using a narrow definition of globalization – as economic integration – the only clearly "globalized" portion of the world economy are markets for short-term financial assets in the industrialized economies. Other financial markets may be interconnected, and national markets for goods have opened, but national segmentation remains important. Using a broader definition of globalization, as complex interdependence, the industrialized democracies also remain unique. These spatial limitations mean that conclusions can be applied to the rest of the world only under restrictive assumptions: that the spread of information technology and the processes of economic integration will transfer to those regions over time with the same consequences observed in the more integrated regions.

If neither technological change nor global consequences are in fact global, neither are they completely novel. Historical comparisons complicate an evaluation of the effects of new technological developments. Although revolutionary rhetoric has been applied to the growing importance of the Internet and advances in computing and telecommunications, global phenomena that are traced to these technologies can be found in earlier eras with very different technological endowments. Global economic integration before 1914 was on some measures more complete than it is at the close of the twentieth century, and nineteenth-century transnational political networks preceded

---

1 These firms, clients of the International Finance Corporation, could also be regarded as elite companies in their national economies. The barriers to wider use of the Internet appeared to be founded in national telecommunications infrastructure. (Daly and Miller 1998)

the current efflorescence of non-governmental organizations. Conversely, innovation in communications technology has not always been associated with growing economic integration. The decades from 1920 to 1950 witnessed a peculiar convergence of new technologies, particularly broadcast and telecommunications, that were adopted by governments exerting control over their economies and populations. Such historical comparison permits a clearer assessment of the effects of current technologies (or certain dimensions of those technologies) on the features of global politics described above. Rather than crude associations between technology and these changes, a more nuanced set of causal relations can be outlined.

Too often the rhetoric of both globalization and cyberspace has disguised beliefs about technology similar to those driving the current boom (or bubble) in Internet stocks: a strong but vague sense of its importance, but no clarity about the scale of its effects or how to measure them. Separating the effects of technology from other explanations has been even less successful. In too many cases, if the technological footprint is present, its prominent role in the outcome is assumed.

In the following evaluation of the role of this networked wave of information technologies on world politics, assumptions of worldwide effects and historically unprecedented transformations will be avoided. Several other widespread and unacknowledged assumptions will be subjected to particular scrutiny. One is the assumption of normative affinity: social and political consequences will resemble the technologies in question. Technologies that are decentralized and horizontal in their application (as opposed to centralized and hierarchical) and easily extended beyond borders will, on this assumption, favor organizations of similar character. Since the nation-state is hierarchical and territorially delimited, technological innovations are believed to undermine the authority of the nation-state. Linked to this assumption is a more instrumental one: that these technologies are more readily deployed by organizations and institutions of a particular sort (for example, non-governmental organizations), and that other organizations (for example, conventionally configured corporations) will have difficulty exploiting them. Finally, technology is often assumed to be the driver of global political change. The possibility that it might create countervailing effects that could limit its ultimate influence is seldom entertained.

Information networks in the hands of governments: capabilities and vulnerabilities

Since the formation of an international system based on territorial states, most technologies have been deployed within those states and their geographically based institutions. The newest wave of technological innovation could also be captured by states and become simply another addition to their capabilities. Much of the debate over the impact of information technology on warfare and military capabilities revolves around technological consequences within a system in which warfare remains the domain of national states. The most conservative view, based on one reading of history, argues that "technological advantages in warfare have generally proved ephemeral," and that new technologies do not sweep away old weapons in a Darwinian fashion; the new is simply added to the old. (Henry and Peartree 1998, 123). This limited view of technological impact suggests that existing military organizations and the states that support them will simply incorporate information technologies into existing organizations and strategies.

The revolution in military affairs (RMA) endorses deeper consequences from successful adoption of information technologies throughout military organizations in the form of enhanced real-time intelligence capabilities (ISR); the addition of information processing to older conceptions of command, control and communications; and advances in the use of force with greater speed and precision, as witnessed in the Gulf War and later military strikes against Iraq (Nye and Owens 1996). In this view, successful adoption of the new technologies requires more radical (and possibly painful) transformation of military organizations, calling into question conventional hierarchies and at the same time permitting military commanders to "micro-command," reinforcing centralized, hierarchical control in battlefield situations (Cohen 1996).

If this intensive level of technological penetration is accepted, debate surrounds the independent influence of technology on capabilities. Some view the relatively low cost of the new technologies as a sign that the international military hierarchy could be radically revised in the face of a "David effect" that favors the (conventionally) weak. (Rothkopf 1998) The weak could rise rapidly to become the new great powers if they possess the economic resources to obtain modern weapons in which the new technology is embedded. Others remain skeptical of a systematic effect in favor of those catching up, arguing that technology cannot be obtained "off the shelf," and that its effectiveness in building military capabilities are dependent on other national characteristics, such as a technologically sophisticated, industrialized economy and high human skill levels. (Nye and Keohane 1998, 87) Past RMAs did not witness radical reversals of national fortune unless the challengers had successfully industrialized, the historical equivalent of constructing a knowledge-intensive economy.

Information technologies could also produce new forms of warfare that will not be waged solely by states, warfare that centers on vulnerabilities created by deeper integration of information technologies into national societies. If these portraits of cyberwar or information warfare are correct, technology may create a different international order. Such capabilties are usually portrayed as threatening the most extreme leveling, in which individuals or groups, armed with readily available hardware and skills, could seriously weaken the most technologically sophisticated societies. The key to this vulnerability is the rapidly falling cost of most information technology: information warfare can be waged on the cheap. Information warfare, even more than preceding variants of warfare in this century, could also target civilian populations and their livelihoods, the entire economic infrastructure of advanced industrial societies. In this vision of the future of warfare, international conflict is no longer waged between coherent national states wielding conventional, if transformed, military instruments. Instead, the boundaries of states have been compromised by information networks, and the traditional hierarchy of force between great powers and others in the system has been undermined by the widespread availability of the new technologies.

From simple incorporation of information processing capabilities in existing weapons systems, the role of information technology, even in this well defined realm of global politics, expands to threaten the conventional view of military competition among states. At each level of information warfare, the independent effect of technology is the subject of controversy: more skilled soldiers versus cheap, off-the-shelf technology; advanced economies reinforcing their existing military edge with soft power versus rogue states or terrorists who easily penetrate information-dependent societies. In one sense, this debate is an old one between the dominance of offense or defense. From another, more radical perspective, information technology extends the twentieth century trend of total warfare, to the point of transforming the nature of warfare itself.

Networks as constraint: governments and economic globalization

Even expansive views of the future of information warfare include a central role for national states, however vulnerable they may become. In the domain of global economic integration, spurred by technological change, the autonomy of states is often portrayed as far more compromised. Although reductions in transportation and communication costs have driven the process of economic integration since the mid-nineteenth century, technological innovations that have driven down the costs of computation and telecommunications since the 1950s have ever more sharply reduced the cost of cross-border transactions in goods and capital markets and reduced the segmentation of national markets.

These technological changes – with telecommunications and computing in the forefront – have also altered the character of firms and enhanced their ability to organize economic activity across national borders. The costs of coordinating activities within and between firms have diminished dramatically. John Dunning argues that information networks of increasing power have created a knowledge-based alliance capitalism, characterized by a less hierarchical and more open form of organization than more easily spans national frontiers through interfirm cooperative ventures, increased levels of foreign investment, and new forms of intrafirm organization. (Dunning 1997) Information technology industries are themselves among the most globalized, illustrating the trends that they have deepened.[2]

Increases in international economic integration (the operational definition of economic globalization adopted here), like the penetration of the new technologies, are differentiated by sector. Information technology has had its greatest effects on cross-border activity in finance, since financial services firms concentrate on information gathering and processing (Herring and Litan 1995, 13). Even among the industrialized countries, however, the world is far from complete financial integration; developing country participation in private capital markets has been concentrated in the most

2 Foreign affiliates of US computer companies produced 40% more than the parent companies produced in the home market (OECD 1997a, 7). In the large industrialized economies, the share of exports in production is much higher than other industries (OECD 1997b). In 1995, more US firms accounted for more than 80% of world hard disk drive production. However, less than 5% of the drives were assembled in the United States (Gourevitch, Bohn, and McKendrick 1998).

successful industrializers and has been characterized by great volatility. In markets for goods, even in highly integrated regional markets, national borders still matter. In labor markets the world does not approach the relative ease with which labor crossed national borders in the late nineteenth century.[3]

If economic integration and the constraints that it imposes on governments were wholly driven by technology, one would expect a pattern of steady increase, broken by sharper upturns as the result of technological innovation. The decades from 1920 to 1950, however, were marked by a decline in international economic integration, despite continuing technical innovation that reduced communication and transportation costs. That decline can be attributed in large measure to government policies that discouraged economic integration and reinforced the boundaries between national markets.

Government policy choices are constrained by technological change and globalized economic activity, but they also remain important determinants of the diffusion of technology and the progress of integration. The technological changes that drive integration require supportive government choices in infrastructure development and regulation. Technologies are vested in particular economic interests that will typically use the political process to create advantage. The political battles surrounding telecommunications policy in the United States and elsewhere demonstrate that the deployment of technology is shaped by political conflict.[4] Assigning an appropriate causal weight to the policy-driven and technological causes of economic integration is difficult. Ralph Bryant attempted to do so in the case of financial integration, but he concluded simply that "the interaction between non-policy innovations and changes in government policies was itself an important part of the history. Each set of evolutionary changes reinforced the effects of the other" (Bryant 1987, 69).

The costs of government efforts to roll back existing levels of economic integration tend to increase over time, and politically feasible choices may therefore be altered. Governments are far from powerless, but their menu of choices and the benefits and costs assigned to those choices are often sharply altered by technological development and economic integration. For example, financial liberalization and the rapid growth in global financial flows has made it difficult if not impossible for governments to maintain a pegged exchange rate and an autonomous monetary policy. Powerful arguments have been made that, for most economies, the choices available have become either monetary union (as in the European EMU) or freely floating exchange rates. Another alternative is capital controls, recently imposed by Malaysia in the wake of the Asian economic crisis. The debate over capital controls underlines the degrees of freedom that remain to governments. Whether Malaysia will pay future costs in access to capital markets remains to be seen. For many, however, the most telling argument against such controls is their erosion over time in the face of an integrated global financial environment and access to technologies that permit evasion.

---

3 For an account of the level of economic integration pre-1914, see IMF 1997, 112-116.

4 On this point, see Neumann, McKnight and Solomon 1997, 155-246.

If government policies are constrained by economic opening, it is likely that they will attempt to achieve economic results through different means. In sharp contrast to the pre-1914 era, electorates expect governments to produce positive results through active economic management. (Even in authoritarian states, such popular expectations have grown over time.) Interests that are damaged by economic openness and technological advance will lobby governments to arrest those changes. This tension between governments both constrained and impelled to intervene on the one hand and economic agents pursuing cross-border trade and investment on the other sets up two sources of conflict surrounding the advance of technologies that further economic integration.

The first is compatibility of diverse national systems of regulation and governance in a world of increasing cross-border flows. Friction between national policy regimes takes two, mirror-image forms. Governments, pressed by their international traders and investors, complain that national policies in other countries do not permit free and fair market access. As barriers to international exchange at the border become increasingly ineffective or undesirable, governments will satisfy domestic demands for protection by policies behind the border that at first glance appear "domestic." Increasingly, international scrutiny falls on these policies, which were preserved from international surveillance in earlier decades. These policies include government decisions over information and telecommunications regulation and infrastructure that have important consequences for private agents inside and outside national markets.

At the same time, governments are petitioned to defend national regulatory regimes by an array of interests protected by those regimes, whether they shield the environment, labor practices, corporate governance, or consumer safety. Information and telecommunications technology, by lowering the cost of exit for private economic agents – rendering national boundaries far more porous – is often perceived as the accomplice of policy convergence among integrated economies. Governments, anticipating the preferences of private agents – whether firms or highly skilled – tailor their policies to fit those preferences. This simple model of policy convergence or regulatory "races to the bottom" is undermined by evidence that private agents do not respond rapidly or in uniform fashion to national regulatory divergence and by evidence of policy convergence in relatively few policy domains (Garrett 1998, Kahler 1998).

Constraints on national policy, concerns over market access, and fears that economic integration will erode valuable and politically popular regulatory regimes suggest international governance as a solution. What governments cannot accomplish on their own vis-à-vis integrated markets, they may be able to accomplish by coordination with other governments. Friction over the rules of market access and harmonization of regulatory regimes may also be dealt with in the context of international institutions. However, international governance by governments is itself called into question by the ascendancy of integrated markets and fragmented political jurisdictions. Proponents of the Internet and its revolutionary implications have argued for self-regulation or private governance from the bottom up, a vision of spontaneous coordination among a multitude of private actors. This argument in favor of governance without governments is strengthened if the capacities of governments are fatally impaired by the consequences of technological innovation. Although greater ease of exit from national economies is one such consequence, the erosion of economic hierarchy may be equally important. In financial markets and product markets the possibilities for direct connection between the ultimate consumer and producers or suppliers become more feasible. Long-standing monopolistic or oligopolistic clubs of intermediaries and brokers are challenged. Government regulation and oversight has been based on such intermediaries and their market-making functions.

One recent example can serve as a powerful illustration: the spread of electronic trading by individuals in the United States equity markets. With the advent of electronic-communications networks (ECNs), transactions costs for individual investors have declined, creating a burst of growth for low-cost stock trading and possibly a challenge to traditional stock exchanges (Buckman and Lucchetti 1999). Transactions cost reduction from such networks could be offset by a decline in the role of old-style intermediaries that curbed volatility in the markets and a concomitant erosion of the ability of governments to regulate financial markets, which depended on those intermediaries and other points at which financial flows are concentrated and can be monitored (Rochlin 1997, 101).

For some observers, the advent of ECNs in the trading of equities, the popularity of amazon.com, and the emergence of widespread electronic commerce at the level of individual investors and consumers, is further confirmation of the end of geographical jurisdictions as sites for many economic transactions (Kobrin 1998). Others, however, note that information technology has had mixed effects on collective governance by states and the erosion of both boundaries and hierarchies. Helleiner, for example, argues that collective government efforts to target money laundering may have been facilitated by the move from cash to electronic flows, most of which leave a record and must move through central "choke points" or clearing houses. Although the advent of powerful encryption options in private hands could render increasing numbers of transactions invisible to government authorities, the threat of fraud may curb those tendencies and render a government role in financial regulation and supervision more attractive to private actors. (Helleiner 1998)

The debate over the implications of electronic commerce in financial markets and other sectors illuminates both the implications of technological advance for global governance and the limits of its influence. Financial markets are a better test than most of the effects of technology, since both technology and government policy changes began the transformation of those markets well before the advent of the Internet. The latest wave of innovation appears to undermine older hierarchies and boundaries that have circumscribed markets in the past. National governments represent one, but only one, of those hierarchies; the effects on private market intermediaries may be as great. As individuals develop the arbitrage possibilities that only firms had held earlier, governments may find additional policy constraints in domains such as taxation.

To leap from such observations to the broader claims of some proponents of cyberspace and globalization would be premature, however. Governments can deploy the new technologies as well (as the proponents of information warfare suggest), although deployment may be less rapid and diffusion less complete than it has been in the private sector. Governments continue to claim important responsibilities for choosing, maintaining, and expanding infrastructure that supports technical innovation and adoption. With infrastructure responsibilities come choices that favor certain paths over others, or, through malign neglect, slow the progress of economic integration. Although the menu of feasible government policies may be altered by technology and the economic integration that it supports, choices remain. Collective governance of markets can reduce friction between competing national systems and enhance regulatory leverage, even as exit options at the national level expand and the hierarchy within both governments and markets is challenged. The "Internet alternative" – spontaneous self-regulation by a multitude of private actors – may prove to be impossible; a government role may appear more attractive as growing numbers of private actors erode trust, and reputation fails to support essential rules of the road.

Networks and global political process: technological bases of global civil society

Corporations, empowered by new technologies of information processing and communication, are not alone in constructing new strategies for operation across national borders. The deployment of new technologies by networks of nongovernmental organizations and activists has produced claims that the tools for constructing a global civil society are at hand. Personal computers, faxes, and the Internet have been used by these organizations to penetrate national boundaries and undermine local and international hierarchies – the same consequences on the political level that constrained governments in conducting economic policy. Technology became a readily transferable means of leveling the field of political competition: "for the first time in history, the forces of peace and environmental preservation have acquired the communication tools and intelligence-gathering technologies previously the province of the military, government, and transnational corporations" (Frederick 1993, 288).

Although some accounts of transnational relations have dealt exclusively with the political dimensions of transnational actors and their success, recent research on the construction and effectiveness of transnational political networks has emphasized the role of information in the formation of transnational coalitions. In their investigation of transnational advocacy networks, Keck and Sikkink place information at the center: "Information bind network members together and is essential for network effectiveness." (Keck and Sikkink 1998, 18) Although advocacy networks on issues such as slavery and women's rights have existed since the nineteenth century (when an earlier revolution in communications and transportation lowered the costs of coordinating political activity), their numbers have grown substantially in the past three decades. Keck and Sikkink associate that growth in part with technological change (the availability of cheap air transportation and the declining cost of cross-border information flows), but their accounts do not attempt to trace the independent effect of technological change on patterns of political action. In the development of advocacy networks for human rights, the environment, and women's rights, the key transformation has occurred across the North-South divide, as resources in the industrialized countries have flowed to disenfranchised groups in the developing world. What occurs is a form of political arbitrage: groups in the developing world that face authoritarian or unresponsive governments use both technologies and political space afforded by groups in the industrialized world in order to exert pressure on their home governments. The logic of this arbitrage, facilitated by technological change, is not dissimilar to the arbitrage across regulatory regimes that is observed in international financial markets.

Technical transfer in favor of transnational political organization began at about the same time as innovations that produced the networking technologies of the 1990s. Frederick documents the use of "highly decentralized technologies," particularly the personal computer, in the construction of PeaceNet and other projects of the Association for Progressive Communication (APC). Those successive projects eventually became the Institute for Global Communication (IGC), a large computer system dedicated to advocacy in the areas of peace, human rights, and environmental preservation.[5] A more recent and strikingly successful effort at advocacy dependent on Internet and other forms of electronic communication is the International Campaign to Ban Landmines (ICBL). Launched in 1992 by a coalition of sixteen organizations representing advocacy networks in human rights, peace, development, women's rights and the environment, the ICBL became a network of networks the eventually linked over 1,300 groups in more than seventy-five countries.[6] Its record of rapid success in lobbying for an international treaty is probably unparalleled in the history of international relations. Through transnational lobbying and the support of sympathetic governments (the Ottawa process), ICBL and its allied organizations produced a treaty to ban antipersonnel mines in December 1997, just five years after its formation; the ICBL was awarded the Nobel Peace Prize in the same year.[7] The campaign for ratification continued after the treaty was signed, and the nongovernmental organizations that are part of the ICBL will be part of an international network of monitors that will oversee treaty implementation.

Assessing the role of radically reduced costs for information processing and communication in the evolution of transnational political movements is difficult. Many of the societies that are the target of such campaigns are not tightly integrated into the world economy, nor do their populations share widely, if at all, in the key technologies of computing and telecommunications. Rather, the key to success across the large divide between the networked industrialized world and developing countries has been the construction of links that enable activists in the developing world to break government monopolies on information and to mobilize nongovernmental allies outside their countries. Those allies in turn can exert pressure on both their own governments and the government that is targeted by the original group of activists. (Keck and Sikkink 1998, 13) Each link in this causal chain, however, raises questions about the more expansive claims that have been made for these networks, despite their growth and their apparent success.

---

5 Frederick 1993. A description of the IGC's current activities can be found at www.igc.org.

6 A summary of the ICBL's history and activities is available at www.icbl.org.

7 The treaty is the Convention on the Prohibition of the Use, Stockpiling, Production and Transfer of Antipersonnel Mines and on Their Destruction.

The first claim concerns the relative power of governments and transnational political networks. Proponents of economic globalization have argued that government power has been permanently undermined by increased threat of exit by economic actors and an erosion of economic hierarchies. In similar fashion, some advocates of nongovernmental networks predict the creation of a political structure that lies outside and in opposition to conventional national politics and governments. Although such networks can undermine government monopolies on information more easily through their links to wider networks of information and activism, their success is dependent on access to those networks and an inability (or unwillingness) of their government to control that access. Given the underdeveloped character of telecommunications networks in many developing countries, a government's ability to discourage such access remains large; even neglect of infrastructure can seriously impede the network's expansion from a fragile outpost to the core of a national political apparatus. China is one of the most important tests of a government's ability to monitor and control the growing activities of economic and political networks that spill over national borders. A recent account suggests that a government intent on economic development and on obtaining the international information resources required by that strategy will have difficulty in retaining control over alternative uses of information networks. The task of controlling nongovernmental access is made even more difficult when its critics work assiduously to undermine its censorship. (Smith 1998).

The success of such networks has been dependent not only on undermining government control over information and information networks, however, but also on attracting the support of governments to implement changes in policy, whether the banning of landmines or an end to political repression in other countries. Governments continue to exert authoritative, if incomplete control over the policies that transnational networks wish to have changed, and their strategies must include framing information in a way that will mobilize political support in support of those changes. These strategies and the avenues of influence that they employ are altered by the availability of transnational information networks. They do not appear radically different from earlier democratic politics, however.

Observers of transnational political networks have portrayed these networks as a different form of social and political organization, "neither hierarchical nor reducible to market relations." (Keck and Sikkink 1998, 200). Parallels between the influence of new technologies on these networks and the emergence of network or alliance capitalism have already been made; the use of information to conduct political or economic arbitrage can be seen as parallel across politics and markets. A core contribution in both instances is the use of high-speed information networks to coordinate the activities of geographically far-flung organizations and individuals.

Hierarchy is not absent from these networks, however. Most accounts, typically written by those sympathetic to their causes, portray a highly egalitarian mode of organization. However, resources and technologies flow from the industrialized countries to the developing countries, and with that asymmetry comes agenda control, the ability to frame or edit information that enters the network, and the selection of acceptable interlocutors in the developing world. This asymmetry was clear in the contribution that the Internet made to the Zapatista uprising in Chiapas after 1994, often held up as the shape of things to come. The Internet permitted the Zapatistas to rapidly disseminate information about their cause to a large international audience. As even its supporters admit, however, this information tidal wave was dependent on observers on the ground in Chiapas (who were permitted to enter by the Mexican government). More important, the Zapatista National Liberation Army (EZLN) "played no direct role in the proliferation of the use of the Internet. Rather, these efforts were initiated by others to weave a network of support for the Zapatista movement." (Cleaver 1998, 628).

Finally, research on transnational political networks often endorses a normative affinity between networks based on technology and new forms of organization and the programs that these networks advocate: egalitarian, democratic, open. This supposed affinity overlooks the possibility that these technologies and the organizations that they support can be adapted or co-opted by more hierarchical organizations (governments in particular) or by groups whose normative orientation is far from that supported by the foundations and NGOs of the industrialized countries. Political Islam has been successful in constructing its own global networks, based on the same political and technological logic as environmental and human rights groups. Although technology and its political cognates may not be neutral, there is little evidence that deployment is limited to those endorsing particular political and social programs.

Cross-border networks and new identities

Evidence for the independent influence of new network technologies on global economics and politics is often anecdotal and fragmentary. In assessing the most profound consequence that these technologies might have, the reshaping of existing national and group identities, evidence and argument becomes even more speculative. For those who believe that we are witnessing the replacement of hierarchical structures by "a complex system of networks and alliances," the undermining of the traditional state is accompanied by the growth of new identities and "the emergence of multiple and competing *political* loyalties." (Kobrin 1998, 378). In many cases these are "virtual communities," that are grouped "by interest and value rather than proximity." (Tipson 1995, 13).

These claims of identity formation and transformation fit squarely with anxieties produced by economic globalization: that the rapid transmission of an array of content (increasingly digital) across existing boundaries will undermine more traditional (and once again, hierarchical) institutions of identity formation: church, state, local communities. These fears are fed by the apparent homogenization of the content that emanates from the United States and Europe, by the overwhelmingly English-language character of the Internet, and by the marketing power of American content providers, particularly international media and entertainment corporations.

An alternative view emphasizes the interactive nature of the new technologies, which permit cultural consumer sovereignty of a kind that older, broadcast systems prevented. The decline of the once omnipotent broadcast networks in the United States and elsewhere is symptomatic of the difficulties in forging a profitable niche as a content provider in the new technological environment. A second face of this individualized culture is the ability of threatened cultures to preserve themselves by using the Internet and other innovations. This possibility raises in sharpest form the issue of separating content, which reflects a clear cultural hierarchy, from the technology, which may serve to undermine that hierarchy.

The most interesting case within which this issue can be examined is that of indigenous groups, often threatened with slow extermination by their dominant national cultures, who have enjoyed remarkable success in the past decade. Many of these groups have won a hearing in the larger political culture for their claims to cultural recognition and territorial rights. A recent survey of the Internet and indigenous groups offers some indication of the contribution of technology to this record and the severe limits on technological means to cultural survival.[8] The contribution of information networking is probably greatest for widely scattered diasporas who retain a sense of their separate identity. The Assyrian Christians, for example, have used the Internet as a means to communicate at low cost, strengthening their sense of common identity. Other groups have used technology to preserve and extend their indigenous languages, to share their experience with other indigenous groups (sometimes constructing coalitions in the process), and, perhaps most important, to developing a network of support and activism in societies that are more sympathetic to their cause.

The limitations on such a strategy are both economic and cultural. Without support from outside their local economies, most indigenous groups cannot afford an initial link to the global networks. When their survival depends on economic development, a personal computer and a telecommunications hookup may appear a waste of resources. In the *CSQ* survey, all of the successful indigenous Internet users reside within the affluent societies of North America and West Europe. More typical is the situation in Latin America, where "the availability of information on the Internet has not resulted in large or significant indigenous participation." (Delgado, P. and Becker 1998, 27) The Internet, as a conduit for outside cultures, also poses a threat as well as an opportunity for indigenous peoples. Cisler notes that the Amish, who are deeply embedded in rich societies, forbid the personal computer (and thus the Internet) as part of their strategy of cultural preservation. (Cisler 1998, 21) Since many of these cultures are hierarchical and dominated by cultural traditionalists, the Internet and the information it provides may also have an internally disruptive effect on existing political and social institutions.

The question of identities and how they are constructed raises the question of whether culture can be treated as information or commodity, the two reigning images of what flows over global information networks. The individualist, anti-hierarchical, and global viewpoint that is reflected in much writing about the Internet may not mesh well with existing cultural institutions and preferences. For individuals and groups that are threatened by traditional national institutions – whether indigenous peoples at odds with dominant cultures or religious and ethnic minorities – these modern technical innovations may serve to preserve and defend identities that are older than the nation-

8 *Cultural Survival Quarterly* 21, 4 (Winter 1998).

state. However, this strategy could result in a Pyrrhic victory: cultures could be preserved against one threat (national absorption) at the cost of fundamental alteration through contact with a wider global and technological environment.

Conclusion: the coexistence and co-optation of states and networks

Revolutionary rhetoric that has surrounded the Internet and the spread of other innovations in communications and information technology has claimed that a networked world will be a world in which traditional forms of organization based on hierarchy and boundaries, most notably the nation-state, will be undermined or transformed. Many of the claims made for the new technologies are colored by unexamined assumptions and supported by a fragile empirical base. The geographical scope and spread of these innovations remains circumscribed by inequalities in global income. Much of the world's population is affected by these technologies, but does not use them on a daily basis. As the personal computer becomes a cheap household commodity and access to telecommunications is altered by the spread of wireless and other media, penetration will deepen outside the most affluent societies, but even then, adoption may be slowed by older, robust alternatives that have served poor communities well.

This circumscription of the use of information and telecommunications technologies makes an evaluation of their effects on global politics difficult. Within the democratic core of the world economy, many other trends have produced porous national boundaries and networked rivals to hierarchical organizations. Little rigorous research has attempted to discriminate among the independent effects of technological change on the one hand and political choices that can both limit and reinforce those effects on the other.

In any wave of technical innovations initial predictions adopt the metaphor of a tidal wave that will sweep away incompatible institutions and practices. An evolutionary perspective would predict rather that some institutions will adapt quickly to a given technical change, while other will lag. However, at least some of the lagging institutions are likely to adapt to and adopt the new technologies over time. Governments have not been rendered ineffectual or obsolete by economic integration and technological innovation, but their practices will change (as the phrase "reinventing government" implies), and the relative importance of their functions will also shift. Maintaining fixed exchange rates and protective barriers at the border may have become fruitless and self-defeating quests for individual national governments that are bent on economic growth in an increasingly integrated world economy. Setting standards, overseeing the evolution of national regulatory regimes, and providing infrastructure may become even more important. Given new technologies, coordination among governments at the regional or global level may become easier as well as more essential. As governments grope toward a new understanding of their roles in this altered environment, there is also little reason to believe that the outcome will be "less" government. Steering under conditions of democratic accountability has become hazardous, but electorates show little sign of wanting to give up either steering or accountability. More contingent hypotheses are needed regarding the longer term effects of technological change on the institutions and actors of world politics; at present, we have very few.

Finally, investigation of technological effects on world politics must be purged of the assumption of normative affinity. In the next wave of institutional adaptation produced by the converging technologies of the 1990s, organizations and groups that oppose the norms that many see embedded in these technologies may adopt those technologies to their own ends. One does not need to predict an inevitable backlash against globalization or international openness to suggest that those who are threatened by contemporary economic and political trends may use the same technological tools to achieve different goals. Technology is not neutral in its effects, but it would be very unusual if a technology were only placed at the service of one political program or one vision of the international future.

References

Berkowitz, Bruce D.: Warfare in the Information Age. In: Issues in Science and Technology (Fall 1995): 59-66

Biddle, Stephen: Victory Misunderstood: What the Gulf War Tells Us about the Future of Conflict. In: International Security. 21, 2 (1996), 139-179

Bryant, Ralph C.: International Financial Intermediation. Washington, D. C.: Brookings Institution 1987

Buckman, Rebecca / Aaron Lucchetti: Electronic Networks Threaten Trading Desks on Street. In: Wall Street Journal (23 December 1998), C1

Cisler, Steve: The Internet and Indigenous Groups. In: Cultural Survival Quarterly. 21, 4, 20-22

Cleaver, Harry M. Jr.: The Zapatista Effect: The Internet and the Rise of an Alternative Political Fabric. In: Journal of International Affairs, 51, 2 (1998), 621-640

Cohen, Eliot A.: A Revolution in Warfare. In: Foreign Affairs. 75, 2, 37-54

Cooper, Jeffrey R.: Another View of Information Warfare: Conflict in the Information Age. In: *Stuart J. D. Schwartzstein* (ed.), The Information Revolution and National Security. Washington, D. C.: The CSIS Press 1996

Cowhey, Peter: Building the Global Information Highway: Toll Booths, Construction Contracts, and Rules of the Road. In: *Drake, William J.* (ed.), The New Information Infrastructure: Strategies for U. S. Policy. New York: The Twentieth Century Fund Press 1995

Daly, John A. / Robert R. Miller: Corporations' Use of the Internet in Developing Countries. Washington, D. C.: The World Bank 1998

Delgado-P., Guillermo / Marc Becker: Latin America: The Internet and Indigenous Texts. In: Cultural Survival Quarterly 21, 4 (1998), 23-28

Dunning, John H.: Technology and the Changing Boundaries of Firms and Governments. In: OECD Proceedings: Industrial Competitiveness in the Knowledge-Based Economy. Paris: OECD 1997

Estabrooks, Maurice: Electronic Technology, Corporate Strategy, and World Transformation. Westport, CT: Quorum Books 1995

Frederick, Howard: Computer Networks and the Emergence of Global Civil Society. In: *Harasim, Linda M.* (ed.), Global Networks. Cambridge: MIT Press 1993

Garrett, Geoffrey: Global Markets and National Politics: Collision Course of Virtuous Circle? In: International Organization, 52, 4 (1998), 787-824

Gourevitch, Peter / Roger Bohn / David McKendrick: What is Globalization? Lessons from the Hard Disk Drive Industry. Unpublished paper, University of California, San Diego. November 1998

Helleiner, Eric: Electronic Money: A Challenge to the Sovereign State? In: Journal of International Affairs, 51, 2 (1998), 387-409

Henry, Ryan / C. Edward Peartree. Military Theory and Information Warfare. In: *Henry, Ryan / C. Edward Peartree* (ed.), The Information Revolution and National Security. Washington, D. C.: The CSIS Press

Herring, Richard J. / Robert E. Litan: Financial Regulation in the Global Economy. Washington, D. C.: The Brookings Institution 1995

International Monetary Fund: World Economic Outlook. Washington, D. C.: International Monetary Fund 1997

Kahler, Miles: Modeling Races to the Bottom. Paper presented at the 1998 meeting of the American Political Science Association, Boston, 3-6 September 1998

Keck, Margaret E. / Kathryn Sikkink: Activists Beyond Borders: Advocacy Networks in International Politics. Ithaca, NY: Cornell University Press 1998

Keohane, Robert O. / Joseph S. Nye. Power and Interdependence in the Information Age. In: Foreign Affairs 77, 5 (1998), 81-94

Kobrin, Stephen J.: Back to the Future: Neomedievalism and the Postmodern Digital World Economy. In: Journal of International Affairs 51, 2 (Spring), 361-386

Neumann, W. Russell / Lee McKnight / Richard Jay Solomon: The Gordian Knot: Political Gridlock on the Information Highway. Cambridge MA: MIT Press 1997

Nye, Joseph S. / Robert O. Keohane: Power and Interdependence in the Information Age. In: Foreign Affairs, 77, 5 (1998), 81-94

Nye, Joseph S. / William A. Owens: America's Information Edge. In: Foreign Affairs 75, 2 (1996), 20-36

Organization for Economic Cooperation and Development (OECD). 1997a. Information Technology Outlook: Editorial.

Organization for Economic Cooperation and Development (OECD). 1997b. Information Technology Outlook.

Rochlin, Gene I.: Trapped in the Net: The Unanticipated Consequences of Computerization. Princeton, NJ: Princeton University Press 1997

Rothkopf, David J.: Cyberpolitik: The Changing Nature of Power in the Information Age. In: Journal of International Affairs 51, 2 (1998), 325-359

Smith Craig S.: In China, a Thousand News Stories Bloom on the Web. In: Wall Street Journal, (18 January 1999), B1

Tipson, Frederick: Global Communications and the Sovereignty of States. Unpublished paper, Council on Foreign Relations Study Group on Sovereignty, Non-State Actors, and a New World Politics 1995

Raymund Werle

The Impact of Information Networks on the Structure of Political Systems

Introduction

At its outset, the public debate about the political effects of information networks was biased towards the impact on democracy. While it would be an exaggeration to suggest that terms like "Teledemocracy" (Arterton 1987), the "Electronic Republic" (Grossman 1995) or "Electronic Democracy" (Browning 1996) – to mention just a few of the catchwords that characterized this debate – were misleading, they did stimulate normative argumentation rather than analytical scrutiny. As a result, the debate has tended to oscillate between two extreme poles. On one hand, we have the optimistic stance that information networks will significantly improve the political system by making it more democratic; on the other, there is the pessimistic attitude that the networks will enhance the capacity of governments and the political elite to control and manipulate citizens and eventually lead to a decline in democracy.

In this paper I would like to highlight a few aspects of the information networks that will most likely affect political structures and discuss how they might exert this influence. This is less ambitious than trying to assess the relationship between technology and democracy. However, focusing on structural aspects of the political system has the following advantage: It makes it possible to include changes which affect the way a political system functions without posing the question concerning a polity's democratic quality in the sense of classical theory of democracy.

Modern society is a "society of organizations" (Perrow 1991). Organized collectives, both public and private, have come to play a predominant role in the process of policy formation. Political negotiations and the exchange between organizations in a more or less pluralistic system of checks and balances rather than direct participation of the citizens is the crucial feature of the political process in this type of society. Therefore, this paper will deal primarily with organizations.

In the first section of this paper I will argue that a distinct organizational field has evolved whose importance parallels the growing significance of information networks. This organizational field is comprised of issues and actors pertinent to these networks and the Internet in particular. The second section focuses on how these and other organizations utilize the networks. Concentrating on associations and interest organizations, I will examine how the organizations and their individual members make use of the facilities of internal and external information exchange and communication. This will lead to a preliminary general assessment of the role of information networks in politics, which constitutes the third and final section of the paper. The focus here is on government agencies, parliaments and citizens, and it comes closest to what is currently being discussed under the heading "Internet and democracy."

Many speculative studies on this topic start from technology and not from society sharing the implicit suggestion that technology determines society. However, rather than determining society or driving history (cf. Smith/ Marx 1994), technology has an interactive relationship to society: It is shaped by, but also shapes society. In this sense, technological determinism can be regarded as one possible explicative scenario, but there are other ways that society can make use of technology (cf. Barber 1988). Digital technology in particular can be flexibly used for many different purposes by individuals and organizations. How any given society incorporates "the same" technology differs from country to country and from one institutional setting to another. A few aspects of such differences will become visible in the following comparison of the USA with Germany.

Information Networks in the Ecology of Policy Domains

Information networks have been gaining political significance in the recent years and have already left their imprint on many political structures. One must adopt a structural model of the political system in order to identify structural changes. Such a model has been developed by Laumann, Knoke and their associates for the area of public policy and state policy formation (Knoke/Laumann 1982; Laumann et al.1985; Laumann et al. 1991).

According to this organizational approach to state policy, a political system can be regarded as a number of delimited policy domains. The material substratum of a policy may be a technology, an industry or a set of moral norms and beliefs; a domain can also comprise a mix of heterogeneous elements. The relevant criterion separating one domain from another is inductive and focuses on actors. A policy domain is identified by specifying a common orientation among a set of actors. The set of actors is delineated by a common concern with formulating, advocating and selecting a course of action that is intended to resolve a given, substantial problem (Knoke/ Laumann 1982: 256). Participants in a policy domain include all actors in both the public and private sector whose interests, strategies and capacity to influence the outcome of group decisions must be taken into account by the other actors. More often than not, such relationships of mutual relevance lead to networks of routine interaction, but not every actor is integrated in such a network. Also, several actor networks that are only loosely linked and represent divergent political camps frequently co–exist in a policy domain (Schneider/ Werle 1991). Based upon analyses of agriculture, energy, health and labor, Laumann and Knoke have shown that policy domains differ with respect to their institutional composition,[1] the constellation of interest groups, the level (intensity) and forms of political conflict and also with respect to their internal organizational structure. This latter aspect indicates that a policy domain may be divided into several subdomains.

Laumann and Knoke's structural model of the political system together with their concept of policy domains can be used to illustrate the structural effects of information networks.[2] In terms of this approach, the political system can be viewed as a landscape or an ecology of policy domains which presumably has been changed by the advent of information networks. If these networks constitute more than a negligible element of the societal infrastructure – more than, say, an appendix to the telephone network – one would expect that a respective policy domain has emerged. In order to prove this suggestion, which in retrospect seems obvious, let us briefly skim over the development of the Internet which has become the core of today's information network.

Apart from its early military background, the Internet began as an American research and education network; a product of science (and technology) policy, it was created to benefit different segments of the scientific community in the USA. Designed to provide access to remote supercomputers and to provide a testbed for experiments in data transmission and switching, the network simultaneously facilitated electronic communication via e–mail. The National Science Foundation's involvement in research and education networking in the middle of the 1980s was a crucial element in the history of the Internet. The NSF launched the NSFNET – the backbone to which

1 E.g., involvement of government and regulatory agencies, a cabinet–level department, formal procedures of rulemaking, adjudication or licensing.

2 In their research project, the authors rely on highly sophisticated methods of sampling, data collection and statistical analysis and they aspire to develop a causal model of political negotiation and exchange. This level of sophistication can by no means be matched in this paper.

regional and local networks could be connected – and took responsibility for coordinating the growth of the national research and education network. In this role, however, the NSF was only the *primus inter pares* in a social network of coordinating, sponsoring and regulating organizations which can be regarded as the nucleus of an Internet policy domain. Diagram 1 provides a structural overview of this domain in 1987/88.

A detailed description of the organizations included in diagram 1 would go beyond the scope of this paper (see Werle 1997; 1999). Most organizations were involved in science and technology policy or were committed to coordinating, developing and operating the network. Central issues included the provision of financial support and the creation of a framework of expectations, expertise and rules within which the research and education network could evolve (CSTB 1988). Business organizations played a minor role in the initial policy network. They were indirectly represented through the Federation of the American Research Networks (FARNET), an organization set up by the regional networks to advance their interests vis à vis the NSF, and through EDUCOM, a consortium of higher education institutions geared towards facilitating the introduction and use of information resources in teaching, learning and research.[3] On the other hand, a large number of volunteers served on the Internet Architecture Board (IAB) and in the Internet Engineering and Internet Research Task Forces (IETF and IRTF). According to their own definition, these were independent committees of researchers and professionals with a technical interest in the health and evolution of the Internet, and they formed the core of self–governance regarding the network's technical and organizational coordination.

The initial Internet domain assumed no prominent status in the ecology of policy domains. It can be regarded as a subdomain of science and technology policy (cf. Rogers 1996; 1998) with weak ties to the policy domains in the area of telecommunications and computing. The Internet domain evolved in a policy niche. In a way this can be attributed to the often criticized fragmented institutional and regulatory structure of US policy in the telecommunications sector in particular but also in some parts of science–based high tech industry (cf. CSTB 1992: 76f, Geller 1995; also Branscomb 1993).

---

3 MCI and IBM were involved at the operational level, and were responsible for providing physical lines and routers for the NSFNET.

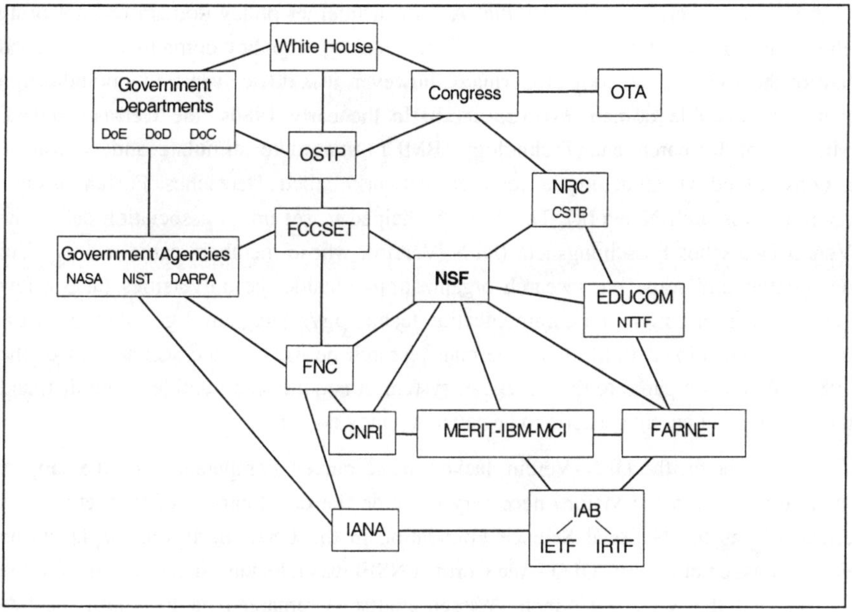

Diagram 1: Initial Internet Policy Domain in the USA (1987/88)

CNRI	Corporation for National Research Initiatives
CSTB	Computer Science and Telecommunications Board
DARPA	Defense Advanced Research Projects Agency
DoC	Department of Commerce
DoD	Department of Defense
DoE	Department of Energy
EDUCOM	Consortium of higher education institutions
FARNET	Federation of the American Research Networks
FCCSET	Federal Coordinating Council for Science, Engineering and Technology
FNC	Federal Networking Council
IAB	Internet Architecture Board
IANA	Internet Assigned Numbers Authority
IETF	Internet Engineering Task Force
IRTF.	Internet Research Task Force
MERIT	Consortium of Michigan Universities, IBM and MCI
NASA	National Aeronautics and Space Administration
NIST	National Institute of Standards and Technology
NRC	National Research Council
NSF	National Science Foundation
NTTF	Networking and Telecommunications Task Force
OSTP	Office of Science and Technology Policy of the President of the USA
OTA	Office of Technology Assessment

Certainly the emergence of the initial American Internet policy domain did not bring about any significant structural changes in the ecology of policy domains in the second half of the 1980s. If we look at Germany, however, it is difficult to find any indication that a comparable domain evolved at all. In the early 1980s, the German Federal Ministry of Research and Technology (BMFT) started to stimulate and coordinate actions aimed at launching a research network called Deutsches Forschungsnetz (German Research Network). The Ministry helped to set up an association called the Verein Deutsches Forschungsnetz (DFN–Verein), whose members came mainly from universities and some big research organizations outside the universities (also a few vendors of information and communication technology). Diagram 2 gives an overview of the organizational field of the German research network in the second half of the 1980s. When compared to the American system, it is quite small and less pluralist, and it does not meet enough criteria to be called a policy domain.

The central actor, the DFN–Verein, lacked the resources, competency and the support (and perhaps even the vision) necessary to guide the development of the network as effectively as the National Science Foundation in the USA. Early on, the Deutsche Forschungsgemeinschaft (DFG – the German NSF) was reluctant to commit itself to the project, and the Science Council (Wissenschaftsrat) remained passive until the late 1980s (Leib/Werle 1997). Concerning the provision and operation of the network the DFN–Verein relied on the Deutsche Bundespost. At the time, the Bundespost was a kind of a public enterprise under the Federal Ministry of Post and Telecommunications and enjoyed a monopoly in the operation of public networks and the provision of public telecom services. It did not consider research networking attractive or challenging. As a result the German research network did not position itself in a way comparable to the NSFNET and subsequently to the Internet (Zorn 1998).

Details of the breathtaking career of the Internet in the 1990s need not be recapitulated here. In the second half of the 1990s, the Internet developed into a policy domain of its own right in many countries, with the USA leading the world in this development. It is no longer merely a subdomain of science policy or other domains. The pervasiveness of the Internet and its increasing commercial viability provide opportunities and present risks that have turned into political issues. Many individuals and organizations take an interest in how this technology must be shaped and institutionally embedded in order to exploit its potential benefits.

We have more than anecdotal evidence that the Internet – and more generally the new information networks –has recently drawn more attention than ever from the U.S. government and the Congress. When the 105th Congress came to a close in October 1998, it had left its mark on the Internet with a plethora of new laws ranging from the Child Online Protection Act over a multitude of rules for the electronic economy – including a three–year net tax ban – to the Government Paperwork Elimination Act. The 105th Congress filed more than 300 bills that included the word Internet, four times as many as the previous Congress. For the first time, a majority of members of Congress had e–mail addresses and web pages.[4]

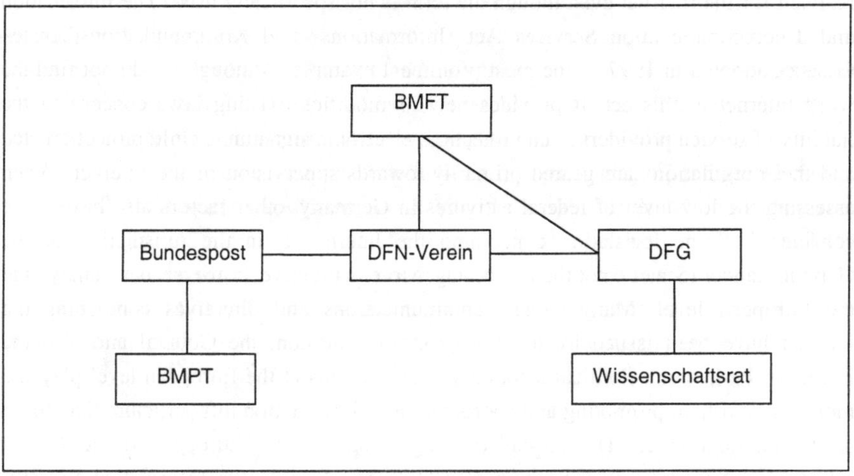

Diagram 2: The German Research Network Policy Domain (1987/88)

BMFT	Bundesministerium für Forschung und Technologie
BMPT	Bundesministerium für Post und Telekommunikation
DFG	Deutsche Forschungsgemeinschaft
DFN	Verein Deutsches Forschungsnetz

Also in Germany we can observe an increasing visibility of the Internet in parliamentary debates, motions and questions though at a significantly lower level than in the USA. A survey on Internet related activities of the Bundestag in the 13th election period[5] shows that there were no more than 22 parliamentary actions such as questions and debates that included the word Internet.[6] If we rely solely on the frequency of the word Internet as a measure of importance, however, we run the risk of underrating the

4 See for instance:"Congress spends the year online" CNET News (http://www.news.com /News/Item/0,4,30402,00.html),
"Government and the Internet Got Acquainted in 1998" New York Times – Cybertimes (http://www.nytimes.com/library/tech/98/12/cyber/articles/28congress.html),
"Legislation Affecting the Internet – 105th Congress" Internet Telecommunications Project (http://www.cybertelecom.org/legis.htm)

5 In the Bundestag's electronic files at http://dip.bundestag.de/.

6 It was not until early 1998 that the parliamentary advisory committee (Ältestenrat des Bundestages) granted the members of parliament the right to set up individual homepages on the server of the Bundestag. Less than 100 out of 672 members of parliament had an individual homepage in summer 1998 (cf. Stradtmann 1998). Through the parliament's server, all members of parliament can be reached by e–mail.

significance of the Internet for the parliament and the Federal Government in Germany. More often than not, legislation – including decrees of government departments – is relevant for the Internet even though the term is not specifically used. The Information and Telecommunication Services Act (Informations- und Kommunikationsdienste-Gesetz), adopted in 1997, is the most prominent example. Although we do not find the word Internet in this act, it provides new or modifies existing laws concerning the liability of service providers, data protection, electronic signatures, child protection etc., and these regulations are geared primarily towards supervision of the Internet. When assessing the low level of federal activities in Germany, other factors also have to be considered. Some legislation concerning the Internet is in the jurisdiction of the German Länder (States), not the Bundestag. More instructive, however, is an analysis at the European level. Many papers, communications and directives concerning the Internet have been issued by the European Commission, the Council and also the European Parliament. Political actors and organizations at the European level played a more active role in promoting and coordinating an information infrastructure than those at the national level. The so–called Bangemann–Report "Europe and the Global Information Society" and the action plan "Europe's Way to the Information Society" were adopted in 1994, one year after the U.S. government launched the National Information Initiative, but two years before the German Department of Trade and Commerce issued the policy plan "Info 2000. Deutschlands Weg in die Informationsgesellschaft" (Germany's Movement into the Information Society).[7]

Given the differences concerning the direct salience of the Internet on the official political agenda in Germany and the USA, it comes as no surprise that the respective policy domains differ in size and contour. Internet policy is no longer a subdomain of science policy in either country, although actors involved in science policy are still around. Neither the NSF nor the Verein Deutsches Forschungsnetz have disappeared. Indeed, even new science policy actors have entered the scene in the USA. These include the American Internet 2 Consortium and the related University Corporation for Advanced Internet Development (UCAID), which is committed to upgrading campus networks, providing connections to regional gigabit networks and furnishing the facilities for advanced applications; their goal is to maintain U.S. leadership in research. Internet policy has established itself as a domain of its own right with the computer, the telecommunications and the media sectors, which are, of course, immediate neighbors.

Diagram 3 and 4 give an impression of the overall structure of the Internet policy domains in the USA and in Germany. In contrast to the diagrams above, these new diagrams only show clusters of organizations rather than single organizational units. This is due to the fact that their number has increased significantly. This does not mean that Germany can be compared to the USA. The population of the U.S. Internet policy

---

7 For a brief comparison of the U.S. and the European development to an information society see Schneider (1997).

domain is significantly larger and more heterogeneous than that of Germany. In the USA, for instance, more than 6,500 service providers – small and medium sized as well as large enterprises – co–exist and compete with one anther, whereas the respective number of German service providers is not much higher than 200. Several interest associations represent the service providers in the USA. The groups include the Commercial Internet eXchange (CIX) Association, which is the oldest, or the Internet Service Providers' Consortium (ISP/C), which is the most visible of the political lobbyist. Other business actors in the American Internet policy domain are vendors of dedicated Internet software and hardware (such as Netscape and Cisco) and network operators (companies like Qwest, Level 3 or IXC), who stepped in and provided data networks which compete with the incumbent telecommunications carriers. Depending on their resources, these organizations either run their own offices located in the netbelt, join interest associations, or forge temporary alliances – all founded with the goal of lobbying Congress and the White House. Another cluster of organizations in the Internet policy domain is focused on technical coordination and self–governance of the network. The traditional bodies which emerged in the early NSFNET days have been complemented and partly replaced by organizations such as the Internet Society, the World Wide Web Consortium, the Global Internet Project (a group of senior business executives), or the new Internet Corporation for Assigned Names and Numbers (ICANN). These organizations have an international membership and regard the scope of their responsibility as worldwide. Their headquarters, however, are located in the USA, and the central focus of their activities is the U.S. Internet policy domain. The same holds true for those organizations in what we may call the civil rights cluster, where free speech, privacy or the participation of the netizens in regulating the Internet are the issues at stake. The Electronic Frontier Foundation, the Center for Democracy and Technology, and the Computer Professionals for Social Responsibility are examples of this type of organization. Last but not least, the Congress, the WhiteHouse[8] and several government departments and government agencies will continue to play a decisive role in the Internet policy domain although, as has been repeated time and again, the government is determined to keep its hands off the Internet and leave it to private actors whenever possible.

The American Internet policy domain is multifarious, pluralist, decentralized and well established in the ecology of policy domains. The belief that the Internet constitutes the crucial infrastructure of the information society is widely shared by the individuals and organizations in this domain, and their common interest lies in accommodating the institutional environment in a way that promises the greatest benefit of this network. Opinions differ, of course, with respect to what this might mean and how it can be realized. With many new actors and new issues in this new policy domain, traditional identifications, commitments and political alliances are seemingly being scrambled in

8 Primarily Vice President Al Gore.

an unpredictable way (Magaziner 1998). Recently, many issues in the Internet policy domain have arisen from the blurring of technical boundaries between electronic media, computers, telecommunications systems and the Internet. Before discussing this convergence issue, let us look at the German Internet policy domain.

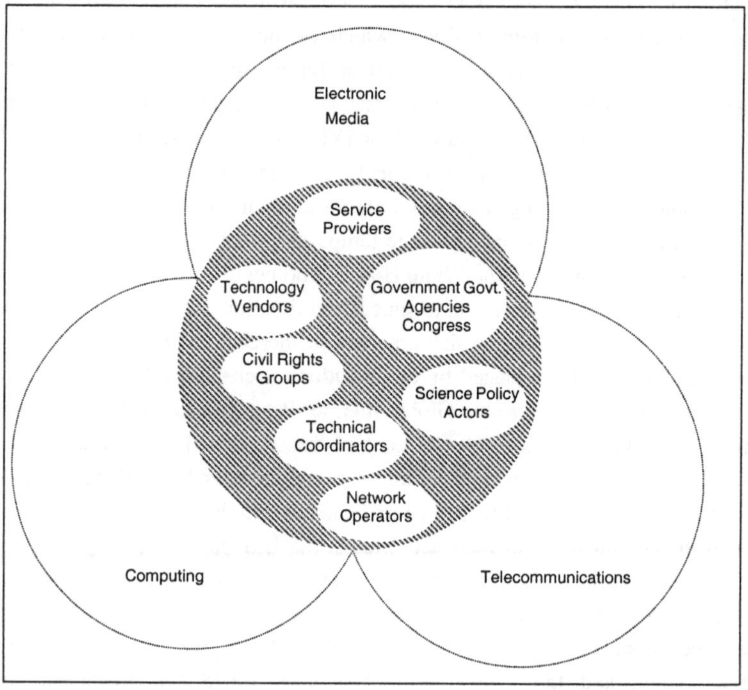

Diagram 3: The American Internet Policy Domain

We have already seen that the German government and the parliament are becoming increasingly aware of the Internet, even if this awareness has brought about comparatively little political activity. This lack of political interest can only be understood against the background of the relatively low social significance of the Internet in this country. One reason for and at the same time a result of the lower prevalence is that Internet utilization by private households and by business firms is by far not as widespread as in the USA. Many German business firms hesitate using the Internet for commercial transactions and external communication, although they rely on internal Internet technology (Intranets). Private households are suspected to be generally less optimistic than their American counterparts concerning the possible benefits of the Internet. But apart from these suggested explanations, which point to cultural differences, the high rates charged for accessing the Internet via the telephone network – which only started to go down after the market was opened to competition last year – and a lack of attractive services provided in the German language account for the lower utilization of the Internet in Germany.

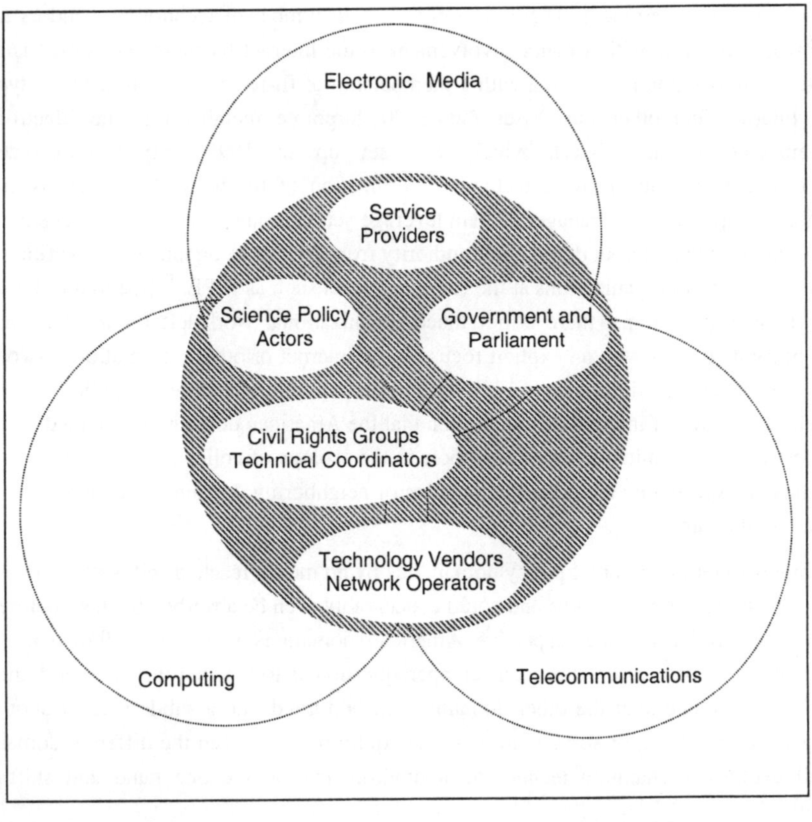

Diagram 4: The German Internet Policy Domain

Accordingly, the Internet policy domain in Germany appears to be rather small and not as differentiated as in the United States. There is the familiar circle of science policy actors with the Verein Deutsches Forschungsnetz who seems to have recovered from the policy failures that mark the history of the German research network. A look at the cluster of political actors shows that the Federal Chancellery (Bundeskanzleramt) and – following the American model – advisory committees such as the Technologierat (Technology Council) have gotten involved, and the governments of the Länder have also gained some leverage.[9] The Ministry of Post and Telecommunications has been replaced with a regulatory authority to oversee the liberalized telecommunications market, but not directly the Internet. The more than 200 Internet service providers form a cluster which also includes alliances set up to represent common commercial interests vis à vis the government. There are only a small number of technology vendors and network operators with a major involvement in the Internet business. The only visible interest association in this area with a membership of firms involved in different types of Internet and other businesses (some 70 corporate members) is the Electronic Commerce Forum (ECO), which was set up in 1995 (http://www.eco.de/). Organizations which provide technical coordination of the network as well as civil rights groups have not managed to gain leverage yet. German organizations focusing on coordinating the Internet derive their authority from American organizations working in this area or from organizations at the European level such as RIPE.[10] Due to the success of these organizations, there is not much organizational work left for the Germans. Civil rights groups with an explicit focus on the Internet or other information networks play an even less significant role.[11] As a result, the German Internet policy domain lacks the degree of internal differentiation that the American domain has attained, and it is less clearly delimited from its neighbors in the ecology of policy domains. In diagram 4, this is indicated by the dotted boundaries of neighboring domains that cut across the Internet domain.

While the German Internet policy domain has by no means reached self–sufficiency vis à vis its neighboring domains and could conceivably even be absorbed by them before it can develop further, the respective American domain is poised to collide with its neighbors. In both cases, it remains an open question as to whether the Internet domain will predominate over the other domains, will be turned into a subdomain of another organizational field, or some kind of stable equilibrium between the different domains will evolve. A changing technological environment on the one hand and shifting

9 Also, a special commission of the Bundestag prepared a report on Germany's development with respect to the information society: "Zukunft der Medien in Wirtschaft und Gesellschaft – Deutschlands Weg in die Informationsgesellschaft" (1998).

10 RIPE (Réseaux IP Européens) is a collaborative organization open to all parties operating in wide area IP networks in Europe. The objective of RIPE is to ensure that the administrative and technical coordination needed to enable a pan–European IP network to be operated is in place (see: http://www.ripe.net/info/ripe/ripe.html. See also the German Network Information Center DENIC at http://www.denic.de/Denic/). The German Internet Society was organized as a chapter of the American parent organization (http://www.isoc.de/).

11 Most popular in the German Internet Community is the Chaos Computer Club set up by a group of hackers more than a decade ago. It portrays itself as "a galactic community of human beings of all ages, genders, races and social positions. We demand unlimited freedom and flow of information without censorship" (http://www.ccc.de/WarmWelcome.html). One organization with a membership of political groups and labor unions is the Initiative Informationsgesellschaft, Medien, Demokratie (http://staff-www.uni-marburg.de/~rillingr/imd/imd.html). Another group of professionals and experts is the Internet Medienrat (http://www4.bdaserver.de/bda/int/medienrat/index.html).

organizational strategies on the other are the forces driving this process of domain competition and overlap. As previously mentioned, the blurring of technical boundaries between electronic media, computers, telecommunications systems and the Internet strongly suggest that traditionally separated sectors will merge, forming an unified multimedia complex. Technical features and services developed in the Internet domain play a crucial role in this process. The world wide web, with its capacity as a mass medium, serves as an example as do the protocols and services facilitating Internet telephony. More important than the growing technical potential are the emerging organizational strategies which make use of or react to new technologies. In an era of mergers, takeovers, joint ventures and strategic alliances, large businesses in telecommunications, in electronic media and in the computer domain are combining forces with Internet organizations or setting up an Internet branch to exploit the business opportunities in this sector. As a result, anti–trust and regulatory agencies are considering intervening in the Internet domain. Organizations rooted in this domain are reacting to these developments, occasionally supported by government agencies and science policy actors (cf. Drake 1995). They are struggling to preserve the structure and the cultural traditions of this domain, but their aim is not to prohibit other organizations from gaining access to and becoming active in the Internet.

Indeed, in the eyes of many actors in this domain, the Internet has the potential to advance a model of society as a de–centralized heterogeneous system with a loosely defined national or territorial identity. Its social structure would then mirror the technical structure of the network of networks. The units are loosely integrated in the system, i.e., they keep as much autonomy as possible without this being detrimental to the links connecting the units. Organizations interact on a peer–to–peer basis rather than in a hierarchical mode. Power, control and authority is distributed, and the system is open and responsive to bottom–up initiatives (cf. Eisner Gillett/Kapor 1997). This stylized picture, which also includes an example of the individual Internaut that will be touched upon in the last section, stands in sharp contrast to the structure found in other policy domains. Without going into detail, one could say that these domains have inherited monopolistic or oligopolistic structures and that they are subject to regulatory and anti–trust intervention which shall maintain competition and prevent abuse based upon economic power (Kahin 1997). As consumers, users play a passive role ("couch potatoes"). However, it would be an exaggeration to argue that these domains are fundamentally different from that of the Internet. Yet, even moderate distinctions make a difference, and the structure of the Internet policy domain appears to be more in line with the structural prerequisites of a democratic society than the other domains.

We can only speculate about future of the Internet. It is unclear if this policy domain will be able to resist the pressure to conform to the structures of the other domains. The sociological theory of institutional isomorphism suggests that constraining mechanisms force one unit in a population of organizations to conform to other units that are exposed to the same set of environmental conditions (DiMaggio/Powell 1991: 66). This suggestion refers to the features – such as the form, the structural components and rules – of single organizations that constitute the units of what DiMaggio and Powell call an organizational field. Our analysis deals with policy domains which share properties of but are not identical with organizational fields, and our focus is not on single organizations but on these domains. However, transferring the basic idea of DiMaggio's and Powell's approach from the level of organizations to that of organizational fields leads to the following inference: An analogous process of change towards isomorphism takes place when policy domains overlap due to technical developments and organizational strategies. This hypothesis concerning the convergence of structural and institutional properties of single domains in an ecology of policy domains still leaves the question about the model the domains will converge on open. Will it be the Internet domain type or another type? The largest domain or the domain with the most efficient structures may well predominate in the end – to the disadvantage of the Internet domain. However, as sociological institutionalism has shown, efficiency is only one and often not the decisive factor determining survival. Political legitimacy and support also secure survival and growth (Meyer/Rowan 1991). Indirect political support of the Internet domain in the USA and other countries is provided by various information society and information infrastructure initiatives. The U.S. NII builds on the Internet as the model of a broader societal strategy to "realize the information future" – and not merely the multimedia future (CSTB 1994; Kahin 1997). This opens a window of opportunity for the Internet policy domain, allowing it perhaps to dominate in the USA and carry its success over into other countries – including Germany, in which the respective domain still depends on external support.

Interest organizations and information networks

Our analysis of the ecology of policy domains is based on a structural model of the political system, with organizations serving as the domains' prevailing units. For the organizations in the Internet policy domain, the network of networks serves as a reference point, providing a source of orientation for their choices, strategies and evaluations. They endeavor to structure the technology and the embedding institutions in a way that they can serve their political, commercial or technological interests. Many organizations other than those in the Internet policy domain utilize information networks, and this utilization is always done – regardless of the type of organization – in such a way as to further organizational needs and preferences. The majority of organizations using electronic networks are private businesses. However, in our analysis of the repercussions of the Internet and other information networks on the political sphere, not every type of organization is equally important. Therefore, in this section we will focus on political organizations that, while involved in politics, are not at the core of the political system, as are government agencies, public administrations and political parties. These entities include private and public interest organizations – often associations – with a voluntary membership. As intermediaries, they aggregate interests and represent them in a policy domain. They represent functional (special interests) and not territorial interests.

The organizations are created by individual actors (or other organizations) who, through transferring rights and resources, empower the organizations to act on behalf of their members. The underlying assumption is that these organizations are more effective in their use of resources than are the members. The members, of course, expect the organizations to act in accordance with their preferences. With reference to action capacity and control, these organizations appear to be what Coleman calls corporate actors (Coleman 1974; 1990). Corporate actors have a constitution which defines their legitimate domain and operational rules. Analogous to human actors, corporate actors are analytically treated as having goals, interests, preferences and strategies. They develop informal practices and have an interest in autonomy, survival, growth and domain expansion (cf. Mayntz 1997). The constitution provides the corporate actor with some freedom to act. Full freedom would give the greatest power to the corporate actor in his interactions with other organizations, but it would simultaneously leave the members without any means of control and is for this reason unattractive. Other aspects can also reduce attractiveness. Many voluntary associations, for instance, have difficulties attracting members because they work for the public good and are unable to provide incentives for membership.

Corporate actors, in particular these types of the interest organizations with voluntary membership, are torn between two partially contradictory logics (Schmitter/ Streeck 1999). The inward bound "logic of membership" requires organizations to be open for participation, transparent, receptive to the needs of members and representative concerning their interests. On the other hand, the "logic of influence," which guides interaction with other organizations in a policy domain, requires the capacity to act quickly and flexibly, embark on political bargaining behind closed doors, forge instead of find a high level of consensus of the members and accumulate resources to maximize external power.

Private and public interest organizations may see in information networks a useful resource that could help to meet both requirements. However, inasmuch as political leverage remains their primary goal, the logic of influence – and not the logic of membership – will guide their action.[12] On the other hand, the level of influence is most often dependent on the membership – for a large membership serves to legitimize any given organization and, naturally, increases the resources made available by the members – such that organizations nevertheless try to invite participation.

12 This is in line with what the corporate actor model of organizations would predict.

When beginning our analysis of how organizations make use of and are affected by information networks, we must first distinguish between interaction with other organizations and interaction with the public. The structure of the U.S. political system is pluralist and dispersed, and it is relatively open. The principle that information should be free and open to the public has obliged government agencies to share its information with the public (freedom of information act), and the expectation that the public have access to such information has been carried over into the domain of political interest organizations. It is necessary to mobilize broad support in order for political initiatives to be successful in the competitive political system. In Germany, we have a strong corporatist tradition with comparatively few organizations being involved in policy making, although differences between more corporatist and more pluralist policy domains can be observed.[13] Public support of interest organization's political initiatives is helpful, but often bargaining takes place behind closed doors and public response is avoided. In Germany, protection of information and privacy rules are more prevalent than principles of open access.

This background has to be taken into account when assessing the utilization of information and communication technology by interest organizations. Generally speaking, the use of information networks, in particular the Internet, can reduce transaction costs and increase flexibility and the speed of information exchange and communication. In a pluralist system such as the USA, where many organizations are involved in politics, e–mail and mailing list services as well as other means of group communication facilitated by the Internet are frequently used. The Internet appears to be the most fitting communication system for a pluralist polity. In this regard, the network stabilized – rather than altered – the system, and has a tendency to make it even more pluralist as cost barriers to effective communication have been reduced. In a corporatist polity such as Germany, the Internet's communicative capacity is of minor significance. However, because networks of communication between many organizations can be set up at little cost, it does provide an opportunity to foster change towards pluralism.[14] On the other hand, the other pre-existing barriers, which hinder new interest organizations in their attempts to enter into the network of incumbent interest organizations, remain unchanged. Thus, political pressure, exerted in an effort to open up small circles of established, elite organizations, will be needed to foster pluralism. Such pressure is likely to come from the European Union, which is significantly more pluralist than Germany, though not necessarily more democratic in the classical sense.

---

13 The differences are also reflected in the German and the U.S. Internet policy domain.

14 We cannot rule out that fragmentation and political disintegration could result as a by product of pluralism. Modeling the effects of the Internet in science, Van Alstyne/ Brynjolfsson (1997: 27) come to the general conclusion that "Internet users can seek out interactions with like–minded individuals who have similar values, and thus become less likely to trust important decisions to

Interaction of interest organizations in organizational networks via the Internet or other information networks does not appear to have changed the structural features of the German and the U.S. system significantly. However, when we look at the interaction between interest organizations and the public we get a different picture. These organizations also use the technology to further their cause; in this case they employ the technology primarily to present themselves to the public. They propagate their political goals and beliefs, and publicize current activities and often their relationship to other organizations as well. In particular, social movements use the Internet extensively. This network offers a new channel with which they can address the public without having to rely solely on mass media. Other kinds of interest organizations also profit from this new medium. Mobilizing public support can help immensely when trying to achieve political goals. Even small organizations can reach the public via the Internet. Small organizations often demonstrate their integration in a broader movement by providing links from their websites to their allies – national and abroad. By setting up links to but not merging with other organizations, they can retain autonomy and at the same time appear as an important actor in a large, virtual organization.[15] Small organizations in particular gain power through such networks of organizations, and this reinforces pluralist structures. Also, public access to information concerning, for instance, membership, goals and various activities of the interest organizations is enhanced significantly by the Internet. However, it remains an open question as to whether this public access to the interest organizations means that the public has a stronger hand in shaping organizational strategies and influencing organizational goals, i.e., if this public access will eventually bring about a change in political structures.

With this question we move from the logic of influence to the other guiding rationale of organizational action, i.e., the logic of membership. Time and again organizational studies have provided evidence that organizations deploy information and use communication technology primarily for internal purposes. They often set up so–called Intranets, which are dedicated to internal communication and are protected from the outside by "firewalls". Due to our focus on public and private interest organizations, however, we are interested in the electronic communication of organizational elites with a broad membership, rather than in the internal communication of an organization's staff. Many organizations provide special services for members which cannot be used by the public. The minutes of board meetings, reports from special

people whose values differ from their own. This voluntary balkanization and the loss of shared experiences and values may be harmful to the structure of democratic societies."

15 The "Association for Progressive Communication" (APC) provides an example of a kind of portal organization linking several networks to one another. A non–profit association of 25 member networks working together, APC provides online organizational and collaboration tools meant to support the worldwide movement struggling for social, environmental and economic justice (http://www.apc.org/english/about.html). "Global Response" (GR) serves as another example. It has created a worldwide network of people and organizations referring environmental crises to GR, which organizes collective reactions to the problem (http://www.globalresponse.org/).

committees or task forces and other strategically important information is made available only to members. They can address the organization's CEO, president or board members directly via e–mail, and they have the opportunity to hold discussions with other members if they are listed on the internal mailing lists. By eliminating cost barriers and providing tools which can efficiently retrieve and analyze organizational documents, the Internet has helped organizations become more open to membership influence. Herein lies a significant advantage of the net over conventional mail and telephone services.

It is difficult to assess the impact of the members' use of the Internet on organizational policy formation and strategy. Most organizations have not yet adapted their constitutions and by–laws to accommodate the opportunities made available by the Internet. Provisions which allow for electronic voting and balloting are missing or are restricted to issues of minor political significance. The logic of influence often prevails over the logic of membership. However, gradual changes can be observed. A survey of four hundred environmental organizations in ten countries shows that those utilizing the Internet (on–line groups) are more "politicized" than off–line groups. The results concerning the extent to which the Internet is shaping the organizations' policy are ambiguous (Zelwietro 1998). Another study shows that in the preliminary stages of the UN World Conference on the Status of Women in Huairou/China 1995, several non–governmental organizations, their members and other interested women used the Internet to exchange and publish documents and to explicate the programmatic positions of the participating organizations. But the organizations' programs have not been changed significantly by these activities. There was an interesting side effect: The status and influence of those women who were familiar with the new technology increased within these organizations (Greve 1997). Again, the standing of smaller organizations were strengthened as a result of being a member of an encompassing virtual network of organizations.

National differences concerning the role of information networks in defining the relationship of interest organizations to one another, to the public and to their own membership are difficult to discern. When organizations make use of the Internet, they do so to further their own interests. As corporate actors they tend to act more in accord with the logic of influence rather than the logic of membership. However, members seem to be gaining leverage gradually through the Internet. The prerequisite for this is, of course, that organizations use the Internet and that members have access to the net. In this respect we find differences between the USA and Germany, which we discuss in the following section.

Politics and information networks

In the introduction I argued that many debates about and speculations concerning information networks deal with their impact on democracy. They focus on the participation of citizens in the process of governance. We already touched on this point in our treatment of the relationship that the public and private interest organizations have to the public. In this case, the citizens' impact on politics is mediated by these organizations (intermediaries). If information networks allow the unorganized public to bypass the intermediaries and thereby significantly enhance its ability to directly participate in governance, the legitimacy and authority of the intermediaries might erode. This would bring about serious structural changes in the policy domains and in the political process. Thus, corporate actors cannot be expected to support direct citizen participation without any reservations, for it endangers their growth and survival. This threat of losing their intermediary function, however, may force these organizations to begin acting more in accord with the logic of membership rather than the logic of influence.[16]

One vital prerequisite for citizens' participation via the Internet is access to the net. It is well known that even in the U.S. only a minority has access to the Internet. According to various sources, some 70.2 million people (35% of the population) had access to the net in June 1998 – more than double the percentage in Germany. Here, 15% (12.2 million) had access in September 1998. With a growing number of people using the net, the initial bias towards a class of users consisting of young white male college graduates from the high–income bracket is disappearing. It will, however, require a universal service policy combined with financial support for low–income households and funding of network literacy programs to ensure a distribution rate for the Internet and online services which compares with that of the telephone (Civille 1995).

Access to the net is a necessary but not a sufficient condition for the public's electronic participation in government. Citizens want to see some tangible return from their political engagement via the Internet. Once they have started using the network as a medium to acquire political information and to communicate their interest, the citizens must have the feeling that they are influencing politics or gaining some other benefits from their involvement. Otherwise, they will cease to use the net as a political medium.

The early Internet users, the prototypical members of the so–called Internet community, had a strong belief in self–determination, free speech and civil rights and tended to be skeptical of formal authority. They also had a certain degree of technical expertise; this helped them to protect themselves from harmful repercussions from the network and to

16 A similar point has been made with reference to the role of political parties in democracies which, thanks also to electronic media, provide increasing opportunities for the direct participation of citizens in the decision–making process through voting. Parties will continue to play an intermediary role, responding to citizens by organizing the election, and stimulating the turnout and political discussion (Budge 1993).

participate in its technical development. This somewhat idealized picture of the past still persists and is shared by many Internet activists of today. To infer from this picture, however, that today's "community" of Internet users are a homogeneous, cohesive, and collegial group with similar values, objectives and skills would be misleading (cf. Rutkowski 1997). Furthermore, the early users were by no means political activists. They wanted to keep official politics off the Internet and create their own "cybersociety," technically coordinated by the IANA, the IAB and the IETF and governed by themselves. This model or vision – had it ever materialized – could not have been maintained in face of the growing economic viability of the network.

In United States, the Internet pioneers were followed by a group of political professionals, a group which included party officials, the government staff, elected political representatives, and also the media and public activists. Not only these élites, but also governments themselves, "have aggressively and enthusiastically undertaken a massive project in experimentation with the Internet as a tool of politics" (Bimber 1998: 18). Most of the activists are committed to the goals and strategies of their organization to the benefit of which they try to shape and use the Internet. Therefore, it comes as no surprise that – as already mentioned – governments, public agencies, parliaments and their members at the federal, the state and the local level have their web sites and e-mail addresses in the USA as well as in Germany. This is also the reason why (ongoing) research focuses, for instance, on the "openness" and "effectiveness" of organizational use rather than on the mere presence of political organizations in the Internet.[17]

By contrast, the general public has been slower than the political Internet professionals to begin using the net, and in the USA it has already been observed that some users drop out again (Katz/Aspden 1998). Not very many people try to participate in political discussions and debates with government officials and political representatives.[18] Even those wanting to communicate with members or offices of parliament are often disappointed. Only a minority of the members of the U.S. Congress use e-mail to communicate with their constituents – even if they receive e-mail from constituents –, and it should be mentioned that, for the time being, members of Congress are not being overwhelmed with electronically mediated demands and opinions from citizens. Personal letters sent by the conventional mail service, telephone calls and especially personal visits have proven to be significantly more effective than e-mails when citizens want to get the attention of a member of parliament (OMB Watch 1998). We have no systematic empirical evidence for Germany in which use of the Internet is not as widespread as in the United States anyway; thus, we can only guess that the general

17 See the activities of the Cyberspace Policy Research Group at the University of Arizona (Tucson). The long term project aims at documenting "the rise and consequences of webbing government across cultures and policy circumstances" (http://www.cyprg.arizona.edu/Mission.htm).

18 As a rule, we find that public and private interest organizations and "experts" (professionals) actively participate in this type of electronic communication.

pattern is similar to what has been observed in the USA. Political parties, governments and members of parliament use the Internet for political announcements and declarations rather than to communicate with its citizens (Stradtmann 1998).

Obviously, the Internet's theoretical potential to encourage the citizens to participate in the democratic process does not automatically increase the actual and effective participation (cf. Leib 1998). The higher the level of politics, the lower the probability that citizens will participate. The Internet reduces transaction costs of political communication which are a barrier to participation, yet the net does not reverse this general rule. A rational reaction to this problem seems to be to use information networks only as a tool to keep an eye on what government officials, members of parliament and other political élites are doing and to keep citizens informed about what is going on. Projects such as "Vote Smart" rely on the traditional mechanisms of democratic control, but use electronic networks (in addition to conventional practices) to make them more efficient.[19]

Assuming that it is easier for citizens to participate directly in low politics than in high politics, we should find more electronic activities at the municipal and local levels. Indeed, political activism in what has been called community networks often deals with local matters. The "virtual community" (Rheingold 1993), which is based on electronic networks and services, often has a local or regional identity (Bonchek 1995). In the USA, community networks provide opportunities to participate in local politics. But in keeping with the early tradition of the Internet, they are also used to facilitate self-governance. As a result, community networks serve to blur the boundary between the public and the private domain rather than fend off politics. In a way, they modify local political values, but keep them local. Concerning community networks, again Germany is lagging behind the USA. But emergence of such networks does not only depend on time. Community networks in Germany usually need government or other external support to get started and reach a critical number of participants.[20] This reliance on such support makes these networks vulnerable to external interference and control, and this may reduce their attractiveness.

All in all, only a fraction of the citizens use information network to gain access to and participate in the political process. The emerging usage patterns suggest that in low politics – and in particular at the local level – community networks facilitate the

---

19 Vote Smart is a national non–partisan, non–profit organization. It "researches, tracks and provides to the public independent factual information on over 13,000 candidates and elected officials. Voting records, campaign issue positions, performance evaluations by special interests, campaign contributions, backgrounds, previous experience, and contact information are available over a toll–free Voter's Research Hotline, manuals and other publications, and the Vote Smart Web site" (http://www.vote-smart.org/about/).

20 We have good reason to believe that the absence of competition in the German telecommunications market accounts for the comparatively small amount of support of community networks received from the telecommunications industry.

participation of socially active citizens in debates and discussions focusing on community issues such as schooling or housing. Yet, civic intervention into high politics remains difficult, if not impossible. Government officials, members of parliament and other members of the political elite do not generally esteem electronic forms of communication and information exchange as highly as conventional forms. They tend to use the Internet to present themselves to the public rather than to communicate with the people. If we draw a distinction between talking politics and doing politics, civilian electronic interactions with political actors are generally restricted to talking.

Conclusion

The impact of information networks on the structure of political systems is not as spectacular as many speculative essays suggest. The networks have developed into the core infrastructural component of the information society and have thereby become technically, economically and politically significant. Correspondingly, these networks, and especially the Internet, have changed the ecology of policy domains and triggered the emergence of an Internet policy domain in its own right. Many new business firms and their interest organizations, new political groups and other actors along with established organizations are convinced that the Internet is the very blood of the information society, and they are working to accommodate the Internet's institutional environment in order to reap the greatest gains from this network. In many respects, the Internet policy domain is different from other domains and seems to have more of the building blocks of a democratic society in its foundation than most of its neighboring domains. Whether or not the Internet domain will be able to preserve its structure and principles and not be overwhelmed by its neighbors remains to be seen. In Germany the respective domain has not yet reached a point of saturation and might be assimilated by other domains before it has had time to develop.

The level of impact that information networks have on political structures and democracy depends to a large degree on how organizations shape and make use of these networks. If we focus on private and public interest organizations whose actions and strategies follow primarily the logic of influence, we find that using information networks is attractive to them due to their flexibility, speed and affordability. The networks enhance the organizations' capacity to interact effectively with other organizations in a pluralist political system – an asset that is especially advantageous for the smaller organizations. This reinforces pluralism and helps to make corporatist systems such as Germany more pluralist. In the majority of cases, the members' influence on the strategy of and action taken by their interest organizations has not changed significantly by the advent of the information networks. The organizations' formal constitutions would have to be adapted to accommodate the possibilities made available by the new networks for the logic of membership to guide organizational action as much as the logic of influence.

The members of various interest organizations have the ability to bypass their respective organization and express their opinions and demands directly to governments and parliaments via electronic networks. This exerts an indirect pressure on these organizations to reform their constitutions and internal structures in order to enhance their responsiveness. However, for the moment at least, government agencies and members of parliament do not appear to be very responsive to electronic input from the public – neither in Germany nor in the USA. Only in low politics, predominantly at the local level, do we find indications that citizens participate in governmental processes. The community networks in the USA are particularly good examples of this. Of course, this does not mean that most citizens take advantage of this opportunity. The majority does not even have home access to the Internet.

Thus, if we look at the input of citizens into the political process via electronic networks, the technical potential to participate exceeds by far the actual use of the available technology. If, however, we evaluate the political output resulting from communication, information exchange and negotiations between organizations, we find indications that the process has become more transparent and receptive to collective interests represented by a great number of organizations. This does not necessarily lead to a significant increase in direct civilian participation (input), but it seems to improve government performance (output). To some degree, information networks account for this inasmuch as they reinforce pluralist structures at the level of organizations.

References

Arterton, F. Christopher: Teledemocracy. Can Technology Protect Democracy? Newbury Park: Sage 1987

Alstyne, Marshall Van / Erik Brynjolfsson: The Net Effect: Modeling and Measuring the Integration of Electronic Communities. Paper presented at the Twenty–Fifth Annual Telecommunications Policy Research Conference. Alexandria, VA, September 27–29, 1997 (http://www.si.umich.edu/~prie/tprc/abstracts97/CyberBalkans.pdf)

Barber, Benjamin, B.: Pangloss, Pandora or Jefferson? Three Scenarios for the Future of Technology and Democracy. In*: Plant Raymond / Frank Gregory/ Alan Brier* (eds.), Information Technology: The Public Issues. Manchester: Manchester University Press 1988, 177–191

Bimber, Bruce: The Internet and Politics in the USA. In*: Eisel, Stephan / Mechthild Scholl* (eds.), Internet und Politik, Sankt Augustin: Konrad–Adenauer–Stiftung (1998), 17–26

Bonchek, Mark S.: Grassroots in Cyberspace: Using Computer Networks to Facilitate Political Participation. Paper Presented ath the 53rd Annual Meeting of the Midwest Political Science Association Chicago, IL on April 6, 1995 (http://institute.strategosnet.com/msb/ppp/grassroots.html)

Branscomb, Lewis M.: Empowering Technology Policy. In: *Branscomb, Lewis M.* (ed.), Empowering Technology. Implementing a U.S. Strategy. Cambridge, MA/ London: MIT Press (1995), 266–294

Browning, Graeme: Electronic Democracy. Using the Internet to Influence American Politics.Wilton, CT: Pemberton Press 1995

Budge, Ian: Direct Democracy: Setting Appropriate Terms of Debate. In: *Held, David* (ed.), Prospects for Democracy. Cambridge: Polity Press (1993), 136–155

Civille, Richard: The Internet and the Poor. In: *Kahin, Brian / James Keller* (eds.), Public Access to the Internet. Cambridge, MA: MIT–Press (1995), 175–207

Coleman, James S.: Power and the Structure of Society. New York: Norton 1974

Coleman, James S.: Foundations of Social Theory. Cambridge, MA: The Belknap Press 1990

CSTB, Computer Science and Technology Board: Towards a National Research Network. Washington, D.C.: National Academy Press 1988

CSTB, Computer Science and Telecommunications Board: Keeping the U.S. Computer and Communications Industry Competitive: Systems Integration. Washington, D.C.: National Academy Press 1992

CSTB, Computer Science and Telecommunications Board: Realizing the Information Future. The Internet and Beyond. Washington D.C.: National Academy Press 1994

DiMaggio, Paul J. / Walter W. Powell: The Iron Cage Revisited: Institutional Isomorphism and Collective Rationality in Organizational Fields. In: *Powell, Walter W. / Paul J. DiMaggio* (eds.), The New Institutionalism in Organizational Analysis. Chicago: The University of Chicago Press (1991), 63–82

Drake, William J.: The National Information Infrastructure Debate: Issues, Interests, and the Congressional Process. In: *Draje, William J.* (ed.), The New Information Infrastructure. Strategies for U.S. Policy, New York: The Twentieth Century Fund Press (1995), 305–344

Eisner Gillett, Sharon / Mitchell Kapor: The Self–Governing Internet: Coordinating by Design. In: *Kahin, Brian / James H. Keller* (eds.), Coordinating the Internet, Cambridge, MA/ London: MIT Press (1997), 3–38

Enquete–Kommission "Zukunft der Medien in Wirtschaft und Gesellschaft – Deutschlands Weg in die Informationsgesellschaft", 1998: Schlußbericht: Deutschlands Weg in die Informationsgesellschaft. Bundestagsdrucksache 13/11004, vom 22.6.98. Bonn: Bundesanzeiger

Geller, Henry: Reforming the U.S. Telecommunications and Information Process. In: *Drake, William J.* (ed.), The New Information Infrastructure. Strategies for U.S. Policy. New York: The Twentieth Century Fund Press (1995), 115–135

Greve, Dorothee: Internet und soziale Bewegungen. In: *Werle, Raymund / Christa Lang* (eds.), Modell Internet? Frankfurt a.M.: Campus (1997), 289–304.

Grossman, Lawrence K.: The Electronic Republic. Reshaping Democracy in the Information Age. New York: Viking 1995

Kahin, Brian: The U.S. National Information Infrastructure Initiative: The Market, the Net, and the Virtual Project. In: *Kahin, Brian / Ernest J. Wilson III* (eds.), National Information Infrastructure Initiatives. Vision and Policy Design. Cambridge, MA, London: MIT Press (1997), 150–189

Katz, James E. / Philip Aspden: Internet Dropouts in the USA. The Invisible Group. In: Telecommunications Policy, 22, 4/5 (1998), 327–339

Knoke, David / Edward O. Laumann: The Social Organization of National Policy Domains: An Exploration of Some Structural Hypotheses. In: Marsden, Peter V. / Nan Lin (eds.), Social Structure and Network Analysis. Beverly Hills: Sage (1982), 255–270

Laumann, Edward O. / David Knoke/ Yong–Hak Kim: An Organizational Approach to State Policy Formation: A Comparative Study of Energy and Health Domains. In: American Sociological Review 50 (1985), 1–19

Laumann, Edward O. / John P. Heinz / Robert Nelson / Robert Salisbury: Organizations in Political Action: Representing Interests in National Policy Making. In: *Marin, Bernd / Renate Mayntz* (eds.), Policy Networks. Empirical Evidence and Theoretical Considerations. Frankfurt a.M./ Boulder, CO: Campus/ Westview Press (1991), 63–95

Leib, Volker: Wissenschaftsnetze und Bürgernetze. Vom selbstgesteuerten Internet zur elekronischen Demokratie. In: *Gellner, Winand / Fritz von Korff* (eds.), Demokratie und Internet. Baden–Baden: Nomos (1998), 81–94

Leib, Volker / Raymund Werle: Wissenschaftsnetze in Europa und den USA. Die Rolle staatlicher Akteure bei ihrer Bereitstellung. In: Werle, Raymund / Christa Lang (eds.), Modell Internet? Entwicklungsperspektiven neuer Kommunikationsnetze. Frankfurt a.M.: Campus (1997), 157–185

Magaziner, Ira: Democracy and Cyberspace: First Principles. 1998 (http://media-in-transition.mit.edu/conferences/democracy/session4_m1.html)

Mayntz, Renate: Soziale Dynamik und politische Steuerung. Theoretische und methodologische Überlegungen. Frankfurt a.M.: Campus (1997), 168–185

Meyer, John W. / Brian Rowan, 1991: Institutionalized Organizations: Formal Structure as Myth and Ceremony. In: *Powell, Walter W. / Paul J. DiMaggio* (eds.), The New Institutionalism in Organizational Analysis. Chicago/ London: The University of Chicago Press (1991), 41–62

OMB Watch,1998: Speaking Up in the Internet Age: Use and Value of Constituent E–mail and Congressional Web Sites. (http://www.ombwatch.org/ombw/npt/reports/emailsurvey.pdf)

Perrow, Charles: A Society of Organizations. In: Theory and Society 20 (1991), 725–762.

Rheingold, Howard: The Virtual Community. Homesteading on the Electronic Frontier. New York: HarperPerennial 1994

Rogers, Juan D.: Implementation of a National Information Infrastructure: Science and the Building of Society. University of Virginia. Dissertation 1996

Rogers, Juan D.: Internetworking and the Politics of Science: NSFNET in Internet History. In: The Information Society 14, 3 (1998), 213–228

Rutkowski, A.M.: Factors Shaping Internet Self–Governance. In*: Kahin, Brian / James Keller* (eds.), Coordination the Internet. Cambridge, MA/ London: MIT–Press (1997), 92–104

Schmitter, Philippe C. / Wolfgang Streeck: The Organization of Business Interests. Studying the Associative Action of Business in Advanced Industrial Societies. MPIfG Discussion Paper 1/99, Köln: MPIfG 1999

Schneider, Volker: Different Roads to the Information Society? Comparing U.S. and European Approaches from a Public Plicy Perspective. In*: Kubicek, Herbert / William H. Dutton / Robin Williams* (eds.), The Social Shaping of Information Superhighways. European and American Roads to the Information Society. Frankfurt a.M./ New York: Campus/ St.Martin's Press (1997), 339–358

Schneider, Volker / Raymund Werle: Policy Networks in the German Telecommunications Domain. In: *Marin, Bernd / Renate Mayntz* (eds.), Policy Networks. Empirical Evidence and Theoretical Considerations. Frankfurt a.M./ Boulder, CO: Campus/ Westview Press (1991), 97–136

Smith, Merrit Roe / Leo Marx (eds.): Does Technology Drive History? The Dilemma of Technological Determinism. Cambridge, MA: MIT Press 1994

Stradtmann, Philipp: Deutschland auf dem Weg in die elektronische Demokratie? Das Internet als neues Medium der politischen Kommunikation und Partizipation. Dipl.Arbeit: Hochschule für Musik und Theater Hannover 1998 (http://www.politik-digital.de/e-demokratie/37/gesamt.doc.)

Werle, Raymund: Academic–Industry–Government Relations and Cross Sectoral Coordination in the Development of Research and Education Networks (REN). In: *Enslow, Philip / Pete Desrochers/ Irene Bonifacio* (eds.), Global Networking '97. Volume II: Policy, Social Applications. Amsterdam: IOS Press (1997), 401–408

Werle, Raymund: Zwischen Selbstorganisation und Steuerung. Geschichte und aktuelle Probleme des Internet. In: *Wilke, Jürgen* (ed.): Massenmedien und Zeitgeschichte. Konstanz: UVK Medien (1999), 499–517

Zelwietro, Joseph: The Politicization of Environmental Organizations trough the Internet. The Information Society, 14 , 1 (1998), 45–56

Zorn, Werner: Verfehlte Entwicklung. In: *Leggewie, Claus / Christa Maar* (eds.), Internet & Politik. Von der Zuschauer– zur Beteiligungsdemokratie. Köln: Bollmann (1998), 194–206

Saskia Sassen

The Impact of the Internet on Sovereignty: Unfounded and Real Worries

There is a growing debate about the Internet and its impact on sovereignty. A good example in the legal scholarship is the recent special issue of *the Indiana Journal for Global Legal Studies*. The major lines of the debate are increasingly polarized among those who believe that the Internet undermines state sovereignty and those who believe that it strengthens liberal democracy. Not unrelated to these two positions is the parallel debate between those who assert that it is impossible to regulate the Internet versus those who maintain that there are various legal instruments available to states for regulating Internet transactions.

I want to argue here that one of the reasons for the polarization in views evident in these debates has to do with, on the one hand, misconceptions about the architecture of the Internet and, on the other, an uncritical assumption that national sovereignty is a given, an unchanged feature of national states. In short, part of the problem is that both the conception of the Internet and that of sovereignty fail to incorporate the finer grain of each and their recent transformations. What has happened in this debate to some extent is a shaping of the interpretation of the Internet's impact on sovereignty in terms of two major long-standing positions in the political theory and legal scholarhsip on the nature of state power – the Realist and Liberal conceptions of state power. Left out of this debate are the specific features of the Internet, let alone the fact that the Internet itself is a dynamic entity. Left out also is the possibility that these two major theories are themselves inadequate to understand state power and national sovereignty in today's context of globalization.

I am concerned about the broader theoretical and political implications of the faulty characterization of the two fundamental concepts in the debate. Among the key issues I want to focus on concerning the Internet are a) the confusion between privately owned digital networks and public digital space, b) the multiple meanings of commercialization of the Net, and c) the possibilities for regulating the Net. Very briefly, my argument will be that it is the enormous growth of private digital networks – especially the case of the global financial markets – rather than the Internet, which is having the greater impact on national sovereignty and indeed transforming it. Secondly, the rapid growth of commercial uses on the net is not necessarily a democratising dynamic, as is often argued under the assumption that markets are a condition for a free society. Commercialization may well create new forms of inequality in digital space – what one could think of as cybersegmentations. Finally, there are features of the Internet today which suggest that regulation is possible, and that it is not necessarily a space of total freedom, a sort of new wild west. But it is a radically different version of regulation from what we have associated with the modern state over the last half century.

When it comes to sovereignty, we see a tendency towards a somewhat unproblematicized acceptance of this category. Taking sovereignty as if it were a fundamental given is particularly inadequate in the current period when we are seeing some rather important transformations in that specific form of power and legitimacy we call state sovereignty. The uncritical acceptance of sovereignty as a given is evident both in so called Realist conceptions of the state, with their emphasis on the power of the state, and Liberal conceptions, with their emphasis on democratic mechanisms as explaining the power of the state. My argument is that economic globalization and technology have brought with them significant transformations in the authority of national states. Especially important here is the growth of new non-state centered governance mechanisms which have transformed the meaning of national territorial sovereignty independently from whatever impact the Internet has so far had, and further, the formation of partly digitalized global financial markets which can deploy considerable power against the will of national states.

In brief, we cannot take either of these two categories – the Internet and sovereignty – as givens. They are dynamic conditions subject to a variety of pressures. Even the Internet, with its young history, can already be thought of as having had two phases and entering a third one. Making problematic the two basic categories in the debate – the Internet and sovereignty – introduces a number of qualifyers into some of the dualities running through the debate, notably the Realist/Liberal opposition in theories of the sovereign state and the interpretation of the Internet as representing either a fundamental revolution or basic continuity in technologies of communication. Liberals have tended to view it as a revolution with enormous potential while Realists tend to take the second view and argue that the state will find ways of regulating the Net and indeed is already capable of doing so. This duality in a way misses the point: the specificity of the Internet in terms of sovereignty is going to have to do in good part with the kinds of uses and practices enacted in the Net and the extent to which commercialization and privatization, including copyrighting, create new forms of concentrated power and inequality on the Net.

I. The Internet's Third Phase: Novel Implications for Democracy

There is little doubt that the Internet is an enormously important tool and space for democratic participation at all levels, the strengthening of civil society, and the formation of a whole new world of transnational political and civic projects.[1] But it has also become clear over the last few years that the Internet is no longer what it was in the 1970s or 1980s; it has become a contested space with considerable possibilities for segmentation and privatization. We cannot take its democratic potential as a given simply because of its interconnectivity. We cannot take its "seamlessness" as a given simply because of its technical properties. And we cannot take its bandwidth availability as a given simply because of the putative exponential growth in network capacity with each added network.[2]

This is a particular moment in the history of digitalnetworks, one when powerful corporate actors and high performance networks are strenghtening the role of private digital space and altering the structure of public digital space, that is, the Internet. Digital space has emerged not simply as a means for communicating, but as a major new theater for capital accumulation and the operations of global capital. Yet much of the writing about electronic space and network power has been shaped by the properties of the Internet, more precisely what one can think of as its first two phases.[3]

To recap a familiar story, the first phase of the Internet was confined largely to a community of insiders – scientists and select government agencies. That community invented communication standards and communication protocols that ensured access for all the members of that community. The second phase of the Internet, centered in the decade of the 1980s, strengthened the democratic and open character of the Net and made it a space of distributed power that limits the possibilities of authoritarian and monopoly control. It is by now well known that the particular features of the Internet are in part a function of the early computer hacker culture which designed software that strengthened the original design of the Net – openness and decentralization – and which sought to make the software universally available for free.

But with the establishment of the World Wide Web in 1993, and its large scale discovery by business by 1995, we can say that the Net has entered a third phase, one characterized by broad-based attempts to commercialize it.[4] Commercialization is often regarded as an

1 In the broadest sense the Internet consists of the technologies that support TCP/IP. In speaking about the Internet as a public space the reference is more specifically to the uses made through software design and distribution of those technical capacities.

2 Indeed carrying capacity has grown enormously, probably surpassing Moore's Law exponential growth rate. Techical developments over the last two years raised the carrying capacity of fiber optic cable from 20 gigabits per second in 1996 to 400 in 1998.

3 I have developed this specific argument in Globalization and its Discontents (1998) chapter 9.

4 Commercialization can enter the Net in several ways. One is the emergence of firms that sell access services to speed up access. This is not an essential service to gain access, but it is a convenience, and an option for those with the income to pay for it. Another is the possibility of adding value (including commercial value) to Net features through the incorporation of voice and image, which consume enormous bandwidth and hence will eventually be more easily subjected to premium pricing mechanisms than is e-mail for instance. When we consider the enormous amount of software design effort that is right now going into producing programs that can ensure safe credit card processing and other types of electronic payment, then we can see that commercialization is likely to increase even though today it is minor. This could stimulate the creation of Web sites that

extension of the positive aspects of the Net. But if carried too far it may in fact have negative consequences for the civic and political potential of the Internet, and in that regard, negative impacts on Liberal state agendas. This commercialization is pursued through the development of software that can simultaneously capitalize on the Net's features **and** implement billing/payment systems, and it is pursued through the extension of copyrights – in other words, the opposite of the early hacker culture. There is insufficient recognition of the tension between some of the features of the Internet which promote openness and interconnectivity, on the one hand, and, on the other, the rapid growth since 1995 of software that seeks to facilitate and expand private appropriation and use of the Net and that would allow for the implementation of copyrighting on a scale we have never seen before.

Yet much of the thinking about digital space and about questions of power and democracy, has been shaped by the properties of the Internet's first two phases. What stands out especially in the second phase is the condition of the Internet as a space of distributed power that limits the possibilities of authoritarian and monopoly control. While this remains a feature of the Internet, too many other dynamics have also been set in motion for us to just stay with this rather utopian view. In this regard, it seems to me that we need to re-theorize digital space and uncouple it analytically from an exclusive focus on the properties of the Net which have so sharply shaped our understanding.

The polarization between Internet romancers, on the one hand, and the logic of business and markets, on the other, is contributing to a parallel polarization in the discourse about digital space, quite independently from the Realist vs. Liberal view, when it comes to the state. There is a utopian approach that emphasizes the decentralization and electronic democracy of the Net, and a dystopian approach that emphasizes the global power of the large corporations.

Neither account is adequate today. While corporate forces have immense power in the shaping of digital networks, it is also a moment when we are seeing the emergence of a fairly broad-based civil society – though as yet a minor share of world population – in electronic space, particularly in the Net, which signals the potential for further developing democratic features of the Net. Further, each of these accounts rests on assumptions that limit the possibility of critical appraisals and future potentialities.

The assumptions that run through much of the discourse of the Internet romancers veil the existence of new forms of concentrated power that may undermine the better features of the Internet; nor do these assumptions help us understand the limits of such new forms of concentrated power, an important political issue. One assumption is that it will always be the open, decentralized space it was designed to be; this makes it ahistorical. John Perry Barlow's 1996 "A Declaration of the Independence of Cyberspace" probably epitomizes this view. Besides this political utopian vision there now is also an economic utopian view, especially strong in the U.S., which sees the Net as offering the possibility of a whole new

incorporate the latest developments of voice and image and could charge for access. I think of the growing use of voice and image for non-essential uses as a de-greening of the net. E-mail is a system of astounding efficiency and "ecological soundness." Voice and image with their enormous consumption of bandwidth are much less so.

type of market economy, one truly open and democratic. The California based *Wired* magazine is a key axis for this line of thought. The second assumption, tightly interlinked with the first, is that digital space is a purely technological event, and in that sense an autonomous space to be read in technical terms. One implication of such a technological reading is the notion that it can escape existing structures of power and inequality in the wider society.

The dystopian view of the Internet has its own limiting assumptions: Big capital will take over and the new high-income transnational class will also become a virtual class, with its spatial mobility further enhanced by digital mobility. Most people will be left out and at best reduced to passive consumers of Internet commerce.[5]

Both the utopian and the dystopian view of the Internet rest on assumptions that limit our understanding of current conditions and developments. The utopian view excludes the fact that electronic space is embedded in actual societal structures and is internally segmented, both conditions with enormous implications for current and future developments as well as for the theorization of networked space and power. The dystopian view excludes the limitations and complementary dependencies of the new digital technologies – no technology is an absolute: it cannot replace all other technologies aimed at similar functions, in this case communication and interactivity. And it excludes the fact of growing contestation between powerful economic actors and civil society in public electronic space, a fact which in itself may lead to new forms of political engagement and in that sense be a force for strengthening political activity.[6]

The Internet, then, has not only undergone significant transformations, but also is caught up in polarizing representations about its key features.

II. Public Digital Space: Contested and Threatened

In my research I have come to regard the Internet as a space produced and marked through the software that gives it its features. There are significant implications attached to the fact that the leading Internet software design focus in the last few years has been the design of "firewalls" and, more recently, of so-called virtual business networks that operate over the Net via "tunnelling" and/or encryption.[7] Both of these represent private appropriations of a public space.[8] The rapid growth of this type of software and its use in the Internet does

---

5 A different type of dystopian view is centered on questions of subjectivity: the transformation in the conditions through which our subjectivity is formed due to the overwhelming presence of technology intermediated sociability. This is a cultural pessimism derived from a notion that the new digital technologies will replace all other technologies through which people connect: the telephone replaced by e-mail, work in office buildings by tele-work from home, social visits by on-line chat clubs, business travel replaced by video conferencing, actual experiences by virtual reality games.

6 For instance, the development of so called "insular technologies" centered on low-cost high frequency radios rather than depending on the fiber optic network and hence on the telecoms that control it. For a full description see the archival material and ongoing debate on Nettime. The idea is the possibility of a world-wide build out of TCP/IP connectionless networks as a low-cost and effective option to the multi-trillion US$ PSTN worldwide dominated by large telecoms.

7 This saves companies the cost of private computer networks, with the requisite staffing and servicing, and the cost of frame relay connections.

8 An additional issue, one which I am not referring to here, is the privatization of infrastructure that

not necessarily strengthen the public-ness of the Net. This is especially significant if there is less production of software aimed at strengthening the public-ness of the Net.[9] Further, this type of software also sets up the conditions for copyrighting, particularly the possibility of copyrighting use/access, including every single use/access.

In my reading, far from strengthening the Internet's democratic potential as many liberal and neo-liberal commentators maintain, excessive commercialization can threaten it. Much of the commercial potential and economic activities often attributed to the Internet, are actually part of private digital networks or firewalled (i.e. privatized) sites in the Internet, a subject I return to later. But even the currently far more limited world of commercial uses possible on the Net, as compared to private digital networks, can bring some problematic consequences to the democratic potential of the Net.

Although the Net as a space of distributed power can thrive even against growing commercialization, and today's non-commercial uses still dominate the Internet, the race is on. Considerable resources are being allocated to invent ways of expanding electronic commerce, ensuring safety of payment transactions, and implementing copyrighting. These are not easy tasks. At last year's Aspen Roundtable on Electronic Commerce, an annual event that brings together the CEOs of the main software and hardware firms as well as the key venture capitalists in the sector, it was once again established by these insiders that there are considerable limits to the medium and that it probably will always cater to particular niche markets, with a few possible exceptions.[10]

The Internet may continue to be a space for de-facto (i.e. not necessarily self-conscious) democratic practices. But it will be so partly as a form of resistance against overarching powers of the economy and of hierarchical power, rather than the space of unlimited freedom which is still part of its representation today in many milieux. The images we need to bring into this representation increasingly need to deal with contestation and resistance, rather than simply the romance of freedom and interconnectivity or the new frontier. In this regard the reawakened interest among non-commercial digital organizations and digital activists in open-source systems, notably Linux, is worth noting. We are seeing the rapid growth of a new generation of alternative organizations and of individuals knowledgeable about digital technologies who are working on the public dimensions and free access questions.[11]

---

has also taken place over the last two years.
(see Globalization and its Discontents, chapter 9).

9 See for example the failure of Digital City Berlin and of Digital City Vienna. The original Digital City, Amsterdam, remains a lively and dynamic public space. It has taken enormous work and time on the part of a group of dedicated founders and members to ensure its survival.

10 The Global Advance of Electronic Commerce. Reinventing Markets, Management and National Sovereignty. A Report of The Sixth Annual Aspen Institute Roundtable on Information Technology. (Aspen, Colorado, August 21-23, 1997) David Bollier, Rapporteur. Washington, D.C.: The Aspen Institute, Communications and Society Program 1998.

11 See for instance the recent (March 1999) Next Five Minutes meetings in Amsterdam and Rotterdam, especially the technical workshops, and the upcoming Wizards of OS meeting in Berlin (July 1999).

There is an incipient literature that enacts this negotiation. Among the more important is the ongoing work of the recently created collective Nettime (1997; Lovink 1998) formed by people who are very knowledgeable about the Internet, many of whom are Net activists, but at the same time critical of the romancing of the Net I described above.

One aspect important to the positive democracy effect of the Net, is that there has been a proliferation of non-commercial uses and users. Civil society, whether it be individuals or NGOs, is a very energetic presence in cyberspace. From struggles around human rights, the environment, and workers strikes around the world to genuinely trivial pursuits, the Net has emerged as a powerful medium for non-elites to communicate, support each other's struggles and create the equivalent of insider groups at scales going from the local to the global.

The political and civic potential of these trends is enormous. It offers the possibility for interested citizens to act in concert. Several authors have examined the possibility of enhancing democratic practices through the formation of communities on the Net and the possible role of governments in supporting them.[12] The possibility of doing so transnationally at a time when a growing set of issues are seen as escaping the bounds of national states makes this even more significant. We are also seeing a greater variety of subcultures on the Net in the last few years after being dominated by young white men, especially from the US. The growth of global corporate actors has also profoundly altered the role of governmemt in the digital era, and, as a consequence has further raised the importance of civil society in electronic space as a force through which a multiplicity of public interests can, wittingly or not, resist the overwhelming influence of the new global corporate world.

III. State Regulation and the Internet

A different issue about sovereignty is raised by the possibilities of regulating the Net. It seems to me that if there is to be some kind of regulation it is going to be very different from what we have usually understood by this term. It is certainly the case that in many ways the Net escapes or overrides most conventional jurisdictions.

Here I would like to focus briefly on a fact that is too often left out of the discussion: there **is** a kind of central authority overseeing some of the crucial features of the Net having to do with addresses and numbers granting.[13] This does not mean that regulation is ipso facto possible. It merely signals that the representation of the Net as escaping all authority is simply inadequate.[14] The nature of this authority is not necessarily akin to regulatory authorities but it is a gate keeping system of sorts and raises the possibility of oversight

---

12 Digital City 1997; Calabrese and Borchert 1996; Calabrese and Burgelman 1999; Rheingold 1993. See also my review of various web sites of this type in Artforum November 1998 p.30

13 There are also more specific issues that may affect the regulation of particular forms of digital activity through a focus on infrastructre. There are different types of infrastructure for different types of digital activities, for instance, financial markets versus consumer wireless phones. This subject I have elaborated elsewhere. See "The State and the Global City" in Globalization and its Discontents.

14 For the most extreme version of this representation see John Perry Barlow's "Declaration of Independence of Cyberspace."

capacities. Even though these oversight capacities would entail considerable innovation in our concepts about regulation, they signal that there are possibilities overlooked in a faulty characterization of the architecture of the Net.

This centrally managed function of the Internet involves the control and assignment of the numbers that computers need to locate an address.[15] It therefore can instruct all the top "root servers" of the Net – the computers that execute address inquiries – and these will accept these instructions. This is, clearly, a power of sorts. For a long time it was not formalized, in good part because its origins lie in the first phase of the Internet. It is the power held by the group of computer scientists who invented the communication protocols and agreed on the standards that make the Net work today. They worked at debugging the systems over the last twenty years and did so not necessarily under contract by any agency in particular. It is a de-facto group which worked at making the Net workable since its beginnings. The particular function of assigning addresses is crucial and was for many years under the informal control of one particular scientist who named this function the "Internet Assigned Numbers Authority."

In the summer of 1998, the Internet Corporation for Assigned Names and Numbers (ICANN), now the group assigned to oversee the Net's address system, was established. It represents a formalization of the earlier authority.[16] It was basically started as a group of insiders with fairly lose and ineffective by-laws. By early 1999 it had implemented conflict-of-interest rules, opened up some board meetings, and worked towards developing a mechanism to elect board members in an effort to build in more accountability. It is today the subject of growing debate among various digital subcultures (e.g. see Nettime for summaries of the debates).

As the Net has grown and become more international there appears to be growing concern that a more organized and accountable system is necessary. This signals the presence of sectors with the will to strengthen and develop this central authority.

The US government's "Framework for Global Electronic Commerce," a blueprint for Internet governance, argues that because of the Internet's global reach and evolving technology, regulation should be kept to a minimum. It also suggests that in the few areas where rules are needed, such as privacy and taxation, policy should be made by quasigovernmental bodies such as the World Intellectual Property Organization (WIPO) or the OECD.

One of the issues with this type of proposal is the absence of transparency and the problems it brings with it. These become evident in one of the first big Net policy dilemmas: cybersquatting. (Private speculators seizing valuable corporate brandnames on the Internet

---

15 One could consider the community of scientists who have worked on making the Net workable and who have had to reach many agreements on a broad range of technical matters, as a sort of informal central "authority." In most other cultural settings they would probably have become a formal, recognizable body – with, one might add, considerable power. There is an interesting sociology here.

16 With the growth of business interest in the Net, the de-facto authority of the early pioneers of the Net and their logic for assigning addresses began to be criticized. For instance, firms found that their names had already been asigned to other parties and that there was little they could do; the whole idea of brandnames and intellectual property rights over a name was not part of the early Net culture.

and selling them back, at an enormous price, to the firms carrying those names.) Net addresses are important for establishing an identity online. So companies want to establish a rule that they are entitled to any domain names using their trademarks. But the Net is used for more than e-commerce, so consumer advocates say this rule would unfairly restrict the rights of schools, museums, political parties and other noncommercial Net users. However, in the deliberations that have taken place at WIPO, it is largely the large firms who are participating, in meetings that take place mostly behind doors. This privatizes the effort to design regulations for the Net.

While the purpose of these governing mechanisms is not about regulation as we have know it, their existence and, perhaps more importantly, the necessity of some such bodies, represents a significant operational opening for some sort of regulation/governance. This is often overlooked in many discussions about the Net and its freedoms.

IV. Distinguishing Private and Public Digital Space

The Internet is only one portion of the vast new world of digital space, and many of the dramatic features attributed to the Internet's power to neutralize sovereignty are actually features of private digital networks, such as those used in international finance. Many assertions about economic processes, dynamics and potentials are happening in private digital space and have little to do with the Internet. I consider this a serious, though fairly common, confusion.[17] Most financial activity and other significant digital economic activities take place in private digital networks.[18] Further, as I already mentioned, much of the use firms make of the Net today asumes the form of firewalled web sites and, increasingly, privatized "tunnels" – the new citadels on the Net. This is not likely to strengthen democratic practice.

Further, we must recognize that private digital networks are also making possible forms of power other than the distributed power made possible by public digital networks. The financial markets illustrate this well. The three properties of electronic networks: speed, simultaneity and interconnectivity have produced orders of magnitude far surpassing anything we had ever seen in financial markets.

Before the financial crisis in Asia hit the global market, turnover value was estimated at US$ 75 trillion – a figure that dwarfs the value of cross-border trade and investment. The consequence has been that the global capital market now has the power to discipline national governments, as became evident with the 1994-5 Mexico "crisis" and the 1997-8

17 When it comes to the broader subject of network power, most computer networks are private. It might be worth repeating that even if we just consider Internet Protocol compatible networks and we take the figures for the period preceding the explosion of business interest in the Net, also then most networks were private: Just counting networks as opposed to traffic volume, in 1994 there were about 40,000 IP compatible networks, but the Internet itself accounted for about 12,000 of these. That leaves a lot of network power that may not necessarily have the attributes of the Internet. Indeed, much of this is concentrated power and reproduces hierarchy rather than distributed power.

18 The growth of direct online investment does often use the Internet. It is mostly retail and represents a minor share of the overall global financial market. Even factoring in its expected tripling in value over the next 3 or 4 years will not give it the type of power of the global financial market I am discussing here.

Asian crisis, when investors were capable of leaving en masse taking out US$55 billion, and the foreign currency markets had the orders of magnitude to alter exchange rates radically for some of these currencies.[19]

It also may be significant that although in some ways the power of these financial electronic networks rests on a kind of distributed power, i.e. millions of investors and their millions of decisions, it ends up as concentrated power. The trajectory followed by what begins as a form of distributed power may assume many forms, in this case, one radically different from that of the Internet. It signals the possibility that digital network power is not inherently distributive. Intervening mechanisms can re-shape its organization. To keep it as a form of distributed power requires that it is embedded in a particular kind of structure.

Digital space, whether private or public, is partly embedded in actual societal structures and power dynamics: its topography weaves in and out of non-electronic space. In the case of private electronic space, this feature carries enormous implications for theory, for the results of the digitalization of economic activity, and for the conditions through which governments and citizens can act on this new electronic world of the economy and power. The embeddedness of private economic electronic space entails the formation of massive concentrations of infrastructure, not only worldwide dispersal, and a complex interaction between conventional communications infrastructure and digitalization. The notion of "global cities" captures this particular embeddedness of global finance in actual financial centers.[20]

There is no purely digital economy and no completely virtual corporation. This means that power, contestation, inequality, in brief, hierarchy, inscribe electronic space. And although the digitalized portions of these industries, particularly finance, have the capacity to subvert the established hierarchies, new hierarchies are being formed, born out of the existing material conditions underlying power and the new conditions created by electronic space.

V. Beyond the Internet's Impact: Sovereignty Reconfigured?

The growth of the Internet as a significant space for practices of various kinds is taking place at a time when we see a number of major transformations in national sovereignty. I find it quite impossible to consider the impact of the Internet on sovereignty as if sovereignty itself were a stable condition.

There are two issues here. One is the historicity of the character of sovereignty located in the state – that particular kind of intermediary. Over the last few years we have seen a shift of some components of this sovereignty to other entities – supra and sub-national as well

19 The other half of this argument has to do with questions of normativity — the fact that the global financial markets are not only capable of deploying raw power but also have produced a logic that now is seen as setting the criteria for "proper" economic policy. IMF conditionality has some of these features. There is an emerging literature on this. I have discussed this issue and some of the literature in Losing Control? chapter 2.

20 I examine some of these issues in "Global Financial Centers" Foreign Affairs, Vol.78, January/February 1999. The growth of electronic trading and electronic network alliances between major financial centers is allowing us to see the particular way in which digitalized markets are partly embedded in these vast concentrations of material resources and human talents which financial centers are.

as non governmental. Who gains legitimacy as a claimant under these new conditions? There are different capacities in different sectors. The Net could become an extrememly important public space for strengthening the claims of non-state actors that lack the resources of globally oriented corporations or of other sectors with considerable resources.

The second issue is the need to examine the assumption about the state as the exclusive representative of its people.[21] It is no longer simply a matter of the Liberal vs. the Realist interpretation. I find this frame confining in much of the debate about the Internet and sovereignty, even though I would agree with one of the lines of argumentation which holds that different states can be characterized either way and that depending on this they will be more or less affected by the Internet. Different intermediaries may emerge between the state and what it represents (i.e. the people), including private bodies in arenas where it used to be public bodies that governed.[22] Seeing the rise of markets and of transnational corporate actors, I cannot help but ask whether Liberal theory and its enactement in political or state practice necessarily imply a liberal state: we have historically perhaps seen this, but today the elements are there to reconfigure this association. At least some scholars argue that we are seeing the neo-liberal rather than the liberal state coming out of liberal policies.[23]

Further, if we are going to consider issues of sovereignty and democracy, then we must ask a critical question about what actors are gaining influence under conditions of digitization and whose claims are gaining legitimacy. For instance, it could be argued (and it is my argument) that private digital space has had a far sharper impact on questions of sovereignty than the Internet. The globalization and digitization of financial markets have made these markets a powerful presence. Indeed, the logic of the global capital markets is today not merely a condition of raw power but one with normative potential. The logic of these markets has contributed to the elaboration of a set of criteria for what is proper government conduct on the economy. This new power of the financial markets is partly a consequence of the orders of magnitude they have reached in good part through their digitalization and the fact that they are globally integrated, two conditions that are mutually reinforcing. The capacity of these markets to affect existing meanings of sovereignty is considerable and in my view, thus far has been greater than that of the Internet.[24]

New transnational regimes and institutions are creating systems that strengthen the claims of certain actors (corporations, the large multinational legal firms) and correspondingly weaken the position of smaller players and of states.[25] Ruggie has pointed out that the issue is not whether such new institutions and major economic actors will substitute national states but rather the possibility of major changes in the system of states: "global markets and transnationalized corporate structures...are not in the business of replacing states" yet they can have the potential for producing fundamental change in the system of states.[26]

---

21 See, for example Franck 1992; Jacobson 1996

22 For instance, the new public voice of some NGOs and of First-Nation people in international fora. For a more general discussion see Losing Control? chapters 1 and 3.

23 See, e.g. Cox, 1987; Panitch 1996.

24 I develop this in Losing Control?, chapter 2. See also The Global City. (Princeton University Press 1991).

25 I discuss this in Losing Control? chapter 1.

26 Ruggie (1993: 143)

What matters here is that global capital has made claims on national states and these have responded through the production of new forms of legality.[27] The new geography of global economic processes, the strategic territories for economic globalization, had to be produced, both in terms of the practices of corporate actors and the requisite infrastructure, and in terms of the work of the state in producing or legitimating new legal regimes.[28] One possible reading of recent developments in the earlier Mexico crisis and in the current Asian crisis, but also in a more structural context – the adoption of neoliberal economic principles by governments wanting to join the global economic markets – is that these markets have emerged as nonstate "actors" whose claims have acquired legitimacy.[29]

This then invites us to raise a whole set of questions about how certain actors have gained this legitimacy in their claims, and in the case of the specific concerns here, how has the development of digitalization favored some over other actors. Put this way, it still leaves unadddressed the question about the future impact of the Internet. And here I would say that commercialization as discussed earlier may well dampen the impact of the Internet in terms of political practices. I return to my earlier point about the importance of strengthening the variety of cultures active on the Net, the importance of struggles for greater bandwidth for civil society actors and for those organizations who cannot pay for increasingly scarce bandwidth.

In my reading the risk on this particular issue is self complacency about the democratic potential of the Internet. The potential is there but we cannot take it for granted, nor can we assume that commercialization is simply going to strengthen this democratic potential. It may well be the case that in the context of the former centrally planned economies of Central Europe and the former Soviet Union, commerce on the Internet is a democratizing practice – at least for a while. But the growing practice of privatizing portions of the Net, electronic commerce and the – almost inevitably associated – strengthening of intellectual property rights on the Internet are to be taken seriously. If uses by civil society multiply, grow, strengthen, raise the interconnections among various nonstate actors in various locations across the globe, then there is probably less to worry about. But right now, there is not enough of this, and the risk that we are left with a poor man's Internet, with slow connections, in competition for bandwidth with entities that can pay for expensive, or for that matter not so expensive but still involving costs that often cannot be afforded by many community organizations or underfunded sectors of civil society.

---

27 In many ways the state is involved in this emerging transnational governance system. But it is a state that has itself undergone transformation and participated in legitimating a new doctrine about the role of the state in the economy. Central to this new doctrine is a growing consensus among states to further the growth and strength of the global economy.(See, e.g. several chapters in Mittelman 1996).

28 Representations that characterize the national state as simply losing significance fail to capture this very important dimension, and reduce what is happening to a function of a putative global-national duality – what one wins, the other loses. I view deregulation not simply as a loss of control by the state but as a crucial mechanism to negotiate the juxtaposition of the inter-state consensus to pursue globalization and the fact that national legal systems remain as the major, or crucial instantiation through which guarantees of contract and property rights are enforced.

29 There are two distinct issues here. One is the formation of new legal regimes that negotiate between national sovereignty and the transnational practices of corporate economic actors. The second issue is the particular content of this new regime, one which contributes to strengthen the advantages of certain types of economic actors and to weaken those of others.

VI. Conclusion

The Internet is only one portion of the vast new world of digital space, and many of the dramatic features attributed to the Internet's power to neutralize sovereignty are actually features of private digital networks, such as those used in international finance. Similarly, the key about many of the current transformations and their potential to limit sovereignty may not be the elimination of sovereignty but its unbundling and partial relocation to other supra-, sub and non-national institutions.

References cited

ADILKNO. The Media Archive. World Edition. New York: Autonomedia, and Amsterdam: ADILKNO 1998

Cox, Robert: Production, Power, and World Order: Social Forces in the Making of History. New York: Columbia University Press 1987

Franck, Thomas M.: The Emerging Right to Democratic Governance. In: American Journal of International Law. Vol. 86, 1 (1992), 46-91

Calabrese, Andrew / Mark Borchert: Prospects for elecronic democracy in the United States: rethinking communication and social policy. In: Media, Culture and Society. Vol. 18 (1996); 249-268

Calabrese, Andrew / Jean-Claude Burgelman (eds.): Communication, Citizenship and Social Policy. New York: Rowman & Littlefield 1999

Dencker, Klaus Peter (ed.): Labile Ordnungen: Netze Denken. Hamburg: Verlag Hans Bredow 1997

Garcia, Linda: The Globalization of Telecommunications and Information. In: Drake, William J. (ed.), The New Information Infrastructure: Strategies for U.S. Policy. New York: Twentieth Century Fund Press 1995, 75-92

Graham, Stephen / Simon Marvin: Telecommunications and the City: Electronic Spaces, Urban Places. London and New York: Routledge 1996

Kroker, Arthur / Marilouise: Hacking the future: stories for the flesh-eating 90s. New York: St. Martin's Press 1996

Lovink, Geert: Grundrisse einer Netzkritik. In *Dencker* (ed.), 1997, op. cit: pp. 234-245.

Nettime: Net Critique. Compiled by *Geert Lovink* and *Pit Schultz*. Berlin: Edition ID-Archiv 1997

Munker, Stefan / Alexander Roesler (eds.): Mythos Internet. Frankfurt: Suhrkamp 1997

Rapp, L. 1995: Toward French Electronic Highways. The New Legal Status of Data Transmissions in France. In: *Rapp, L.* (ed.), Telecommunications and Space Journal. Vol. 2 (Annual Edition), 1995, 231-246

Rotzer, Florian: Die Telepolis: Urbanität im digitalen Zeitalter. Mannheim: Bollmann 1995

Jacobson, David: Rights Across Borders: Immigration and the Decline of Citizenship. Baltimore: Johns Hopkins Press 1996

Mittelman, James (ed.): Globalization: Critical Reflections. Yearbook of International Political Economy. Vol. 9. Boulder, Colo.: Lynne Riener Publishers. 1996

Panitch, Leo: Rethinking the Role of the State in an Era of Globalization. In: *Mittelman* (ed.), 1996, op cit.

Ruggie, John Gerard: Territoriality and beyond: problematizing modernity in international relations. International Organization 47, 1 (Winter 1993), 139-174

Sassen, Saskia: Globalization and Its Discontents. Selected Essays. New York: New Press 1998

— Losing Control? Sovereignty in an Age of Globalization. The 1995 Columbia Univ. L. Hastings Schoff Memorial Lectures. New York: Columbia University Press 1996

— The Global City: New York, London, Tokyo. Princeton University Press 1995

Stiftinger, Edeltraud / Edward Strasser (eds.): Binary Myths: Cyberspace-The Renaissance of Lost Emotions. Vienna: Zukunfts- und Kulturwerkstätte 1997

Christoph Engel

The Internet and the Nation State*

Creative destruction is how *Joseph Schumpeter* described the effect of competition[1]. Of course this sounds scornful in the ears of the affected companies, their shareholders and employees. Today, nation states also suffer from competitive pressures and consequently feel similarly affected. Under competition their performance degenerates to being providers of a bundle of services. Many of the elements of this bundle are available from other government or private providers. Economically speaking, monopolistic competition[2] reigns instead of the monopoly of the state. This term is used by economists to describe a state of affairs in which a competitor offers a reasonable substitute, not an identical product.[3] The Internet is, of course, not the only reason for the competition between various systems growing more intense.[4] But, the Internet is simultaneously both a factor and an indicator of globalisation. Conversely, the effect of the Internet on the nation state is not restricted to the possibility of avoiding national regulation.This is just the phenomenon which has drawn the greatest public attention to itself.

While technology does not determine social and political processes, it is not without influence.[5] This examination therefore begins with a short description of the Internet phenomenon. Less of relevance is the Internet in its present form, as its potential for the future. Because of its stormy development, a forecast is only possible assuming a whole series of indeterminate factors (II) Since this is the case, the effect of the Internet on the nation state is not a causal one (III). It does, however, result in consequences for domestic power (IV) as well as external sovereignty (V). It follows from both that many tried and tested solutions of the international community for overcoming international conflicts are losing their effectiveness (VI). On the other hand, the need for supranational solutions will become greater rather than smaller on account of the Internet (VII). But this does not necessarily mean anarchy. However, grounds do exist for searching for newer solutions that are better suited to the characteristics of the

---

* The original German version of this paper has been prepared for the German Society for Public International Law. It has been presented at the Kiel meeting of the Society in March 1999. It will be published in the *Berichte der Deutschen Gesellschaft für Völkerrecht*. I am indebted for the translation to *Patricia Adler* and for valuable comments to *Adrienne Héritier* and *Christoph Knill*.

1 *Schumpeter, Joseph A.*, Kapitalismus, Capitalism, Socialism and Democracy, New York 1942 (German version Kapitalismus, Sozialismus und Demokratie, Tübingen 1993) 134 et seq.; see also *id.:* Theorie der wirtschaftlichen Entwicklung. Eine Untersuchung über Unternehmergewinn, Kapital, Kredit, Zins und den Konjunkturzyklus, 1917 /Berlin[9] 1997, 88 et seq.

2 *Wolf Schäfer:* Globalisierung: Entmonopolisierung des Nationalen ?, in: *Hartmut Berg* (editor): Globalisierung der Wirtschaft: Ursachen - Formen - Konsequenzen (Schriften des Vereins für Socialpolitik NF 263) Berlin 1999, 9-21 (10 and passim).

3 The concept has been developed by *Edward H. Chamberlin:* The Theory of Monopolistic Competition. A Reorientation of the Theory of Value, Cambridge, Mass. 1933; *Joan Robinson:* The Economics of Imperfect Competition. London 1933. A modern overview is offered by *Jean Tirole*, The Theory of Industrial Organization, Cambridge, Mass. 1988 (chapter 7).

4 Enlightening on this concept the collective contributions in the following volume *Lüder Gerken* (Ed): Competition among Institutions. Houndmills 1995.

5 More under III.

Internet (VIII). Looking at these solutions as a whole, the elements of a new international order of both power and values can be found (IX).

I. Characteristics of the Internet

The reason why the Internet potentially has considerable influence on social and political processes can be deducted from a short list of its characteristics. The Internet is global (1), decentralized (2), timeless (3), very cheap (4), very simple (5), digital (6), individual (7) and, if so desired, also wireless (8), very secure (9), secret (10) and anonymous (11).

1. Global

In the Internet, distance no longer plays a role.[6] This is true both economically as well as technologically. Internet users only pay telephone charges for the connection between their Internet provider and the next interface point. Nowadays, such interface points are to be found in almost every local loop. Frequent users of the Internet can avail themselves of package offers. Having no infrastructure of its own, the Internet uses all transmission paths currently available.Technically speaking, the Internet is a service rather than a net. The infrastructure of the Internet is completely international.[7]

The ordinary user is often unable to tell where an addressee is permanently resident. This is because of the so-called domain names. In order for two computers to be able to communicate via the Internet, both must have an a unique address. This occurs with the aid of so-called IP-addresses. But no person could remember the long series of numbers that one needs in order to be able to correctly identify all the computers around the world that have been networked. The task of the domain name is to transform these combinations of numbers into abbreviations with which our imagination can identify. Two parallel systems exist according to the rules used to date. One class of domain names ends with a national abbreviation, for example .de. This signifies a country classification. But there is no national abbreviation .us, a circumstance which is easy to explain, since the Internet originated in the United States. Even today, by far the majority of Internet users are Americans. A second system exists with the abbreviations .edu, .com, .net, .org, .gov, .mil and .int. All these classes of domain names are used globally, and not just in the USA.[8] The email address of a German customer of America Online reads, for example, ...@aol.com.

Most users cannot infer the place of origin from a domain name, but a state can do so. However, it must then conduct a considerable amount of investigation work. It becomes

---

6 *David G. Post:* Governing Cyberspace, in: Wayne Law Review 43 (1996) 155: [at footnote 15]: "Cyberspace [...] does not merely weaken the significance of physical location, it destroys it"; [at footnote 16]: "events in cyberspace [...] do not cross geographical borders [...], they ignore the existence of borders altogether".

7 *Ditmar Brock:* Wirtschaft und Staat im Zeitalter der Globalisierung. Von nationalen Volkswirtschaften zur globalisierten Wirtschaft, in: Aus Politik und Zeitgeschichte, 33-34/97, 12-19 (16 et seq.).

8 A very good, easy to read introduction into the system of domain names by *Klaus W. Grewlich*: Governance in "Cyberspace". Access and Public Interest in Global Communications [forthcoming], Chapter VII.

even more difficult when the use of the Internet technically also no longer takes place within a single territory. There are mainly two reasons for this. From the point of view of an Internet user, distance hardly plays a role any longer. But it does make a difference to the network architecture whether an Internet page has to be downloaded from the USA or whether it is available on a local server. That is why Internet pages that are commonly used are 'mirrored' onto local servers. They are then available for downloading not only once, but possibly many times in the most diverse variety of countries.

In addition, the situation arises more and more frequently that data is processed on a combination of several computers rather than on a single computer. A classic example is the employee who dials from home into his company's central computer and works on a document with his colleagues there.[9] Lufthansa, for example, processes used flight tickets in India.[10] Surfing the Internet, possible through the use of hypertext, also belongs at this juncture. Hypertext is commonly highlighted in blue on most Internet pages. Clicking on it brings the user to another page. In this manner, the user often changes back and forth between servers in various countries during a single session.

2. Decentralized

Regulation is much easier when it only has to control a few linked interfaces instead of thousands of people or processes.[11] That is why it is of significance for the likelihood of regulation that the degree of centralization in the Internet is extremely small. It was originally created in order to maintain communication paths in the event of a nuclear strike.[12] One can state, without exaggeration, that 1% standardization stands in opposition to 99% diversity.[13] The only items that are standardized are the routing of the signal, quality standards, protocol standards, the IP addresses already mentioned and the domain names.[14]

Since the Internet is not a single network but a net of networks, control of it is, on the one hand, made more difficult but, on the other hand, entry into the market of network providers is facilitated. To be an Internet provider, one only needs a single server, costing less than US $ 50,000.[15] The customers of this one provider are not only able to communicate amongst themselves, but also with people and computers all over the world. Economically speaking: since the Internet is standardized at such a low level, it is easy for a new provider to exploit the network externalities of the whole Internet. The

---

9 *Michael Dertouzos:* What Will Be. How the New World of Information Will Change Our Lives. San Francisco 1997, 109 et seq.

10 More under IV 2 c) on the interconnected possibility of cutting value creation chains.

11 The plastic notion "regulation targets bottlenecks" comes from *Paul David.*

12 Fitting on the history of the Internet is *Raymund Werle*: The Impact of Information Networks on the Structure of Political Systems. in: *Christoph Engel/Kenneth Keller (Eds.):* Understanding the Impact of Global Networks on Local Social, Political and Cultural Values 159-185 (177).

13 *Sharon Eisner Gilett/Mitchell Kapor:* The Self-Governing Internet. Coordination by Design. http://ccs.mit.edu/CCSWP197.html (15.02.199) [8-10].

14 Id.

15 *Henry H. Perritt:* Cyberspace and Sovereignty, in: Journal of International Legal Studies 3 (1997) 155-204 (161).

critical mass problem that represents a key market entry barrier for other network goods plays only a marginal role with the Internet.[16]

3. Timeless

The composer *Wolfgang Rihm* described the Internet as the medium "in which time and space meet".[17] Initially, this sentence appears to have a very superficial meaning, but those academics who work together with American colleagues quickly learn to value e-mail and not only because of its cost effectiveness. It is more a case of the marginalization of time zone differences between the two continents in their communication exchanges. They no longer need to squeeze everything into the short afternoon interval, in which both are seated at their desks. Companies that are globally active possess even finer-tuned instruments in order to maximize quasi-simultaneous timing.[18] Nowadays, some multinational companies develop products 24 hours a day. When a German engineer goes home, he hands his half-finished product to his American colleague who, in turn, passes it to a Japanese colleague several hours later.

The Internet bridges long periods and not just ones of a few hours length. This characteristic is shared with all retrieval services. However, in contrast with services such as pay-per-view, the decentralized Internet is missing a regular clean-up facility. It also lacks a culture of forgetfulness.[19] Information which is made available on the network stays there for an indeterminate amount of time. Search engines will discover it even years later and give it - almost[20] - the same weighting as a message from the same day. Even if the originator wanted to remove the message, he cannot be sure of success, thanks to the mirror technology already mentioned. The fact that the message is erased from the original server does not remove it from the net. While a special search software does exist that is also intended to find mirror images, it does not normally enjoy complete success.

4. Very Cheap

It costs the same amount to communicate via Internet with one's neighbours as with an islander from Fiji, and this amount is minute. This not only holds true for transmission costs to the next interface, but also for the activities of an Internet provider and for the services that can be used via the network. Free e-mail is almost standard, and some companies even exist that charge users no fee at all for their whole Internet access.[21] It is

---

16 Main texts on the economic background: *Michael L. Katz/Carl Shapiro:* Technology Adoption in the Presence of Network Externalities, in: Journal of Political Economy 94 (1986) 822-841; *id.:* Product Introduction with Network Externalities, in: Journal of Industrial Economics 40 (1992) 55-83; an overview of the literature published since then is provided by *Manfred J. Holler:* Modellierung von Netzwerkeffekten und Ansätze industriepolitischer Aussagen, in: Jahrbuch für Neue Politische Ökonomie 16 (1997) 90-114.

17 I thank *Ernst-Joachim Mestmäcker* for this tip.

18 *Dertouzos* (footnote 9) 93 and passim.

19 I owe this thought to *Nicole te Heesen*.

20 All search engines sort the hits. Under the criteria there is also regularly the number of occurrences in which they have recently been accessed.

21 They must then of course finance themselves indirectly; more on this under II 3b).

almost an integral part of the Internet's culture for a user to be able to access any services offered free-of-charge. Those seeking user fees must offer very attractive contents indeed.

All these reasons point to Internet use being a low-cost decision. In the past few years, economists have shown much interest in such decisions.[22] People act differently in such situations. Cost calculations are relegated to playing only a marginal role. People even forego the consequent pursuit of a coherent utility function. The desire to participate, the feeling of solidarity, or even a type of activity on the off-chance, increases. Instruments to control human behaviour that assume rational behaviour, no longer fit. It therefore makes little sense to make decisions a little cheaper or a little more expensive. That does not mean that such behaviour is completely incapable of being guided. But the state's well-tried knowledge in directing people in high-cost situations is of little use in this one.[23]

5. Very Simple

The Internet community uses its own language. What is generally called a letter by most people, is derogatively called snail-mail. E-mail is not only much faster, but is also a lot simpler for a computer user, since he would also write an ordinary letter on the computer. Now, instead of having to print it out, put it in an envelope, attach a stamp and bring it to the postbox, with e-mail, he simply points the mouse to the 'send' icon or key. Responses to incoming mail can be made within two minutes using the 'reply' function. One can also simultaneously send the same piece of mail to an infinite number of persons via a mailing list. Academics working from home soon value access to databanks and electronic newsletters. Instead of previously having to go to a library and switch on a photocopier, an academic now has the necessary information at his fingertips on a PDF-file within the space of a minute. He can even conduct electronic research on the file.

All this appears trivial, but it brings about a fundamental change in the user's behaviour. Hardly anyone would exchange 30 letters a day with others, but no-one considers 30 e-mails to be shocking. Because it has become so simple, one sends three lines to someone with whom one would previously not even have corresponded. It costs scarcely any additional effort to allow other persons to participate in the exchange of ideas via copies or blind copies. Those who threaten to sink under the weight of information can use filters to divide it into manageable units.

---

22 This thought is primarily attributable to *Gebhard Kirchgässner.* He expounded on this idea in three essays: Towards a Theory of Low-Cost Decisions, in: European Journal of Political Economy 8 (1972) 305-320; *Gebhard Kirchgässner/Werner Pommerehne:* Low-Cost Decisions as a Challenge to Public Choice, in: Public Choice 77 (1993) 107-115; *Gebhard Kirchgässner:* Bemerkungen zur Minimalmoral, in: Zeitschrift für Wirtschafts- und Sozialwissenschaften 116 (1996) 223-251.

23 This is one of the reasons why the Internet leads to the restructuring of statehood, more under IV 4 and V 7.

6. Digital

All Internet communication takes place digitally. Texts, sounds and images are separated into yes/no combinations. This has a series of important consequences. Firstly, all these types of content can employ the same method of transmission. There is no more need, technically speaking, for separate channels for data transmission, for different telephone and television cables.[24] More precisely formulated: all these transmission paths are in competition with each other.

In addition, digital information can be attached to any chosen product. Users can add images, sounds or video sequences to their home pages. Individual components can also be compiled ad hoc from diverse sources and the visible or audible information can be given control signals. In this manner, a differentiated copyright protection can be established.[25]

A final point is that one can also compress digital information. Using video sequences as an example: images not registered by the human eye are immediately cut out of the amount of information via a special programme. Moreover, the retina gains the impression of moving images through the rapid sequencing of static pictures. But only a small part of the image changes from one static image to the next, an effect which is exploited by image compression, which only transfers changes in previous images. Since compressed files need much less band width and memory, narrow band information channels can also be used to transfer complex contents.

7. Individual

The Internet is an ideal instrument for transforming mass media into an individual medium. The coarsest filter is a search engine. Those who know how to operate these engines elegantly can find the information they seek relatively quickly by connecting several search terms. Frequently used search sites can be stored. Some newspapers supply filters that the user places like a grid over the complete range of news offers. This procedure can be expanded to the whole programme of a publishing house, or even larger parts of the Internet.[26] Even more effective are search engines with a learning ability. They store information about what sites a user has actively accessed in the past, and then compare this user profile with those of other users. This allows technology, so to speak, to draw analogies with a good success rate.[27] The recommendation lists of Amazon.com function in this fashion. Each book offers links to other books that previous buyers have also purchased in significant numbers.[28]

8. Wireless

Since only yes/no data are transported via Internet, it basically makes no difference whether a wire or wireless transmission path is used. The residents of thinly-populated, rural areas will therefore in future be less severely disadvantaged from the outset than

---

24 See II 2 below on band-width problems.

25 See further VII 2.

26 More on this by *Dertouzos* (footnote 9) 121.

27 *Dertouzos* (footnote 9) 114 f. describes an example for a choice of music.

28 See VII 3 and VIII 6b) concerning obvious data protection problems.

previously the case. Or, more specifically formulated towards the situation in Germany: a wired universal service for the Internet is technical nonsense. In thinly-populated areas, it is sufficient to have a wireless connection, which is consistently much cheaper.

Wireless transmission also opens up completely new possibilities of use. Bluetooth, the most advanced wireless project, comes from the United States. It uses radio frequences, and produces wireless connections with up to one Mb/s at distances of up to 10 metres.[29] Using this technology, the electronic household has become a real possibility. By carrying a small transmitter and receiver, one can simultaneously control all household appliances while walking past. Small transmitter and receiver stations, for which one could, for example, consider using the small telephone boxes on the street, would allow practically permanent online use.[30]

The international impact of the Internet is further increased by satellite transmission. In this respect, however, the traditional direct transmission satellites are of lesser importance. They are put into orbit in such a way as to appear to be located at a fixed point above the earth. However, this point is so far away that a great deal of energy is expended for the return journey. Energy is the scarcest good in space, because it can only be stored via solar collectors. This is where the technical preference for lower orbitting satellites comes in. However, even here, the signal's transmission takes a few fractions of a second which, although not detrimental to some services such as retrieval services or e-mail, poses a big disadvantage to interactive services.

While the lower-flying satellites permit global communication betweeen businessmen, they also represent an attractive alternative for reaching users in countries that cut themselves off completely from the international flow of information or in countries that attempt to force this information to flow through the eye of a needle controlled by them. North Korea and Myanmar belong to the first category[31], China and Singapore to the second.[32] A preliminary system is already on the market. A cellular phone for use with this Iridium network currently costs around US-$ 1,800, with the company charging 80 cents per minute of use, but these prices are expected to drop. The second system, Teledesic, is due to go into service in 2002. It will have a much higher band width and will also allow the transmission of moving pictures, but be no more expensive than Iridium is today. This system is also noteworthy because almost all of its intelligence will be located inside the satellite. Practically the only possibility that will be left to nation states will be to proceed directly against users.[33]

---

29 Technical and economic details can be found on the following website: http://www.sss-mag.com/ssnews.html#3 (23.02.1999).

30 See *Dertouzos* (footnote 9) 113-138 on the fairly futuristic sounding social consequences.

31 *A. Michael Froomkin:* Flood Control on the Information Ocean. Living with Anonymity, Digital Cash and Distributed Databases, in: University of Pittsburgh, Journal of Law and Commerce 15 /1996) 395 (445).

32 *Jack Goldsmith:* Against Cyberanarchy, in: University of Chicago Law Review 65 (1988) 1199-1250 (1228 with references)

33 I owe all this information to *Robert Spinrad*.

9. Very Secure

Internet communication is very secure. Indeed, as already mentioned, it was originally created in order to maintain communication channels even in the event of a nuclear war.[34] The technical reason for this lies in the packet-switched character of transmission.[35] The complete message is broken down into small data packets. Each packet is wrapped up, so to speak, with details that give information about the sender and recipient and which assign the packet to precisely this message. These data packets can now take completely different paths through the network. If a package fails to arrive or is not fast enough, the recipient sends an error message to the sender. The missing packet is then sent via another transmission path.[36] This all serves to provide protection from the collapse of transmission paths and also from deliberate disruptions by an intervening state.[37]

10. Secret

Microsoft has just learned the painful lesson in the current cartel process being filed against it: e-mails are no more secure than postcards. The American cartel authorities have intercepted almost 6,000 e-mails from Microsoft and are now able to present an almost perfect trail of evidence against the firm. Users therefore have a great deal of interest in encrypting the contents of an e-mail before transmitting it. Encryption also serves as a tool for authentification purposes. It ensures that the transmitted contents really do originate from the person sending the e-mail and that they have not been changed in the meantime.[38]

The development of data encryption technology has come a long way. Of greatest practical use are solutions employing two different keys: a public and a private one.[39] The use of two different keys prevents the key itself being transmitted directly from the sender to the recipient. This is important, because it could be quite easily intercepted at this point. However, with the two key system, the technical instrument needed to de-encrypt the message, i.e. the public key, can be transmitted quite openly. In practice, many people state it on their homepage. They then only have to prevent someone acquiring the second, private key.

Those who would like to do so, may proceed a step further. If an encrypted message is intercepted, only jumbled-up data is received, but one is then immediately aware that someone has sent or received an encrypted message. In western industrial nations, this will hardly be of significance, since most people will routinely encrypt their electronic

---

34 See no. 2 again above.

35 *Grewlich* Cyberspace (footnote 8) Chapter Two. 3..

36 I owe all these details to *Robert Spinrad.*

37 In the words of *Miles Kahler:* "jamming is hard to implement in the net".

38 *Grewlich* Cyberspace (footnote 8) Chapter Six.

39 An overview of other solutions is given by *Grewlich* Cyberspace (footnote 8) Chapter Six. 1.; for further details see *Dertouzos* (footnote 9) 99-107 and for a comprehensive overview *Kenneth W. Dam/Herbert S. Lin* (Eds.) Cryptography's Role in Securing the Information Society. Committee to Study National Cryptography Policy. Computer Science and Telecommunications Board. Commission on Physical Sciences, Mathematics and Applications. National Research Council, Washington (National Academy Press) 1996 and in particular the appendices on pages 343-676.

traffic.[40] This will not fail on account of the cost, since a very good and effective encryption system, Pretty Good Privacy, is available free-of-charge on the Internet.[41] This will be different, however, in totalitarian states. But it technically presents no difficulties to hide an encrypted message behind an apparently quite harmless one. This is how a pornographic picture can manage to get into an Arabian country, encrypted as a religious hymn.[42]

No encryption system is perfect. Secret services or criminal investigation authorities are able, albeit with much difficulty, to de-encrypt coded messages. The USA traditionally view encryption technologies as weapons and subject them to strict export controls.[43] Furthermore, security authorities in many countries insist that the private key is deposited in a location which they can access in an emergency.[44] But there is, once again, a relatively simple countermeasure to this as well. One initially encrypts a message with a private key that has not been deposited. This message that has been encrypted once is then encrypted a second time, with a code whose private portion has been deposited at the deposit location. The message is then unobtrusive to scanners owned by the state. They appear to have been encrypted in a permissible manner.[45] The only real weak spots that remain are a) the moment in which the signal is coded and b) the moment in which it is encoded.[46] If the computer is offline at this point, however, it is extremely difficult for the supervisory authorities to exploit these weak spots.

11. Anonymous

Anonymous letters have always been in existence. But the Internet combines the availability of fairly extensive anonymity together with very little effort needed to employ it. Chat groups even expressly cultivate a culture of pseudonyms, whose attraction lies precisely in the fact that the persons do not meet in real life and that they therefore do not need to fear their pseudonyms being exposed. This is a type of electronic masquerade. If he so desired, the person running the chat group could pull the mask off each visitor's face, because the transmission of the data packets, as we know, only works because each computer is uniquely identified via an IP address.[47] An investigator doesn't even have to simultaneously determine the communications path, since who spoke with whom at any particular time is noted in the so-called log files.

Just as an extortioner is able to put on a pair of gloves and stick letters onto a piece of paper from a glossy magazine, an Internet user can make it very difficult for others to identify him. First of all, he can make the IP address illegible, by passing the connection via an anonymizer. These are so-called remailers. They expressly see their task as removing the sender's original IP address and replacing it with their own IP address. If

40 See further details under VIII 6 b) on encryption as a means of aiding oneself.
41 http://www.nai.com/default_pgp.asp (15.03.1999)
42 This plastic example is from *Dertouzos* (footnote 9) 290.
43 The investigation of this policy is the central theme of the report Cryptography's Role in Securing the Information Society (footnote 39) 113-166 and 249-264.
44 See footnote just quoted for a comprehensive explanation, 167-215 and 265-285.
45 *Grewlich* Cyberspace (footnote 8), Chapter Six. 2. 2. 3..
46 I owe this tip to *Robert Spinrad.*
47 See no. 9 already quoted above.

one uses several remailers, the prosecution authorities cannot even resort to applying pressure to the remailer because only the first remailer would be able to establish a connection to the sender[48]. The user can also employ an electronic agent that executes search and download operations in a preprogrammed, anonymous manner.[49]

If the user is part of a larger community, he can additionally hide behind the firewall which separates the Intranet from the Internet. The task of such firewalls is to precisely make visible no more than a relatively large address space, not the actual IP addresses. And finally, one can normally log into internal networks from any of the computers attached to that net. So even if an investigation authority was able to find out the IP address, it would still not know who had used that computer.[50] The same problem is posed by Internet cafes, of which a poignant example exists: For years, Francois Mitterand hid his cancer problems from the French people. After his death, his doctor wrote a book about this concealment. Just before the book was delivered to retailers, Mitterand's family successfully obtained a court order preventing its delivery to retailers. But a few days later, the cunning owner of a pre-publication copy scanned in the complete text in an Internet cafe and made it available on the net.

II. Unknown Factors

This paper argues *de lege ferenda*, not *de lege lata.* A glance at today's reality allows us to judge whether the Internet poses a problem at all for the nation state. In particular, it helps us determine to what extent features of the Internet clash with historic conditions for the nation state. A reaction by the legal system only makes sense, however, if these effects are still present at the moment the legal instruments are actually employed. We thus face the task of a three-fold prognosis. The Internet can change, and the nation state and the society which supports it can take on a different character. Finally, we have to assess what influence the instruments on hand will have on the changed nation state. The most robust part of this task is an analysis of the effects of technology on state and society.[51] To forecast the effect of governance tools is already much more demanding. This is because they impact on social and political processes, and not on a process belonging to natural science.[52] Even more challenging is the prognosis of how reality will develop under these influences. We are already uncertain as to how quickly the Internet will spread (1). The qualitative development of the net also contains some unknown factors (2). It is particularly hard to forecast the extent to which the net and the services offered on it will become commercialized (3) and whether the Internet will differentiate into language and culture zones (4). Finally, although there is more or less agreement that the decisive problem in the age of the Internet will be an information flood rather than information scarcity, much remains to be done in developing corresponding instruments to resolve this problem (5).

---

48 See *Froomkin* for more on anonymity techniques UPittsbJIC 1996 (footnote 31) 414-427.

49 *Dirk Baecker:* Networking the Net, in: *Christoph Engel/Kenneth Keller (Eds.)* Understanding the Impact of Global Networks on Local Social, Political and Cultural Values 93-111 (102).

50 I owe this information to *Thomas Feldkamp.*

51 See also below III.

52 See more under IV - V.

1. Market Saturation

It is already hard enough to make reliable statements about the number of persons who are currently able to use the Internet. One estimate, which is probably somewhat optimistic, assumes that, in June 1998, 70.2 million persons in the USA (12.2 million in Germany) had access to it. This corresponds to around 35% of the U.S. and around 15 % of the German population.[53] It is even harder to predict future penetration rates. It can only be said with certainty that the opening of markets in industrial countries is proceeding at a stormy pace.

A conceptional reason can at least be found for this that lies in the dynamic characteristics of network goods, as already discussed.[54] There are two thresholds, if one stylizes the experience that has so far been gained with the spread of such goods. The first threshold decides on whether the service on offer can continue to exist or whether it must be removed from the market. This threshold has almost certainly been passed with the Internet. A second threshold makes the network good almost indispensible to certain circles of people. In Germany, for example, almost no-one can imagine living without a telephone nowadays. This second threshold has almost certainly not been reached for the whole of the German population as far as the Internet is concerned. But, in some circles, it is becoming more and more difficult to image not being able to be reached electronically. A good example is found in the sciences, where e-mail is almost obligatory for anyone wishing to maintain international contacts.

The speed with which the Internet will reach large circles of the German population will probably depend on two inter-related factors: price trends and making signals pass the last mile. At this juncture, the development of the completely decentralized Internet therefore ultimately also rests on the development of the local networks that were up till now completely centralized. Or, to formulate it more figuratively: national telecommunications policy is also a central factor in the development of the Internet. In Germany, it is not yet settled whether real competition can develop on the last mile among several network operators, or whether just highly regulated service competition on the networks of Deutsche Telekom will prove feasible.[55]

2. Qualitative Network Development

Three paths in network development have particular importance for user behaviour and thereby also a social and political effect. The most important question is how bandwidth will develop. As long as considerable advances fail to be made in this regard, moving pictures and multimedia applications will remain at the periphery.[56] The real bottleneck

---

53 *Werle* in *Engel/Keller* (footnote 12) 159-185 (177).

54 See point 2 above.

55 Further details, see *Christoph Engel/Günter Knieps:* Die Vorschriften des Telekommunikationsgesetzes über den Zugang zu wesentlichen Leistungen. Eine juristisch-ökonomische Untersuchung (Law and Economics of International Telecommunications 37) Baden-Baden 1998.

56 Technically, however, the possibility exists of using up to 1 Mb/sec already today. Moving pictures can be transferred in real time without impairing quality. Since the architecture of the net was not originally intended for this, this however disturbs many other users; more on this from *Michael Hutter:* The Commercialization of the Internet. A Progress Report, in: *Christoph Engel-*

here, both currently and in the foreseeable future, is again the last mile.[57] At the moment, long-range connection capacity is also in short supply, but both technical and economic solutions to this problem are certain to be found soon.[58]

The next indeterminate factor also principally results from the uncertain future of the last mile. A private Internet user typically logs in just for the period in which he uses it and then immediately leaves the net. While there is, meanwhile, a whole range of Internet providers who charge fairly reasonable prices for 24 hour use of the net, most telecommunications suppliers levy prohibitively expensive charges for a quasi-permanent connection to the local network. Where connections to the local network are offered by competitors of Deutsche Telekom, a few, fairly cheap, flat-rate arrangements are however already in existence. If such tariffs achieve a breakthrough, the behaviour of users will change. Only then will one be able to speak of 'living on the web' in Germany.

Finally, uncertainty remains concerning the development of net and service architecture over the coming years. To date, Internet traffic has primarily been conducted via the classic telecommunications networks. If completely identical or similar contents are to be sent simultaneously to many people, the switches of this net will be burdened heavily. Technically and economically, it therefore makes sense to create nets with a hybrid architecture appropriate for hybrid services lying midway between personal and mass communication, alongside the traditional net for point to point traffic. Mailing lists or customized, filtered, news services could then be distributed much more effectively.[59] It is equally unclear how the system's facade of computers, the so-called portals, will develop. The operating system traditionally served as the technical bridge for connecting varying hardware and software configurations. Since more and more computers are networked, the browser is increasingly taking over this function.[60] If this

---

Kenneth Keller (Eds.) Understanding the Impact of Global Networks on Local Social, Political and Cultural Values 73-92 (76).

57 In most countries, it consists of an analogue telephone wire/cable. It simultaneously combines two disadvantages. The original digital signals must then be converted into analogue signals with a modem and reconverted into digital signals by the receiver with a second modem. In addition, a telephone wire only has a capacity of 60 Kb. Germany belongs to the few countries with a relatively large number of ISDN connections. They are digital and have double the bandwidth. Larger capacity cables to consumer's homes are found in California and Massachusetts; more detail from: Realizing the Information Future. The Internet and Beyond. Renaissance Committee. Computer Science and Telecommunications Board. Commission on Physical Sciences, Mathematics and Applications. National Research Council. 1994, 179. Seriously being considered are also asymmetric solutions with a narrow control channel from the end user to remote servers and a relatively wide back channel.

58 The most probable technical solution consists of a transition to complete optical transmission, since a single optical fibre possesses a capacity of 40GB. Several hundred optical fibres can be bundled together to form a cable. This solution becomes possible because purely optical switches are now available; see *David J. Farber*: Predicting the Unpredictable - Technology and Society, in: *Christoph Engel/Kenneth Keller (Eds.):* Understanding the Impact of Global Networks on Local Social, Political and Cultural Values 29-38 (30 et seq.).

59 I owe this reference to *Martina Zitterbart.*

60 *Dertouzos* (footnote 9) 109/336.

trend gains momentum, the design of the browser will become the decisive factor for the impact of news on public debate.[61]

3. Commercialization

There is hardly a question being discussed in such a lively manner as the one surrounding the commercialization of the Internet.[62] This is, of course, initially an economic question. Net (a) and services (b) are scarce goods, for whose production someone must bear the costs. However, commercialization of the Internet would simultaneously also diametrally alter its culture. Even developments that make economic sense could fail to materialize because they are not desired by a large number of users (c).

a) Network

Traditional paths are being followed to finance the last mile of the net. That is precisely why telecommunications policy has so much influence on the Internet's technical range.[63] The backbone, i.e. the long-range connections are, from a practical point of view, primarily an American problem, since the Internet originated in that country. Its architecture leads to the fact that, even today, most of the world's traffic passes through the USA. This also applies to the communication between users from other countries. Historically, the majority of the Internet's backbone has been financed from the U.S. federal budget.[64] Avowedly, however, the U.S. government is increasingly withdrawing its financial support.[65] Up till now Internet providers have been making flat payments to those operating the long-distance connections in its stead.[66]

A multitude of suggestions has been put forward to change this situation and to implement usage-based tariffs.[67] Technically, this is possible using so-called ATM technology, which allows information about its priority level to be added to each individual data packet. Priority traffic would then be transported particularly quickly or via a particularly large bandwidth.[68] From an economic viewpoint, such solutions make sense, for the backbone has a big peak load problem, whereas its basic load only represents about 5% of its capacity.[69] In addition, the various services on offer burden the net to quite different degrees. An unformatted word, such as is often used in e-mails, only uses an average of around 44 bits. A non-compressed video, on the other

61 The fight for the distribution and design of the so-called portals is being fought correspondingly intensively. I again owe this reference to *Robert Spinrad*.

62 Comprehensively *Hutter* in *Engel/Keller* (footnote 53); see also *Baecker* in *Engel/Keller* (footenote 49).

63 See 1 above.

64 Details in: Realizing the Information Future (footnote 57) 175 and in *Jeffrey K. MacKie-Mason/Hal R. Varian:* Some FAQs about Usage-Based Pricing, ftp://alfred.sims.berkeley.edu/pub/Papers/useFAQs.html (13.02.1999).

65 The history of the backbone's financing is portrayed in *Grewlich's* Cyberspace (footnote 8) Chapter Two. 3. 7..

66 *MacKie-Mason/Varian* (footnote 64) 2.

67 Just above and passim; further suggested solutions described by *Hutter* in *Engel/Keller* (footnote 12) 75.

68 I owe this information to *Martina Zitterbart.*

69 *MacKie-Mason/Varian* (footnote 64).

hand, uses 100 mb/s, representing a ratio of 1 : 2 million.[70] However, critics counter that the Internet's frequent blockages are not the result of current pricing policies but of unpredictable growth.[71] Economically speaking, this would then be a dynamic problem, rather than one of allocation.

If usage-based tariffs became effective, some uses would then perhaps cease to be low-price decisions.[72] This would simplify the state's influence on user behaviour. The state could then not only obtain information about access to the net by controlling the payments, but also set behavioural changes in motion by means of pecuniary incentives.

b) Services

Although Internet providers pay for use of the backbone, they do not pay for their customers' access to web sites. Until now, such access was mostly free-of-charge, which was also due to technical reasons. From a practical point of view, only credit cards could be used for payment. As long as effective cryptography is not generally available[73], a fairly large risk exists that third persons will learn the credit card number and commit fraud with it.[74] Principally, however, transaction costs for credit card payments are much too high. Only the advent of e-cash would permit micro payments to be made[75], such as they are needed for individual access to the offers of a news agency.

Consumer habits must be added to the technical reasons. The Internet began its victory march among universities, where the costs of producing and distributing its contents were already paid for out of university budgets. Academics themselves have an interest in publicizing their ideas. Many commercial providers therefore found it advisable to finance their services indirectly, for example, via banner advertising or pop-up windows through which the user must first navigate in order to reach his desired contents. Other providers offer the general public their main service free-of-charge and make their profits by offering profitable complementary products. Standard examples are Netscape or the Acrobat Reader, both of which earn money by selling software to the content providers which uses the possibilities of the browser or reader in an optimal fashion. The question crops up again here, of whether the old, low-cost situation will disappear through commercialization.

c) Internet Culture

The differentiation between high-cost and low-cost situations does not, however, exhaust the problem. Moreover, the university history of the net has left its mark much, much deeper. A clear indication of this is the fact that the Internet community reacts as

---

70 *MacKie-Mason/Varian* (footnote 64) 3. A further figure is equally explicit: multimedia applications only account for around 0.01% of Internet usage, but use around 20% of the bandwidth, *Grewlich* Cyberspace (footnote 8) Chapter Two. 4..

71 So, particularly *David Farber* in *Farber's* discussion in *Engel/Keller* (footnote 58).

72 See above, I 4.

73 See above, I 10.

74 See however below VIII 6d) on collective solutions to this problem.

75 Further on this under V 3.

strongly to the sending of unsolicited advertising, as to pornography or propaganda.[76] A large group of persons is willing to work voluntarily in committees who keep the net functioning and who continue its development.[77] The traditional Internet community therefore reminds one particularly of phenomena which *Elinor Ostrom* examined in relation to fisheries, mineral deposits and environmental problems. A relatively homogeneous social group prefers to organize itself in a collective manner, instead of coordinating its behaviour decentrally via prices.[78] Will this culture succeed in spreading to the many new Internet users? Will it, at least in its own partial area of the net, be able to continue in existence? Will it therefore be possible to succeed in organizing a co-existence between a commercialized Internet for the occasional user and a traditional Internet community with completely different motivations?[79]

4. Breakdown into Language and Culture Zones

One further, cultural question is far from being answered. Internet observers from the social sciences are worried that the American Way of Life will, via this vehicle, finally become dominant all over the world.[80] However, in actual fact, communication researchers have observed that the Internet has diversified rapidly into language and culture zones.[81] This apparently applies particularly to the Japanese, but equally so to the French and Germans. If this development continues to gain ground, the net would perhaps technically have a global range but, as a communications area, would once again primarily correspond to the societies that have been generated by history. The truth probably lies somewhere in between. The elite class all speak English anyway, and anyone living in an authoritarian country who seeks to reach a world public, will use this language. Those who are denied access to popular web sites by domestic laws or by their social surroundings will have an incentive to learn the necessary English vocabulary.

5. Attention Management

Even before the existence of the Internet, academia was drowning in too many publications. A glance into a book store at a train station demonstrates how necessary it is for a reader to be selective in his choice. Even so, the Internet represents a quantum

---

76 See further below VII 3, VIII 5b) and 6; compare also *Dertouzos* (footnote 9) 28: 'Info-feudalism by a few princes is intolerable to the serfs of a computer community'.

77 More from *Werle* in *Engel/Keller* (footnote 12) 162.

78 *Elinor Ostrom:* Governing the Commons. The Evolution of Institutions for Collective Action (The Political Economy of Institutions and Decisions) Cambridge 1990.

79 The question has much to do with the basic problem of constructivism. Ideas by *Michael Thompson:* Global Networks and Local Cultures. What are the Mismatches and what can be Done About them?, in: *Christoph Engel/Kenneth Keller* (Eds.): Understanding the Impact of Global Networks on Local Social, Political and Cultural Values 113-129.

80 Insistent reference on this topic *Kenneth Kenniston:* Cultural Diversity or Global Monoculture. The Impacts of the Information Age, in: *Christoph Engel/Kenneth Keller (Eds.):* Understanding the Impact of Global Networks on Local Social, Political and Cultural Values 131-140.

81 I owe this reference to *Günter Müller.*

leap. One only needs to feed a search engine with a relatively well-known term in order to understand why one is lost without information management.

This problem is particularly urgent in the Internet, but the chance of overcoming it is also greater. If the user takes care of the search himself, he will refine his search technique. We have already become acquainted with the terms filter, frequency distribution and intelligent search engines.[82] In the age of an information abundancy, political effect and commercial success are decided by the provider's ability to attract the public's attention. We can be certain that technical and journalistic creativity will be pointed to precisely this question. But, up till now, the most important solutions have only been apparent on the horizon. We have already spoken about portals.[83] The pop-up window is another push technology that the user must first click away from before he arrives at the site he is actually seeking. Anyone who knows which mechanisms search engines use to order to rank the sites found, can also attempt to manipulate this order.[84] Will users permanently allow this to happen? Or will they then, in turn, develop protective mechanisms in order to retain control of their own attention? This is not only a technical question, but also a cultural one. By consciously discarding certain pieces of information, the users namely also decide themselves in which type of society they wish to live.[85]

III. Effects

Our interest is directed at the effects of the Internet on the nation state. More generally speaking, it concerns the relationship between technology and political institutions. Of course, this relationship is not a deterministic one.[86] On the other hand, technological development is not irrelevant for the way that institutions work.

One can best describe this connection using the categories of system theory. The new technology is not part of the subsystem 'politics', but belongs instead to its environment. In the short term, politics can completely ignore technological change. Speaking in terms of system theory, they then treat it like irrelevant environmental noise. However, technological development alters the restrictions within which politics are made. Hence, this element of the environment can increasingly disturb the self reference of the political system. It is therefore worthwhile for a social subsystem to invest in mechanisms that can estimate the potential for disruption and attempt to integrate the new element into its own system in a timely fashion.[87]

---

82 See above I 5.

83 See above I.

84 Technically, this occurs with the aid of so-called meta-tags in the source code. The user does not see this information and therefore does not notice the manipulation. *Florian Rötzer:* Aufmerksamkeit - Rohstoffe der Informationsgesellschaft, in: *Andreas Brill/Michael de Vries (eds.):* Virtuelle Wirtschaft. Virtuelle Unternehmen, virtuelle Produkte, virtuelles Geld und virtuelle Kommunikation. Opladen 1998, 174 - 191 (195).

85 *Thompson* in *Engel/Keller* (footnote 79) 116f..

86 *Werle* emphasizes this point in *Engel/Keller* (footnote 12) 160, as does *Thompson* in *Engel/Keller* (footnote 79) 118.

87 Compare *Baecker* in *Engel/Keller* (footnote 49) 93-95.

The Internet's potential for disruption is occasionally based on the fact that completely new possibilities are created for exerting political influence. We will take a closer look at the best example: e-cash as private money.[88] But qualitative effects are by far outweighed by quantitative ones. The Internet allows, namely, previously marginal phenomena to become ubiquitous. Of course, even in the past, one was able to purchase foreign newspapers in Germany. But the use of other foreign mass media was already more difficult. For instance, although most British TV programmes are transmitted via the same Astra satellite as the one used by German channels, British channels do not sell the codes to Germany for encrypted British programmes due to copyright reasons. On the contrary, every piece of content that is put on the Internet anywhere abroad is immediately available on every networked German computer. Other regulatory problems are not ubiquitous in the Internet, but they are so important that they can no longer be ignored. Neonazis, for example, had of course linked up with each other before the advent of the Internet. But they are now able to organize themselves much more effectively with encoded e-mails and web pages than was previously the case. Finally, some regulatory problems have only succeeded in attracting public attention thanks to the Internet. This appears to be the case with child pornography. Fortunately, new pictures rarely appear to be the subject of e-mail exchanges. But via organizations such as Cyberangels, the public at large has become aware just how many people wish to see these perverse pictures from the 1960s and '70s.

Many effects of the Internet are not monocausal. In particular, states, as regulatory bodies, are not only being exposed to more lively international competition via the Internet. It is more a case of the Internet representing only one factor and also being an indicator of the more general phenomenon of globalisation.[89] Ultimately, the relationship between technology and political institutions is not one-sided. National and international actors are not only exposed to globalisation; they often use it for their own strategic interests.[90] This may be an attractive strategy, because technology alters the restrictions on political action. Sometimes, technological development also allows for a battle of the forum. It is mainly the Internet's digital technology that has provided such an opportunity. All forms of mass and private communication are namely now available using the very same technical infrastructure.[91] In Germany, the relationship between the federal government and the states has brought this question to a head. The result is a fragile compromise laid down in two largely harmonized documents, the Treaty on Media Services concluded by the German Länder, and the Federal Statute on Information and Communication Services.[92]

---

88 See below V 3.

89 More detail under IV 2, V-VI.

90 More from *Saskia Sassen:* Losing Control? Sovereignty in an Age of Globalization. New York 1996; see also *Dertouzos* (footnote 9) 291: technology can be the pretext in older conflicts of interest.

91 As long as the bandwidth problem is unresolved, this does not however apply to television, see above II 2.

92 *Martin Bullinger/Ernst-Joachim Mestmäcker* think through this problem from the federal government's point of view: Multimediadienste. Struktur und staatliche Aufgaben nach

Moreover, technology is not alone as far as change is concerned; state, society and political institutions are also changing. It may well be that personality and society are no longer the same, when the Internet belongs to the everyday life of a larger proportion of the population.[93] Political institutions may succeed in developing completely new control instruments to tackle the new regulatory problems, which might make the state even more powerful.[94] And, finally, our analytical zest should not make us lose modesty. It has, for example, taken hundreds of years to recognize the real social importance of the printed book[95], and automobiles were initially welcomed in the United States as eliminating the problem of horse manure from the streets.[96]

IV. Consequences for Domestic Rule

The Internet's consequences for domestic rule in a nation state become apparent in a distinction made by *Albert O. Hirschman*. A state is an organization of which its citizens are its members. From this perspective, the government, administration and the courts represent its management. Just like in a holding company, members of the management exert influence either via voice (1) or via exit (2). In the first case, they do not question membership, but use their legal and political possibilities of influence. In the second case, however, they threaten to rescind their membership if the management refuses to change its behaviour.[97] The Internet increases both the possibility of voice and also of exit. But sometimes it can simply lead to destabilization (3). States see themselves forced to employ more demanding governance tools than previously (4). The result is a change in the character of statehood (5).

1. Voice

The Internet expands citizens' possibilities of influencing the decisions of state institutions[98]. In this regard, that which we in general saw about its effects, applies: some really new avenues for voice appear. But, above all, voice now becomes much more simple and its probability therefore increases. Some people and groups would previously have been incapable of mounting an effective opposition. The opportunity costs of voice fall for everyone.[99] Taking a letter as an example: for most people, the decisive factor is not that a stamp is more expensive than a telephone unit for sending an e-mail, but that they are more likely to use the latter because it costs less time and effort.[100] Often, voice will now even become a low-cost decision, so that an individual's cost calculations no longer play any role at all.[101] Ultimately, voice carries particular

deutschem und europäischem Recht (Law and Economics of International Telecommunications 30) Baden-Baden 1997.

93 I owe this thought to *Winfried Hassemer*.

94 See also VIII 1 below on this point.

95 *Baecker* in *Engel/Keller* (footnote 80), 101 [12].

96 *Keniston* in *Engel/Keller* (footnote 80) 140.

97 More detail in *Albert O. Hirschman:* Abwanderung und Widerspruch. Reaktionen auf Leistungsabfall bei Unternehmungen, Organisationen und Staaten (Schriften für Kooperationsforschung A 8) Tübingen 1974.

98 See *Schäfer* in *Berg* (footnote 2) 11.

99 The term 'opportunity costs' fits here better than the general one of 'costs'.

100 See above I 5.

101 On this concept see previous ref. I 4.

weight if the person voicing the opposition can also threaten to rescind his membership. That is why the simultaneous expansion of both possibilities through the Internet is so important.

The Internet initially expands opportunities to control government (a). It also becomes much easier to exert ad hoc political influence (b). Intermediaries become vulgarized (c). Diffuse interests can organize themselves (d) and opportunities for political power are redistributed (e).

a) Control

Anyone seeking to exercise control must know the activities of those being monitored. This is traditionally not an easy feat in Germany. Both the government's and the administration's style are characterized by secrecy. Even those formally participating in administrative proceedings must follow strict rules in order to view administrative files. General freedom of information for the public at large does not exist. But, admittedly, the statutes on the law of the press of the Länder do allow for a right to information by the press. And now, under pressure from the European Union, the Environmental Information Act has led to a change in this partial area. Of course, even in the age of the Internet, the government can still manage to protect true state secrets; we have already spoken of the possibilities of cryptography.[102] But, with the Internet, information that has at some time or other been made public once has the potential of becoming available to everyone. New information intermediaries can specialize in compiling registers of sinners in the administration. They do not even have to wait until someone paints an incriminating case. An electronic sniffer programme can do their work. In the USA, consumer complaints stations already monitor the behaviour of doctors in the same manner.[103]

Also, as we know, the Internet is timeless.[104] Governments therefore lose the possibility of collective amnesia. They can never be sure when a search engine will once again reveal a bad deed committed at the beginning of a legislative period. In the Internet, citizens also receive unpredictable and, because of the economic competition, unmonitored information about parallel solutions to social problems in other countries. It therefore becomes easier for them to break free of political thought blockages, expose bogus arguments and make alternative solutions ready for acceptance.

b) Ad-hoc Influence

In a representative democracy, the influence of citizens is channelled through elections and votes. Of course, even in the past, politics was never completely isolated from other forms of influence. But, in the past, those who had previously organized themselves were able to exert influence much easier, with the media and organized interest groups being the most important instruments thereof. Citizens' initiatives and demonstrations remained for other parts of the population. The Internet now expands the possibilities of

---

102 See above I 10.
103 More detail from *Dertouzos* (footnote 9) 166 f.
104 See above I 3.

exerting political influence ad hoc. In the USA, this has been coined 'civil society'.[105] In the Internet it is sufficient for a single person to obtain knowledge of a problematic issue. This is how Greenpeace's electronic warning system functions.[106] Using a mailing list, a political protest or a consumer boycott can be organized within hours.[107] In this way, people have even occasionally succeeded in overturning a political decision at the last minute. Such was the case with a draft amendment to American copyright law, which would have particularly favoured the database of the company West Law.[108]

Even in the age of the Internet, not a single person among 80 million Germans succeeds in overturning politicial decisions by himself, but permanent ties to organized parties or associations are no longer necessary. Much less structured, ad hoc interest groups, even if they have been specifically formed for the purpose, can also suffice. To use an old term:[109] instead of an organization, a simple social movement suffices.[110] This makes it more probable that many of the "speechless millions of this earth" will be heard.[111]

c) Vulgarization of the Intermediaries

In order for people to organize ad hoc opposition to a political decision, they must already be severely affected by it. In addition, ad hoc movements are poorly suited to the formulation of political orientations. It is therefore no accident that they come together much sooner, in order to oppose a solution that has been formulated by someone else. This is why, even in the age of the Internet, political intermediaries will not become superfluous. But the Internet will force them to change their character.[112] It will be much easier to create new ones. These new intermediaries will act differently to their predecessors, thus causing the traditional intermediaries to come under pressure.

New intermediaries are sometimes referred to as Samisdat media.[113] Since the Internet is globally standardized, setting up new media is technically so simple. This is why anyone can effortlessly become his own publisher.[114] Economically speaking, barriers to market entry are plainly low. A homepage is usually sufficient, for which one needs nothing

---

105 *Lawrence K. Grossman:* The Electronic Republic. Reshaping Democracy in the Information Age. New York 1995; *Graham Browning:* Electronic Democracy. Using the Internet to Influence American Politics. Witlon, Conn. 1996; *Henry Perritt:* Cyberspace Self-Government. Town Hall Democracy or Rediscovered Royalism? In: Berkeley Technology Law Journal 11 (1997) 413-482.

106 *Thompson* in *Engel/Keller* (footnote 79) 124.

107 *Ulrich Beck:* Das Demokratie-Dilemma im Zeitalter der Globalisierung, in: aus politik und zeitgeschichte 38/98, 3-11 (7).

108 I owe this example to *Herbert Burkert.* Er formulates the following four conditions for the success of such a strategy: a) speed is useful because for example politicians only expose the most decisive element just shortly before a vote takes place; b) there is already a place on the Internet at which similarly-minded people gather information; c) the situation is politically unstable; d) the group receives support via traditional media for the decisive move.

109 - but one which has however been misused by the National Socialist (Nazi) movement -

110 *Werle* in *Engel/Keller* (footnote 12) 175 speaks of "social-movement-type-organizations".

111 *Yehudi Menuhin* formulated the hope: "When are all these technologies finally going to let us hear from the voiceless millions of this earth?", cited to *Dertouzos* (footnote 9) 284.

112 *Perritt* (footnote 105) JILS 1997, 163.

113 Dertouzos (footnote 9) 161.

114 *Grewlich* Cyberspace (footnote 8) Chapter Two. 3. 7..

more than a computer and access to the Internet.[115] But the Internet's biggest advantage is more of a journalistic nature. As a research medium, the Internet permits simple, rapid access to information, which is the raw material of every intermediary. In the Internet, even informal polls can be organized with little effort. It will hardly disturb the new intermediaries that they will not normally be able to match professional statistical standards, since percentages obtained in this manner will still have suggestive power.[116]

Distribution is also very simple. While addressees still have to locate a website, search engines and, even more so, hyperlinks facilitate this task, resulting in a type of network comprising of information offers. Anyone seeking a better overview can also use the relevant link lists. Push technologies are not limited to large companies. A classic instrument in this regard is that of crossposting in mailing lists. If a widely accessed mailing list exists covering a related field, one can post a cross-reference therein to one's own list or web site. In one important respect, such new intermediaries can even beat their classic competitors: they possess far better possibilities of reducing scatter losses, since they can generate as small series as they wish. If that seems more attractive to the intermediaries, they set up a bulletin board, to which the addressees actively go when they seek pertinent information. A hybrid form is the despatch of link lists via e-mail. In the USA, the term 'narrowcasting' has established itself for these new intermediaries, which differentiates them from classic broadcasting.[117]

The typical result is an intermediary who is only concerned with a very specific topic.[118] The border between private and public communication becomes permeable. What appears to one user to be a new intermediary, is a regular electronic meeting place to another. Only the e-mail address needs to be altered, in order to swap from private to public communication. This is what often happens in mailing lists. Information important enough for everyone is sent to all the addressees on a list and, from this, a private e-mail exchange may result. Or, conversely, private communication with another addressee on the list may at some point become important enough to be made public.

Through the Internet, the previous intermediaries come under pressure as well, primarily for two reasons. Until now, the services of many intermediaries were coupled with other products and distributed at single price. For example, information and editing, as the editorial services of a newspaper office, were previously paid for jointly, not separately. In the Internet, access to individual news items is no longer a scarce good. It therefore remains to be seen whether there is sufficient willingness to pay for the editorial services alone.[119] Additionally, since it will be easier to establish new intermediaries, the traditional ones will be subjected to competitive pressure, thus forcing many of them to attend to the wishes of their members more precisely. Thus, even within the intermediaries, we encounter the logic of exit and voice.[120] This does

115 See I 4 above for details on the figures.

116 Compare *Dertouzos* (footnote 9) 161/216.

117 *Thompson* in *Engel/Keller* (footnote 79) 118.

118 *Perritt* (footnote 105) JILS 1997, 160 speaks of "unbundling" media into single pieces of information.

119 I owe this reference to *Miles Kahler*.

120 See above IV 1-2.

not necessarily strengthen the intermediaries. The logic of influence often stands in contrast to the logic of membership.[121]

d) Organization of Diffuse Minorities

The new possibilities of voice have the greatest practical meaning for those interests which were scarcely capable of being organized in the past. This reduces the importance of *Mancur Olson's* classical insight considerably. He had noted that, almost exclusively, organized interests, as opposed to diffuse ones, have a chance of exerting influence on political decisions. Key political decisions were therefore traditionally systematically skewed against diffuse interests.[122] The Internet, however, now offers the possibility of being virtual neighbours[123], a type of community without propinquity.[124] Of course, it is much simpler if the persons concerned have seen each other at least once[125] or if a previously weak interest group is now strengthened.[126] But, if worse comes to worse, the group can even find together without. In the USA, for example, adult sufferers of childhood polio have got together and convinced the conventional school of medicine that, although supposedly fully healed, their illness has often led to long-term effects in need of treatment.[127] The Internet is even more important in countries with a badly developed infrastructure. There, politics is no longer confined to densely populated areas.

Anyone with economic training will, however, object that, up till now, the discussion has only centered on the technical possibilities for organizing diffuse interests. So far, we have said nothing on incentives to use these new possibilities. By itself, the Internet will not alter the fact that individuals act almost irrationally, if they stand up for the common interest of their group. A dynamic problem, of which we are already aware, also appears. Even interest groups become more valuable to their members as more and more people join them. A critical mass problem therefore also exists here. Even interest organizations are network goods.[128] But even from a strictly economic angle, the more severely the interests of a minority group have been previously ignored, the less weight these arguments will carry. Activism is even easier to predict, if we remember how cheap communication via the Internet is. In this low-cost situation, a willingness to become active for a common cause becomes quite plausible.[129]

---

121 This pair of terms comes from *Philippe C. Schmitter/Wolfgang Streeck:* The Organisation of Business Interests. Studying the Associative Action of Business in Advanced Industrial Societies (Max-Planck-Institut für Gesellschaftsforschung Discussion Paper 1/99); *Werle* makes the connection to the Internet in *Engel/Keller* (footnote 12) 173-174.

122 *Mancur Olson:* Die Logik des kollektiven Handelns. Kollektivgüter und die Theorie der Gruppen (Die Einheit der Gesellschaftswissenschaften 10) Tübingen3 1992.

123 The term comes from *Dertouzos* (footnote 9) 157-160.

124 This term comes from *Thompson* in *Engel/Keller* (footnote 79) 118.

125 *Dertouzos* (footnote 9) 9.

126 Just above 201.

127 Details in *Dertouzos* (footnote 9) 137.

128 I owe this reference to *Günter Knieps*.

129 See above I 4.

e) Redistributing the Opportunities for Political Power

While political decisions are tied to the wishes and preferences of its citizens, they do not simply arise from the aggregation of individual preferences with the aid of formal decision-making rules. Political power is the most important ingredient for the assertion of one's own interests in the political process. Many attempts have been made to draw up a concept for the phenomenon of power but, at this point, the one by *Jack Knight* must suffice. Knight understands political decisions as being the result of negotiations between organized interests. It is hard to deny the plausibility of the concept for German politics. Negotiating with one another are the parties of a coalition, the various ressorts of the government, the government officials with associations and the government with the opposition in the Bundesrat. According to Knight's ideas, the result of these negotiations depends on a combination of five factors: Those who are able to live well with the status quo have a stronger threat point.[130] Those who invest more resources in the political struggle also have more opportunities.[131] Patience often pays dividends during the negotiating process.[132] Persons who can employ political risk to productive purposes will also have more success.[133] One has to recognize when one can afford to raise an objection, but then also actually do so when the situation warrants it. After all, a credible threat of retaliation can alter the outcome of the negotiations.[134]

The Internet exerts influence on mainly one of these elements: it changes the resources that promise success in political disputes, thus redistributing the opportunities for political power.[135] Traditionally, it was a question of organizing interests in a professional manner[136], but also one of the funds needed to employ experts. Nowadays, however, thanks to information technology, professionalism has become widely available. This process is already well advanced in the case of word processing. Via the Internet, it now also covers the actual organization of interests.

However, the Internet is primarily of use in an asymmetric way to persons who previously had little or even no power. The successful use of these new possibilities demands three characteristics: technical competence, good knowledge of the English language and above all, the ability to skip back and forth with agility between different roles. It has alway been common for the political elite to speak and write English. It is the other two factors though that have the potential of redistributing power. Many of those who hold the keys to political power today, did not grow up with the computer or the Internet. Some are simply shy of these new technical media. They are in any case usually much less comfortable using them than the present generation. Up to the present

---

130 *Knight* makes this more precise and talks about the collapse value ("Zerschlagungswert"): *Jack Knight:* Institutionen und gesellschaftlicher Konflikt (Die Einheit der Gesellschaftswissenschaften 9) Tübingen 1997, 141.

131 Just above 144.

132 *Knight* speaks more precisely about time preferences (footnote 130) 142.

133 *Knight* speaks of risk attitude (footnote 130) 146.

134 Immediately above 149.

135 Compare *Grewlich* Cyberspace (footnote 8) Chapter One. 2. 1.: The Internet brings about a "redistribution of professional opportunities, wealth and social status".

136 Just above d).

time, widely strewn networks of personal relationships formed the most important resource in the political game. While these have not lost their importance, the Internet is accelerating the differentiation of society into more and more subsystems, and also more specialized ones. The most decisive social ability will therefore be the masterful handling of a multitude of roles. A multitude of virtual neighbourhoods will exist alongside the physical one.[137] Anyone seeking success must simultaneously lead a life among several cultures.[138] The central picture is of the "urban villager", who is virtually connected with persons from all over the world, but at the same time only seldom needs to leave his local surroundings.[139] In other words, the world is again taking a leap forward to a new form of modernity.[140] People succeed more easily in this regard the earlier they have gained the relevant experience, again favouring the younger generation over the older one that previously held power.

2. Exit

a) Introduction

The Internet increases the possibilities of both voice to political decisions and exit from the political system.[141] Normally, the opportunity of exit means the possibility of arbitrating between different systems of rules.[142] As is mentioned in the introduction, the Internet then increases the competition between the systems.[143] As a provider of rules, the state sees itself come under pressure from competition.[144] The state transforms itself from a monopolist into a club. The Constitution becomes the club's Articles of Association and the state becomes the provider of a bundle of public goods.[145]

System competition and exit are, however, not identical, since the idea of competition between systems assumes that the previous one is being replaced by a new form of social order. Exit, on the other hand, can also have an anarchistic element, leading not to a new order, but simply destabilization. This question is especially important for the Internet.[146]

One can also explain the political importance of exit with a concept that Gerhard Wegner developed in his habilitation paper. He has pointed to the fact that the state's

---

137 *Dertouzos* (footnote 9) 159.

138 *Keniston* in *Engel/Keller* (footnote 80) 135 speaks of a second culture of 'Americanization' as a connector to the world.

139 *Dertouzos* (footnote 9) 280f.

140 That is the central theme of *Wolfgang Kersting:* Global Networks and Local Values. Some Philosophical Remarks from an Individualist Point of View, in: *Christoph Engel/Kenneth Keller:* Understanding the Impact of Global Networks on Local Social, Political and Cultural Values 9-27.

141 Compare *Schäfer* in *Berg* (footnote 2) 11.

142 *A. Michael Froomkin:* The Internet as a Source of Regulatory Arbitrage, in: *Brian Kahin/Charles Nesson:* Borders in Cyberspace, Information Policy and the Global Information Infrastructure, Cambridge, Mass. 1997, 129-163.

143 See already above I.

144 *Wolfgang Kerber:* Erfordern Globalisierung und Standortwettbewerb einen Paradigmenwechsel in der Theorie der Wirtschaftspolitik?, in: Ordo 49 (1998) 253-268 (254f).

145 Just above 256f.

146 See closer under 3.

governing impulses hit addressees who are able to react creatively. A regulator therefore never knows beforehand whether the addressees will simply adapt their behaviour lineally to the new restrictions. In the most desirable case, the impulses instigate technical or institutional innovation, which then strengthens the state's span of control. Conversely, via innovation, the addressees can succeed in making the impulse to govern ineffective.[147] Exit is one such adverse creative reaction. The Internet's new possibilities of exit are particularly dangerous to politics, since they interfere subsequently with a regulatory structure that is already in place. The political powers were therefore not able to reflect about minimizing the risk of exit as a precautionary measure.

The business of governing will become more difficult in the future, since the new possibilities of exit not only devalue the monitoring potential of command and control regulation, they also affect governance tools that the state has only just acquired. This applies in particular to negotiations in the shadow of hierarchy, that have since become fashionable.[148] In principle, such negotiations are a very effective instrument. The state threatens with rules that impose unilateral burdens and thus causes an industry branch to exercise self-regulation. This not only improves implementation to a very far-reaching extent; at the same time the state also overcomes the knowledge barriers that were put up against its unilateral intervention.[149] But all this only functions if an industry association is really capable of guiding the behaviour of its members. If the members are able to exit from the power of the association by rescinding their membership, then the association is no longer an attractive negotiating partner for the state.

The extent of competition between systems does not solely rest with the Internet. It is more a case that the Internet's importance can only be understood in the inter-relationship with other driving forces of globalization. It dramatically reduces the costs of overcoming space and time.[150] That is of such importance because, simultaneously, transport costs have sunk, the legal boundaries between different economies have diminished thanks to the GATT and WTO, and institutional innovation is capable of overcoming much more complex situations than was previously the case.[151]

Competition between systems is no different to competition between products: a supplier is not only disciplined by current competitors, but also by potential ones. This observation allows us to conceptionally link exit and voice.[152] The credible threat of exit emphasizes voice. In addition, national actors can build up international negotiating power which they can then exert at national level. Environmental associations, in

147 *Gerhard Wegner:* Wirtschaftspolitik zwischen Selbst- und Fremdsteuerung - ein neuer Ansaty (Contributiones Jenenses 3) Baden-Baden 1996; on this topic see also *my* book review in: RabelsZ (1999) 191-196.

148 The evocative term comes from *Fritz W. Scharpf:* Games Real Actors Play. Actor-Centered Institutionalism in Policy Research (Theoretical Lenses on Public Policy) Boulder 1997, 205 f.

149 More detail in *Christoph Engel:* Selbstregulierung im Bereich der Produktverantwortung. Instrumente und deren Ausgestaltung (Preprints from the Max-Planck Project Group on the Law of Common Goods 1998/7).

150 See above I 1 and 3.

151 See *Ulrich Steger (ed.):* Wirkmuster der Globalisierung (Ladenburger Kolleg Globalisierung verstehen und gestalten) Ladenburg 1998.

152 Compare under IV 1-2.

particular, understand this well.[153] Occasionally, national interest groups even build a coalition with a foreign sovereign. American data protectionists, for example, only gained influence in American politics when the European Union threatened with the extra-territorial application of its data protection laws.[154]

Just how intense the competition between systems is, depends on the extent to which the regulatory addressees are mobile.[155] But we should not artificially restrict our view to one of physical exit (b). The Internet is more important for partial (c) or even merely virtual exit (d). In addition, it also facilitates tax evasion (e), thereby removing the state's ability to manoeuvre.

b) Physical Exit

The virtual reality of the Internet cannot protect anyone from physical capture by the constables of the state. But the Internet can facilitate the decision to physically migrate. It is, namely, much easier nowadays to maintain contact to one's old habitat via e-mail, discussion groups and Internet newspapers. If he so chooses, a person can carry his entire medical history on a smart card.[156] Anyone who leads a mobile life can also search immediately for a cultural home among an international elite that maintains contact over the Internet in between occasional meetings.

c) Partial Exit

The Internet has a by far greater bearing on what one might call partial exit. This mainly comes to the fore when companies cut the value chain into small units to an extent not seen before.[157] This is because the Internet reduces the transaction costs for international business.[158] Firms can now organize the purchase of inputs on a worldwide basis[159] and have the primary products delivered just-in-time. This applies equally to both goods and services. A Maroccan firm takes care of the computerized layout of 20% of all books published in France.[160] An American firm contracts out thousands of doctors' bills to a firm in a small Irish village.[161] Lufthansa has transferred its accounting center for used flight tickets to India.[162]

---

153 *Grewlich* Cyberspace (footnote 8) Chapter One. 3. 1..

154 I owe this reference to *Henry Perritt;* more on data protection under VII 3 and VIII 3b).

155 *Kerber* (footnote 144) Ordo 1998, 253.

156 More from *Dertouzos* (footnote 9) 169.

157 *Friedrich L. Sell:* Anforderungen an immobile Produktionsfaktoren vor dem Hintergrund der Globalisierung, in: *Hartmut Berg (ed.):* Globalisierung der Wirtschaft: Ursachen - Formen - Konsequenzen (Schriften des Vereins für Socialpolitik NF 263) 69-101 (80).

158 *Christian Kirchner:* Kommentar [zu Hannelore Weck-Hannemann: Globalisierung: Herausforderung oder Anwendungsfall der neuen politischen Ökonomie?, in: Jahrbuch für neue politische Ökonomie 17 (1998) 84-107], in: Jahrbuch für Neue Politische Ökonomie 17 (1998) 108-112 (108f).

159 *Henning Klodt:* Globalisierung: Phänomen und empirische Relevanz, in: Jahrbuch für Neue Politische Ökonomie 17 (1998) 7-34 (9).

160 *Jörg Becker/Daniel Salamanca:* Globalisierung, elektronische Netze und der Export von Arbeit, in: aus politik und zeitgeschichte 42/97, 31-38 (31).

161 Just above.

162 Just above 32f.

But the Internet not only makes trade much easier; it also facilitates the business of organizing firms at arm's length, thereby providing additional impulses to the search for hybrid solutions between contract and organization.[163] The term 'virtual companies' is on the march.[164] Firms exist, for example, in California that accept orders for tailor-made goods and then have them made up by subcontractors in Asia at low wage rates.[165] Other firms put together ad hoc teams for each new entrepreneurial activity, comprising both in-house employees and persons not employed by the firm.[166]

Finally, foreign direct investment will be much simpler via Internet. An investor wishing to avoid the state's grasp therefore no longer needs to restrict himself to portfolio investments. He can instead place a direct investment. As the owner, he has a much greater influence on the business risk. He therefore no longer needs to spread his foreign risks as widely. He receives the risk premium himself instead of it being received by the company in which he has invested his capital.

Partial exit allows the uncoupling of state services. Economically speaking, the state has traditionally produced a highly-aggregated bundle of services, which encompasses everything from national defense and domestic security, to children's education, as well as antitrust and private law. Inhabitants were unable to unfasten this bundle. Hence, anyone not wishing to avail themselves of all these services thought very carefully about the question of emigrating abroad, since in a new country they would also only be able to receive a different but similarly aggregated bundle of state services. Partial exit provides precisely the means of splitting up this bundle. Those who are clever can treat the state like a cafeteria, only sampling palatable dishes.

The possibilities of unbundling public services go even further. With the aid of the Internet, well-organized social actors can also take on tasks of which only the state was traditionally capable, since the Internet drastically sinks the transaction costs of many activities. An extreme example is private money. Up till now, only the state was able to provide a uniform yardstick of value, an instrument for transferring values and postponing consumption into the future.. To do this, the state used its central bank. Recently, however, serious plans to introduce private money have been announced. It would primarily be used to effect micro payments.[167] In the past, the organization of markets was also only generally possible with the assistance of the state. Classic examples are stock exchanges. Organized markets were needed to allow some goods to become tradeable items in the first place. Others could , without access to an organised market,only be traded among a small number of persons, such as is the case with stocks

---

163 Such hybrid forms are the central research theme of *Oliver E. Williamson:* Die ökonomischen Institutionen des Kapitalismus. Unternehmen, Märkte, Kooperationen (Die Einheit der Gesellschaftswissenschaften 64), Tübingen 1990, 187-237.

164 *Sell* in *Berg* (footnote 157) 80.

165 Just above 80.

166 *Michael de Vries:* Das virtuelle Unternehmen. Formentheoretische Überlegungen zu Grenzen eines grenzenlosen Konzepts, in: *Andreas Brill/id. (ed.):* Virtuelle Wirtschaft. Virtuelle Unternehmen, virtuelle Produkte, virtuelles Geld und virtuelle Kommunikation. Opladen 1998, 54-86 (59).

167 An overview of projects and possibilities is provided by *Froomkin* (footnote 31) UPittsbJLC 1996. 450-471; see further under V 3.

and shares.[168] In the age of the Internet, many companies no longer need this assistance. Classic examples are computer exchanges.

Finally, the Internet makes it much simpler to protect oneself from the interfering influence of third parties. The possibilities of self-help will occupy us more closely.[169] At this point, it suffices to say that government is then also no longer needed as a protective state.

d) Virtual Exit

The last exit option, that of virtual exit, is based on a feature of most legal orders. In this case, the regulatory object proper is left completely untouched, but the regulatory addressee manages to give his behaviour an appearance such that the unwelcome legal rule no longer has an effect.

Occasionally, this already succeeds on the level of material law. This is where, for example, the old legal argument of antitrust law belongs concerning the correct determination of the relevant territorial boundaries of a market. Companies regularly attempt to convince the antitrust authorities and courts that they should take into consideration the global market rather than the German one. This is particularly relevant for those provisions of antitrust law that are based on market domination, since those who appear to be dominant players in the German market may not be anywhere near so in the much larger global market. The Internet supplies new arguments for this, since the transaction costs for global trade are sinking. It will, however, only come to virtual exit if the company succeeds in convincing the cartel authorities that the foreign competition is greater than in reality, since otherwise, the company really would be controlled by the global market. German cartel law would then indeed have no reason to intervene.

More important from a practical point of view is virtual exit where a company creatively plays with the rules of conflict of laws. The rules of private international law decide on which national law is applied to cases with foreign contact. They rest on the basic idea of harmony in international decisions. States are thus prepared, in principle, to allow their own law to take a step down. This willingness is primarily restricted to private law.[170] Which law finds application is decided by conflict law with the aid of connecting factors. In accordance with article 15 I, combined with article 14 I 1 EGBGB, for example, the validity of an agreement on property and income is governed by the laws of the state to which both spouses belong.[171] For reasons of legal security and practicality, conflict of laws uses very simple connecting factors, which in this case is the joint nationality of the spouses. The further the connecting factor is away from the regulated phenomenon, the more easily an area for virtual exit is created. The regulatory

168 Stimulating in regard to organized markets *Rudolf Richter/Eirik Furubotn:* Neue Institutionenökonomik. Eine Einführung und kritische Würdigung (Neue Ökonomische Grundrisse [1]) Tübingen 1996, 309-351.

169 See below VIII 6.

170 See more below under VIII 3c).

171 In reality, of course, things are much more complicated. See for instance the many further regulations in art. 14 and 15 EGBGB, the rules of art. 4 (1) EGBGB on *renvoi* and the rules of art. 6 EGBGB in regard to the *ordre public*.

addressee can, namely, simply restrict himself to changing the connecting factor, without removing the regulated activity from this country.[172]

e) Tax Evasion

The opportunities opened up by the Internet for physical, partial or virtual exit lessen not only the state's direct regulatory possibilities; every single one of them also has an effect on the tax laws. Capital, which is already more mobile than labour, becomes even more so via the Internet, thereby removing it more and more from the access of the treasury. Partial exit often precisely serves the purpose of moving those portions of the value creation chain abroad that are burdened by high taxes. Finally, the highly complex German tax laws open up a possibility every now and then for virtual exit. These are then popularly known as tax evasion holes.

The erosion of the tax base is not only of significance for the tax laws. Financial means are taken away from the state that it could otherwise employ to guide the behaviour of its citizens. New subsidies are, for example, only possible if the state reduces other services. The comparatively expensive implementation of command and control regulation can thereby become prohibitively expensive. The state can already see itself pressured for fiscal reasons into grasping at other governance tools such as the voluntary restraint agreements which have already been mentioned.[173]

3. Destabilization

The terms exit and voice have positive connotations. They describe how the members of an organization will manage to succeed in ensuring that the management, by and large, really does subjugate itself to the wishes of its members. The positive connotation implicitly assumes that the traditional and the newly-created governance tools are functionally equivalent. This supposition does not always hold true. If it does not, the Internet can then lead to destabilization. More carefully and probably more accurately formulated: suitable governance tools have yet to be found for the new possibilities of action that individuals now possess.

The Internet can have destabilizing economic, political and social effects. In an economic sense, it can increase the inherent stabilization problems present in every market economy. They are most apparent in the cyclical risks in financial markets[174]. Many economists fear that these risks will be increased through private electronic cash.[175] International trade in foreign exchange is mainly handled electronically. In

172 German conflict law is increasingly influenced by a trend coming from the USA. It brings the connecting factors closer to the regulated problem. This can be clearly seen from art. 29 EGBGB in regard to consumer contracts and from art. 30 EGBGB regarding labour relations. As a result, the room for virtual exit shrinks. I owe this reference to *Wolf Osthaus.*

173 See above footnote 149.

174 See also *Martin Hellwig:* Systemische Risiken im Finanzsektor, in: *Dieter Duwendag (ed.):* Finanzmärkte im Spannungsfeld von Globalisierung, Regulierung und Geldpolitik (Schriften des Vereins für Socialpolitik NF 261) Berlin 1998, 123-151.

175 More detail under V 3.

1995 already, a fifth of annual global trade in goods and services was turned over on the foreign exchange markets in a single trading day.[176]

The worry about political destabilization can be traced back to the anarchic potential of the Internet. Suppliers of outlawed contents might manage to remove themselves from all forms of state control. German national socialists, for example, are already tightly organized through the Internet.[177] In addition, key political decisions for a population of 80 million can only be made if the room for maneouvre has been previously restricted to just a few possibilities.[178] This agenda setting become less likely, the more the traditional media lose ground in favour of single issue intermediaries.

On the border between political and social effects the fear exists that the Internet could lead to a disintegration of society.[179] In addition, in the age of globalisation, the flexibility for redistribution ordered by the state becomes smaller. This directly results from the difficulties in taxing mobile factors.[180] One of the most important instruments for reducing social tension thereby loses its efficacy. Finally, the Internet leads to the creation of a new class in society. The privileged ones are those who possess the technical, language and psychological ability to use the advantages of the Internet.[181] The greater the number of people unable to do so, the more attractive the flight into simplicity becomes. This could give religious sects new impetus. Such doctrines of salvation could finally gain influence on state decisions. Some even fear a new 'Holy War' against all that is modern.[182]

4. Transformation of Statehood

Ultimately, the Internet forces a deep-seated transformation of statehood, partly by itself and partly in joint cooperation with other globalisation elements. The new possibilities of voice[183] shatter the rigid German idea of a representative democracy. In the long run, the constitution will have to react toincreased political influence between elections by liberalizing referenda and votes. The vulgarization of the intermediaries will, in the long term, undermine the privileged constitutional position of the parties and mass media. The desire will grow to meet the increased factual possibilities for information with formal freedom of information. While the state can attempt to influence self-regulation

---

176 *Edzard Reuter:* Recht und Ökonomie im Zeitalter der Globalisierung. Gedanken zu einem schwierigen Wechselverhältnis (Juristische Studiengesellschaft Karlsruhe 220) Heidelberg 1997, 2: Daily foreign exchange trade amounted to $1.35 trillion, annual global trade in goods and services around $6 trillion. The gross domestic product of German industry in 1994 amounted to $3.3 trillion.

177 See also below VII 3.

178 In the economic thought experiment, there may either be just two possibilities or no more than two actors. More detail on the so-called *Condorcet* paradoxon *Peter Bernholz/Friedrich Breyer:* Grundlagen der Politischen Ökonomie. II Ökonomische Theorie der Politik. Tübingen3 1994 54-69. The unorderly political reality manages to be ready even with a somewhat more complicated situation. But it also cannot manage to fit many objects or interest groups together.

179 More details on this under V 5.

180 See just 2e).

181 See above 1e).

182 *Keniston* in *Engel/Keller* (footnote 80) 136-138 reports the fear of Benjamin Barber of a "jihad" or an exclusively cultural nationalism.

183 See above 1.

and self-assistance as the most effective instruments of governance, even if it succeeds, democracy and the rule of law will considerably lose ground.[184]

V. Consequences for External Sovereignty

The Internet is capable of restricting the sovereignty of the state in many ways. It does not stop at national boundaries (1). It impedes the sovereignty of nation states in regard to information (2), currency (3) and values (4). This is why it has the potential of disintegrating the nation states (5). Autonomy becomes prohibitively expensive for a nation state (6). The traditional forms of statehood will be affected (7). New international conflicts arise (8).

1. Territorial Sovereignty

State boundaries play neither a technical nor an economic role in the Internet.[185] This weakens sovereignty in a two-fold manner. If the state considers a technical or economic aspect, or a question of content, to be in need of regulation, the regulatory object lies outside its jurisdiction to a large extent. Even its sovereignty over persons and institutions scarcely helps it further. From a political science viewpoint, the state therefore sees itself confronted with a problem of multi-level governance, much as is the case with protecting the climate or the atmosphere.[186]

However, the Internet is no natural phenomenon. It is both made and used by people. These people do not necessarily have the world's general well-being or the well-being of a particular nation state in mind. On the contrary, they will often seek their own advantage. The Internet expands the possibilities of exerting strategic influence on national regulations. This applies firstly to regulation of the Internet itself. The USA would, for example, like to regulate electronic gambling, but have problems with this approach, because the gambling operators have, as a precaution, established their businesses in the Caribbean. And we already know that the Internet presents new possibilities for exit in many other areas of life.[187] They also simultaneously weaken the sovereignty of the state.

2. Sovereignty of Information

Even in the past, states never had complete sovereignty of information. Flyers jettisoned from aircraft, the spill-over of terrestrial frequencies and direct-transmission satellites allowed the penetration of foreign content.[188] People travelled and communicated by telephone, thus allowing information to spread abroad. But both the former have become so much easier with the Internet that the idea of a state's sovereignty on

184 See *Engel* Selbstregulierung (footnote 149) .

185 See above I 1.

186 Compare *Steger* Globalisierung (footnote 151) 61: "Das Auseinanderfallen des staatlichen Handlungsraumes und der Reichweite der Probleme stellt die Funktion des Nationalstaats auf den Prüfstand".

187 See above IV 2.

188 On the older discussion in public international law see *Christoph Engel:* Das Völkerrecht des Telekommunikationsvorgangs, in: RabelsZ 1985, 90-120.

information no longer makes much sense.[189] This is because the Internet is not only very cheap and very simple, it is also very safe and, if desired, secret and anonymous.[190] Of lesser concern is propaganda of a foreign state. Yet the people do receive an insight into foreign ways of life, get to know know other political institutions and are capable of comparing their own country much more precisely with other countries. This is not only useful to foreign states, but also to non-governmental organizations. With the aid of the Internet, environmental organizations succeeded in making certain topics the subject of international negotiations.[191] Anyone wishing to gather information can access foreign data bases.[192] National security mongering often falls apart in a networked world because of foreign openness. Anyone wishing to read secret German government documents can often obtain them with the aid of the American Freedom of Information Act, because the German government has seen itself forced to consult its American partner on a particular issue and has sent them a copy of the pertinent documentation for the purpose.

In contrast, it is becoming more and more difficult for nation states to hide events in their territory from the eyes of the world public. Students of an American law school, for example, ensure that information from Bosnia and Kosovo is constantly available on the Internet.[193] In this way, foreign states and non-governmental organizations can exercise much better control as to whether a state upholds its obligations to its people under public international law.

3. Currency Sovereignty

We have already spoken several times about the possibility of private electronic money.[194] Technically, this is possible.[195] Economically, electronic money is so attractive because this is the only way that micropayments can be made.[196] Anonymous electronic money is also the securest method of preventing personality profiles being deduced from electronic payments.[197] Since electronic money represents a substitute for credit cards, it remains to be seen, however, whether the credit card companies can prevent the creation of this new market. Visa has in any case just purchased the technically most ambitious project, Mondex.[198]

---

189 Compare *Brock* (footnote 7) apuz 33-34/97, 17: "Die Verbreitung von Wissen [ist] wesentlich schwerer einzudämmen oder zu kanalisieren [...] als der Export von Gütern".

190 More details above I 4 and 5 as well as 9-11.

191 More from *Perritt* (footnote 105) JILS 1997, 155.

192 Immediately above.

193 Both initiatives are originate from the Chicago-Kent College of Law, http://pbosnia.kentlaw.edu (2.3.1999); http://www.kenntlaw.edu/kosovo (2.3.1999); further examples in *Froomkin* (footnote 31) UPittsbJLC 1996, 506.

194 See above II 3b) and IV 2c).

195 Overviews are provided, inter alia, by *Achim Bühl*: Cybermoney oder die Verflüchtigung des Geldes, in: *Andreas Brill/Michael de Vries (eds.)* Virtuelle Wirtschaft. Virtuelle Unternehmen, virtuelle Produkte, virtuelles Geld und virtuelle Kommunikation, Opladen 1998, 224-240; and *Aleksander Berentsen:* Digitales Geld, Geldmenge und Geldpolitik, id. 251-264.

196 See already above II 3b) and *Froomkin* (footnote 31) UPittsbJLC 1996, 454.

197 Id.

198 I owe this reference to *Saskia Sassen*.

Electronic money could allow *Friedrich-August von Hayek's* vision of private money[199] and *Knut Wicksell's* of an economy based totally on credit[200] to become reality. Central banks would lose their ability to control the quantity of money in circulation. Anonymous electronic money is even more anonymous than cash.[201] One thing both have in common is that the payment record cannot be traced. But on top of that, with anonymous electronic money, the buyer and the purchaser can even avoid meeting personally.[202] This will facilitate money laundering and, to a very great extent, withdraw monetary assets from the control of the state.

4. Sovereignty of Values

Values fulfill individual and social functions. They facilitate an individual's orientation and decisions. Both ultimately fuse together, since without preconceptions, an individual cannot comprehend his environment. However, this preconception is inevitably based on value judgements.[203] The social function of values can best be explained in terms of system theory. In order for individuals to be able to live together, values create the code that allows communication in the first place.[204] Values are conveyed about education, socialization and enculturation. Admittedly, cultures were never completely identical, confined to the borders of a single state, and culture was always more of a social phenomenon than one of the state. But cultural ties were normally more territorial and local than personal. If they were personal, they were primarily linked to nationality. That is why the state and society were able to form a joint culture.

This has become more difficult in the Internet. Space and time play no role here.[205] People come into contact with foreign cultures much more frequently and intensively than before.[206] Missionary type cultures can actively attempt to expand their sphere of influence. The less the Internet differentiates into language and culture zones[207], the more it could lead to a global monoculture of English and the American Way of Life.[208]

---

199 *Friedrich August von Hayek*: Denationalisation of Money: the Argument Refined. An Analysis of the Theory and Practice of Concurrent Currencies (Hobart Paper Special 70) London 1990.

200 *Knut Wicksell*: Geldzins und Güterpreise. Eine Studie über die den Tauschwert des Geldes bestimmenden Ursachen, Jena 1898 (Aalen2 1984).

201 This holds at least true for the Internet payments offered by the e-cash system of the company DigiCash. Compare *Aleksander Berentsen:* Monetary Policy Implications of Digital Money, in: Kyklos 51 (1998) 89-117 (92); *Jörg Bibow/Thorsten Wichmann:* Elektronisches Geld. Funktionsweise und wirtschaftspolitische Konsequenzen, in: RWI-Mitteilungen 47 (1997) 115-139 (124).

202 Compare *Richard W. Rahn*: The New Monetary Universe and ist Impact on Taxation, in: *James A. Dorn (ed.)*: The Future of Money in the Information Age, 81-89 (82).

203 For details see *Hans Albert:* Traktat über rationale Praxis (Die Einheit der Gesellschaftswissenschaften 22) Tübingen 1978.

204 For details see *Baecker* in *Engel/Keller* (footnote 49); on both functions and their inner connection *Kersting* in *Engel/Keller* (footnote 140).

205 See above I 1 and 3.

206 *David*: The Internet and the Economics of Network Technology Evolution, in: *Engel/Keller* Understanding the Impact of Global Networks on Local Social, Political and Cultural Values 39-71 (42).

207 See above on this II 4.

208 Details in *Keniston* in *Engel/Keller* (footnote 80) 131-136 and passim.

Alternatively, the various cultures could differentiate themselves more and more according to specific stratums of society, career origins or ideological orientations. The elites might become culturally homeless.[209] Many people will be able to live in several cultures simultaneously. An optimistic version connects a local bond in the stricter sense with other professional or ideological links that are not tied to a particular place. Precisely this modern solution to the problem could generate another problem of its own. People not able to cope with the virtuoso game of playing several roles could grasp the flight into simplicity and search for their identity within firmer ideologies.[210]

It is hard to predict which one of these trends will ultimately succeed, but all agree that a loosening of the congruence between cultural zone and the nation state will occur[211]. At the same time, people's access to information will differentiate itself more and more. News filters will lead to customized media.[212] People will no longer necessarily take notice of the news all at the same time. It remains to be seen how successful push technologies will become.[213] A process thus gathers impetus that already began with the differentiation of the print media and the privatization of electronic media. We no longer see only a few intermediaries who, so to speak, set the people's political agenda themselves. Finally, political institutions also lose terrain as governance instruments. Many questions are more effectively able to be overcome via self-regulation or self-help. That is why it would be irrational if individuals turned their attention mainly to the activities of political institutions.[214]

5. Disintegration

Political institutions do not serve a purpose in themselves. When historic cultures come to an end, initially only nostalgic regret is sparked off. It is different, however, if people's whole behaviour is altogether less embedded in values rather than simply one value being replaced by another, or one culture by another. The "cognitive card" of these individuals, will then, namely, become much more uncertain.[215] Social cohabitation becomes more difficult. Much which was previously taken for granted, now needs to be secured via rules of law.[216] People need to exert much more effort in order to create a reliable intersubjective information system.[217] This impacts on the functioning of a market economy, since only in the case of a spot contract for a standardized good do the contractual parties go their own separate ways immediately following the agreement's conclusion. If a delivery is made on credit, or if the purchaser cannot immediately evaluate the quality of the wares, the parties are necessarily bound to each other for a longer period. This is particularly the case when, within a company, exchange is

---

209 *Henning Klodt:* Globalisierung: Phänomen und empirische Relevanz, in: Jahrbuch für neue politische Ökonomie 17 (1998) 7-34 (9f.); see also *Brock* (footnote 7) apuz 33-34/97, 18: national cultures are replaced by globalized cultures of experts.

210 See already above IV 1 e).

211 I owe this thought to *Fritz W. Scharpf.*

212 *Dertouzos* (footnote 9) 121.

213 See above II 5.

214 Compare a formulation that I owe to *Saskia Sassen:* "The political space is being reconfigured".

215 *Knight* (footnote 130) 88f.

216 *Knight* (footnote 130) 194f.

217 *David* in *Engel/Keller* (footnote 11) 64.

replaced by the principle of organization, or if one of the endless hybrid forms between agreement and organization is employed.[218] All these forms yield gains from cooperation only if and when the parties can bring with them a minimum willingness to bear a risk. If they want to cover themselves against every possible risk, the agreement will, at best, be a zero-sum game.[219] Without a minimum of trust, particularly towards persons whom one has not known previously, a market economy cannot increase the general prosperity. Until now, this trust has had its roots in the common culture of the parties to the transaction.[220]

The Internet could have the potential of eroding the embeddedness of behaviour in values, for which there is a psychological as well as a sociological indicator. Psychologists point to the fact that intrinsic motivation is easy to destroy but difficult to build.[221] In the Internet, people are confronted frequently and intensively with other cultures. No-one initially notices if their attitude leans away more and more from that of their own cultural heritage. The originating culture therefore has little opportunity to strengthen a shaken orientation of values. Those who wish, can almost completely avoid other people in the Internet. They can at any rate remain anonymous.[222] Even those giving their name do not come face-to-face with a conversation partner in the Internet. If one omits the virtual communities, people in the Internet often meet each other in a decontextualized environment.[223] All this has considerable psychological significance. For it is precisely by face to face contact and by context that value orientations are strengthened.[224]

From a sociological perspective, the problem is not one of changing values. Society's stock of values was never stable. That taboos are broken is also not a problem. On the contrary, the cohesion of a society becomes manifest in the common defence of a taboo. But social cohesion becomes more difficult when the Internet demands changing values in rapid succession from a society, or when many values are simultaneously affected. For not only the building up of intrinsic motivation needs time - the grouping of a society or a social subsystem around a new code also does.[225]

---

218 Compare the reference already mentioned in footnote 163.

219 *Scharpf* Games Real Actors Play (footnote 148) 97.

220 Economics is now beginning to take on these questions. One analysis which is not convincing in each and every aspect is offered by *Tanja Ripperger:* Ökonomik des Vertrauens. Analyse eines Organisationsprinzips (Die Einheit der Gesellschaftswissenschaft 101) Tübingen 1998.

221 More details from *Bruno S. Frey/Iris Bohnet:* Die Ökonomie zwischen extrinsicher and intrinsicher Motivation, in: Homo Oeconomicus 11 (1994) 1-20.

222 Compare *Froomkin* (footnote 31) UPittsbJLC 1996, 405: "digital anonymity exacerbates the trends that are producing a society of strangers"; *Thompson* in *Engel/Keller* (footnote 79) 118 then talks of "propinquity without community".

223 I owe this reference to *Robert Adams.*

224 More details from *Iris Bohnet:* Kooperationen und Kommunikation. Eine ökonomische Analyse individueller Entscheidungen (Die Einheit der Gesellschaftswissenschaften 98) Tübingen 1997, especially 30-34.

225 I owe this thought to *Dirk Baecker.*

6. Prohibitive Costs of Autonomy

Even the Internet cannot change territorial jurisdiction. In most states it corresponds now as then with the factual power over activities in its own territory. But even if it so desired, a state would find it hard to prevent every connection to the Internet within its borders, since digital signals can also be transmitted via satellite.[226] Additionally, wired transmissions use existing telecommunications lines.[227] The state thus cannot simply forbid every physical connection to the Internet, if it does not wish to simultaneously cut itself off from worldwide telephone traffic. At the very most, it can attempt to filter all signals that have been transmitted as packets.[228]

But it is primarily the costs of such an autarkic strategy that are prohibitive – a course upon which only North Korea and Myanmar have embarked.[229] This is because the Internet does not only transport problematic signals that are capable of endangering the inner stability or cultural homogeneity within a country. Its main function is as a tool for international exchange in the sciences and economics. China and Singapore are, nonetheless, still attempting to attach strict conditions to Internet access in their countries.[230] Yet Singapore has already had to accept a number of setbacks in this regard. Initially, it had only issued a licence for a single Internet access provider. In 1995, out of fear of pornographic pictures, the government forced this provider to scan 80,000 files with the suffix .gif, an action which did actually also succeed in unearthing five pornographic pictures. The government has not repeated this one-off experiment, because foreign companies with a subsidiary in Singapore feared that, in this manner, their confidential e-mails would be exposed.[231] In the meantime, Singapore has relaxed its policy even further. Only households are still obliged to use this access provider, whereas companies can now obtain direct access to the Internet. They only have to commit themselves to ensuring that their employees consume only permissible content.[232]

At best, all other countries around the world intercept Internet use on a random basis. This has repercussions on their freedom to choose an economic constitution and an orientation towards a particular set of values. The Internet namely destabilizes authoritarian regimes and stabilizes liberal and flexible ones.[233] The Internet therefore brings about an acceleration in the modernisation of state and society.[234] In the end, this could also alter the political culture in Germany. While Germany is a democratic country, it is more corporatist than liberal. The corporatist interplay between many inwardly relatively closed groups can profit much less from the new technical,

---

226 See above I 8.

227 More details above I 2.

228 More details just above.

229 *Froomkin* (footnote 31) UPittsbJLC 1996, 445 and references.

230 More from *Goldsmith* (footnote 32) UCLR 1998, 1228.

231 *Froomkin* (footnote 31) UPittsbJLC 1996, 446f..

232 I owe this reference to *Herbert Burkert.*

233 *Henry Perritt,* reported by *David G. Post:* The "Unsettled Paradox": The Internet, the State and the Consent of the Government, http://www.cli.org/sov.html (12.02.1999) 2.

234 *Kersting* in *Engel/Keller* (footnote 140).

journalistic and economic possibilities of the Internet than the individualistic American society. In the attempt not to fall behind either economically or politically, the political culture in Germany could simultaneously undergo change.[235]

7. Transforming Statehood

Statehood will be transformed not only on account of the new possibilities of exit and voice, but also on account of the new shake-ups in sovereignty. For one, the state will become less important as a protective entity. It has neither power on its own nor with the cooperation of other states to control the activities taking place in the Internet. It is therefore unable to provide this protective service to its citizens.[236] In this respect, the Internet is part of the globalisation process. It forces states to define themselves for the most part by way of issues with a genuine link to territory: inner and outer security, use of land and the resolution of local environmental problems. Participation in national politics therefore becomes less attractive to citizens.[237] The power of regulation migrates to the international community and to self-steering mechanisms. We will see that democratic, legitimate national parliaments can exert influence[238], but they no longer carry sole responsibility for regulatory activity and also do not exercise complete power over same.

In addition, the possibilities of exit[239] force the nation states to strike at weaker substitutes with their regulations. A glance into the rules of attribution contained in the Media Services Treaty of the German Länder and the Federal Information and Communications Services Act is very informative in this regard.[240] Of course, German justice would prefer to prosecute the originator of illegal contents. But this is often a hopeless undertaking in the Internet, because the originator chooses either a state with liberal rules or one that has no effective enforcement powers. In order to overcome this, German law then strikes out at the user. In accordance with 184 StGB (criminal code) it is thus not only the person who fabricates pornographic material about children who commits a criminal offence, but also anyone distributing, purchasing or even viewing it. For the criminal investigation authorities this rule represents a Danaer gift. For instead of controlling a few manufacturers, they must now attempt to control the whole consumer scene.

The Media Services Treaty and the Information and Communications Services Act also allow, in principle, for the prosecution of an organized online service provider who offers problematic content, instead of against its originator. At first glance, this improves the regulator's situation, since it covers providers such as T-Online, AOL or

235 *Werle* in *Engel/Keller* (footnote 12) 160, 170 and passim.

236 *Saskia Sassen:* Sovereignty and the Internet, in: *Christoph Engel/Kenneth Keller* (Eds.): Understanding the Impact of Global Networks on Local Social, Political and Cultural Values 189.

237 Compare *Steger* (footnote 151) 41.

238 See below VIII 4.

239 See above IV 2.

240 Media Services Treaty of 01.08.1997, GVBl. Hessen 1997 I 135; Informations- und Kommunikationsdienste-Gesetz of 22.07.1997, BGBl. 1997 I 1870. The rules of attribution are laid out in paragraph 5 of both documents.

CompuServe. But, in the medium term, this is not very helpful. The problematic contents move to less well-organized services or services that are completely unorganized. It is no coincidence that the majority of problematic contents are simultaneously especially attractive commercially. This is particularly true of sex and crime. If organized providers do not wish to be pushed out of business they will also organize themselves in the long run in such a way that regulation can no longer tangent them. In the end, all that remains is the plain Internet provider. German law is provident enough not to attribute the Internet's contents to it. Even if a legal system sought to proceed differently, it would scarcely be of use, since we already know that one needs practically no capital in order to become an Internet provider. Backyard providers would therefore still keep mushrooming. If there is sufficient willingness to pay, the users can in any case deviate to low earth orbit satellite systems. In the case of Teledesic, virtually all its intelligence is located on the satellite. So not even the provider's technical headquarters remain as a hostage on Earth.[241]

In other regards, too, the Internet forces national regulators to revert to weaker substitutes. Thanks to packet transmission, states can mostly only just determine that someone has accessed a problematic site, but they are unable to prevent the use of its contents.[242] The only course that remains is to subsequently proceed against the user by means of criminal law or command and control regulation. If this user has been tipped off, he will encrypt the signal.[243] In this case, it is then only possible to determine that he has received or sent an encoded signal. If he also uses a remailer[244], it can only be determined that he made an anonymous communications transaction.

8. Potential for International Conflicts

The potential for international conflicts increases on account of the Internet, as every state is now a potential neighbour. Most conflicts therefore gain a multilateral character. Conflicts of jurisdiction increase.[245] It becomes more difficult to organize the co-existence of different ideologies, state constitutions and economic orders. Many of these are existential conflicts, not merely conflicts of interest.[246] From the point of view of an individual state and its government, the more vibrant competition between systems is felt as an international conflict.[247]

At the same time, nation states are forced more and more to coordinate with other nations, because only thus can they achieve their political objectives.[248] But this makes tolerance towards other ideologies even more painful.

Finally, the destabilization of national societies and states is a source of new, international conflict. States defend themselves when foreign groups seek to gain

---

241 See above I 8.
242 See above I 9.
243 See above I 10.
244 See above I 11.
245 See more details under VIII 3b) on the extra territorial application of national law.
246 *Kersting* in *Engel/Keller* (footnote 140) 9-27.
247 See above before I and IV 2.
248 *Beck* (footnote 107) apuz 38-98, 6f.

influence on their political way of life, or even join up together with domestic groups. Taking the Kurds as an example, it has just become quite apparent how effective minorities can meanwhile organize themselves across borders. Defensive reactions of local cultures prepared to use force can even lead to civil war and, in turn, endanger international peace.[249]

Additionally, the Internet brings changes in the comparative economic and political advantages of states.[250] This can lead to further impoverishment of the poorer nations.[251] Alternatively, previously successful nations fall behind on account of competition. This could happen precisely to Germany, if it turns out to be correct that a corporatist society cannot use the new opportunities well.

Finally, the technology itself creates new conflicts. Many developing countries refuse to accept that the satellite systems close to the Earth, Iridium and Teledesic, necessarily cover every place around the globe, since these developing countries have no influence, of course, on the commercial and journalistic decisions of the operators.[252]

VI. Efficacy Losses of the International Community's Traditional Solutions

Tried and tested solutions of the international community lose their effectiveness through the Internet. This primarily concerns sovereignty (1), possibilities for the legal management of co-existence (2) and opportunities for overcoming international conflicts via a treaty (3).

1. Sovereignty

The cornerstone of international law is the sovereignty of states. It effectively organizes communities. If Germany and France have a problem, it is not necessary for 130 million people to negotiate with each other. Two governments negotiate on their behalf instead. The Internet and globalisation do not abrogate sovereignty, but certainly weaken it. There are two reasons for this, which we have already noted. States are no longer monopolists: they are subjected to substitution competition from other states.[253] In other words: they are no longer complete masters in their own houses. In addition, many of the Internet's regulatory problems can only be resolved through international cooperation or self-regulation mechanisms.[254] Economically, both can be understood as the attenuation of political property rights.[255]

---

249 Again see *Kenniston's* reference in *Engel/Keller* (footnote 53) 140-141, to *Benjamin Barber* and the worry of a Jihad.

250 *Grewlich* Cyberspace (footnote 8) Chapter One. 2. 2., Chapter Six. 2. 2. and passim.

251 *Dertouzos* (footnote 9) 240-243 describes the disadvantages of black Africa.

252 *Dertouzos* (footnote 9) 324f.

253 See above in front of I.

254 See already above IV 4 and more under VIII 4-5.

255 I owe this analogy to *Giandomenico Najone;* for a comprehensive overview of the economic concept of property rights see *Thrainn Eggertsson:* Economic Behaviour and Institutions. Cambridge 1990.

2. Co-existence

Traditionally, international law has considered the organization of co-existence between states to be its most noble task. It was precisely **not** concerned with pushing through a uniform concept of good politics or ethics for the entire world. On the contrary, each country was to the maximum extent possible supposed to be able to proceed in its own manner. The primary instruments for achieving this objective are the exclusive granting of sovereignty and the prohibition of intervention. Only one central area of conflict remained: the overlapping area of sovereignty over territories and nationals, which has led to the rules of public international law on the treatment of foreign nationals. Although after the Second World War, human rights and some material principles of the international community were added, they are still understood as rules of negative coordination. Their concern is that a state might intervene too much into the protected sphere of individuals. This orientation of general international law was sufficient and appropriate as long as power was mainly executed by means of command and control. As has already been suggested several times, this type of regulation is however only in exceptional cases suitable for regulating the Internet.[256] Even national legal systems find it hard to exert control over self-regulation or over self-help.[257] Much less well developed are the instruments of international law in regard to context governance.

It is hard for the international community to organize its co-existence in the Internet because the Internet has no headquarters. This is why the solutions found for the closely-related area of telecommunications policy provide no assistance here. In telecommunications policy, the International Telecommunication Union ITU has meanwhile successfully managed to organize the co-existence of diametrally-opposed telecommunications orders.[258] This was comparatively easy since, traditionally, there were just the national monopolies. In any case, telecommunications signals are transmitted continuously and from one point of the Earth's surface to another[259], and the networks have a clearly-defined, mainly hierarchical structure. Conversly, in the Internet, signals are transmitted in packets, using unforeseeable transmission paths.

3. Agreement

Finally, the possibility of concluding treaties will also be shattered, since states will in many cases no longer be in a position to make credible commitments. Exit and voice mean that governments are no longer complete masters in their own households. We can also draw on another pair of terms: the alien state can no longer be sure that the logic of influence will always retain the upper hand over the logic of membership[260].

256 See more details under VIII 2-3.

257 See *Engel* again, Selbstregulierung (footnote 149).

258 More from *Christoph Engel:* Wege zur Bewältigung der Konflikte in der globalen Informationsgesellschaft, in: *Ernst-Joachim Mestmäcker (Ed.):* Kommunikation ohne Monopole II. Ein Symposium über Ordnungsprinzipien im Wirtschaftsrecht der Telekommunikation und der elektronischen Medien (Law and Economics of International Telecommunications 23) Baden-Baden 1995, 179-210.

259 This will not alter until non-geostationary satellites are positioned, see above I. 8. Up till now, however, they were unable to permanently shake national telecommunications orders.

260 See above footnote 121.

Additionally, outwardly, states can no longer promise with certainty that a third country will not be able to interfere in their domestic sphere, thereby frustrating the agreement. If the potential contracting party is able to do this himself, then the conclusion of a treaty will be less attractive to him. He can obtain the object of his desires by himself, without having to make contractual concessions. Economic contract theory can precisely explain why an international treaty then loses its effectiveness. This is exactly the consequence of attenuated political property rights.[261] The subject of international treaties is, namely, the exchange of such rights. If these property rights are no longer well-defined, the mechanism of exchanging promises is weakened.

VII. New Demand for Supranational Rules

If we only had classic international law, an almost tragic situation would arise, in that this instrument would lose its effectiveness just at the moment when the need for it increases. Internet trade needs protection against the abuse of national sovereignty rights (1). The more international daily reality becomes, the less satisfying are institutions of a private law society that are grounded in national legal orders (2). The correction of market failure caused or increased by the net often only makes sense at international level (3). The following examples illustrate the demand for regulation.

1. The Removal of Obstacles to Internet Trade

The Internet is plagued by one of the oldest co-existence problems of the international community. Especially Germany, with its divided territorial history, has gained particularly intensive experience with this. If the next barrier at which customs duty is levied comes every few kilometers, international trade cannot flourish. It is equally bothersome if every transit state levies and collects its own tax. This problem is particularly serious in the Internet because precisely at the outset it is not clear which path the data packets will take.[262] Not surprisingly, it is mainly the United States that is working on making Internet trade free of customs taxes, or at least a zone in which harmonized tax rates will apply.[263] Since 1998, it has made such trade tax-free for three years as far as its own laws are concerned.[264] In the World Trade Organization (WTO), it was only able to push through a standstill arrangement.[265]

2. International Institutions of a Private Law Society

Traditionally, international law has simply assumed the existence of private law orders on a national basis. At best, international agreements have unified the rules for coordinating these private law orders, by means of treaties harmonizing private international law. However, adjacent to this, uniform substantive rules have always existed, i.e. institutions of a private law society have been directly embedded in

261 See just above 1.

262 See above I 1 and 9.

263 http://www.whitehouse.gov/WH/new/commerce/index-plain.html (11.12.1998).

264 *Werle* in *Engel/Keller* (footnote 12) 164.

265 More in *Grewlich* Cyberspace (footnote 8) Chapter Four. 2. 2..

international agreements.[266] Typical examples are the conventions pertaining to laws on bills of exchange and also cheque laws. Through the Internet, the need for uniform rules has suddenly increased.[267] Copyright law[268], digital signatures[269], the electronic conclusion of contracts[270], as well as electronic payments[271] are classic legal institutions. However, uniform rules concerning technical standards[272], the unique addressing of computers via IP-addresses[273] and their transformation into domain names[274] are also needed. Ultimately, national antitrust authorities have a hard time preventing market dominance over Internet activities, a danger of whose existence the public at large became aware through the Microsoft case. The work being carried out in the context of the WTO on an international antitrust law is therefore also important for the Internet.[275]

3. International Correction of Market Failure

There are certain goods with which markets cannot come to terms. With others, the question of whether alternative institutional arrangements can come to terms better than the market is not at all a trivial one. As is well known, economics speaks in both cases of market failure. There are sufficient examples of both in the Internet. It lies outside the power of a single nation state to overcome these problems.

Sometimes the Internet community has so far been unable to define or enforce property rights. Electronic violence can ensue, for example, by entering viruses into the system.[276] In a dispute, someone blocks the mail server of another person by sending enormously large programmes as attachments, or he sends messages in the name of a third party which damage that person's reputation.[277] Data security also belongs at this juncture.[278] Documents are falsified. The same is also done quite easily with pictures once they have been digitally scanned.[279]

---

266 Comprehensively *Jan Kropholler:* Internationales Einheitsrecht (Beiträge zum ausländischen und internationalen Privatrecht 39) Tübingen 1975.

267 See again the White Paper from the White House on Internet Trade (footnote 28) Principle No. 3, Recommendations No. 1-9.

268 Comprehensively on this point *Grewlich* Cyberspace (footnote 8) Chapter Eight.

269 More id. Chapter Six. 2. 1. with references.

270 More id. Chapter Two. 3. 5. 1..

271 See above V 3.

272 More from *Dertouzos* (footnote 9) 83.

273 See above I 2.

274 Comprehensively on this point *Dertouzos* (footnote 9) 83.

275 Compare *Ernst-Ulrich Petersmann*: Proposals For Negotiating International Competition Rules in the GATT-WTO World Trade and Legal System, in: Außenwirtschaft 49 (1994) 231-277 and the contributions to *Wolfgang Fikentscher/Ulrich Immenga (eds.)*: Draft International Antitrust Code, Baden-Baden 1995.

276 Details in *Dertouzos* (footnote 9) 287.

277 *Dertouzos* (footnote 9) 287 reports of antisemitic remarks, which a Canadian sent in the name of an American Internet provider.

278 The American government considers the lack of data security to be one of the biggest obstacles to the development of Internet trade, White Paper (footnote 267), Recommendation No. 6.

279 *Dertouzos* (footnote 9) 148-150 therefore reckons that electronic pictures will in future count as having as little authenticity as a typed text.

Particularly vulnerable groups or interests demand protection. This is where data protection[280], consumer protection from fraud in the net[281] or from unsolicited advertising belong.[282] Even more pressing is the fact that the Internet lacks selection mechanisms and also institutions enabling it to forget[283], rules on the management of information waste, so to speak.[284] Last, but not least, there are contents that many, if not all states, detest: child pornography, hate speech and instructions for building atomic bombs being only the most distasteful.[285]

VIII. Solutions

1. Introduction

"Where there's danger, there's also a saviour," or so wrote Friedrich Hölderlin. Even in the Age of the Internet, the world will not sink into anarchy. States will not fall apart like clay giants. The Earth's system of political power has always demonstrated its ability to meet new challenges. Viewed absolutely, not a single legal system around the globe can protect the legal goods defined by it. It suffices therefore when problematic developments again become marginalized. It sometimes also suffices if public attention is turned to other matters.[286] Pragmatic willingness, not a Cassandra call, is needed to find reasonable solutions via trial and error. Historically, the development of statehood has always followed along the same lines as the possibilities of being able to exert power.

Moreover, it would be wrong to take a one-sided view at the loss of traditional instruments of power. For a long time in the USA, the discussion about the political effects of the Internet has even been formulated as the opposite of Athen to Orwell.[287] The state therefore also gains new instruments of power in the Internet of a technical, journalistic and economic nature. Once people transmit the majority of their communications via the Internet, many new monitoring possibilities open themselves up to secret services and investigation authorities[288], as a person's whole communication behaviour is reflected in the log files;[289] electronic watermarks prove the falsification of documents[290]; a sniffer finds documents wherever they are located on the net; or a buddy alarms the monitoring authorities, as soon as someone logs into the net. If the

280 See also on this just White Paper (footnote 267) Recommendation No. 5.

281 *Grewlich* Cyberspace (footnote 8) Chapter One. 2. 1..

282 The Internet community then speaks of spamming. According to its code of ethics, it is one of the most serious crimes. More from *David R. Johnson:* Self-ordering for the Internet, http://www.cli.org/selford/problems.htm (12.02.1999).

283 I owe this plastic term to *Nicole te Heesen.*

284 Compare *Dertouzos* (footnote 9) 238, who speaks of "info-junk".

285 More in *Christoph Engel:* Inhaltskontrolle im Internet, in: AfP 1996, 220-227.

286 See already above III.

287 Details from *Thompson* in *Engel/Keller* (footnote 79) 118, who, however, rightly considers it to be an impermissible abbreviation.

288 A horror scenario is found in *Dertouzos* (footnote 9) 293, who, however, believes it to be overemphasized.

289 See above I 11, but also at this reference the possibilities of anonymization.

290 Sometimes, however, the watermark can be removed via compression and subsequent decompression of the document.

state issues wireless identification cards, it can even depict a person's mobility behaviour.[291]

The new journalistic possibilities of the Internet are not only used by minorities. They can be equally applied by the state for a clever public relations campaign or a propagandistic shaping of the political preferences of its citizens. Finally, it is not a settled state of affairs that the state always sees itself cast back to weaker substitutes.[292] On the contrary, some believe that new targets will materialize to which the state will be able to apply regulation better than was previously the case.[293] The very fact that the Internet is itself a net, speaks for this thesis. Most of the Internet's uses also have network character. We already know that network goods represent a dynamic problem, in that a critical mass must first be reached. If a provider succeeds in this aim, subsequent competitors with more or less identical goods have an extremely difficult time. This insight has double importance for the regulator. The number of providers is endogenously kept small. And goverment can try to influence the attempt to gain critical mass.[294]

The possibilities of governing the Internet can be divided into five categories: a community of states can conclude a treaty (2); a single state can employ its legal system (3); non-state actors can create legal rules and enforce them (4), but they can also employ non-legal governance tools (5); and finally, people can completely manage without central control and resort to self-help (6).

2. Solutions by the International Community of States

In public, the impression is often gladly created of the community of states being powerless and therefore inactive in regards to the Internet. That is not correct. The international law system had already attended to some problems before the Internet was created. As far back as 1910, a treaty existed to combat the distribution of illicit publications.[295] The treaty concerned "illicit papers, drawings, pictures or objects that have an international character".[296] This also fits electronic transmission. The treaty obliges the contractual states to proceed against such publications and to support one another in their pursuit.[297] The Convention on the Prevention and Punishment of

---

291 More detail by *Farber* in *Engel/Keller* (footnote 58) 32f..

292 See above IV 4.

293 See the thesis of *Paul David* and *Klaus W. Grewlich*.

294 This should not, however, be viewed as a cure-all remedy. The state interferes with the incentives for creatively changing the system the more it has previously regulated the system. At the same time it provides an impulse for greater decentralisation. Hence regulation possibly prevents network externalities being taken profit from. Finally, the regulated firms will attempt to dissect the value creation chain so that they are no longer tangented by the regulation.

295 Treaty of 04.05.1910, RGBl. 1911, 209, as well as protocol of 04.05.1949, UNTS 30, 3 consolidated edition UNTS 47, 159. The Federal Republic has however not yet signed the changed treaty.

296 Article 1 I Nr. 1 of the Treaty.

297 In a strict sense, the treaty does not however effect any legal harmonization, because in Article 1 I 1 only refers to such acts that prove to be at variance with municipal law. If one looks more closely, however, it must be determined to which provisions of municipal law the treaty refers. This demands an autonomous term of "illicit writings".

Genocide, dating from 1948[298], obliges the parties to that agreement, inter alia, to criminalize the "direct and public incitement to commit genocide".[299] That is also the case where such a demand is made in the Internet. The fact that the user first has to download it is just a means of dissemination. The International Convention on the Avoidance of All Forms of Racial Discrimination dating back to the year 1966[300] forbids not only racially discriminating acts, but also racially discriminating words.[301] The United Nations' Human Rights Pact from the same year[302] protects not only human rights; it also forbids war propaganda[303] and "every encouragement of nationalistic, racial or religious hatred, which incites discrimination, animosity or violence.[304] In addition, there is a UN convention on the right of correction from the year 1953[305], to which the Federal Republic has not yet acceded.

There are also recent international agreements, the most important of which being the Treaty of the World Intellectual Property Rights Organization WIPO on the Protection of Copyright in the Internet[306]. The G-8 states have scheduled negotiations regarding international agreements on a whole series of questions relating to the Internet: child pornography, sexual abuse, drug dealing, money laundering, electronic fraud, computer piracy, as well as industrial and state espionage[307].

Customary law also has its merits for the Internet. It is created decentrally, often fashionably described nowadays as "bottom up", which is why it can react to a decentralized phenomenon like the Internet better than a central regulator.

However, international agreements and especially international customary law have a decisive disadvantage in that their development needs time. The delay may be endurable in some cases. Child pornography, for example, remains child pornography no matter what technical dissemination method is used. But many regulatory intentions are concerned with a particular technology or a particular use of the Internet. The danger then arises that an international rule is already out-of-date before it comes into existence.[308] But the international community can also react to that such as in the ITU, for example. In its international founding agreement, only a few material principles are laid down; it mostly contains principles concerning organizational and procedural

298 Convention of 09.12.1948, BGBl. 1954 II. 729.

299 Article III c of the convention.

300 Convention of 07.04.1966, BGBl. 1969 II 961, compare also BTDrs. 13/1883.

301 Article IV of the Convention

302 International Pact on Civil and Political Rights of 09.12.1966, BGBl. 1973 II 1533.

303 Article 20 I of the Pact.

304 Article 20 II of the Pact; compare also Article 26, whereby everyone has a right to protection against discrimination.

305 Convention on the International Right of Correction from 31.03.1953, UNTS 435, 192.

306 Agreement of 20.02.1996, WIPO Document CRNR/DC/94, published in: International Journal of Industrial Property and Copyright Law 1997, 208-213 or http://www.wipo.org (15.03.1999).

307 They have primarily referred to the work of the so-called Carnegie Groupe, http://www.iid.de/iukdg/carnegie_e.html (15.02.1999); more on the G8-discussions from *Goldsmith* (footnote 32) UCLR 1998, 1230-1232.

308 Compare *Grewlich* Cyberspace (footnote 8) Chapter One. 3. 1.: The Internet alters communication in a revolutionary way, whereas international law moves, at its best, in an evolutionary manner.

matters for the formation of rules. That is why this international organization can not only keep pace with technological developments, it can also influence them to a considerable extent via its standardization committees.[309]

But this also only functions if the international community is in agreement about material standards or, more precisely: they must be prepared to at least tolerate deviating concepts.[310] This prerequisite is often not found in the Internet, since states not only argue about concrete regulation projects; more often they clash over entirely different orientations regarding a desirable economic and social order.

3. Solutions Without the International Community

Even an individual state is not powerless against the Internet. Sometimes it even succeeds in dampening the competitive pressure on national regulation that is generated by the Internet (a). The greater its political power and its cleverness, the sooner a state can give its own regulatory ideas an extraterritorial effect (b). A promising venture is primarily the silent coordination of different national policies with the aid of private international law (c).

a) Strategic Dampening of the Competition between Systems

System competition, like competition in the product markets, is not an external power beyond the reach of those affected by it. On the contrary, in order to stay in the picture, they can endeavour to tone down the pressure from competition through their own market behaviour. At this point, we are only interested in unilateral market behaviour.[311] The state even has it particularly easy in this regard since, not only can it change its range of services, it can also employ those of its sovereign powers that remain unaffected by system competition.

As we already know, however, technical solutions have a very high price - eventually leading to autarky.[312] More promising are strategies that make exit so expensive that it no longer represents an attractive proposition. There are models for this from other areas. Canada and the USA struck at cross-border territorial radio as far back as the 1970s with a legal tax instrument. Canadian firms advertising on American radio stations were not able to set off the costs as company expenses from their taxes.[313] The USA reacted with the same rule for American advertising on Canadian programmes.[314] The lack of employee cross-border mobility also has to do with benefits that are coupled

309 Comprehensively *Andreas Tegge:* Die Internationale Telekommunikations-Union. Organisation und Funktion einer Weltorganisation im Wandel (Law and Economics of International Telecommunications 21) Baden-Baden 1994.

310 More detail from *Engel* in *Mestmäcker:* Kommunikation ohne Monopole II (footnote 258) 191-205.

311 But the parallels to a cartel do of course exist. That is precisely the conclusion of an international agreement that sets standards.

312 See above V. 6.

313 *Nicolas Matesco Matte/Ram S. Jakhu:* Law of International Telecommunications in Canada (Law and Economics of International Telecommunications 3) Baden-Baden 1987, 82 et.seq.

314 *Stefan R. Barnett:* Regulation of Mass Media, in: ders./Michael Botein/Eli Noam: Law of International Telecommunications in the United States (Law and Economics of International Telecommunications 4) Baden-Baden 1988, 189f.

to remaining in the country. For example, it is often difficult to transfer social insurance rights.[315] There is also a direct application example pertaining to the Internet: the American government is attempting to circulate the encryption standard it favours by obliging its use for all data exchange between the government and U.S. firms. So, if a firm does not wish to work with several different standards, it is obvious that it will then continue to use this standard in its communication with private parties as well.[316]

b) Extraterritoriality

The classic reply of national regulators to crossborder phenomena is the extraterritorial application of their own laws. In principle, this option presents itself for regulating the Internet as well. An individual state can therefore also influence processes that take place outside its territory.[317] Precisely Germany has come out in favour of this option. Bavarian prosecutors have forced CompuServe to deny access to newsgroups with pornographic content.[318] Since the managers responsible for Germany at CompuServe had omitted to take the advice of German authorities about other pornographic sites sufficiently seriously, a criminal case was brought by the Bavarian magistrate's court (Amtsgericht) and the chief executive officer of the German branch was sentenced.[319] Data protection provides another example: the European Data Protection Ordinance permits the transmission of personal data to a third country only if one of three criteria are fulfilled: either the Commission has determined that a suitable level of protection exists in that state;[320] sufficient ad hoc protective measures have been taken (which is the normal situation, whereby transmitter and user conclude protection agreements);[321] or, finally, one of the very strictly interpreted exceptions occurs, allowing a transmission that is justified by the overriding interests of the person concerned or an important public interest.[322]

However, the above example also simultaneously illustrates how precarious the extraterritorial application of national law actually is. Since how does one state ensure that the law of the destination state does not specifically prevent the application of these standards?[323] Contractualized data protection will only work if similar data transmissions take place repeatedly.[324] And a regulator will only be able to rely on contractual assurances if the reputation of internationally-active firms acting as a kind of

---

315 More from *Sell* in *Berg* (footnote 157) 73 f.

316 More from *A. Michael Froomkin:* It Came From Planet Clipper. The Battle over Cryptografic Key "Escrow" in: University of Chicago Legal Forum 1996, 15-75 (50-60, compare also 32).

317 Convincing *Goldsmith* (footnote 32) UCLR 1998, 1202-1205 and passim.

318 Reported by *Axel Kossel/Frank Möcke:* Pornowächter versus Internet, in: c't 1996/2, 14-17 (14).

319 More details from *Gunnar Bender:* Bavaria vs. Felix Somm. The Pornography Conviction of the Former CompuServe Manager, in: International Journal of Communications Law and Policy 1998/1, 1-4 http://www.digital-law.met/ILCLP/1_1998/ijclp_webdoc14_1_1998.html (18.02.1998).

320 Article 25 II Data Protection Directive (Directive 95/46/EC of 24 october 1995), OJ 1995 L 281/31.

321 Article 26 II of the Ordinance.

322 More explicitly GD XV D 5025/98, 3f. and passim; see and also comprehensively *Grewlich* Cyberspace (footnote 8) Chapter Four. 2. 3. 3. as well as Chapter Nine. 1. 4. 3..

323 GD XV D 5025/98, 22.

324 Id. 23.

hostage is available to him.[325] In addition, the extraterritorial application of national law leads to diplomatic conflicts. In the 1980s, antitrust law gained much experience in this regard.[326] It also raises questions of publicinternational law. For the extraterritorial application of national law is regarded as an unlawful intervention in foreign sovereignty, if the acting state cannot rely on a genuine link to the regulated activity.[327] Since location no longer plays a role in the Internet[328], it appears to be particularly doubtful whether the effects doctrine applies. That would, namely, be tantamount to foregoing any specific point of attachment, since all Internet contents can be downloaded from within every state around the globe.[329]

c) Conflict of Laws Provisions

States fight against the extraterritorial application of foreign economics law, because they consider it to be intervention by a foreign sovereign into their domestic affairs. This defensive behaviour is foreign to international private law. It is based on the basic idea of international decision unity. Instead of material justice, territorial justice seems to take its place. Those who have to adjust their lives to living with different legal systems should not get trapped between the wheels of the mill.[330] In private law, therefore, the state voluntarily allows itself to be the henchman of foreign legal systems. In this manner, it comes to coordinated enforcement of national laws. Speaking in terms of political economy, it is a form of coordinated behaviour between several sovereigns. This technical term from competition theory has been chosen with care. It expresses the idea that the coordinated behaviour is specifically not based on a binding agreement. Rather, the basis in every individual case is the revocable conviction that it is best for all states to proceed in such a manner.[331]

It is precisely the very number of states who are necessarily affected by every attempt at regulating the Internet that makes the mutual coordination of private law instruments an attractive option. The Internet could therefore become the initiator for a return to private

---

325 Id. 23f.

326 Illustrative the contributions to the symposium of the Max-Planck-Institute in Hamburg published in: RabelsZ 52 (1988) 1-302.

327 Comprehensively *Werner Meng:* Extraterritoriale Jurisdiktion im Öffentlichen Wirtschaftsrecht 1994; see also *Christoph Engel:* Die Bedeutung des Völkerrechts für die Anwendung in- und ausländischen Wirtschaftsrechts, in: RabelsZ 52 (1988) 271-302 and from the perspective of private international law *Anton K. Schnyder:* Wirtschaftskollisionsrecht. Sonderanknüpfung und extraterritoriale Anwendung wirtschaftsrechtlicher Normen unter besonderer Berücksichtigung von Marktrecht. Zürich 1990; *Stefan Habermeier:* Neue Wege zum Wirtschaftskollisionsrecht. Eine Bestandsaufnahme prävalenter wirtschaftskollisionsrechtlicher Methodologie unter dem Blickwinkel des kritischen Rationalismus (Saarbrücker Studien zum Internationalen Recht 6) Baden-Baden 1997.

328 See above I 1.

329 On this discussion, see *Grewlich* Cyberspace (footnote 8) Chapter Ten. 1. 3.; *Stephan Wilske/Teresa Schiller:* International Jurisdiction in Cyberspace. Which States May Regulate the Internet? In: Federal Communications Law Journal 50 (1997) 117-179; *Christine E. Mayeski:* The Presence of a Website as a Constitutionally Permissible Basis for Personal Jurisdiction, http://www.law.indiana.edu/ilj/v73/no1/mayeski.html (13.2.1999).

330 More details from *Jan Kropholler:* Internationales Privatrecht, Tübingen3 1997, pp. 24-40.

331 More from *Scharpf* Games Real Actors Play (footnote 148) pp. 107-112.

law.[332] A prerequisite, however, is the willingness of states to first bring the principles of conflict laws in this area more closely into line with each other than was previously the case.[333] In particular, it will scarcely be possible to retain, in international tort law, the principle that the law of the place applies where the protected good has been violated. For, in an Internet tort, this might be un unforeseeable multitude of legal orders, each demanding application to one and the same activity.

4. Solutions Without the State

The Internet acts as a stimulant to both conflict of laws and private legal ordering. One can interpret this as a form of self-regulation.[334] Encouraged by the American government, this is how the International Uniform Commercial Code for Electronic Trade[335] was able to be developed by industry associations and not by governments. It contains provisions for the settlement of online disputes via arbitration clauses.[336] Indeed, a suggestion has even been made to set up virtual arbitration tribunals for the resolution of net disputes.[337]

While private legal rules are not decreed by the state and arbitration decisions do not come before its courts, this does not mean that the legal system has no influence on private law or private jurisdiction. There is therefore no need for it to simply tolerate these processes; it can also prompt, prevent or change them. Ultimately, of course, this could occur via state decrees or prohibitions, but other mechanisms exist that are more elegant. Selective incorporation manipulates the interface between private rules and state law. Legally, there are three possibilities. In the first case, private rules or decisions directly become part of the legal order via incorporation, which is especially problematic from a constitutional point of view.[338] This is the reason why mere presumptions are more common in the German legal order. In product liability law, for example, it is presumed that a product is free-of-defects if it corresponds to DIN standards. While this presumption can be rebutted, only someone greatly disturbed by the DIN standard will take the trouble to bring forth counter evidence. Finally, private rules and decisions can also merely represent facts relevant for the application of general clauses of state law.[339]

---

332 I owe this thought to *Wolf Osthaus;* see also *Scharpf* Games Real Actors Play (footnote 148) p. 110: "It would be interesting to speculate, nevertheless, whether the simultaneous evolution of world-wide systems of communication and world-wide economic exchange might also increase the speed of mutual adjustment at such a rate that even in the presence of continuous external change, social interactions might now benefit from temporary equilibria that previously were too short-lived to be realized".

333 Compare White House (footnote 267), Principle No. 5: "The legal framework supporting commercial transactions should be consistent and predictable regardless of the jurisdiction in which a particular buyer and seller reside".

334 A type of law merchant is created, *Goldsmith* (footnote 32) UCLR 1998, 1206 et seq.

335 White House (footnote 267), Recommendation No. 3.

336 Suggestion thus made by *Goldsmith* (footnote 32) UCLR 1998, pp. 1244-1250.

337 More from *Hutter* in *Engel/Keller* (footnote 56) 84.

338 Leading case BVerfG 01.03.1978, BVerfGE 47, 285, 287/311 - notary fees.

339 This technique is primarily discussed in international economics law for foreign intervention standards, see for example *Peter O. Mülbert:* Ausländische Eingriffsnormen als Datum, in: IPRax 6 (1986) pp.140-142.

The incentive effects of an incorporation of private rules or decisions into the legal system are however ambivalent. The incorporation gives the regulation or decision additional authority. If the mechanism for creating the rules is under competitive pressure, incorporation can also strengthen its competitive position. But the very same effect can turn itself into a competitive disadvantage. Due to the incorporation, the private rules and decisions namely simultaneously serve two purposes: the original private one and the new state one. Since the legal consequences of state law depend on the contents of these regulations or decisions, the mechanisms for the design and application of the rules will come under additional pressure. The private rule-making body then loses flexibility: at the utmost extreme, even any ability to carry out its original function. The problem has become apparent in broadcasting. Since the latest reform was undertaken, the law on media concentration control has been geared to viewer market shares. The regulator takes his figures from the GfK (*Gesellschaft für Kommunikationsforschung*). Previously, this company generated these figures in the exclusive interest of the advertising industry, which wanted to know how effective an advertising spot was. Given this new and additional task, the firm fears that it might in future not be able to react as quickly and flexibly to the changed desires of the advertising industry.[340]

A more careful form of control by the state does not immediately start off with the content of private rules and decisions, but centres instead on the organization and the process of creating rules and applying them. This is where the decades old discussion about the usefulness of a Standardization Act belongs. Conceptionally, it is a form of context control. It is based on the idea, inspired by system theory, that there is a sufficiently direct connection between organization and process on the one hand, and the content of the rules on the other hand.[341] The legal system steps back yet another step further when it limits itself to maintaining a lively level of competition between different institutions in the creation and application of private rules. For the regulator, control of the content, context control and a competitive system for the competition between institutions therefore act as substitutes.[342]

Finally, with all three of these mechanisms, the state leaves the material decision on the content of these rules to a private instance, but this need not be so. Rather, it can, so to speak, proceed in two stages and negotiate with a private association about the contents of rules promulgated by the association. This state-controlled self-regulation arises in the shadow of hierarchy.[343] In order for private actors to agree on traded rules, the state needs something with which it can either encourage or threaten. In practice, on the domestic front, it primarily uses the threat of issuing rules that will impose a burden.[344]

340 More details from *Christoph Engel:* Die Messung der Fernsehnutzung als Voraussetzung eines Marktanteilsmodells zur Kontrolle der Medienkonzentration, in: ZUM 1995, pp. 653-666.

341 More from *Christoph Engel:* Regulierung durch Organisation und Verfahren, in: FS Ernst-Joachim Mestmäcker. Baden-Baden 1996, pp. 119-138.

342 More from *Christoph Engel:* Rezension von *Jack Knight:* Institutionen und gesellschaftlicher Konflikt. Tübingen 1997, erscheint demnächst in RabelsZ.

343 More from *Scharpf* Games Real Actors Play (footnote 148) pp. 197-205.

344 *Engel* Selbstregulierung (footnote 149).

That is problematic for the Internet because the addressees of the state's threat can often avoid such a burden.[345] But states could be successful in cases where the coexistence of legal systems needs to be organized, in order for Internet trade to blossom. We saw that this affects customs duties and taxes.[346] Even more promising is the fact that Internet trade depends to a remarkable extent on international institutions of private law.[347] States could attach their agreement to pertinent international treaties on condition that self-control solves the most important market failure problems of the Internet.[348]

5. Solutions without Law

Self-regulation often takes place outside the legal system. Private actors tend to draw up either technical (a) or social norms (b). Self-control is even more effective if addressees accept it as part of their own set of values instead of as a restriction (c).

a) Technical Norms

Technical norms can, of course, be drawn up as legal regulations. This is seldom the case, however. In addition to this formal difference, there is primarily also a material difference. Technical norms are formulated much more precisely than legal regulations. Therefore the application of technical norms really does correspond more or less with the picture of syllogism. There is often only a rare chance of flexibility through interpretation. The norm really determines behaviour. We encounter not only "false" but also often "right". The enforcement of technical regulations is then exclusively a problem of control rather than one of interpretation. Ultimately, technical regulations are mostly self-executing: anyone not adhering to them is excluded from communication.

Technical standards in the Internet are found in the compatibility standards that make communication possible.[349] The rules on the issue of IP addressees and on their transformation into domain names are also based on technical standards.[350] Since the Internet was originally conceived by technicians, there is however a tendency to look for the solution of more complex social problems in technical standards. Some would even like to prescribe the application of defined filter software to the providers of online services.

b) Social Norms

Social norms differ from legal rules by the grounds on which their validity is based. These lie in the social relationships of a group rather than in the legal system. Sanctions are taken from the social network. The strictest sanction is that of being expelled from the group. The creation of social norms does not normally follow a formalized process. Often, they are not even written down.

345 See above, IV 2.
346 See above, VII 1.
347 See above, VII 2.
348 See above, VII 3.
349 See above, I 2.
350 See above, I 2.

Although the so-called 'netiquette' has achieved fame[351], its effectiveness is often overestimated. It is mainly a collection of harmless rules: for example, that a line of e-mail should be no longer than 65 strokes in length. Other social norms drawn up by the Internet community have more bite. The community reacts almost angrily, for example, to the unsolicited receipt of electronic advertising, so-called 'spamming'. Some social norms have their own enforcement mechanism. The CyberAngels, for example, constantly search for dirt and sleaze in the net and electronically pillory the originator.[352] The Internet community has specific sanctions. In spring 1994, for example, an American law firm sent 1.2 million e-mails to Internet users in which it offered its services to participants in the annual Green-Card lottery. As a reaction, users clogged its e-mail connection with 600,000 replies, thus making it unusable for any other purpose.[353]

c) Intrinsic Motivation

Social norms are a form of central control. They are enforced by means of social sanctions, thus setting new restrictions on the behaviour of a group's members. For a considerable part of the social reality of the net, this concept is misleading. The idea that the traditional Internet community treats the net like a common pool resource is much more apt. Although they are scattered around the globe, these people view themselves as members of a group, held together by the common willingness to make the Internet function for everyone and to improve it.[354] These technicians and academics, empirically speaking, bear the hallmarks that *Elinor Ostrom* has often found in regimes for the exploitation of limited natural resources.[355] Control is then activated in the heads of those involved, rather than by an outside source. The willingness to stand up for commonly-used goods thus comes from intrinsic motivation. Connected with this appears to be the willingness to intervene against misuse.[356] We have, however, already seen that commercialization of the Internet is proceeding at a rapid pace.[357] No-one can predict today whether the original Internet culture will manage to survive, or even possess the power to reach new users.

6. Solutions Without External Assistance

Even self-regulation is a form of regulation, i.e. of central control. This is not the only possibility of overcoming the social problems of the Internet; in reality, much more decentralized forms of self-help also exist.[358] This solution implies an unusual distribution of property rights (a). Technical solutions become possible (b). An

---

351 Its contents are repeated by *Sally Hambridge:* Netiquette Guidelines, http://www..cybernothing.org/cno/docs/rfc 1855.html (15.2.1999).

352 Spiegel 11/1996, p. 78.

353 *Stephan Detjen:* Rechtsprobleme internationaler Datennetze, in: AfP 1996, pp. 44-46 (45)

354 *Thompson* in *Engel/Keller* (footnote 79) 115f..

355 *Ostrom:* Governing the Commons (footnote 78).

356 Economically speaking: the second order prisoner's dilemma is overcome through intrinsic motivation.

357 See above II 3, in particular c).

358 The plastic term comes from *Kenneth W. Dam:* Self-Help in the Digital Jungle (Chicago John M. Olin Law & Economics Working Paper 59) Chicago 1998.

individual can also employ the assistance of protective intermediaries (c), or insure himself against the risk of inappropriate behaviour by third parties (d). Self-help is an effective instrument, but it can also lead to regulatory problems itself, if the objective is overshot (e).

a) Property Right of the Disrupter

The legal profession has been educated to find fair and just solutions to social conflicts. Economically speaking, they therefore always keep an eye on the distributional effects of a solution. This explains why, implicity, they generally assign property rights to the person whom they consider has been disturbed. Blanket clauses of the type set out in paragraph 823 I BGB (civil code) provide the dogmatic justification for this, since almost every new social conflict affects one of the protected goods, namely, life, health, freedom and property. Economists start off on a different tack. Their basic problem is the scarcity of goods. They look for incentive mechanisms that cause the scarce resources to move to their most productive location. This demands the definition of property rights. Only when they have been exhaustively determined and assigned to a single person, can the market unfold its full effect. The right to interfere in the protected sphere of another person can also represent a trading commodity. Someone purchases, for example, a pipeline right. Alternatively, the object of trade can also be the right to forbid a third person to interfere in one's sphere.

As far back as the 1960s, *Ronald Coase* had shown that it is irrelevant for the allocative question whether the property right, legally speaking, lies with the disrupter or the person being disturbed. If the economic plans of both people can be realized better by an exchange of property rights, this exchange will then take place. But this proposition only holds true in a fictitious world without transaction costs. In reality, it takes effort in order to define, defend and transmit a property right. From an allocative point of view, a comparison of the transaction costs must therefore decide on whether it is better for the property right to originally lie with the disrupter or with the one being disturbed.[359]

It should be noted, however, that this is not simultaneously a recommendation for distribution policy. The science of economics only recommends the separation of allocation and distribution. If it is better, in terms of incentives, to give the property right to the person being disturbed, the distribution problem must be overcome in another manner. Economists would normally recommend using the general tax-transfer mechanism, whose advantage lies in the fact that a distributive measure causes a minimum of disruption to the mechanism of allocation.

b) Technical Solutions

These theoretical considerations have great significance for the solution of the Internet's social problems. If one gives the property right to the person being disturbed, he must, namely, be capable of successfully defending it against interference. No legal system can desire to see him countering violence with violence, so only central control mechanisms remain. But we have just seen that legal protection in the Internet is a

359 *Ronald H. Coase:* The Problem of Social Cost, in: Journal of Law and Economics 3 (1960) pp. 1-44.

matter requiring that a great deal of preconditions first be met. Even central control by society is often unable to assist.

If, on the other hand, one allocates the property right to the disrupter right from the outset, the person being disturbed will seek protective measures by himself. There are numerous examples of well-functioning technical safeguards in the Internet. Anyone wishing to protect himself or his children from problematic contents can employ electronic filters. Since the property right lies with the disrupter, competition to improve these filters gets under way all by itself. Competition acts, as it always does, as a process of discovery and constantly brings with it the emergence of improved safeguard systems. A limit is set only by the users' willingness to pay. No court in the world could create such effective safeguards, since innovation does not occur by way of commands.

Anyone worried that third parties will take away the gains from his work, can encrypt its contents. During encryption, he can individually define under what conditions customers can access it and pass it on to other persons.[360] Encryption also ensures protection from fraud. The use of a defined code ensures, namely, that the contents really are the authentic work of the author and have not been modified in the meantime.[361] Anyone fearing that hackers will penetrate his computer and expose his secrets or will cause damage, can protect himself via a firewall. Anyone worried that third parties can draw up a personality profile can make his electronic communications anonymous.[362] On the other hand, those wanting nothing to do with anonymous electronic mail can demand its encryption. In order to decode it, the sender must then make known his public key. This allows conclusions to be drawn about the sender.[363]

c) Protection Intermediaries

The potentially disturbed person must not necessarily take on the task of self-help himself. He can instead employ the assistance of protection intermediaries. Organized online providers are a classic example.[364] In the proprietary area of their services, they can set up rules of admittance and behaviour. If users do not stick to the rules, they can employ sanctions. The threat of sanctions is a credible one, because the providers can simply take unpopular services out of their programme.[365] Insofar as they allow their users access to the non-proprietary part of the Internet, these providers also work with filters. One example has occupied the American courts: the company Cyberpromotions is specialized in direct advertising via e-mail, which most Internet users consider to be spamming and would prefer not to receive. AOL has therefore constructed its gateway to the Internet in such a way as to prevent mails being received that have a return address from Cyberpromotions.[366] Intermediaries also exist that have exclusively specialized in self-protection for the Internet community. Economically speaking, they

360 *Dam* (footnote 358) p. 6 and 8 et seq.

361 *Grewlich* Cyberspace (footnote 8) Chapter Six. 1..

362 *Froomkin* UPittsbJLC 1996 (footnote 31) pp. 399 and 498.

363 *Dertouzos* (footnote 9) p. 148.

364 As T-Online, AOL or CompuServe.

365 *Johnson* http://www.cli.org/selford/Spam.htm (12.02.199).

366 *Cyberpromotions, Inc. V. American Online,* C.A. nos. 96-2846, 96-5213 (C.D Ba. Nov. 26, 1996, cited by *Post* (footnote 6) *Wayne LR* 1997 [at footnote 30].

offer self-protection as an item itself, i.e. uncoupled from other services. One example is the organization a.c.e.n.a, which initially reacts to spamming with organized e-mail protests to the originator. If that does not help, it sets a killer software going that picks up and deletes such messages everywhere in the net.[367] As is otherwise the case with intermediaries, users must weigh up the advantages and disadvantages. An intermediary will never be able to target the preferences of an individual user 100%. Thanks to economies of scale and scope, an intermediary is, however, much cheaper and better in his work than an individual ever could be. Competition between different intermediaries leads to a diversification of solutions.

d) Insurance

Electronic filters and protective intermediaries are a causal therapy. They get rid of the malady at its roots, which is possible because the malady itself has an electronic character. If these protective mechanisms fail, it is in any case subsequently difficult to carry out any treatment. Both these factors are different when it comes to trade in physical goods via the Internet. This is the reason for a different solution being found as far as consumer protection is concerned. Credit card companies do not demand payment from their customers if the business on hand has not been conducted in a proper manner.[368] Economically speaking, this is an insurance solution. The customer has neither a need to get involved in the consumer protection legislation of totally different nations, nor does he need to place his faith in court decisions being accepted at the seat of the seller that have been made by his home country in the application of its national law. The customer only has to deal with a single global player, who applies published, uniform rules and regulations to all his international transactions.[369]

Credit card companies of course do this in their own interests. Only thus can they increase customers' faith in this payment method and expand their business.[370] Like all insurers, credit card companies try to limit their insured risks. They estimate the creditworthiness of the companies which they accept as contractual partners. They supervise their behaviour[371] and agree to invert the burden of proof between customer and delivery merchant in the case of disputes about the delivery or quality of goods.[372] Parallel to this, credit card companies have established safeguards that, for example, are intended to minimize the fraudulent use of credit cards.[373] Ultimately, which risks credit card companies are prepared to bear rests on the possibility of being able to control such risk. They are particularly hesitant in the case of disputes regarding the quality of the

---

367 *Perritt* (footnote 105) *Berkeley* TLJ 1997, pp. 438-440.

368 I owe my reference to this phenomenon from *Henri Tjiong*. Details are found in an OECD document: Consumer Redress in the Global Market Place. Chargebacks, OECD/GD (96) 142, Paris 1996.

369 OECD/GD (96) 142, 30 (compare also 25).

370 Just above, 8.

371 See above, 14.

372 See above, 30.

373 See above, 7.

goods or pretended violations of the terms of trade, once goods have been ordered, paid and delivered.[374]

e) Protection from Self-Protection?

Some forms of self-protection are purely defensive in nature. A customer insures himself against the risks of electronic trade, or protects himself from undesirable content via a filter. Third parties will hardly be able to object to this. Criticism is more justified, however, if the insurer, for his part, carries out checks on people's behaviour, or if standardised filters no longer give certain providers a chance. And third parties will certainly defend themselves when they become the victim of aggressive protection techniques. We have already become familiar with the example of killer software. Besides, the use of many protection techniques is ambivalent. While anonymity protects from personality profiles being made, it also reduces the risk of being exposed while conducting illegal or socially unacceptable behaviour.[375] The opportunity arises of destroying the relationship between freedom and responsibility.[376] Ultimately, instruments that were developed for self-protection purposes, can also be employed for purely aggressive intent. In the meantime, for instance, a whole range of services have sprung up that are specialized in obtaining unlisted telephone numbers, bank account numbers, telephone data recordings, criminal records registers, medical data or data on financial assets.[377] Censorware is not only employed for the protection of adolescents; it is also employed to supervise employees.[378] And e-mail bombs are also employed by environmental organizations in order to force companies to come to the negotiating table.[379]

Within limits, competition between various self-protection mechanisms may provide assistance against such abuse, but this demands that a sufficiently large number of self-protection inquirers does not wish to be brought into contact with such abuses. Besides, all the central control mechanisms that we have put together can be deployed in order to prevent the abuse of protective techniques.[380] Above all, the third parties concerned will strive to develop their own protective measures against the abuse of other protective measures. Self-protection is therefore the most effective solution to protect against self-protection.

---

374 See above 7/15/30; see also just above 49 et seq. for a list of risks, for which chargebacks are normally acceptable.

375 *Froomkin* (footnote 31) UPittsbJLC 1996, 402 et seq.

376 For this reason, Justice *Scalia* in the USA is vehemently opposed to the constitutionally guaranteed protection of anonymity, *McIntyre v. Ohio Elections Commission* 115 S.C.t 1511(1537) (*Scalia J.*, dissenting), cited to *Froomkin* (footnote 31) UPittsbJLC 1996, p. 405/410.

377 Evidence in *Rötzer* in *Brill/de Vries* (footnote 84) p. 185.

378 Just above, 185-188.

379 Reports found in *Thompson* in *Engel/Keller* (footnote 79) 125.

380 See above, 2-5.

IX. Elements of a New International Order of Governance and Values

1. The Normative Objective

The interim balance of our considerations is not a bad one: while the new regulatory needs thrust up by the Internet have not yet been exhausted, there are grounds for optimism. Regulatory problems are being understood better and better, and more and more effective instruments to provide solutions to them are being found. But to date we have, so to speak, only come to terms with the small problems of the Internet. In conclusion, we must return to the bigger problems. In their most general form, they can be described as system retention and system development. With system retention, we are concerned with the key words power, justice and peace, whereby anarchistic elements must not be allowed to gain the upper hand. The majority of the people must accept control as being legitimate and should have no reason to believe in fatalism or a flight into simplicity. The chances for domestic peace and also peace between nations are then at their greatest.

Besides, we must retain the humus in which individuals and social cohabitation have so far evolved. An analogy to biology is enlightening.[381] As is well known, international law has taken on the task of protecting biodiversity[382], in order to maintain the current gene pool as far as possible, since it increases the adaptation and development possibilities of natural organisms. For many years, cultural anthropology has produced an analogy between natural and social organisms. What genes are to a natural organism, are memes to societies.[383] This suggests that the diversity of societies and their cultures should not be disturbed unnecessarily.

2. Elements of a Solution

This diversity of normative objectives reminds us to take care in the search for solutions. International law can certainly adapt. It can remind itself that it has never separated spheres of influence from each other exclusively on a territorial basis. Historically, the territorial state is in any case a young occurrence. Even in recent history, political units have existed alongside it that have been primarily, or even completely, defined in terms of people. The Maltese Order is minor example. Personality, however, was of great significance for the Jewish state of the 19th century.[384] For the purposes of the Internet, the rules of attribution in public international law could differentiate even further along functional lines. A type of 'nationality' for data packets could be the end result of this development.[385] Above all, international law will have to apply its mechanisms for solving conflicts of sovereignty and adapt it to thecharacteristics of the Internet.

---

381 *David* in *Engel/Keller* (footnote 11) 47.

382 Convention on Biological Diversity of 1992, 31 I.L.M. 818 (1992) = BGBl. 1993 II 1742.

383 Stimulating *Robert Boyd/Peter J. Richerson:* The Evolution of Norms. An Anthropological View, in: Journal of Institutional and Theoretical Economics 150 (1994) pp. 72-87.

384 I owe this reference to *Raimund Bleischwitz.*

385 Compare *David R. Johnson/David G. Post:* The New "Civic Virtue" of the Internet, http://www.cli/org/paper4.htm (12.02.1999), p. 2: Online-Jurisdictions are supposed to exist; compare also 10 et seq.

Since states cannot control the Internet by themselves, international law will have to adjust to a more complex network of power relations. Politically speaking: multi-level governance will become the norm.[386] It is more of a pragmatic question, as to whether international law will attempt to absorb these forms of power. It then ought to allow the non-governmental organizations more room than it has done up till now. Even individual private companies would have to receive their proper places as actors, and not merely be subjects of national legal systems. But it may possibly be smarter for international law to remain with the previous, narrower definition of its jurisdiction. From this perspective, self-regulation and self-assistance are mere facts to which international law reacts.

Multi-level governance is a hybrid form of exercising power. The discussion in private law about hybrid forms between contract and organization has shown that such control instruments can be just as effective and suitable.[387] Such systems allow a balance between stability and innovation to be achieved more easily. There are, therefore, even grounds for optimism in regard to the bigger problems. So far, only two inter-related problems still need to be overcome. People will profit to varying degrees from the new possibilities of a flexible system of power. A problem of distribution will thus remain. This is of such significance because globalisation also diminishes the nation states' room for maneouvre in regard to distribution. States can no longer levy high taxes on mobile production factors, since this would only result in their exit. In contrast, the production factor labour is, in the long term, immobile. But, up to now, the distribution policies of the state were primarily intended to assist employees. It is not evident to date that a supranational distribution policy could take its place.

In addition, the increased complexity is making individuals insecure to varying degrees. The ability to live with this condition, or even profit from it, is no anthropological constant. This brings forth the need for the formulation of an educational programme. But for this, no solutions have yet been found. This is an urgent matter, in order to avoid a destructive flight into simplicity that endangers both domestic and external peace.

---

386 *Gary Marks/Lisbet Hooghe/Kermit Blank*: European Integration from the 1980s: State-Centric v. Multi-Level governance, 1996.

387 This is a summary of the results of the discussion about *Williamson's* thesis (footnote 163).

Lorenz Müller

Global Networks and Local Values

Discussion Report*

* Report on the Discussions held during the 1st Symposium of the Max Planck Project Group on the Law of Common Goods and the Computer Science and Telecommunications Board of the National Research Council, February 18 – 20, 1999 in Dresden

The purpose of the symposium was to analyze the interaction between global networks and local cultures and values. It was divided into five sessions. The report on the discussions does not follow a chronological order, nor does it attempt to provide an exhaustive description; rather, it attempts to offer a systematic account of the contributions.

A. Local Values

The panel discussed the meaning of "local values" in several sessions. Different positions were expressed with respect to both concepts of value (I) and concepts of locality (II).

I. Concepts of Values

With reference to the definition of value, the participants discussed the substance of values (1), the approach of Cultural Theory (2) and Systems Theory (3) towards values, the rhetoric and reality of values (4), and similarities between values with technical norms (5).

1. Substance of Values

In his presentation, Mr. Kersting had described values as formal. Substantial values were defined as traditional values upon which the traditional world had been grounded. They lost their cultural importance with the success of the enlightenment. Therefore, people today have to develop value profiles without substantial values. They have to develop more flexible and responsive attitudes and the ability to deal with ethical and religious pluralism. Substantial values were not necessarily better in solving integration problems than the supporters of the idea of substantial values believed.

This view was questioned by Mr. Engel. He discussed two functions of values, one for the individual and one for the society:

For the individual, values had a cognitive function. It would be impossible to enter the heuristic circle completely devoid of all substantial values. Also, values are not gained by birth, but learned from society. Therefore, it is difficult to imagine a state in which individuals would have only formal values.

Values have a societal function as well. No society can exist without substantial values. On the contrary, even the most liberal societies, e.g. the U.S., have a narrowly and strictly defined set of substantial values. Mr. Engel asked whether this is a mere accident of history or whether the fact that societies worldwide are being tied together by substantial values is not proof that societies cannot work without substantial values.

Other discussants objected to Mr. Kersting´s position, too. Historically, there might have been a shift towards more modern values in the west, but not a complete move; the conventional dualism of traditional and modern concealed more than it revealed, said Mr. Thompson. People had a right to roots and culture and needed roots in form of local cultures and values, argued Mr. Keniston.

2. Cultural Theory

According to Mr. Thompson's presentation, a distinction is made in Cultural Theory between the fatalist, hierarchist, individualist and egalitarian attitudes as the four forms of solidarities within a society. Mr. Hutter asked him to relate Cultural Theory to local values. Mr. Thompson answered that in Cultural Theory one would investigate the patterns of disagreement and contention between the solidarities at different levels or countries. Differences between the relative strength of the four solidarities in different localities would show differences in local political cultures and local values.

3. Systems Theory

Mr. Baecker had described the Internet as a perturbation to existing systems. In order to become communication, these perturbations have to be coded. Coding means making sense of these perturbations that are coming in from the environment. Mr. Engel asked whether, in the language of Systems Theory, the term of local values could be seen as being the code of communication in defined societies. Mr. Baecker affirmed this question.

4. Rhetoric and Reality

a) Realities behind Rhetoric

Mr. Burkert made a distinction between the rhetoric of local values and the prevailing reality of values. To have a rhetoric of local values would be useful because it would help a society to find an own identity and to perceive the other side more clearly. But in international negotiations, for instance, it would be often helpful to show that a part of the own rhetoric of values is a part of the reality of the other side. This could be also a good approach for research. It would be useful to show that there are other realities behind the rhetoric of local values, and it would be interesting to find out why these other realities do not appear in the rhetoric of values.

b) Values as Asserted Representations or Stereotypes

Mr. Adams said values were either asserted representations that people give for themselves and which are, therefore, subject to some doubt, or they were stereotypes that one applies, i.e., categories into which one fits things. He suggested that it would be preferable to deal with people in terms of intentions and associations and the behaviors that could be, in empirical situations, derived from those rather than values.

5. Values and Technical Norms

Mr. Werle described the similarities between technical norms and social values. He asked whether local values were selected in a way similar to local technical standards and whether the terminology of the economics of standardization could be used in the analysis of values.

Mr. David answered that the apparatus of the economics of standards could be used by asking where social norms come from — whether they are de facto customs or conventions which have emerged without being chosen by anyone, or whether they are imposed by some authority. One might feel differently about the two cases. One might say that some norms have been imposed by an authority. Therefore, it is by no means clear that people, if left free to do things once again, would return to the same norms; hence, they are not fixed points. Then one might ask whether further protection and entrenchment against the competition of other possible norms should be allowed. That would lead to the question concerning the type of legitimacy of norms. An answer to this question would need to take into consideration many issues, such as subjectivity, situational ethics and the existence of a hierarchy in the quality of norms. It would be easier to talk about norms in a technical sense insofar. Nevertheless, some scholars argued that there is an equivalent of method standards in the area of normative value.

II. Concepts of Locality

1. Locality and Propinquity

Ms. Sassen argued that the very notion of "local" is being transformed by the process of globalization in general and by the emergence of global information networks in particular.

The "local" is in a process of becoming one modality in a complex global process; it is not a part of a hierarchy of local, regional, national and international spheres. The local sphere is being mobilized on a global level by the Internet, e.g., the international business community or immigrant communities were locals which operate in a cross-border space. Therefore, the notion of "local" could not be restricted to something that is embedded in a particular locality and contained within it. The "local" is rupturing its own boundaries.

Mr. Thompson amended this view with the observation that community is usually understood as propinquity in the sense that people live close to one another and share a community. This view has been modified due to the new communication technologies: Firstly, people can have community without propinquity and, secondly, propinquity without community.

Ms. Sassen added that the Internet could also intensify the interactions in localities. As an example she discussed the Digital-City-Project in Amsterdam, a local website which can be accessed via the Internet and was mostly used by citizens of Amsterdam. Thus, the Internet elaborates and intensifies the local and, at the same time, helps the local to become part of a global network of locals.

2. Locality, Regions and Nations

Mr. Grewlich said that, put simply, on the level of the occidental culture a community of values exists. One would have to break the investigation down to the nations and regions in order to find differences. Politically, culture is a glue that binds a nation together and is also a matter of political control.

Mr. Engel asked whether the local in values could be linked to the four solidarities of Cultural Theory, such that societies can be described to a large extent as being characterized by the hierarchical mode or the individualistic way, for example.

3. Locality and Language Spaces

With regard to Mr. Keniston's presentation, Mr. Engel said that to equate locality with language-spaces implies a very broad understanding of the local. This could be misleading even if vernaculars were understood as languages. Therefore, to equate language-spaces with localities of values may well be a good first start, but it is not adequate for the whole job.

III. Diffferences between the U.S. and Germany and Europe

Mr. Holznagel used Cultural Theory to analyze different approaches to the Internet in the U.S. on the one hand and Germany and Europe on the other. Regarding Germany, he argued that a fatalist view prevailed in East Germany, while the individualistic approach dominated both in West-Germany as well as in the United States. The egalitarian approach was strong in the U.S., but very weak in Germany. Comparing Europe as a whole with the U.S., he said that Europe had a position between the individualistic and the hierarchical approach, whereas the individualistic and the egalitarian approach was predominate in the U.S., excluding the hierarchical approach. In Europe, especially France would not give up the hierarchical approach due to its interest in supporting local industries and preserving local values, e.g. the French language.

This thesis was criticized as being too simplistic by Mr. Grewlich; he argued that, at the political level, there was a division of labor in Europe in the defense of local cultures, which the Germans implicitly accept. He claimed that the French are ready to carry this burden, whereas the Germans, to some extent, were trying to avoid the issue. In his view the defense of local cultural values is an extremely complex issue, particularly in the European Union.

B. Global Networks

The panel discussed the development of global information networks in the future with respect to technological developments (I) and commercialization (II).

I. Technological Developments

The discussion concerning the technological development of global information networks centered on the conditions of technology selection (1), forecasts with regard to band width (2), the universal addressability in the Internet (3) and the security and vulnerability of information networks (4).

1. Conditions of Technology Selection

Mr. Grewlich asked whether competition always ensures that the best standards and the best technology survive, or whether it is rather more likely that poor standards and less than optimal technologies are ultimately successful due to trapped technology or political intervention.

Mr. David answered that the presumption of an invisible hand did not fit into a market given the kinds of externalities that characterize the markets of the information networks. Sub-optimal systems may well be able to survive for a long time, but if some new technology is developed that is so much better than the old, then it dislodges the previous technological regime by making it obsolete. In this case it is possible to escape from a lock-in-situation with a sub-optimal technology.

2. Band Width

a) Predictions

Mr. Farber had predicted that a dramatic increase in band width would even be available at home offices within the next few years. According to this forecast, data rates up to five megabyte per second will be feasible over the existing copper and cable system at prices of under one hundred dollars a month. Using new fiber-optic networks, even multi-gigabyte-connections would be possible.

Mr. David was doubtful that this prediction would come true. His skepticism was based on the assumption that incompatibility problems would prove to be a hindrance. He also suggested that technology would evolve considerably more slowly and with larger sunk costs than Mr. Farber predicted. In light of these problems it seemed likely that we would continue to use the current systems for a while. Therefore, he argued that policy planning should not be based on an engineer's vision. Rather, planning should assume a mixed system with gateways between high speed optical transmission and the rest of the complex which would be essentially inherited and elaborated in keeping with the system already in place.

Mr. Farber responded to this objection in two ways:

Firstly, the speed of the technological development had been underestimated in the past, e.g. by the telephone industry which had believed that it would take 50-60 years before packet-switching would have any impact on the phone industry.

Secondly, development progresses step by step: Many companies in the U.S. are already linked by gigabit connections between their plants. Such connections become more and more usual for large companies. This has an impact on the price structure of the long haul data paths, making high-speed-connections affordable for smaller companies. In the end, even private households could gain access to multi-gigabyte band widths.

However, to reach this goal the congestion problems in the local loop had to be solved. This could be difficult because there are no incentives for local carriers to invest enormous amounts of capital in order to expand their capacity there.

Ms. Zitterbart pointed out that the emergence of mobile systems could effect congestion in the backbone. She suggested that it would be difficult to solve that congestion problem since nobody knows where the users would appear at any given moment and where the traffic would be directed. This problem would become even more difficult with the increased use of multicast communication.

b) Effects on Encryption

Mr. Burkert asked about the effects that the increase of band width would have on the process of encryption. Mr. Farber suggested encryption would become more difficult in fiber-optic networks. At least at present, it would be difficult to encrypt a 60-gigabit path.

3. Addressability

Mr. Perrit asked whether the universal addressability in global networks will be available even in the high-speed and multifunctional networks of the future. Mr. Farber affirmed the question, albeit with the restriction that it would not be possible to continue with the familiar use of IP-addresses. He said that IP will become more of an application interface standard. However, during times of innovation and change, periods of incompatibility could appear. The IP address base will be extended such that an IP address could be assigned to almost every atom. In the future almost everything will have an IP-address and would be able to communicate, even toys.

4. Security

The symposium addressed the possibility of large scale failures of software systems. Mr. Keller asked whether the penetration of network-technologies will increase the vulnerability of the system as a whole and what could be done to limit any possible risks.

a) Proprietary Software Systems

Mr. Farber said that the attempts to develop reliable software engineering had been a failure. In fact, a small amount of progress had been made, but the size of the systems had simultaneously exploded. Furthermore, the shift from largely centralized systems to fully distributed and extremely complex systems presented a problem. Nobody really knew how to engineer appropriate software that was robust and reliable. More progress had been made with respect to hardware. Mr. Farber hoped that the industry will be able to learn from their experiences with hardware and find solutions in the area of software engineering.

b) Open Systems

The problems of developing reliable software have not been solved by open systems like Linux, Mr. Farber explained. He mentioned that, although open source systems are integrating self-correcting steps that are less likely to be in place in proprietary systems, open source systems have no control for security issues.

II. Commercialization of Global Networks

With respect to the commercialization of global information networks, firstly, the question concerning the ability of economics to provide an appropriate methodology to investigate this subject was discussed (1). Apart from this, the symposium dealt with commercialization of the net itself (2) and with commercialization of services on the net (3).

1. Methodology

Mr. Hutter stated that economists had developed fairly little competence with respect to the real issues of the commercialization of global networks. Economists talk in general about material products, but they generally avoid information and communication problems. Thus, problems of finance, problems of what constitutes property and problems of standards usually are not delved into. Therefore, the economist literature might be not the best place to search for investigations of the real issues in commercialization. Investigations in more applied fields might perhaps have more success.

Mr. Engel viewed this position as being too skeptical. In his view, economics are at least able to explain why certain allocation problems within global networks can not be easily solved by traditional markets. Traditional economics faces the problem that a static competition theory is not able to deal with the problems in global networks. Thus, the efforts made in the field of economics to develop a dynamic competition theory have to be considered. Additionally, incentive problems exist in global networks. Therefore, one has to look for institutions with impact on the development of global networks. In this context, economics could contribute a lot. Not everything could be framed in terms of economics, but the conceptual tools in the field of economics could nevertheless be very helpful.

Another objection regarding the methodology of economics was made by Mr. Thompson. He said that economists usually work within the framework of individualist social solidarity. While this is certainly one valid way of framing things, it is only one of several ways, as Cultural Theory shows. The other social solidarities also have to be taken into consideration.

2. Net

Addressing the commercialization of the net itself, the panel discussed the issues of privatization (a), pricing (b) and the specifics of the local loop (c).

a) Privatization

Ms. Sassen described the privatization of telecommunication networks as a hollowing out of the state not only on the technical level, but also on the level of administering, managing and coordinating the systems.

Mr. Perrit stressed in his reply the necessity of distinguishing between privatization and opening the markets. The WTO-agreements on telecommunication dealt not with privatization, but rather with liberalizing the markets. Vices of privatization might exist, but there could be equal or worse anti-democratic vices of a publicly owned, but monopolistic telecommunications company.

Ms. Sassen raised the objection that opening the market has had different consequences in different parts of the world. In many parts of the world, liberalizing the market has meant that foreign investors have been allowed to enter. In the case of many Latin American countries, opening the market meant privatizing rather than eliminating or disciplining a state monopoly. In Argentina for instance, the telephones now work, but many people cannot afford a telephone connection anymore.

Mr. Hutter explained that he believed privatization to be the solution when he began doing research on the subject. Now, however, he had his doubts. Private efforts were most often outpaced by new public efforts, e.g., innovations and investments to set up proprietary systems had often been circumvented. Thus, the attempt to privatize the commons could fail.

b) Usage-based Pricing

For technological reasons the Internet needs no central control or authority, and this fact was described as a problem with respect to financing the capacity of the network. This feature of the Internet has made it impossible to develop a mechanism which permits exacting precise charges for using the net, and "www" has thus become a synonym for "worldwide wait", Mr. David said. There are enormous problems concerning the allocation of resources; for example, the introduction of an improved browser technology has led to the creation of service provisions which have been enormously expensive in terms of band width, such as colored images and movies, etc. If the government does not provide an accordingly high level of band width, as is the case with the Arbornet and NSFnet, then the technical solution will present major problems.

The symposium addressed the question whether usage-based pricing would be an appropriate solution to this problem. The discussion was concerned with the technological possibilities (a) and the desirability of usage-based pricing (b).

aa) Technological Possibilities

Mr. Spinrad confirmed that usage based pricing is technologically feasible. A number of mechanisms were proposed. The implication of a technology called Asynchronous Transfer Mode (ATM), a system which uses net transfer and IP's but adds additional information to the transferred packets, is the solution that will most likely be used. ATM facilitated assigning different classes of value which can be tariffed differently. Though already technical feasable, there is currently a large standards and tariffing debate.

Mr. Werle and Mr. Farber raised doubts about Mr. Spinrad's predictions. Many people were not convinced that ATM is the technology of the future. Traditional network operators are committed to ATM, but new network operators in the area of Internet are not. The possibility of quality-of-service-pricing relied on the assumption that the ATM network would continue to be the one used. It was asserted that his assumption was wrong with reference to IP networks, where it is difficult to introduce quality-of-service-pricing.

Mr. Kahler thought the question concerning the future use of applied technology, i.e., if it be from ATM or not, was irrelevant. His argumentation rested on the fact that future networks will provide different classes or types services.

bb) Necessity and Desirability of Usage-based Pricing

The attitudes towards the necessity and desirability of usage-based pricing differed according to the predictions concerning band width development and congestion.

According to Mr. Farber´s forecast, congestion will no longer be a problem or at least become less significant due to the predicted increase in band width. Usage-based pricing will be very difficult for both people and companies. He thought that it would be better to price by capacity, by the size of the band width a customer has access to. Even if congestion is a problem in the future, it would be an engineering problem, not a load problem. The net-traffic grows and changes too fast to have enough time to properly engineer the net, e.g. to order and install new equipment. The congestion points in the U.S. are the interchange points with little impact on the issue of pricing to the consumer.

Mr. Perrit was of the opinion that the cause of congestion lies in insufficient band width in the local loop. In the local loop, flat rate pricing had always been customary and would be likely to continue to be appropriate. There had been congestion as a result of Internet traffic at the core infrastructure of the telephone system. The reasons could be found in a mismatch between the packet nature of the data traffic and the circuit switched nature of the telephone infrastructure. But most participants expected a blurring of the distinction between voice traffic and data traffic in this new infrastructure. Decision-makers in the part of the market that is open to competition and private decision-making about pricing would move away from usage-based pricing towards flat-rate pricing. Therefore, it is possible that there would be no demand for sophisticated pricing mechanisms. Perhaps other tools like customized long-term contracts would be more successful.

Mr. Spinrad replied that if AT&T and the other carriers had quality of service measures with ATM, they would bill accordingly and there would be a demand. However, this would still leave the great body of usage that could be priced at a flat rate. The idea is that if the carriers can get more money for a guaranteed service, they would be able to charge for it and put in more lines.

Ms. Zitterbart called to the participant's attention the fact that volume is not the only important issue with respect to congestion. Another important issue is delay, e.g. a voice does not produce a high volume, but it has to be transported continuously in order to be understandable.

c) Local Loop

Mr. Engel stated that until not long ago many economists considered the local loop to be a natural monopoly or at least a natural oligopoly. Working on these assumptions, he asked whether it is likely that monopolists or oligopolists will try to abuse their position in order to maintain their old business, i.e., circuit-switched telephony, or whether the competitive pressure from wireless communications is strong enough to control the monopoly position of the wired communications networks.

Mr. Farber replied that the established owners of the local loop are under great pressure. He suggested that in the U.S. a political fight is being waged; telephone companies are being forced to offer access to high band width and a large number of corporations are competing in the marketplace to use that band width at reasonable cost. In his opinion, wireless transmission is attractive in urban areas – but not in the rural countryside - and will work to replace the wired network in the local context.

2. Services

With respect to the commercialization of services on the net, the symposium discussed the issues of setting up properties in general (a), intellectual property protection (b), trade (c) and actors (d).

a) Properties in general

The issue of establishing properties in the global information networks was discussed. Of special interest was the influence of private investors on the activities of non-profit organizations and the options available for protecting properties in open networks.

Mr. Hutter had predicted in his presentation that the community oriented model of non-profit-organizations such as universities would become less important in the Internet due to the financial power of private investors. He expressed the belief that proprietary systems would become more significant in the Internet. Since the financial situation of the public sector is becoming worse, the pressure to sell licenses to private companies will grow. However, he stated that clear benchmarks were necessary in order to answer this question.

Mr. Werle stressed that the community-oriented mechanism of producing the goods created on the Internet would still prevail. New types of producing collective, but also individual goods are being developed. He mentioned that new categories, such as trust in the relationship of individuals within information networks, were necessary in order to distinguish these new methods from traditional means of production.

Ms. Sassen voiced the opinion that the development of technologies in the hacker scene and open source systems like Linux could be seen as a response to the efforts made to protect proprietary goods in information networks.

Mr. Keller said that proprietary goods often need protection guaranteed by governments, but there is growing concern that the power of governments is eroding. He argued that this development does not harmonize with the prediction that proprietary systems will increase in significance. Ms. Sassen replied that the poor applicability of existing regulations in the Internet, on the one hand, and the will to bring in other regulations, on the other, is shaping the Internet. She described the process as being dynamic, incomplete, and in a stage characterized by many new innovations.

b) Intellectual Property Protection

Intellectual property protection was described as an important prerequisite for doing business in information networks. The issue was touched upon with respect to technological possibilities (aa), legal protection (bb) and potential effects of legal protection on competition and technological development (cc).

aa) Technological Possibilities

Mr. Kahler asked how technological protection could be provided for digital projects on the net and about the competition between producers and pirates. He mentioned that software programs are already used to distribute digitized music on the Internet all over the world and that the record company executives are terrified. One such company had indicated that it was working on methods to defeat this software. Without technologies that are capable of protecting digital property, business in the net would decline.

Mr. Spinrad discussed attempts to provide technological protection of intellectual property. A number of organizations around the world, both academic and commercial, were working on digital property rights protection techniques. Basically, they took the idea or the legal notion of copyright and extended it to cover rights other than just the right to copy. Technologically, the information would be protected in a digital envelope, an encryption envelope, whose access points are controlled by a set of pre-specified rights, e.g., the right to copy, to print or to copy until a certain date after which it becomes impossible to reproduce it. All of these techniques relied on so-called trusted systems. This meant that the participants have to agree to follow the rule of law, e.g. that they will use trusted printers and trusted servers. This sort of ethical commerce could have a mechanism to allow for the billing and protection of rights, but it would become more difficult, though still possible, to provide protection from rogue hackers. This could lead to a kind of encryption war between producers and pirates.

bb) Legal Protection

Mr. Dam said that circumvention technologies, i.e., ways of defeating protection standards, were one of the subjects of the Digital Millennium Act, which went through the U.S.-Congress in October 1998.

cc) Potential Effects on Competition and Technological Development

Mr. Dam asked whether patents or copyright protection for computer software could lead to settling on a standard prematurely and whether it might be better to have an intellectual property regime which preserves the competition of standards.

Mr. David replied that intellectual property protection could create a monopolistic position in which the proprietor of the protected software would have an incentive to restrict access by raising the price. In a competition of standards, a number of people with different monopolies try to develop the dominant standard. He commented that, once they had the dominant standard, they were protected in that and could extract the monopoly rates. Since protection offered by patents have a limited duration, it is in the monopolist's interest to gain dominance as fast as possible. Mr. David therefore argued that all that one does by giving software protection would be to increase the size of the total payoff that the winner would take in and to increase the willingness of people to subsidize early use. Certain standards could become essential facilities, particularly in the human/machine interface. Mr. David expressed his concern that this could create a monopoly, since the owner of the standard could effectively block entry. This could result in negative externalities in the networks: Firstly, since monopolist tend to overprice their services and products, people are excluded because they do not buy the product. This led, secondly, to a decrease in the network, such that the users will not get the full network benefits. Based upon this scenario, Mr. David argued that a monopolist should not be rewarded by intellectual property protection.

c) Trade and Services in and with the Net

Mr. Hutter had described three kinds of goods: Firstly, the use of the net; secondly, goods in the net, i.e., the sale of parts of the net or of commodities that can only exist because they are transmitted through the net; and, thirdly, goods that are marketed on the net, basically off-line commodities which can be advertised, ordered and billed, but not transmitted through the net. For the categories one and two, he forecasted a situation in which the initial prices would be very high but would then drop down to very low prices. In category three, the off-net commodities, he thought that prices were not going to change dramatically.

The last prediction was questioned by Mr. Kahler. He argued that the developments in the area of offline-goods and services marketed on the net would lead to a situation in which a whole set of intermediaries who provide services were going to be priced efficiently for the first time and, therefore, might disappear from the market. This could cause significant changes. He cited as an example the recent decline in the number of travel agents. He suggested that a similar process could be observed with financial services; the full service brokering of the past had moved to discount brokerage, and then moved from that stage to online trading. These developments raise the question of whether or not we need these financial intermediaries at all.

d) Actors

In Mr. Werle's description, consumers in global networks are obviously not "couch potatoes", i.e. passive users of mass media like TV, but active users interested in getting information services of all kinds. In his view, economics theorists will have to come to grips with this role.

Mr. Hutter brought up the term "prosumers" in this context. This describes the union of consumers and producers into one figure, a union brought about by the fact that users participate in developing the products. Thus, a very important distinction for economic analysis, production and consumption, would start to merge into one.

Mr. Perrit said the ease of entry of both economic and political actors would be an important part of the forces which are changing the market structure. The layered, modular character of the Internet would make it easy for firms to specialize, especially since they could rely on the standard and open character of the Internet.

III. Differences between the U.S. and Europe

Mr. David said that the number of Internet host sites in both the U.S. and Europe in the nineties were growing at about the same rate and that Europe was about 15 months behind the U.S.. He suggested that the number of Internet host sites was not necessarily a good measure of traffic volume and for services offered. But in his view there seemed to be a great difference for instance between the West Coast of the U.S., where everything traverses through the Internet, and the situation in England, where things are entirely different.

Ms. Zitterbart agreed in general with the thesis that the American technology and American service providers were dominant on the Internet. She suggested that one nevertheless had to take into consideration the fact that mobile networks and IP-telephony would be a part of the Internet technology of the next generation. In these areas some niches would exist in which Europe and Germany would be in a better position since ISDN knowledge would be useful for these technologies.

Apart from this, Ms. Zitterbart discussed the difficulties involved in describing the state of the art of Internet technology in Europe as a whole. The Scandinavian countries have to be treated separately. Sweden, Finland and Norway have even a better infrastructure than the U.S. or at least a similar one due to their low density of population.

Mr. Werle agreed with regard to the technological state of the art in Scandinavian countries, but considered the low density of population to be of minor importance. He said that the crucial point was the different technology policy concerning research and education and data networks in Scandinavia. The Scandinavian countries were the only ones that were open to TCP/IP more or less from the beginning, while the other national governments committed themselves to OSI, the open system interconnection, and standardized data networks differently.

Mr. Werle argued that for this reason TCP/IP-related politics needed to be considered in order to explain why some countries are lagging behind.

C. Starting Points for Analyses of Interactions of Global Networks with Local Cultures and Political Structures

The panel discussed different questions regarding starting points for analyses of the interactions of information networks with cultures and local values, in particular the potential of technology assessment (I) and methodological approaches (II).

I. Possibilities and Limits of Technology Assessment

Mr. Keller raised the question concerning prospects of separating the effects of new communication networks from effects with other causes. He suggested that one examines how transitional stages dealing with the introduction of new technologies are managed. It may possibly make sense to figure out ways of asking a set of questions that infer not so much an equilibrium change in the nature of the institutions as a need to manage the introduction of technology in a sensible way. Time scale matching would be an important factor, for example the question if there are time scales that match the institutions in this transient period. The question would not be whether or not the available institutions are no longer functioning, but how it is possible to use them quickly to anticipate the coming changes.

Mr. Kahler replied with the remark that the ability to anticipate coming changes requires an enormous amount of foresight coupled with an understanding of how technology becomes taken up and promoted by other institutions. He suggested that governments respond not to technology but to the political forces that promote technology; such a second order effect would be very hard to predict.

Mr. Thompson stressed the impossibility of anticipating all of the effects of a new technology. In his view, most of the consequences of a new technological innovation can not be anticipated. Technology assessment consists much more in technological options assessment. Even options assessment could not be regarded as complete. To go the whole way would mean to accept that technology is a social and cultural process, that the technology is intimately bound up in social and cultural lifes and that the way the whole bundle evolves is inherently complex; that there is an order within it, but its future states are unpredictable.

Mr. Spinrad expressed the opinion that technological forecast would be notably unsuccessful. Nevertheless, techniques of scenario planning exist, of looking at a range of potential outcomes given the technological change within a time frame of five to ten years.

II. Methodological Approaches

1. Determinism and Social Systems Theory

Mr. Keniston held the position that technology is not deterministic. Mr. Engel basically agreed, but hesitated to deny any impact of technology on social and political developments. According to Systems Theory, a new element of technology was a perturbation, and this perturbation could be ignored by the existing loop. It could be treated as noise. But if it is treated as noise, it would come back, and at the second stage the perturbation increases, and, finally, people would no longer be willing to ignore it. Because they know that this point will be reached if they don't react soon enough, they tend to intervene at an earlier stage and adapt the noise. This view of a new technology as a new restriction to which the system is responding with a bit of liberty would be a good way of conceptualizing the interrelationship between technology and culture or power.

2. Cultural Theory

Mr. David described the approach of Cultural Theory as useful, with the Internet depicting a potentiality and people having an image of it. The way in which it comes to be used would be effected not only by its technical potentiality, but also by the supporting structures that are put into place and which would privilege one or another of these sorts of templates. From a perception theory approach, it would be less interesting to examine what the Internet is and more interesting to investigate what people will make of it. What they will make of it is not be determined simply by technical potential but also by the supporting mechanisms and institutions which regulate social interaction and create and protect rights. All of this affects society.

Mr. Thompson stressed the importance of the constructionist approach inasmuch as the impact of the perception and behavior of people have a considerable impact. But one also has to be aware that there are some real constraints in the world.

Mr. Engel wondered whether societies could be characterized using Cultural Theory, i.e., whether they could be described as being formed by the hierarchical mode or the individualistic way, for example. If this is possible, then the Internet could bring about a much greater confrontation of the different views of the world, since people will not be able to avoid being exposed to different views of the world. This obviously will make living together in a society much more complicated.

3. Economics of Standards

Mr. Engel drew a parallel to technical standards. In the field of technical standards there are ongoing debates on the question of whether substance or gateways should be standardized and how basic or specific the standards could be. Mr. Engel asked whether these questions regarding technical standards could be linked to the question concerning local values, i.e., whether local values could be perceived as standards at a relatively high level. Related to this question was the question on whether or not the effect of the Internet might be to bring communications standards down to a lower level or even to gateway standards instead of having substantial standards; if these presuppositions were true, one could learn from the literature on network externalities how to understand the problem of the interaction of global networks and local values.

Mr. David replied that it would be basically possible to protect local characteristics of a local system while allowing it to be communicative with the outside. He suggested that this would be possible using converters or translators. Since converters were inefficient, the question would be if people are willing to pay for it. If people were willing to pay for the converters necessary to preserve functionality of value systems, another problem would arise from an economist's perspective. Economically, the protection of local values by putting resources into gateway systems which are inefficient would induce people to create more locally specialized idiosyncratic communities. The question should be posed as to whether converters are an asset to those people using them, or whether a gateway system would be in the interest of those who want to sell proprietary products that differ from others on the market such that the latter could then profit from the production of ever more diverse products in the protection of the public sectors.

D. Impact on Languages and Cultures

The symposium addressed the impact of the dominance of English on other languages (I) and, thus, on other cultures themselves (II). The development of translation-technology as a way to overcome language boundaries was described as rather problematic and not feasible in the foreseeable future (III).

I. Impact of English as the Dominant Internet Language

1. Figures

It was stated that more than 90 percent of the content of the Internet is expressed in English. Mr. Adams said that, according to an article in Foreign Policy, only about 380 million native speakers of English existed, but that about a third of the world's population speaks English in some form.

Mr. Keniston replied that an estimate that one-third of the world's population speaks English is an extraordinary exaggeration. Such estimates rest on how one defines “English speaking.”

2. Predictions

Mr. Adams said India would graduate about 50,000 computer scientists a year, 15,000 of which come yearly to the United States for periods of residence. This formed an opportunity structure with pressure that English will remain the language of the Internet in India for the foreseeable future.

3. Impact on other Languages

Mr. Hutter asked whether English expels other languages or whether English develops into a kind of a superlanguage that does not affect local languages.

Ms. Zitterbart said that, despite the penetration of the English language, global networks could support local languages since everybody would have access to information in his language even if she or he is abroad. Everybody abroad could have more contact to their language and culture than ever before due to the information and communication technologies.

A discussant raised doubts concerning the impact of global networks on local languages. The more interesting question is why some local cultures and languages prove to be very resilient while others are less resilient. This question obviously predates the Internet and all other electronic means of communication.

II. Impact of Technical Standards

1. Relationship of Technical Standards and Languages

Two contrasting ways in which standards could be related to local values were suggested. On the one hand, one could say that the loose standardization of the Internet by Anglo-Saxon or Anglophonic norms would impose a kind of hegemony of the Anglo-Saxon world on many other non-Anglo-Saxon cultures. This would most likely lead to a condition in which many cultures felt threatened by the dominance of language web sites. In this sense, standardization could be seen as a threat to local values. On the other hand, standardization in a technical sense would be a prerequisite for the preservation of local values in a world of global networks. Without local language conventions and technical norms concerning how to use the computer in German or in Yiddish or in other languages, it would not be possible to use a computer at all. Thus, standardization at this more specific level, at the level for example of ASCII, is a prerequisite for the preservation of local cultures in an age of information power.

2. Operating Systems

Mr. Keniston described the localization of American operating systems as usual for languages like German and French. In the discussion he exemplified the impact of the dominance of Anglo-Saxon technical standards on local languages with a story about Iceland. This is an island with a population of under half a million that has preserved more or less the same language for 700 or 800 years. Icelanders were very proud that they can still read their old sagas in their native language. Yet, they were almost all bilingual and speak English as well as Icelandic. The preservation of Icelandic as a language is a very important issue for Icelanders. An operating system in Icelandic does not exist. Thus, they had asked the U.S.-Software-industry to localize their operating system to Icelandic. The software industry refused because localization was too expensive to provide it for the small population of Icelanders.

III. Relationship of Language and Local Cultures

1. Fundamental Part of Culture

Mr. Hutter asked whether language serves the function of proxy for values and if, therefore, differences in language could serve as a first indication for different values.

Mr. Keniston answered that culture and values are related to language inasmuch as language is the medium that determines what people can perceive and what they can express. Language, culture, values were part of a seamless web in the experience of any individual or any given community. Thus, language would be a fundamental part of culture. Any value would have to be understood as embedded in a context which is broadly cultural. Therefore, it would be difficult to sort values out; talking about a list of values would also be problematic, although both could be useful for certain empirical and research purposes.

Mr. Grewlich described the anxiety of people in cultures with languages other than English as a fear that they would lose the ability to be creative in their own language. This anxiety would be particularly strong in France.

2. Countermovements

Mr. Hutter stated that English pop music is not dominant in the global pop music market despite the dominance of English. He claimed that regional pop music was dominant. Rather thin metropolitan markets used English pop music on a global, worldwide basis. This could perhaps be interpreted as a kind of countermovement. Mr. Keniston agreed partially with respect to India. Indian MTV and pop music were all in Indian languages, but the format, the dances, the presentation and even the announcer of Indian MTV are American.

IV. Machine Translation

Mr. Hutter asked whether machine translation might provide a means of communicating for two individuals who speak two different native languages. Perhaps, translation technology would lead to a future in which it is easy for individuals to use local languages and in which the use of local languages vis-a-vis a global language like English is strengthened.

Mr. Spinrad replied that almost all of the instruction manuals of large companies are already translated to a large extent automatically. However, the sentences have to be very simple, and the richness or subtlety of language has to be avoided in order to render a text which can be translated by a machine. The translation of more complex texts has not yet been very successful. Language translation is difficult since it has to be contextual and must take background notions into consideration. He predicted slow but continual progress.

E. Interactions of Information Networks with Internal Political Structures

The interactions of information networks with internal political structures were discussed in different contexts throughout the whole symposium. Though the discussion concentrated on the effects of global networks on internal political structures (I), the impact of actors in the field of Internet policy on the development of information networks was also addressed (II).

I. Effects of Global Information Networks on Internal Political Structures

1. New Options of Voice and Exit

a) Concept of Voice and Exit

Mr. Engel had used Albert O. Hirschman's concept of voice and exit to analyze the impact of global networks on internal political structures. Mr. Thompson explained that, according to Hirschman, exit is an individualist strategy, and voice an egalitarian strategy. He pointed out that the hierarchist strategy and loyalty was missing, i.e., the strategy to be loyal to the sovereign despite the possibilities of voice and exit.

Mr. Engel replied that he was convinced that loyalty in this sense was not a determining factor. In economic terms, loyalty was only likely to be a factor in low-cost decisions. The more a decision costs, the less loyalty would play a role. Since the decisions in question were not low-cost decisions, it was implausible that those who might want to exit or raise voice would feel hindered from doing so by loyalty.

b) New Voice Options

A source of much contention was the issue of new voice options with respect to the emergence of single interest groups (aa) and the potential of information networks to enhance participation in the democratic process (bb). Apart from the theoretical discussion, examples of political activism in information networks were also presented (cc). Finally, differences between the U.S. and Germany were discussed (dd).

aa) Single Interest Groups

Several participants described the emergence of single interest groups and how this process has been facilitated by the Internet. People who form a society on the Internet frequently pursue a common interest. Many experts have forecasted the rise of non-governmental, cohesive entities which are not necessarily merely another part of the basic society. These entities could possibly become competitive with the society in the future. They may well become virtual societies of a different sort.

Mr. David suggested the ease with which single-interest-groups could be built would encourage a strategy in politics in which compromise is shunned and concerns about the larger social system in which, in the end, all of the constituents have to function, would diminish. This issue is related to the problem of the delamination of society.

Mr. Engel described the problem of single-interest groups with reference to the provision of public goods. The provision of public goods rests on decisions that effect distribution. Those who lose on the distributional side are not very willing to accept such decisions. It would be easier to overcome the distributional problem in societies with more issues to deal with. For they could raise money, build packages and compensate for the losses such that they could dilute the disadvantages of a decision. Therefore, if the Internet really leads to the development of more and more single issue societies, a lot of problems in solving social problems could evolve.

Mr. Perrit said the development of single-interest groups would perhaps mean the demise of the myth of popular democracy. This concept presupposes that people coexist in several cultures at once, and, thus, learn to practice civility, e.g. to find compromises and to lose gracefully. If the Internet facilitates sequential existence rather than simultaneous existence in several cultures, the need for civility, for compromise, and learning how to lose gracefully would decrease. This could become a serious problem in terms of the habits of discourse that are taken for granted in certain sections of civil society.

bb) Potential of Information Networks to Enhance Democratic Participation

The potential of information networks to enhance participation in the democratic process was discussed with respect to the reduction of transaction costs (1), the impact on organizations (2), the potential to increase effective participation (3), and the ability to increase political interest (4).

1) Reduction of Transaction Costs

Participants agreed on that the information networks have the potential to reduce the transaction costs of political communication — costs which are a barrier to participation. The Internet makes it possible to mobilize a politically effective coalition very inexpensively.

2) Impact on Established Organizations

Mr. Werle said that the Internet provided an opportunity to bypass organizations. Citizens are able to address members of government or parliament directly. Although these institutions often do not respond, the technical opportunity could pose a threat to the organizations since they are afraid that they might be bypassed.

This would perhaps have an impact on the organizations themselves. However, predictions based on social theory, especially on organizational theory and corporate actor concepts of organizations, suggest that organizations could initially profit from the Internet.

3) Increase of Effective Participation?

Mr. Werle held the position that the Internet's potential to enhance the citizens' participation in the democratic process would not automatically increase effective participation. The higher the level of politics, the lower the probability that citizens would participate. The Internet would reduce transaction costs of political communication, which are a barrier to participation, but it would nevertheless not reverse this general rule.

Mr. Engel argued, firstly, that Mr. Werle's thesis focused on interest groups as corporate actors as opposed to a totally unorganized environment. Perhaps something exists between these actors, like collective actors, since the transaction costs to set up collective actors would be lower via the Internet, e.g. via mailing lists. Mr. Engel's second comment related Mr. Werle´s arguments to the voting paradox, i.e., that the individual does not have sufficient incentive to get engaged politically because the chance of changing a political outcome is too low. Mr. Engel suggested that this was true from a rational perspective; however people vote even though it might not be "rational" to do so. Mr. Engel thought that this phenomenon could serve to counter Mr. Werle's skepticism regarding the individuals willingness to engage politically via the Internet.

4) Raising Political Interest?

Mr. Engel argued further that the change between periods of high and low levels of political activism and commitment could not be fully explained by rational terms. There also were reasons like fashion, e.g., that it simply was chic or cool in the sixties and the seventies to be politically active and that it is not nowadays. Thus, the question should be asked whether the fact that access to the political forum facilitated by the Internet could make it cool or chic to be politically active again.

Mr. Hutter replied that, due to a loss of interest in the political structure, people who are conversant in the Internet would move into other fields. Business would be a likely candidate since it is currently much more faddish than being politically active.

Mr. Werle answered that individuals and organizations would initially use the Internet as a tool in order to get what they want keeping with their preferences and strategies. In this first step, the pure existence of the Internet would not change anything concerning theses preferences and strategies.

cc) Examples of Successful Political Activism in Information Networks

Mr. Burkert described the results of his investigation of two non-local cases in which the Internet had an impact on the rulemaking process:

The first case was the failure of the Westlaw Amendment in the U.S. Congress, an amendment within in the Paperwork Reduction Act that would have changed Federal Government copyright-law so that Westlaw would have had a kind of monopoly. The amendment failed within a week due to activities on the Internet. The second case was the at least temporary break down of the MAI (Multilateral Agreement on Investments).

According to Mr. Burkert, four elements are essential in order to influence the political process via the Internet. Firstly, there is the speed of communication on the Internet, which has countered the speed advantage of those in control of the regulation. The second important element is the pre-existence of a community with a well known portal or brand name which provides up-to-date information. This could be a mailing list which people subscribe to or an Internet site that is known to that particular community and regularly visited. Thirdly, influence through the Internet assumes a politically unstable situation in which not much energy is necessary to have influence on a decision. In the Westlaw amendment case, the situation was unstable because the Republican party did not want to support this company for political reasons. In the MAI case there had been growing resistance against the agreement. The fourth element required in order to influence the rulemaking process via the Internet is a coupling of influential traditional mass media on the one hand and the Internet on the other. Journalists are increasingly using the Internet themselves to look for stories. In the case of the Westlaw amendment, there was a coupling of the Internet mailing list by James Love and the Wall Street Journal; in the case of the MAI agreement, the non-governmental organization joined forces with Le Monde, Le Monde Diplomatique and the Tageszeitung in Germany.

dd) Differences between the U.S. and Germany

Mr. Werle stated that the German Internet community had not emerged to the same extent as the American; it had remained smaller and was less developed. Concerning community networks, Germany also lagged behind the USA. The emergence of such networks would not only be a matter of time. Community networks in Germany usually needed governmental support or other external support to start and reach a critical mass of participants. From a point of view of democracy or democratic theory, this was a disadvantage since, once the Internet becomes a medium used by the mass of the German population, democratic elements could be missing.

Mr. Holznagel argued that the Internet was in Germany already being heavily used by the right wing scene inasmuch as the right wing parties organize themselves via Internet. They were extremely active and probably the first who used the new technology for internal purposes. Nevertheless he thought it correct to describe the political activity of Germans on the Internet as being rather weak and as reflecting the situation in the society. But this situation could change quickly. If certain issues would arise, e.g. environmental issues, the Internet could quickly turn into a political tool for the younger generation. With respect to the activities on the governmental side, he cautioned that it should be taken into consideration that the political structure in Germany is dominated by a generation of politicians that is not familiar with the Internet. It would take a while until people who are knowledgeable about the Internet move up into areas with decision making power.

c) New Exit Options

Mr. Engel's thesis that the Internet would create new exit options to avoid the regulatory influence of nation states (aa) provoked a controversial debate about the significance of these options (bb).

aa) Phenomenology

Mr. Engel's presentation had described two kinds of new exit options as Internet-related. First, the option of a tailor-made exit, i.e., the splitting of the value chain by a firm in order to leave only less regulated parts in a country and leave more regulated parts out. In this way firms could avoid regulatory burdens easier than before. Secondly, the option of virtual exit, i.e., the possibility of exploiting the rules on the conflict of laws in order to get under a more favorable regulatory regime.

bb) Significance

Mr. Engel said both kinds of new exit options would lead to a loss of leverage of national governments. They would lose their power enabling them to deal with those that are presently in their jurisdictions. Governmental instruments would become much less powerful. The tax-base could be eroded.

This assumption was doubted by several participants. It seems to be uncertain that the Internet will facilitate outsourcing except for certain types of activities. (See also F.I.).

2. Impact on Wealth Distribution

According to Mr. Keniston's presentation, in India only members in the group that is already dominant and ruling have access to computers and global information networks. Their access to computers enhanced their position of control in India. The power of these group members is amended by the fact that they can easily communicate with the rest of the world. But the non-Anglophonic population of India, about 95 percent of the population, has access neither to these empowering new technologies, nor to the communication and the informational resources which these technologies provide.

Mr. Thompson replied that there was a trend to equalize information asymmetries even in India. The privatized Indian Telephone Company installed telephone points in Indian villages. Now for instance, the farmers are able to make the price comparisons on rice for the first time, giving them an option heretofore reserved for the merchants.

In Bangladesh, an even more spectacular joint venture between a Bank and the Norwegian Telephone Company will lead to the installation of a cheap mobile phone system, which will probably also involve laptop computers. Here again, all of this has tremendous implications with respect to the possibility of equalizing information asymmetries. Thus, when one views the communication networks more broadly rather than focussing just on the Internet, it seems likely that the elites' privileged position will not automatically be strengthened.

Mr. Keniston said that one needed to take into consideration that these people in India and in Bangladesh have very little marketing and purchasing power. Therefore, the developments Mr. Thompson described were not brought about by market forces.

II. Impact of Internal Political Structures on the Development of Information Networks

This symposium discussed the influence of different political structures on the development of information networks. Many more political activities had been started in the U.S. than in Germany and Europe (1). In contrast to Europe, the technological development in the U.S. is already embedded in a social setting in which the members are used to the Internet (2). It is difficult even for non-liberal governments to control the whole information-flow crossing their borders (3).

1. Symbolic Political Activities with regard to the Internet

Comparing the activities of American and European politics with regard to the development of the Internet, Mr. Werle stated that there was much more activity in the U.S., even in the narrower field of symbolic politics. Instead of investing large sums of money, sometimes a government merely needs to take part in some symbolic actions in order to provide incentives for certain activities. The Internet is proof of this. Nobody can argue that the development of the Internet was a result of money given by the American government. Government money was involved, but it was not related to an explicit industrial policy or technology policy of the United States. To the contrary, the Internet and the TCP/IP standards have evolved more or less in a university niche that is not commercialized. Thus, sometimes symbolic actions like the National Information Initiative of the U.S. or similar European activities seem to be the right strategy. If one works from the assumption that governments will lose power as a consequence of the growth of information networks and the Internet, then it seems necessary that governments will have to modify their roles and their self-understanding in order to promote developments in a national policy arena.

2. Differences between the U.S. and Europe

Mr. David asked how much the development could be accelerated in the European setting and still remain within acceptable boundaries. He also asked the discrepancy between Europe and the U.S. He was interested in the significance of European policy on the fifth framework, as well, i.e., with reference to extending and improving high speed Internet links in support of the European scientific community.

Mr. Werle answered that Germany and other European countries were reducing the American lead with reference to the number of servers, etc. But diffusion of technology is only one aspect; the development of a social infrastructure the other. Minitel, a technology completely incompatible with the Internet, had been pushed by the French Government; it had at its peak more than seven million users in France. Although it is now being replaced by the Internet, its one time presence provides a social infrastructure which is already prepared for the Internet. From this point of view, differences in Europe were identifiable. Therefore, the time lag could be diminished partly, but Europe as a whole is lagging behind. The programs launched by the European Commission, particularly in the area of research and education networks, could perhaps be viewed as a reaction to this development. On the other hand, the U.S. has also started initiatives like Internet II, which are, perhaps, more powerful for the initiation of a new development than European activities. However, these developments were related as much to social elements and social variables as to technical issues. The U.S. has an advantage since the technological development is already embedded in a social setting which is used to using the Internet.

3. Censorship

The example of Singapore served to illustrate what could happen if the new information and communication technologies fall in the hands of non-liberal governments. Mr. Burkert explained that the policy of Singapore initially had been to lead all local traffic through proxy servers under governmental control. But this policy was harmful for their business because the companies were not able to respond fast enough. Therefore, Internet providers who provide access to companies now were connected directly to the internet. But the head of the company is held personally responsible for his subordinates activities and must be sure that they are doing the "right" surfing on the Internet.

F. Interactions of Information Networks with International Political Structures

I. Impact of Global Information Networks on International Political Structures

International political structures are based on the assumption that national states are sovereign. This was described as undergoing a general erosion process due to the emergence of global information networks (1). New actors are now entering the international level (2). International negotiations are gaining significance with reference to national regulations (3).

1. Impact on Sovereignty

A controversial discussion arose concerning the impact of global information networks on national sovereignty. Mr. Engel had said in his presentation that governments were losing their power to regulate within the national territory due to new options of voice and exit.

Mr. Perrit said, in addition to the weakening of sovereignty due to the influence of foreigners on domestic interest groups, the sovereignty will be also weakened by domestic interest groups which will go abroad in order to reach their goals. This is political arbitrage. An example of this can be found in the interests groups which have sought to increase their copyrights but have not been successful in the United States Congress. Therefore, they have intensified their efforts to impact the negotiations of the World Intellectual Property Organization (WIPO). As a result, they have obtained a treaty that the Congress will have to enforce. The creation of newly valuable information flows has enabled Europe to exercise an extraordinary kind of de facto extraterritoriality sovereignty over U.S. privacy law, inasmuch as the European privacy directive prohibits the flow of information to the United States unless the United States begins to protect privacy. The U.S. have already begun to act accordingly, solely as a response to the perceived threat of this cutoff of the flows. Mr. Perrit claimed that another distinct point should be taken into account: decentralization. The increase of and the more distributed character of bottlenecks would complicate the regulatory process, since regulation usually targets bottlenecks.

Mr. Grewlich argued that governments not only lost, but also gained power due to the increased use of these networks. For the states now have better access to more information, and this gives them more control.

Mr. Engel replied that the loss and gain of state power and control would not be balanced. States would gain a bit, but lose a lot.

Ms. Sassen held the position that the national stake would not disappear at the stage the development is moving to, but that a lot of what was nationalized in the last hundred years would be denationalized. Components of the power and legitimacy of sovereignty would move to supra-national and international organizations, but also to sub-national levels. Thus, the national state would remain but its power would be reduced to an administrative capacity that is nevertheless indispensable for the citizens and even for multinational companies which need the national state in order to gain their legal status.

Mr. David stressed that the economics of the process were not going to spread elsewhere; the threat that some corporations flee to other jurisdictions is not credible. Transnational corporations could live in another legal space, but their assets would be in very concrete places, and they would rely upon the local law and the local structures for their daily functions.

Mr. Dam drew an analogy in the development of the financial market. The attempt of the U.S. to preserve the Bretton-Woods-system by imposing constraints had caused, due to what is now called regulatory arbitrage, an almost immediate move of both lenders and borrowers to London. Similar developments could be brought about by attempts to regulate the Internet.

2. New Actors

Ms. Sassen described the emergence of a new strategic intermediary space with private agents on the international level. New financial intermediaries have already evolved. China, for instance, has decided to launch a hundred-year bond on its national debt with the help of J.P. Morgan. Credit rating agencies and private institutions for international commercial arbitration as a cross-border dispute settlement could be seen as similar examples for new intermediaries. This suggests that the state will be confronted with another set of strategic agents in the international scene who are engaged in the business of governance.

Mr. Perrit stated that the existence of private business organizations exercising functions which are today defined as governmental is nothing new. For instance in the American colonies of the 18th century, most of these functions had been performed by private and economically motivated actors. Therefore, it would be a mistake to suppose that there are certain functions that have heretofore always been performed by governments but are now being privatized. There may well be a development that is a kind of return to privatization, but this is no water shed.

Mr. Grewlich reported that the OECD had issued documents in the Ottawa Conference that had been written and negotiated not only by governments, but also by business groups and public interest groups. Recommendations had been addressed to both governments and non-governmental organizations, and the request was made for all of them to take certain measures. This could be the beginning of an evolution of soft law.

3. Increased Reach of International Negotiations

The reach of international negotiations will now extend very deeply into national regulatory agencies and other forms of domestic governments, Mr. Kahler said. Apart from the WTO and some of the new codes negotiated under the WTO, no real mechanisms for dealing with this new phenomenon exist.

II. Impact of International Political Structures on Global Networks

1. Differences between the U.S. and other Nations

Mr. Grewlich talked about a great discrepancy that exists between the U.S., as the remaining superpower, and the other actors in the world. The superpower had a huge population, continental reach, the greatest military capacity, a strong economy and also a strong national identity. In the technology field, the U.S. had a concentration of power in terms of basic capacity, communication networks and both software and cultural content. These empirical facts needed to be addressed.

2. Strategic Trade-Policy of the U.S.

Mr. Grewlich argued that deregulation and competition are the major driving forces towards "convergence" and the creation of wealth in the multimedia value chain. But reversely, as the emerging new reality of "convergence" feeds back to the regulatory environment and as this may result in regulatory inconsistencies, a certain amount of re-regulation, i.e. an adjustment of existing regulatory schemes might be required. The U.S. example shows that national comparative advantage may emerge from "optimum policy mixes" (for instance "pull effects" of lead markets resulting from proactive liberalisation, R&D superiority together with widely shared political visions) combined with judicious trade policy (market opening including pressures for foreign regulatory adjustment); — possibly perceived as "neo-protectionism" if certain obstacles in the pull/lead market remain (e.g. critical foreign direct investment restrictions).

3. Counterarguments

Mr. Kahler replied that the European Union had a strategic policy, too, which perhaps was not as successful as the American, but definitely present. According to his position, the market power of the U.S. was not particularly new. Although one could argue that American market power in the area of global communications networks is greater than it has been in other areas in the past, the need for market access or the desire for market access would continue to drive negotiations. The U.S. has merely increased its predominance. Rather, the connection between multinational corporations, which use multinational alliances as a means of exerting leverage, is a new phenomenon. The crucial thing is that countries want to change regulatory policies in various ways. The question concerning the national advantage and how to establish a national advantage in the larger sense was discussed by Joseph S. Nye and William A. Owens, who see the reason for the U.S. predominance in information technologies in "soft power" — the attraction of American democracy and free markets. But Mr. Kahler said that this formulation gives perhaps more credit to the coherence of U.S. policy than in fact exists.

Mr. Engel inquired about the possibility of separating the strategic perspective from the four different normative views of the world Cultural Theory. Since it is not rooted in people, but in political institutions defending their own position, the strategic perspective of specific governments are normatively different. Political institutions are instruments, and if a state does not have the best instruments, there is no reason to allow old-fashioned political institutions to defend them against something which is normatively superior.

4. Interplay between Rhetoric and Material Substructure

Mr. David suggested that a distinction be made: On one hand we would have the mobilization of technology as an instrument for the projection of national power or the containment of national power; on the other hand there would be the mobilization of the rhetoric of technology as a surrogate way of seeking to advance certain positions of power or to oppose them by suggesting that this is inevitable or the course of the future. A part of the values conflict would be generated at the level of rhetoric. People could essentially accept the strategy at the level of the rhetoric which becomes packaged as the rhetoric of technology. But they may well react against it at a later stage, perceiving it as an example of American business power and American political influence packaged in rhetoric. Then there would be an interplay between the rhetoric, which would be real in international relations, and the material substructure, which would be also real.

G. Tools for Regulating Global Information Networks

Regarding the tools available to regulate global information networks the symposium discussed public international law (1), rules for conflicts of laws (2) and self-regulation (3).

1. Public International Law

a) Collective Responsibility

With respect to the question concerning the design of a responsive legal system in a situation where the ability of nation-states is attenuated, Mr. David described the research of economic historians. They are re-examining the formation of institutions which supported trade during the Middle Ages. The essential feature that the historians are interested in is the mechanism of collective responsibility that had been developed in lieu of incentives. The goal was to encourage the other parties, to whom an offending individual could possibly flee, to enforce relevant restrictions. This research suggested that it might be possible to establish some of the conditions which existed in a pre-international law environment without having to reconstruct the whole system of international law.

Mr. Engel agreed. He believed that such a mechanism can be found in public international law. The community of states has no formal constitution. It could therefore not simply rely on the constitution as a safeguard for obligations contracted on the operational level of the legal order. He suggested, however, that multilateral treaties serve as a viable substitute. Once a larger number of states have concluded a multilateral treaty, all contracting parties are offended if one party breaches its obligations to a single other party.

b) Regulating Nodes

Mr. David said the use of high speed networks to conduct financial and other kinds of business, indeed, for e-commerce in general, would most likely be highly concentrated at certain nodes, such as it is with the financial networks in New York, London, Tokyo, Frankfurt. He suggested that if these nodes could be regulated by an agreement between the hosting states, then the whole network could be regulated.

The core problem will be friction between the different systems, which will be caused by the confrontation of different regulatory regimes and questions of market access which will not be defined by exit, per se. In fact, market access issues would be about non-exit, about wanting-in rather than getting-out. Thus, the central question will be how to deal with those system frictions, which will likely lead to demands that various attempts to establish harmony be made.

Mr. Engel responded that a small number of actors would actually be easier to regulate than a large number. Actors are dependent on the subsequent willingness of governments to intervene on their behalf. Therefore, governments could negotiate solutions relatively easily. He said, however, that the situation would become more complicated when outside competition emerges. Outside competition would be unlikely in cases of considerable sunk costs. For, considerable sunk costs form exit barriers which is synonym to entry barriers. The question therefore arises as to whether the Internet and globalization will lead not only to a small number of actors but also to high sunk costs for these actors at a given place. Further empirical research is needed in order to answer this question.

Mr. Engel concluded with the comment that aside from this, it remained to be seen to what extent the actors would leave elements of the value chain at the nodes. The concentration on certain nodes would only serve as a solution to the problem if relevant parts of the value chain remained at the nodes.

c) Integration of New Actors

Mr. Grewlich made a case for integrating the new actors on the international political level into public international law.

Mr. Engel replied this would bring about a dramatic change in the structure of public international law. He mentioned that due to the fact that public international law has no central sovereign, this law would depend on whether or not contracts among the subjects of law could be met. It would be difficult merely to establish a contract among 250 states, and the integration of the NGOs would mean that there were thousands or ten thousands of persons between which contracts would have to be established. He thought that it would at best be possible to establish a class system in which the sovereign states are the only ones able to make decisions on a constitutional basis while the other actors are allowed to act but not to change the constitution. However, he thought that even that would be difficult to set up.

d) Regulating Public Interest by Conventions

Mr. Grewlich distinguished between access regulation and public interest regulation as a subject of international negotiations. In the field of access regulation there is a turgid amount of regulations and differences, and he thought that they should be replaced by free market forces. Were this put into place, he thought that the vital area of public interest regulation would remain intact. This would be a field in which new conventions would have to be allowed to develop.

Mr. Engel responded that the idea that public interests could be regulated by conventions was utopian. The common ground shared by different states concerning what legitimate questions of public interest would be is too small. The states have not even been able to set up a common antitrust law, although the necessity of this on a world basis is obvious. Only a few specific public interest issues had been discussed on a worldwide basis. The discussion about child pornography would be perhaps the only one that one could cite as a possible success story.

2. Conflict of Laws (Private International Law)

a) Difficulties of Harmonization

Mr. Engel suggested that one could perhaps find a solution for the problem of regulating global networks in the rules of conflict of laws. Mr. Perrit said that the issue of how to harmonize, express and then enforce the new conflict of laws rule was quite problematic. In the United States, at least choice of law is in complete disarray.

Mr. Engel agreed with this. At the end of the last century the metarules dealing with conflicts of laws were more or less universal, and, therefore, the chances that an unanimous decision based on these metarules was much greater than today. Nonetheless, when compared with extraterritoriality, foreign rulemaking seems to be more acceptable in the form of private international law or private law than in the form of public law. He suggested that private international law would therefore be a better tool to reach mutual adjustment than public law.

b) Impact of Power Relations

Mr. Burkert suspected that "the myth of freedom of contract" would still be a motivating idea behind the idea of private law. This fact means that the impact of power relations between states is being ignored. He thought that a tendency to accept and adopt the law of the hegemonial power was visible, but, on the other hand, this would allow for the development of different sets of law for different players on the same subject. Mr. Burkert cited cryptography law as an example of this. He said that is tacitly understood among governments that national companies are to be provided with the best cryptographic devices that are available in the market, but the governments do not wish to have these devices used by the citizens.

Mr. Engel answered that both the criticism of freedom of contract and the development of a class law assumed that power structures are leading to an unjust outcome.

He believed this to be partly true, but any other option would only function with a strong sovereign, since the only way to combat unjust results of negotiations is a third-party settlement. He did not believe that this type of third-party settlement is still feasible. He thought a lawyers' task not to consist in defending utopia but to look out for the best solution in a given situation. He thought a solution might be to give property rights to the disturber, and then looking for the best way for the disturbed person to protect himself, although this would probably cause problems in terms of distribution and power.

3. Self-Regulation

The discussion on proposed measures for collective self-regulation focused primarily on potential spill-over effects (a) but also touched on the possibility of unilateral self-regulation (b).

a) Spill-Over Effects

Mr. Perrit said that an affirmative shaping of collective private regulation were insufficient. He thought that it would also be necessary to remove prohibitions. In his view one of the principal obstacles to the development of collective private regulation in the United States is the fact that antitrust laws can be violated under the existing case law. He mentioned one of the proposals for self-regulation in the United States made in response to the European privacy directive as an example. This proposal had been made in order to create an opportunity for companies which deal in personal data to join a group. By joining the group, the company agrees to honor certain enumerated norms with respect to personal privacy. These norms are in essence the norms found in the European privacy directive.

According to Mr. Perrit three different kinds of spill-over effects have to be distinguished. Firstly, once competing companies meet in order to reach an agreement on privacy norms, they could also fix prices, etc. Secondly, other companies could be excluded from joining the group. The reason given for this is that these companies allegedly do not adhere to the privacy norms; however, the real reason is to avoid competition with these companies. Thirdly, a spillover problem exists with respect to third parties which the collective has to protect. Mr. Perrit thought it unwise to give the potential actors the right to determine the regulations intended to protect victims who are not part of this collective. However, this solution may be better than nothing, i.e., it may be better to let the companies set the rules and to force the victims to accept these rules and to submit to the jurisdiction of the collective in order to resolve their complaints. But Mr. Perrit claimed that most people did not approve of this method.

Due to this skepticism Mr. Perrit thought that it was likely that a system would evolve in which the victim could choose between the mechanisms defined by the collective or using the usual legal processes, i.e., going to court. Since the substantive law concerning privacy was not very protective in the U.S., the expectation was that most victims would voluntarily elect to resort to the mechanisms established by the collective. Mr. Perrit thought this would nevertheless be a tolerable solution since the degree of protection to the third parties would be enhanced, even though they would not have participated in defining the rules or setting up the enforcement institutions. He thought that it would be more problematic to force the third parties to submit to such a process in which they had no representation.

Mr. Engel basically agreed with this. He mentioned that antitrust problems would be problematic in a self-regulated system because self-regulation causes spill-overs, and the purpose of antitrust law would be to make these spillovers less eminent than they would otherwise be. Self-regulation would not be a perfect solution. He thought that some sort of government institution should monitor this self-regulatory system. Since the use of force would be done by organizations, he thought that it would be easier to provide some control at this level than on the individual level, for it is easier for governments to control organizations than individuals.

b) Unilateral Private Regulation

Mr. Perrit said that in addition to collective private regulation, unilateral private regulation would also be possible. He pointed out that the reaction to the prosecution of the CompuServe executive in Germany had nothing to do with collective regulation; it had to do with the expectations that the targeted intermediary would internalize the norms and figure out a way to enforce them against its own membership.

H. Targets of Regulation – First Normative Attempts

According to the plans of the two symposia of the project, a normative analysis of the need, the extent and nature of policy action was proposed as the subject of a second symposium. In spite of this, the first tentative contributions were made with respect to problems which could create a need for regulation and appropriate solutions. The discussions centered on possible consequences of an possible global monoculture and the question concerning the possible need to protect cultural diversity through active intervention.

I. Dangers of Global Monoculture?

Mr. Keniston defended the thesis that a global monoculture would lead to a "exclusionary cultural nationalism." Reactionary atavisms would be provoked were a perceived cosmopolitanism to undermine or threaten local cultures by subordinating them to second place.

Mr. Kahler replied that he could see no connection to these fears in the empirical world. Empirically speaking, it would be even very difficult to support the claim that exclusionary ethnic or cultural nationalism had grown in the 1990s as compared to other periods. Thus, it would be hard to see an association with the globalization phenomenon in this respect. Even in specific ethnic conflicts, particularly the most violent ones, there was no reason to assume that a motivating factor was a reaction against a global monoculture.

II. Protection of Local Cultures?

1. Active Intervention

In keeping with his concerns about the effects of a global monoculture, Mr. Keniston argued that active intervention of corporate and business leaders and of political leaders who know how to moderate the forces of the market would be necessary to achieve the preservation and deepening of cultural diversity. A similar position was expressed by Mr. Thompson. He said that from the viewpoint of Cultural Theory one could argue for normative efforts made to preserve the tensions which exist between the different solidarities as a way of preserving the proper dynamics of a society. But this idea has only recently developed and is a very tentative suggestion.

2. No Intervention

Mr. Kahler held the opposite position. In his view there is no reason to give national cultures any particular privileged position in being local. Those who express concerns about the development of a monoculture are usually speakers of former top languages. They are not concerned about losing their local cultures but about losing in the race for the second language.

Mr. David said that national governments have repeatedly abused this notion that local cultures and values have to be protected. He thought this idea was dangerous because it allowed national sentiment to be mobilized for aggressive action. He expressed his surprise that the potential of the Internet to preserve some linguistic traditions had not been systematically exploited, a fact that is especially surprising in light of the fact that many people use the Internet to protect biological species and thus biodiversity. He suspected that one reason might be that people do not regard language as something which is part of the endowment of humankind and that they therefore do not think that linguistic diversity is something that people should be interested in preserving.

List of Symposium Participants

Prof. Robert McC. Adams Professor of Anthropology, University of California, San Diego	**Prof. Dr. Dirk Baecker** Witten/Herdecke University;
Dr. Herbert Burkert Senior Researcher, German National Research Centre for Information Technology, St.Augustin, Germany; Assistant Professor for Information and Communication Law, St.Gallen, Switzerland	**Prof. Kenneth Dam** Max Pain Professor of American and Foreign Law, University of Chicago Law School; Member of the Steering Committee
Prof. Dr. Paul A. David Senior Research Fellow, All Souls College, Oxford University; Member of the Steering Committee	**Prof. Dr. Christoph Engel** Director of the Max Planck Projektgroup on the Law of Common Goods, Bonn; Co-Chairman of the Steering Committee
Prof. David Farber Moore Professor of Telecommunication Systems, University of Pennsylvania	**Prof. Dr. Dr. Klaus W. Grewlich** Universities of Freiburg and Bonn Member of the Steering Committee
Prof. Dr. Bernd Holznagel Westfälische Wilhelms-University, Münster, Institute for Information Telecommunication and Media Law Member of the Steering Committee	**Dr. Rolf Hoffmann** Director of the German American Academic Council
Prof. Dr. Michael Hutter Professor of Economics, chair for economic theory, Witten/Herdecke University; Founding Director of the Institute for Economy and Culture, Witten/Herdecke University Member of the Steering Committee	**Prof. Dr. Kenneth H. Keller** Professor of Science and Technology Policy, Hubert H. Humphrey Institute of Public Affairs at the University of Minnesota; Co-Chairman of the Steering Committee

Prof. Miles Kahler University of California, Graduate School of International Relations/Pacific Studies	**Prof. Kenneth Keniston** Andrew W. Mellon Professor of Human Development at the Massachusetts Institute of Technology; Member of the Steering Committee
Prof. Dr. Wolfgang Kersting Christian-Albrechts-University of Kiel, Faculty of Philosophy; Member of the Steering Committee	**Prof. Dr. Henry H. Perritt, Jr.** Dean & Professor of Law Chicago-Kent College of Law, Illinois Institute of Technology; Member of the Steering Committee
Prof. Saskia Sassen Professor of Sociology and the College, Department of Sociology	**Dr. Robert Spinrad** Vice President, Technology Strategy with Xerox, Palo Alto Research Center; Member of the Steering Committee
Prof. Michael Thompson LOS-centre, Bergen, Norway; Director of The Musgrave Institute, London	**Prof. Dr. Hans-Heinrich Trute** University of Technology, Dresden, Department of Law
Dr. Raymund Werle Max Planck Institute for the Study of Societies, Cologne; Member of the Steering Committee	**Prof. Dr. Joachim Wieland** Bielefeld University, Faculty of Law
Prof. Dr. Martina Zitterbart Operating Systems and Computer Networks, Technical University, Braunschweig; Member of the Steering Committee	